The United Nations

The United Nations

75 Years of Promoting Peace, Human Rights, and Development

Kent J. Kille and Alynna J. Lyon

BLOOMSBURY ACADEMIC
NEW YORK • LONDON • OXFORD • NEW DELHI • SYDNEY

BLOOMSBURY ACADEMIC
Bloomsbury Publishing Inc
1385 Broadway, New York, NY 10018, USA
50 Bedford Square, London, WC1B 3DP, UK
29 Earlsfort Terrace, Dublin 2, Ireland

BLOOMSBURY, BLOOMSBURY ACADEMIC and the Diana logo
are trademarks of Bloomsbury Publishing Plc

First published in the United States of America by ABC-CLIO 2020
Paperback edition published by Bloomsbury Academic 2024

Copyright © Bloomsbury Publishing Inc, 2024

For legal purposes the Acknowledgments on p. xi constitute
an extension of this copyright page.

Cover photo: (id-work/iStockphoto)
Cover design by Silverander Communications

All rights reserved. No part of this publication may be reproduced or
transmitted in any form or by any means, electronic or mechanical,
including photocopying, recording, or any information storage or retrieval
system, without prior permission in writing from the publishers.

Bloomsbury Publishing Inc does not have any control over, or responsibility for,
any third-party websites referred to or in this book. All internet addresses given
in this book were correct at the time of going to press. The author and publisher
regret any inconvenience caused if addresses have changed or sites have
ceased to exist, but can accept no responsibility for any such changes.

Library of Congress Cataloging-in-Publication Data
Names: Kille, Kent J., author. | Lyon, Alynna, 1969- author.
Title: The United Nations : 75 years of promoting peace, human rights, and
development / Kent J. Kille and Alynna J. Lyon.
Description: Santa Barbara, California : ABC-CLIO, 2020. |
Includes bibliographical references and index.
Identifiers: LCCN 2020011407 (print) | LCCN 2020011408 (ebook) |
ISBN 9781440851568 (hardcover) | ISBN 9781440851575 (ebook)
Subjects: LCSH: United Nations—History.
Classification: LCC JZ4984.5 .K547 2020 (print) | LCC JZ4984.5 (ebook) |
DDC 341.2309—dc23
LC record available at https://lccn.loc.gov/2020011407
LC ebook record available at https://lccn.loc.gov/2020011408

ISBN: HB: 978-1-4408-5156-8
PB: 979-8-7651-2969-2
ePDF: 978-1-4408-5157-5
eBook: 979-8-2161-6015-1

To find out more about our authors and books visit www.bloomsbury.com
and sign up for our newsletters.

Contents

Acknowledgments   xi

United Nations System Organizational Chart   xii

Part I   United Nations Founding, Purposes, and Principles

Introduction   1

United Nations Historical Background   2

Charter of the United Nations   9

United Nations Purposes   11

United Nations Principles   11

Part II   United Nations Principal Organs

Introduction   13

General Assembly   15

Security Council   21

Economic and Social Council (ECOSOC)   28

Secretariat   33

International Court of Justice (ICJ)   36

Trusteeship Council   40

Part III   The United Nations System

Introduction   47

Specialized Agencies

Food and Agriculture Organization (FAO)   48

International Civil Aviation Organization (ICAO)   52

International Fund for Agricultural Development (IFAD)   55

International Labour Organization (ILO)   58

International Maritime Organization (IMO)   62

International Monetary Fund (IMF)   65

International Telecommunication Union (ITU)   69

United Nations Educational, Scientific and Cultural Organization (UNESCO)   72

United Nations Industrial Development Organization (UNIDO)   77

Universal Postal Union (UPU)   80

World Bank Group   84

World Health Organization (WHO)   87

World Intellectual Property Organization (WIPO)   90

World Meteorological Organization (WMO)   94

World Tourism Organization (UNWTO)   97

Programmes and Funds

United Nations Children's Fund (UNICEF)   101

United Nations Conference on Trade and Development (UNCTAD)   105

United Nations Development Programme (UNDP)   109

United Nations Entity for Gender Equality and the Empowerment of Women (UN Women)   112

United Nations Environment Programme (UNEP)   116

United Nations High Commissioner for Refugees (UNHCR)   119

United Nations Human Settlements Programme (UN-Habitat)   123

United Nations Population Fund (UNFPA)   126

United Nations Relief and Works Agency for Palestine Refugees in the Near East (UNRWA)   130

World Food Programme (WFP)   133

Other Subsidiary Bodies

Disarmament Commission   136

Functional Commissions   139

High-level Political Forum on Sustainable Development (HLPF)   141

Human Rights Council   144

Joint United Nations Programme on HIV/AIDS (UNAIDS)   147

Peacebuilding Commission   150

Permanent Forum on Indigenous Issues   152

Regional Commissions   155

Research and Training Institutes   157

Related Organizations

International Atomic Energy Agency (IAEA)   160

International Criminal Court (ICC)   162

International Organization for Migration (IOM)   165

International Seabed Authority (ISA)   167

Organization for the Prohibition of Chemical Weapons (OPCW)   170

Preparatory Commission for the Comprehensive Nuclear-Test-Ban Treaty Organization (CTBTO)   173

World Trade Organization (WTO)   175

Part IV   Individual Actors in the United Nations System

Introduction   179

Secretaries-General

 Office of Secretary-General   180

 Trygve Lie   182

 Dag Hammarskjöld   185

 U Thant   187

 Kurt Waldheim   188

 Javier Pérez de Cuéllar   190

 Boutros Boutros-Ghali   192

 Kofi Annan   194

 Ban Ki-moon   196

António Guterres   198

Deputy Secretary-General   201

Special Representatives of the United Nations Secretary-General (SRSGs)   203

President of General Assembly   205

President of Security Council   207

Executive Heads of Specialized Agencies   209

Member State Ambassadors and Delegates   211

United States Ambassadors to the United Nations   213

Goodwill Ambassadors and Messengers of Peace   216

Part V United Nations Concepts and Issues

Introduction   219

Arms Control and Disarmament   220

Collective Security   222

Cybersecurity   223

Economic Development   225

Environmental Protection   227

Global Commons   231

Health   233

Human Rights   235

Human Security   239

Indigenous Peoples   241

Membership   242

Nongovernmental Organizations (NGOs)   245

Peacebuilding   247

Peaceful Settlement   249

Peacekeeping   251

Refugees and Migration   253

Regionalism   255

Responsibility to Protect (R2P)   257

Role of Great Powers   260

Self-Determination   262

Sustainable Development   264

Sustainable Development Goals (SDGs)   266

Terrorism   269

United Nations Budget and Financing   272

United Nations Conferences and Summits   274

United Nations Headquarters   275

United Nations Reform   277

Voting and Negotiating Blocs   279

Women and Gender   281

Part VI Documents

Charter of the United Nations   287

Universal Declaration of Human Rights   311

Sample United Nations General Assembly Resolution:
    A/RES/73/241 (2018)   316

United Nations Security Council S/RES/1325 (2000)   320

Appendix: United Nations International Days (as of 2020)   325

Bibliography   331

Index   337

Acknowledgments

The following student research assistants at The College of Wooster provided important research and editing assistance: Ghita Chiboub, Maureen Hanes, Matt Mayes, and Emmy Todd. In addition, Sabrina Harris, a student research assistant at The College of Wooster, receives particular recognition for the level of research collected and organized as well as writing assistance on the United Nations Entity for Gender Equality and the Empowerment of Women (UN Women). Several students from the University of New Hampshire also provided valuable research support and assistance, including Ryan Clasby, Cailee Griffin, Sophia Henkels, Elizabeth Lohmueller, and Madeleine Rousseau.

Alynna and Kent would also like to express their deep gratitude to their families for their support and patience and to their students of International Relations and the United Nations System who continually provide inspiration.

The United Nations System

UN PRINCIPAL ORGANS

GENERAL ASSEMBLY

Subsidiary Organs
- Disarmament Commission
- Human Rights Council
- International Law Commission
- Joint Inspection Unit (JIU)
- Main Committees
- Standing committees and ad hoc bodies

Funds and Programmes[1]
- **UNDP** United Nations Development Programme
  - **UNCDF** United Nations Capital Development Fund
  - **UNV** United Nations Volunteers
- **UNEP**[8] United Nations Environment Programme
- **UNFPA** United Nations Population Fund
- **UN-HABITAT**[8] United Nations Human Settlements Programme
- **UNICEF** United Nations Children's Fund
- **WFP** World Food Programme (UN/FAO)

SECURITY COUNCIL

Subsidiary Organs
- Counter-Terrorism Committee
- International Residual Mechanism for Criminal Tribunals
- Military Staff Committee

ECONOMIC AND SOCIAL COUNCIL

Functional Commissions
- Crime Prevention and Criminal Justice
- Narcotic Drugs
- Population and Development
- Science and Technology for Development
- Social Development
- Statistics
- Status of Women
- United Nations Forum on Forests

Regional Commissions[8]
- **ECA** Economic Commission for Africa
- **ECE** Economic Commission for Europe
- **ECLAC** Economic Commission for Latin America and the Caribbean
- **ESCAP** Economic and Social Commission for Asia and the Pacific
- **ESCWA** Economic and Social Commission for Western Asia

SECRETARIAT

Departments and Offices[9]
- **EOSG** Executive Office of the Secretary-General
- **DCO** Development Coordination Office
- **DESA** Department of Economic and Social Affairs
- **DGACM** Department for General Assembly and Conference Management
- **DGC** Department of Global Communications
- **DMSPC** Department of Management Strategy, Policy and Compliance
- **DOS** Department of Operational Support
- **DPO** Department of Peace Operations
- **DPPA** Department of Political and Peacebuilding Affairs
- **DSS** Department of Safety and Security
- **OCHA** Office for the Coordination of Humanitarian Affairs
- **OCT** Office of Counter-Terrorism
- **ODA** Office for Disarmament Affairs
- **OHCHR** Office of the United Nations High Commissioner for Human Rights
- **OIOS** Office of Internal Oversight Services
- **OLA** Office of Legal Affairs
- **OSAA** Office of the Special Adviser on Africa
- **SRSG/CAAC** Office of the Special Representative of the Secretary-General for Children and Armed Conflict
- **SRSG/SVC** Office of the Special Representative of the Secretary-General on Sexual Violence in Conflict
- **SRSG/VAC** Office of the Special Representative of the Secretary-General on Violence Against Children

INTERNATIONAL COURT OF JUSTICE

TRUSTEESHIP COUNCIL[6]

Research and Training

UNIDIR United Nations Institute for Disarmament Research
UNITAR United Nations Institute for Training and Research
UNSSC United Nations System Staff College
UNU United Nations University

Other Entities

ITC International Trade Centre (UN/WTO)
UNCTAD[1,8] United Nations Conference on Trade and Development
UNHCR[1] Office of the United Nations High Commissioner for Refugees
UNOPS[1] United Nations Office for Project Services
UNRWA[1] United Nations Relief and Works Agency for Palestine Refugees in the Near East
UN-WOMEN[1] United Nations Entity for Gender Equality and the Empowerment of Women

Related Organizations

CTBTO PREPARATORY COMMISSION Preparatory Commission for the Comprehensive Nuclear-Test-Ban Treaty Organization
IAEA[1,3] International Atomic Energy Agency
ICC International Criminal Court
IOM[1] International Organization for Migration
ISA International Seabed Authority
ITLOS International Tribunal for the Law of the Sea
OPCW[3] Organization for the Prohibition of Chemical Weapons
WTO[1,4] World Trade Organization

Peacebuilding Commission

HLPF
High-level Political Forum on Sustainable Development

- Peacekeeping operations and political missions
- Sanctions committees (ad hoc)
- Standing committees and ad hoc bodies

Specialized Agencies[1,5]

FAO Food and Agriculture Organization of the United Nations
ICAO International Civil Aviation Organization
IFAD International Fund for Agricultural Development
ILO International Labour Organization
IMF International Monetary Fund
IMO International Maritime Organization
ITU International Telecommunication Union
UNESCO United Nations Educational, Scientific and Cultural Organization
UNIDO United Nations Industrial Development Organization
UNWTO World Tourism Organization
UPU Universal Postal Union
WHO World Health Organization
WIPO World Intellectual Property Organization
WMO World Meteorological Organization
WORLD BANK GROUP[7]
- **IBRD** International Bank for Reconstruction and Development
- **IDA** International Development Association
- **IFC** International Finance Corporation

Other Bodies[10]

- Committee for Development Policy
- Committee of Experts on Public Administration
- Committee on Non-Governmental Organizations
- Permanent Forum on Indigenous Issues

UNAIDS Joint United Nations Programme on HIV/AIDS
UNGEGN United Nations Group of Experts on Geographical Names
UNGGIM Committee of Experts on Global Geospatial Information Management

Research and Training

UNICRI United Nations Interregional Crime and Justice Research Institute
UNRISD United Nations Research Institute for Social Development

UNDRR United Nations Office for Disaster Risk Reduction
UNODC[1] United Nations Office on Drugs and Crime
UNOG United Nations Office at Geneva
UN-OHRLLS Office of the High Representative for the Least Developed Countries, Landlocked Developing Countries and Small Island Developing States
UNON United Nations Office at Nairobi
UNOP[2] United Nations Office for Partnerships
UNOV United Nations Office at Vienna

Notes:
1. Members of the United Nations System Chief Executives Board for Coordination (CEB).
2. UN Office for Partnerships (UNOP) is the UN's focal point vis-a-vis the United Nations Foundation, Inc.
3. IAEA and OPCW report to the Security Council and the General Assembly (GA).
4. WTO has no reporting obligation to the GA, but contributes on an ad hoc basis to GA and Economic and Social Council (ECOSOC) work on, inter alia, finance and development issues.
5. Specialized agencies are autonomous organizations whose work is coordinated through ECOSOC (intergovernmental level) and CEB (inter-secretariat level).
6. The Trusteeship Council suspended operation on 1 November 1994, as on 1 October 1994 Palau, the last United Nations Trust Territory, became independent.
7. International Centre for Settlement of Investment Disputes (ICSID) and Multilateral Investment Guarantee Agency (MIGA) are not specialized agencies in accordance with Articles 57 and 63 of the Charter, but are part of the World Bank Group.
8. The secretariats of these organs are part of the UN Secretariat.
9. The Secretariat also includes the following offices: The Ethics Office, United Nations Ombudsman and Mediation Services, and the Office of Administration of Justice.
10. For a complete list of ECOSOC Subsidiary Bodies see un.org/ecosoc.

This Chart is a reflection of the functional organization of the United Nations System and for informational purposes only. It does not include all offices or entities of the United Nations System.

PART I

United Nations Founding, Purposes, and Principles

INTRODUCTION

The United Nations (UN) is a universal international governmental organization tasked with maintaining peace and security, as well as promoting economic and social cooperation and protecting human rights across the globe. When the UN was founded in 1945, people around the world were optimistic that the organization would save the planet from the "scourge of war." Since the creation of the UN, there have been no wars between great powers, and the organization has dynamically evolved in its handling of breaches of peace through the creation of peacekeeping, the delivery of humanitarian assistance, and the construction of new security norms, such as the responsibility to protect. Great strides have been made in addressing the social needs of the world's population, including the eradication of smallpox. The UN provided a venue for the creation of many significant international human rights agreements, including the Universal Declaration of Human Rights (see Part VI) and the Convention on the Elimination of All Forms of Discrimination against Women. Since 1945, the UN added over 140 member states, including assisting with the transition of many former colonial territories to independent countries operating as full members of the organization. The UN emphasizes the economic needs of these less economically developed countries, while also extending its mandate to address environmental protection and sustainability. The UN System as a whole is a wide-ranging family of principal organs, specialized agencies, programmes and funds, and other affiliated bodies that have expanded and adapted over time. While there are points of success, there are also visible failures, including the inability to protect vulnerable populations in Rwanda (1994) and Srebrenica (1995) and instances of UN peacekeepers abusing the very people they are tasked with protecting. The UN also faces significant criticism, like many large organizations, for being prone to inefficiencies, redundancies, and coordination difficulties. A key challenge for the UN in the twenty-first century is the fact that the organization is based on respecting member states' sovereign control over their territory, while facing a long list of global challenges that do not conform to country borders. These "problems without passports" include transnational terrorism, environmental devastation, unprecedented refugee pressures, lethal pandemics, and the proliferation of weapons systems that can kill millions. The UN, despite its difficulties, provides a vital organizational setting to bring together almost every country in the world, as well as civil society and the private sector, to address international challenges from a global perspective.

United Nations Historical Background

The founding of the UN in 1945 was an extraordinary event as fifty countries came together and designed an organization to promote international collaboration, the peaceful resolution of conflict, economic and social cooperation, and human rights. U.S. President Harry S. Truman called the organization "a solid structure upon which we can build a better world." The creation of the UN was no easy feat, but several key elements fortuitously came together. First, after two major destructive wars, the world was tired of bloodshed and wanted a different approach to resolving conflict. Second, the most powerful countries at the time were willing to cooperate and, most importantly, to compromise. This included the United States, which up until 1941 had generally been reluctant to become involved in global politics. In addition, previous experiments (particularly the League of Nations) provided a blueprint for how to (and how not to) design a universal international organization. Many scholars and diplomats across the globe view the establishment of the UN as a milestone in humanity's quest to build peace and escape from the vicious cycles of war.

PRECURSORS TO THE UNITED NATIONS

The UN is the result of a range of attempts to address aggressive behavior and regulate international affairs. The UN's earliest point of origin can be traced back to the Treaty of Westphalia signed in 1648. After the Thirty Years' War (1618–1648), the princedoms around Europe agreed to establish the idea of sovereignty (supreme authority and freedom from interference in domestic affairs) to guide their relations. Although the Treaty of Westphalia did not create an organization, the central idea of sovereignty continues to define relations between countries today and is reinforced as a core UN principle. Yet, as countries became more connected, they needed a way to cooperate and began developing organizations to make it easier to meet, communicate, and collaborate.

Many international organizations, including the UN, were created after war. This was true for an early experiment in Europe fashioned by the Congress of Vienna (1814–1815) to reorganize international politics after the Napoleonic Wars ended in 1815. An agreement between the most powerful Europeans at the time (Austria, Britain, Prussia, and Russia) established the Concert of Europe, which became an early model for collaboration between countries. The Concert represents one of the first multilateral alliances where several countries negotiated at the same time, rather than the traditional bilateral (relations between two countries) approach. In this organizational experiment, countries held sovereign equality and attended occasional meetings. The Concert centered on creating regional stability, which was effective in blocking two attempts to unseat the constitutional governments of Italy (1820) and Spain (1822). The Concert is widely considered to be one of the first credible efforts to coordinate global policy and promote peace. However, the fragmented approach taken, along with the lack of permanent headquarters and full-time staff, limited its effectiveness. In addition, the primary method of creating stability was to balance powerful countries against each other.

While the Concert of Europe was focused on political agreements, a legal-based approach to regulating disputes between countries emerged in The Hague, Netherlands. In 1899 and 1907, the city hosted the Hague Peace Conferences, which led to a series of international agreements guiding the handling of disputes and warfare. These Hague Conventions created a model for how countries with different viewpoints could meet and come to agreements. This approach was used in the creation of the League of Nations (1919), the precursor to the UN. The Conventions also created the Permanent Court of Arbitration (1899) to provide an international legal forum. The Permanent Court of Arbitration, which still operates today, served as a forerunner to the League's Permanent Court of International Justice and then the UN's International Court of Justice.

Other more technical organizational predecessors to the UN also emerged in the nineteenth century. Changes in technology and increased economic activity often brought new demands for countries to work together. Developments like the telegraph, steamships, and railroads created interdependence between people in different countries that required coordination and a place for countries to discuss challenges and create shared understandings on rules of engagement across borders. For example, the Central Commission for the Navigation of the Rhine was created in 1815 to ensure freedom of navigation along the Rhine River as it flowed across borders. Other public international unions were also given a narrowly defined focus, including the International Telegraph Union (1865), the Universal Postal Union (1878), and the International Bureau of Weights and Measures (1875).

Overall, these key developments of the nineteenth century set the stage for the UN. The Congress of Vienna and Concert of Europe established multilateral consultation among a set of great powers and a model of an executive council. The Hague Conferences brought in the idea of universality as non-European states (with legal equality) were included, and they helped develop parliamentary procedures with a standard approach to running meetings and voting guidelines along with promoting the use of international courts. In addition, the public international unions highlighted the need for the involvement of specialists and a permanent secretariat to run the day-to-day operations of an organization. More broadly, membership was usually limited to countries (as opposed to nongovernmental organizations), and those members generally had one vote each. Most organizations were created by writing a treaty between the countries. The process usually involved two stages as states had to sign on to the treaty and then ratify (gain approval from their home governments) the agreement. However, these early organizations did not have full jurisdiction over the countries. Instead, countries agreed to comply with the agreements they made in those organizations, often with the ability to opt out of a particular agreement they did not support.

In his 1910 Nobel Peace Prize speech, U.S. President Theodore Roosevelt praised the first Hague Conference for providing "a Magna Carta for the nations." In this address, Roosevelt outlined three pillars for building international peace: strong "treaties of arbitration," enhancing the Hague court system, and creating a "League of Peace" built around an agreement between the most powerful countries of the day. Yet, despite these important developments, less than a decade after the second Hague Peace Conference a war of unfathomable proportion broke out in Europe and over twenty million lost their lives in battle. The balance of power approach used by the Concert of Europe proved ineffective as the conflict between a handful of countries escalated into a world war. With balance of power discredited, and World War I's immense destruction, world leaders were motivated to search for new mechanisms to avert war. Many insisted that a different approach should be based on collective security (an attack on one would be considered an attack on all) to deter countries from aggressive behavior.

THE LEAGUE OF NATIONS

In U.S. President Woodrow Wilson's Fourteen Points speech (January 8, 1918) to Congress, he argued that a "general association of nations must be formed under specific covenants for the purpose of affording mutual guarantees of political independence and territorial integrity to great and small states alike" to help build world peace. Such an organization, which would ultimately take form as the League of Nations, would reform the entire system of international relations. With this model, which many labeled as idealistic, every country would become vested in collective peace rather than pursuing their own country's power. However, although President Wilson supported the idea, in 1919 Congress was in a nationalistic, isolationist mood that, along with domestic political divisions, led to the rejection of international collaboration. Many in the United States were concerned that collective security would undermine American sovereignty and draw the United States into foreign wars in a manner that would challenge Congress' constitutionally granted power to make war. When the Treaty of Versailles, which ended World War I and created the League of Nations, was presented to the Senate for ratification, they rejected membership in the organization by a 39–55 vote.

Despite the lack of U.S. membership, the League of Nations came into existence in January 1920. The organizational structure included an Assembly with universal membership giving each country one vote. The most powerful countries (initially Britain, France, Italy, and Japan) had permanent membership in a separate Council (joined by a limited number of rotating members) that met to discuss threats to international peace and could issue sanctions (verbal, economic, and military) to address countries that were threatening international stability. The League also included a Secretariat (staffed year-round) with headquarters in

Geneva, headed by a Secretary-General, which facilitated and organized meetings. The Treaty of Versailles also created another notable precursor to the UN when it established the International Labour Organization, now a UN specialized agency, to promote social justice through addressing labor conditions.

The League of Nations included several elements that were not adopted by the UN's creators. For example, most of the League's decisions required unanimity, which meant that all countries had to agree. Unfortunately, this often resulted in gridlock within the organization. To resolve disputes that threatened to escalate into conflict, members of the League were to "submit the matter either to arbitration or judicial settlement or to enquiry by the Council" and then "agree in no case to resort to war until three months after" the decision by these bodies (Covenant of the League of Nations, Article 12). Several international crises proved the League's approach to be ineffective, including the Manchurian Crisis starting in 1931 when Japan invaded parts of China and when Italy invaded Ethiopia in 1935. With such disappointments, the idea of creating a "new League" gained momentum even before the outbreak of World War II. In 1937, negotiations between the United States, the United Kingdom, and France looked at issues such as tackling economic and financial structures (as the Great Depression raised concerns about international economic stability), restricting the increase in weapons, and creating a more functional political mechanism to avert war.

THE CREATION OF THE UNITED NATIONS

In August 1941, the Americans and the British signed the Atlantic Charter, which affirmed "certain common principles in the national policies of their respective countries on which they based their hopes for a better future for the world." The December 1941 bombing of Pearl Harbor forced the United States out of an official position of neutrality. At the start of January 1942, China, the Soviet Union, the United Kingdom, and the United States joined twenty-two other countries and signed the "Declaration by United Nations" to ally against the Axis powers. Twenty-one additional countries later signed on to this declaration, which referenced and supported the Atlantic Charter. At the August 1943 Quebec Conference, the United States and United Kingdom approved the idea of drafting a declaration that would include calling for an international organization based on members possessing sovereign equality, which culminated in the October 1943 Moscow Declaration.

However, the great powers disagreed about how to avert war once and for all. The United States wanted to promote collective neutrality, economic development, and disarmament and leave the Europeans to settle the political conflicts. The British indicated that their focus would remain on establishing a foundation for peace and that the economic structures and reduction in weapons should wait. The United Kingdom was also wary of including the Soviet Union and was concerned about whether China could be a reliable partner. Yet, the inclusion of China was key for U.S. President Franklin D. Roosevelt's efforts to balance Japan and to establish that the future organization was more than a private club of European countries.

As World War II progressed, the Allied Powers began to lay out a plan for promoting postwar security. In these discussions, several key issues emerged. UK Prime Minister Winston Churchill recommended creating several regionally based organizations, whereas the United States under Roosevelt wanted an organization where all "peace-loving nations" would be members. Other questions included whether the great powers would control the organization and, if so, how smaller and middle powers would participate. The scope of the organization was also a subject of debate. Would it focus on just peace and security or also address issues of economic development and even human rights? The issue of what to do in cases of threats to international peace dominated several discussions.

The Soviets presented many hurdles to the creation of the UN. In 1939, the League of Nations had expelled the Soviet Union for aggressive acts against Finland. This experience left Soviet leader Joseph Stalin highly skeptical about membership in a new organization. Another controversy erupted over voting in the planned Security Council. The Soviets proposed that great powers would have absolute veto on all matters, including substantive and procedural votes. Stalin also demanded that all of the fifteen Soviet Republics be granted membership in the General Assembly, a request that almost derailed the organization.

When the Soviet Union, the United Kingdom, China, and the United States signed the Moscow Declaration, they acknowledged "the necessity of establishing at the earliest practicable date a general international organization, based on the principle of the sovereign equality of all peace-loving states . . . for the maintenance of international peace and security." At the December 1943 meeting with Churchill and Stalin in Tehran, Roosevelt set out his "four policemen" approach where the great powers would collaborate and step in to enforce the peace if a country began acting aggressively—in essence providing an international police force. The first draft of what would become the UN Charter was set out at the Dumbarton Oaks mansion in Washington, DC, in the fall of 1944. Much of the detailed planning for the UN came from within the United States. Roosevelt created the Advisory Committee on Postwar Foreign Policy within the Department of State. This group drafted the document presented at the Dumbarton Oaks conference. U.S. efforts focused on reviving the institutional blueprint of the League of Nations created by South African diplomat and Prime Minister Jan Smuts that included a permanent secretariat, a large representative body, and an executive council. Many also credit Smuts with writing the first draft of the Preamble to the UN Charter.

During the two-phase Dumbarton Oaks meeting, the four powers reached agreement on the broad design of an institution that would emphasize international security yet also included economic development and a focus on international justice. The great powers established that they would contribute armed forces to enforce the proposed Security Council rulings and suppress aggression, something the League failed to do. Final details, in particular how voting would operate in the Security Council, were worked out in February 1945 in Yalta between Churchill, Roosevelt, and Stalin, and plans for a conference starting April 25, 1945, to establish the UN were announced.

Roosevelt's unexpected death on April 12, 1945, shortly before the UN plans were to be finalized, had the potential to end the American leadership of the process and threatened the creation of the UN. Churchill, Stalin, and Chinese leader Chiang Kai-shek were all shaken by the sudden loss of the president. One of the first questions posed to President Truman as he took office was whether the conference in San Francisco to establish the UN would be canceled or postponed. Yet, Truman was also a supporter of the UN and proclaimed that Roosevelt's policies would continue and that the conference would meet as planned.

The San Francisco Conference on International Organization was a transformative event as delegates traveled weeks to come together to draft the Charter even as World War II raged on. An estimated six thousand people representing their countries, the press, civil society, and international civil servants attended. Although the primary structure and goals of the organization were ironed out before the meeting, several controversies continued. One major debate at the conference involved who could participate. For example, a dispute arose over whether Argentina could attend due to its relationship with the Axis powers. The issue of including the Soviet Republics was resolved in a compromise plan when voting membership for two of its republics (Byelorussia and Ukraine) was granted. There were also questions about the role and powers of the General Assembly and the membership and scope of the Security Council. Many were concerned about the extent of power given to the United States, the United Kingdom, China, and the Soviet Union and wanted to ensure that middle and smaller powers had a voice and a role to play.

Although the great powers had agreed to much of the design, several compromises had to be made to gain the support of the rest of the countries in attendance. The role of regional organizations, like the Arab League (formed earlier in 1945), needed clarification. The transition from occupied territory to political self-determination was also a major issue, leading to the creation of a separate Trusteeship Council. In the face of the Holocaust, delegates also intended to create an International Bill of Human Rights. However, since this provoked numerous controversies, the issue was tabled to prevent disrupting the proceedings and the UN would wait until 1948 to create the Universal Declaration of Human Rights (see Part VI).

On July 28, 1945, the United States became the first country to ratify the Charter as the U.S. Senate approved the document in an 89–2 vote. Within months, enough other countries approved the Charter, and the UN came into legal existence on October 24, 1945, which is celebrated as UN Day. Former U.S. Secretary of State Cordell Hull won the Nobel Peace Prize for his efforts in creating the UN, although he gave extensive credit to Leo Pasvolsky (a U.S. bureaucrat who is viewed as drafting much of the Charter).

In a unanimous vote, the U.S. Congress invited the UN to build its permanent headquarters in the United States. Many Europeans wanted the UN to be headquartered on the European continent, and expanding on the site of the League of Nations in Geneva, Switzerland was a favored option. However, as much of Europe was in the process of rebuilding after the war, and many wanted to avoid the

> **San Francisco Conference on International Organization**
>
> From April 25 to June 25, 1945, San Francisco became the center of global efforts to create peace. With World War II still raging, delegates from fifty countries (representing more than 80 percent of the world's population) came together to create a new international organization. Headquartered at the San Francisco Opera House and Veteran's Building, delegates created four commissions to draft the Charter of the United Nations. The first was tasked with finalizing the requirements for membership, the purposes and principles of the organization, establishing the scope of the Secretariat, and the process for amending the Charter. The other three commissions mapped out the General Assembly, Security Council, and the International Court of Justice. Many raised concerns over the power that the Security Council would bestow upon China, France, the Soviet Union, the United Kingdom, and the United States, as each were given a permanent seat and veto power. The creation of the General Assembly, where all members would have an equal voice, helped to bring many skeptical smaller powers to the table. As many in attendance understood that security also came with economic stability and self-determination, the Economic and Social Council and the Trusteeship Council were created. After weeks of negotiations, around four hundred meetings, and moments of impasse the delegates unanimously signed the Charter on June 26, 1945, and declared their combined goal "to save succeeding generations from the scourge of war." In so doing, the delegates created both a practical constitution and a statement of ideals and aspirations. Although many attendees acknowledged that the design was not perfect, the outcome represented a significant step toward harmonizing countries' policies and created a forum to promote international peace and stability.

legacy of the League as a failure, the United States offered a fresh start. Within the United States, several cities were explored as possible locations, including Boston, Philadelphia, and San Francisco. At the first General Assembly session in January 1946, the member states (meeting in London) voted to build the UN offices in New York City. When John D. Rockefeller Jr., businessman and entrepreneur, donated the funds to purchase eighteen acres near the East River, the decision was finalized. This area on First Avenue between 42nd and 48th Streets is often referred to as Turtle Bay and is considered international territory. Construction got underway in 1948, and the UN's New York headquarters was completed in 1952.

See also: Charter of the United Nations; Collective Security; General Assembly; Human Rights; International Court of Justice; International Labour Organization; International Telecommunication Union; Membership; Regionalism; Role of Great Powers; Security Council; Self-Determination; Trusteeship Council; United Nations Headquarters; United Nations Principles; Universal Postal Union.

FURTHER READING

"A Great Day" Radio Program. January 1, 1955. Available at https://www.un.org/en/sections/history-united-nations-charter/1945-san-francisco-conference/index.html.

Hoopes, Townsend, and Douglas Brinkley. 1997. *FDR and the Creation of the U.N.* New Haven, CT: Yale University Press.

Krasno, Jean E. 2004. "Founding the United Nations: An Evolutionary Process." In *The United Nations: Confronting the Challenges of a Global Society*, edited by Jean E. Krasno. Boulder, CO: Lynne Rienner.

Reinalda, Bob. 2009. *Routledge History of International Organizations: From 1815 to the Present Day*. New York: Routledge.

Schlesinger, Stephen C. 2003. *Act of Creation: The Founding of the United Nations: A Story of Superpowers, Secret Agents, Wartime Allies and Enemies, and Their Quest for a Peaceful World*. Boulder, CO: Westview Press.

Charter of the United Nations

The UN Charter (full text provided in Part VI) is the founding document of the organization. Drafted and signed at the San Francisco Conference on International Organization (April–June 1945) and ratified to enter force in October 1945, the Charter is a binding international treaty that serves as the equivalent of the constitution of the UN and, according to some interpretations, for the global community overall. With a few exceptions, which are explained later, the text of the Charter remains unchanged today. The print version of the Charter, which is published in conjunction with the Statute of the International Court of Justice, famously appears with a UN blue-color cover in pocket size to carry for easy reference (although in honor of the seventieth anniversary of the organization, it was released with a range of different colored covers as well). Across a preamble and nineteen chapters covering 111 articles, the Charter sets out the central purposes, guiding principles, organizational structure, and functions of the UN and details the handling of threats to peace and security, economic and social cooperation, non-self-governing territories, membership, and regional arrangements.

While the current UN System encompasses a wide range of subsidiary bodies, which are in accordance with Article 7(2) on organs as well as the UN's approved relationship with intergovernmental specialized agencies (see Article 57 and other references across the Charter), the Charter focuses on setting out the six principal organs, with each getting its own chapter and related articles. The chapters on the first four principal organs set out their composition, functions and powers, voting, and basic procedures: General Assembly (Chapter IV), Security Council (Chapter V), Economic and Social Council (ECOSOC) (Chapter X), Trusteeship Council (Chapter XIII, building upon the preceding Chapter XI: Declaration regarding Non-Self-Governing Territories, and Chapter XII: International Trusteeship System). The chapters addressing the two remaining principal organs are structured differently. Chapter XIV on the International Court of Justice establishes the status, members, compliance, and ability of other UN bodies to request advisory opinions. Staffing guidelines for the Secretariat are provided in Chapter XV, along with the appointment process for and capabilities of the Secretary-General.

The Charter provides extensive coverage of the maintenance of international peace and security, including several chapters devoted to the topic. Chapter VI covers the pacific settlement of disputes, emphasizing the priority of resolving disagreements in a peaceful manner and explaining the means by which this could be pursued. Chapter VII: Action with Respect to Threats to the Peace, Breaches of the Peace, and Acts of Aggression stresses the central role for the Security Council to counter such situations and the need for the member states to follow the Council's security directives. However, the related Charter provisions set out in this chapter for readily available armed forces and the establishment of a Military Staff Committee to back the Security Council's capabilities have not been met. The chapter also concludes with Article 51, which explicitly provides for the acceptability of self-defense until the Security Council can act. While Chapter XVII outlines transitional security arrangements coming out of World War II, Chapter VIII on regional arrangements remains very relevant to modern efforts to promote peace and security. Although regional organizations in the world today address a number of issues, the Charter is focused solely on the security implications of such bodies. Regional arrangements and action are acceptable and may be encouraged or utilized as well by the Security Council, but the Charter is clear that such activities must fit with the parameters of UN purposes and principles and the Security Council remains the ultimate authorizing authority.

Compared to the variety of chapters connected to peace and security, there is only one distinct, separate chapter on international economic and social cooperation (Chapter IX), with much of this chapter devoted to the ability of the General Assembly, ECOSOC, and specialized agencies to work in this area. The central reference in this chapter is Article 55, which connects "stability and well-being" to social and economic conditions. Although also established as one of the central purposes of the UN, human rights do not have a dedicated chapter in the Charter. However, the vague references to human rights across the Charter, including in Article 55(c) that follows the points on economic and social cooperation, are widely acknowledged as representing a vital step in the development of global human rights protection.

Chapter II establishes the criteria and process for becoming a UN member. Following upon the fifty-one founding members of the UN (Article 3), additional members should be "peace-loving" states that accept and can live up to the "obligations" of the Charter (Article 4). The Security Council is responsible for judging applicants and making a recommendation to the General Assembly for approval, a process that has been used to expand the size of the UN over time to 193, with the latest member (South Sudan) added in 2011. Member states can be suspended, or even expelled, but no such explicit actions under Article 5 or 6 have been taken.

The text of the Charter established in 1945 remains largely unaltered. The growth in membership did spur changes to two of the principal organs, with the Security Council expanding from eleven to fifteen members in 1965 (by increasing the number of nonpermanent members from six to ten) and ECOSOC being enlarged from the original eighteen to twenty-seven in 1965 and further extended to fifty-four in 1973. The process for such amendments is covered in Chapter XVIII, with a two-thirds vote in the General Assembly needed to adopt amendments. Such amendments then require ratification, again by two-thirds of the membership, but this must also include all five permanent members of the Security Council. The member states have been largely unwilling to undertake this process to tackle more significant changes to the Charter.

See also: Economic and Social Council; General Assembly; Human Rights; International Court of Justice; Membership; Office of Secretary-General; Peaceful Settlement; Regionalism; Secretariat; Security Council; Trusteeship Council; United Nations Historical Background; United Nations Principles; United Nations Purposes; United Nations Reform.

FURTHER READING

Goodrich, Leland M., Edvard I. Hambro, and Anne P. Simons. 1969. *Charter of the United Nations: Commentary and Documents.* Third and revised edition. New York: Columbia University Press.

Shapiro, Ian, and Joseph Lampert, eds. 2014. *Charter of the United Nations: Together with Scholarly Commentaries and Essential Historical Documents.* New Haven, CT: Yale University Press.

Simma, Bruno, Hermann Khan, Georg Nolte, and Andreas Paulus, eds. 2012. *The Charter of the United Nations: A Commentary.* Third edition. Oxford: Oxford University Press.

United Nations Purposes

The purposes of the UN are laid out in the Preamble and Article 1 of the Charter. The purposes highlight the main objectives of the UN. Understanding what the organization is set up to achieve is vital for examining and evaluating the UN. Across the Preamble and Article 1, three central purposes appear. First, as the UN emerged from World War II, there is a clear emphasis on maintaining international peace and security. This priority is reflected in many UN activities designed to maintain international peace and security established in the Charter, including the peaceful settlement of disputes. UN practices have also evolved beyond what is explicitly set out in the Charter, in particular the development of peacekeeping. Second, the UN is supposed to promote international economic and social cooperation. UN bodies, such as the UN Development Programme and World Health Organization, are engaged in a wide range of economic and social programs. Third, the UN is designed to promote respect for human rights of all peoples across the globe. Protection of human rights is at the center of many UN activities and organizational bodies, including the Human Rights Council. While the UN remains strongly committed to the purposes laid out in the Charter, the mandate of the organization has expanded over the past seventy-five years to include the promotion of other issues such as environmental protection.

See also: Charter of the United Nations; Economic Development; Environmental Protection; Human Rights; Human Rights Council; Peaceful Settlement; Peacekeeping; United Nations Development Programme; World Health Organization.

United Nations Principles

Article 2 of the Charter establishes the principles of the UN, which can be viewed as the overarching philosophical or moral guidelines for UN affairs. The principles represent how the organization and its member states "shall act" when "in pursuit of the Purposes" set out in Article 1. Thus, the principles provide recommendations for the proper conduct of the organization as well as a blueprint for how UN member states should engage in international relations. While Article 2 presents seven points, these come together thematically around four central principles. Member states are expected to fulfill their obligations under the Charter "in good faith," which provides a strong position for the UN relative to individual members that have signed on to the Charter. However, other principles clearly emphasize member state capabilities. The first principle stresses that the UN "is based on the principle of sovereign equality." All member states, regardless of size or power in the international arena, are considered legal equals within the UN. The focus on sovereignty also dictates that there is no higher authority above a country, which can limit the possibility for independent actions by the UN. This is reinforced by the principle that the UN is not authorized to intervene in the domestic affairs of any member state. Developments in UN practice, such as the responsibility to protect, often center around different interpretations of sovereignty and what is considered to be under domestic jurisdiction. Finally, highlighting the UN's emphasis on maintaining international peace and security, there is a sequence of connected principles. These indicate that member states should not threaten or use force in any manner, must support UN enforcement efforts, require that nonmembers follow the same principles to maintain peace and security (although UN membership is now near universal), and should settle international disputes in a peaceful manner.

See also: Charter of the United Nations; Membership; Peaceful Settlement; Responsibility to Protect; United Nations Purposes.

PART II

United Nations Principal Organs

INTRODUCTION

The United Nations (UN) was established with six main bodies, which are designated as the principal organs of the organization. Each principal organ is detailed in a dedicated chapter of the UN Charter: General Assembly (Chapter IV), Security Council (Chapter V), Economic and Social Council (ECOSOC; Chapter X), Trusteeship Council (Chapter XIII), International Court of Justice (Chapter XIV), and Secretariat (Chapter XV). The UN is largely built upon the basic structure of its precursor, the League of Nations, which had an Assembly, Council, Permanent Court of International Justice, and Secretariat, but expanded with the addition of ECOSOC and the Trusteeship Council. Since the UN's founding, the principal organs have adapted and evolved to different degrees. For example, both ECOSOC and the Security Council expanded in size, and the Trusteeship Council, having completed its mandate, suspended operation. The principal organs are central to the functioning of the UN but also only serve as the "tip of the organizational iceberg" to the broader UN System (as detailed in Part III). While the principal organs do overlap in certain places, they do not play a "checks and balances" role relative to each other. In particular, the General Assembly and the Security Council (the two main decision-making bodies) pass separate resolutions independently, with Council decisions being legally binding on UN members while Assembly resolutions are nonbinding suggestions. The particular voting procedures also vary across the organs. The following entries detail the basic historical roots of each organ, the areas of responsibility, structure, activities and contributions, controversies and debates over, and institutional development and reform prospects.

Resolutions

The decisions or recommendations from a UN body are expressed in a formal text referred to as a resolution. Resolutions are passed by many entities within the UN System, although the resolutions from the main decision-making bodies of the General Assembly and the Security Council are particularly noted by the international community. Only Security Council decisions hold the status of being legally binding on UN members, but nonbinding resolutions are still an important marker of global agreement on an issue. Although a resolution may be several pages long, the format of a resolution is essentially one long sentence, with each part of the resolution carefully demarcated, and a period only appearing at the end of the resolution. A resolution begins with the heading, which clearly identifies which body approved the resolution, the date, and topic. As official UN documents, each resolution is given a distinct number that captures the source and timing, and these are often the short-hand reference for pointing to particular resolutions. For example, S/RES/2325 (2016) indicates resolution number 2325 passed by the Security Council (all Council resolutions are listed in numerical order) in 2016; while A/RES/71/278 designates General Assembly resolution number 278 passed in the 71st session (which took place 2016–2017). Following the heading is a set of preambular clauses, which set out previous work on this topic as well as the need to address this topic. Each preambular clause begins with an italicized phrase such as "Emphasizing," "Guided by," or "Recalling," and the clauses are separated by a comma. The final section has a series of operative clauses that set out what should be done to address the topic. Operative clauses also begin with an italicized phrase but are separated by a semicolon. All clauses can include additional phrasing that indicates the level of seriousness of the phrase, for example, moving from "Noting" to "Noting with deep concern" in the preambulatory section or using "Demands" instead of "Requests" in the operative section. Resolutions are translated into the six official languages of the UN (Arabic, Chinese, English, French, Russian, and Spanish). For examples of General Assembly and Security Council resolutions, see Part VI.

Voting Procedures

Majority

The most common form of voting requires the approval of the majority of the members present and voting. The exact number required for a majority to be reached can vary, with the most common form being a simple majority with 51 percent approval as in the Economic and Social Council (ECOSOC) and the Trusteeship Council. The International Court of Justice rulings are decided by a majority of the judges presiding, although the President of the Court is empowered to break a tie vote. The General Assembly requires a simple majority for most votes, although a two-thirds majority is required for "important questions" as outlined in Article 18 of the Charter. The Security Council requires a minimum of nine affirmative votes (out of the fifteen members).

Negative

The Security Council also employs negative voting. The five permanent members (China, France, Russia, the United Kingdom, and the United States) are allowed to veto a decision by casting a no vote. Thus, even if it is a 14–1 vote, if there is one "no" vote from a permanent member then the resolution fails.

Consensus

Instead of taking a formal vote, decisions can be reached by consensus. Consensus means that there is common consent among all participants that they have reached a satisfactory collective decision acceptable to all, with no objections. Many decisions in ECOSOC and the General Assembly are now taken by consensus, although majority votes are employed as well.

Unanimity

Unlike consensus, where a vote passes as long as there is not dissent, unanimity requires positive votes from the participating countries. This ensures that the decisions taken reflect the full support of all members. The League of Nations was limited by its need to pass decisions unanimously, which led to the alternative voting approach for the UN. Other international organizations still require unanimity, such as the North Atlantic Treaty Organization (although consensus is largely employed).

Weighted

Weighted voting ensures that certain countries have greater voting power, based on factors such as relative population size or financial contribution to the organization. None of the principal organs use weighted voting, but there are other parts of the UN System where this is employed (with some controversy). A noted example is the International Monetary Fund, where the percentage of votes is connected to the level of money contributed.

General Assembly

The General Assembly is the only principal organ at the UN with universal membership. Acting as the UN's plenary body, the General Assembly brings together representatives from every member state to discuss the challenges of the day, inform the international community about local and global issues, and set standards regarding expectations for countries' behavior. The General Assembly is the primary representative institution within the UN and operates with a deep commitment to "one country, one vote." While the General Assembly does not have legal enforcement power, its actions do hold significant symbolic power. Many smaller and middle power countries use the General Assembly as a key venue for their foreign policies.

REPRESENTATION

Along with the 193 member state representatives (as of the addition of South Sudan in 2011), the General Assembly also provides a number of actors with "observer" status. The UN classifies the Holy See (or the Vatican) and Palestine as nonmember states and allows them to maintain permanent observer missions at UN Headquarters in New York. Many international organizations and other entities (such as the African Union, the European Union, the International Committee of the Red Cross, and the Inter-Parliamentary Union) also have observer status with permanent offices and can participate in discussions and negotiations, but they cannot vote. Other international organizations are allowed to participate as observers, but they cannot maintain permanent offices at the UN (such as the Association of Caribbean States, Commonwealth of Independent States, and Pacific Islands Forum). Overall, approximately one hundred international governmental organizations and other entities have observer status. The General Assembly grants one vote for each member, which provides equal representation for every member state. Although there have been efforts to revise this approach, such as attempts to create a weighted voting system that would give countries with more money (and thus financial contributions to the UN) and larger populations more power or say, the General Assembly has remained firmly committed to equal representation.

RESPONSIBILITIES

Most of the responsibilities of the General Assembly are listed in Chapter IV of the UN Charter, although several places throughout the Charter also refer to the body's role and responsibilities. For example, Article 4 of Chapter II discusses the guidelines for the role of the General Assembly in approving membership, and Article 35 of Chapter VI establishes that member states may bring disputes to the attention of the General Assembly (as well as the Security Council). The relationship between the institutions of the UN do not correspond to a "checks and balances" approach, yet there is overlap of responsibilities in several areas, including the appointment of the Secretary-General (in conjunction with the Security Council) and acceptance of new members (through application to the Secretary-General and review by the Security Council). The General Assembly also elects judges to the International Court of Justice (ICJ; again in conjunction with the Security Council) and member states to the Economic and Social Council (ECOSOC), the Human Rights Council, and the Peacebuilding Commission (along with ECOSOC and the Security Council). In addition, the General Assembly is tasked with reviewing reports from other UN agencies. Chapter IV also gives the General Assembly the authority to make recommendations on international political cooperation. Perhaps the most significant power of the General Assembly is the power of the purse, as the Assembly oversees the UN budget and creates the formula that establishes the dues that each member state pays. The General Assembly can also establish new UN entities. For example, this power was used when creating the UN Environment Programme in 1972.

DECISION-MAKING PROCESS

As General Assembly membership is inclusive of countries from across the globe, the majority of the representatives are from developing countries. At the same time, the General Assembly presents a Western approach to discussion and debate as it abides by the rules of parliamentary procedure, majority voting, caucusing, the presentation of resolutions that may accept revisions, and the division of tasks. Like most legislative branches, the work of the body is delegated to several committees. When the General Assembly considers an issue, it usually starts in one of the permanent Main Committees. Each of these committees is guided by a Bureau made up of a Chair, three Vice-Chairs, and a Rapporteur.

There are six main General Assembly committees. The First Committee, called the Disarmament and International Security Committee, has an agenda that includes weapons of mass destruction (both nuclear and chemical), weapons in outer space, conventional weapons, weapons proliferation, and approaches to disarmament. The Second Committee is also known as the Economic and Financial Committee. This committee's discussions include economic policy, poverty eradication, financing for economic development, food security and agriculture development, issues concerning globalization, the use of technology and communication for development, sustainable development, and the authority of Palestinians to control their natural resources. A significant part of the Social, Humanitarian and Cultural Committee's (Third Committee) work focuses on the promotion of human rights, along with issues such as social development, advancement of women, crime prevention, and drug control. The Fourth Committee, called the Special Political and Decolonization Committee, addresses areas, including non-self-governing territories, the effects of atomic radiation, Palestinian refugees, and cooperating on the peaceful uses of outer space. In addition, the committee includes the work of the Special Committee on Peacekeeping Operations, which incorporates all of the member states engaged with peacekeeping missions. The Administrative and Budgetary Committee constitutes the Fifth Committee, which focuses on the UN's general operations budget and the peacekeeping budget. The Fifth Committee establishes the "scale of assessments," which sets how much each member state pays to the UN and also considers oversight issues, such as human resources matters and management reform. The Sixth Committee, or the Legal Committee, provides focus on international law and other UN legal matters. The committee hosts an "International Law Week" each October, which includes an invitation to the President of the ICJ to address the committee. The resolutions, reports, and decisions adopted by the six Main Committees are usually submitted to the full General Assembly for what are called "plenary sessions."

The General Assembly has established rules of procedure and elects a President for each annual session, with these sessions opening on Tuesday of the third week of September. Along with the President, there are twenty-one Vice-Presidents who, together with the Chairs of the six Main Committees, make up the General Committee. There is also a nine-member Credentials Committee, which reviews the credentials of member state delegations. The opening meetings of each General Assembly have become significant media events and many Heads of State come to the UN and make speeches in the General Assembly Hall. Notable speakers in recent years have also included Pope Francis. While the audience is composed of UN delegates, the speakers are also thinking of the audience back home. The ceremonies in September have been described as global political theater due to their more symbolic than substantive nature. In addition, the September meetings now draw organizations and groups from around the world and provide the epicenter of a flurry of global political activity, both formal events within the UN walls and informal events in and around the UN as well as other offices and social gatherings.

Each annual session of the General Assembly is numbered consecutively, with the first regular session opening in 1946 and the 74th session in 2019. Beginning with the 44th session (1989–1990), the General Assembly has been deemed to be "in session" for the entire year. Each session is divided into two parts: the first part (from mid-September to December) is known as the "main" session and includes general debate and most of the work of the six Main Committees. The second part (from January to September) is referred to as the "resumed" session and often includes debates that focus on a particular theme, consultations, and meetings of working groups. Special sessions can be called, and thirty such sessions have been convened as of the latest in 2016. These sessions range from an examination of the global drug problem, consideration of HIV/AIDS, and disarmament, to several focused on specific countries or regions, including Namibia, the racial segregation policy of Apartheid in South Africa, and the status of the Palestinians.

Within the General Assembly, most resolutions require a simple majority (just over 50 percent) to pass. However, some issues, particularly those on the admission of new countries as members, resolutions concerning peace and security, and budgets, require that two-thirds of those voting are in agreement. On more procedural issues, the threshold is lower and the voting requirement is a simple majority. As the agenda is very full and each year similar provisions are passed, the General Assembly often uses consensus rather than a formal roll call vote to move resolutions through the agenda. The President, in consultation with the delegates, can declare that a resolution has support by "consensus," where no member state objects and, therefore, passes without a formal vote.

The resolutions that pass the General Assembly are not enforceable and represent recommendations to the countries of the world. At the same time, the General Assembly has adopted significant policies and proposals that have influenced millions of people. The General Assembly is the primary multilateral venue and has approved several landmark statements, including the adoption of the Universal Declaration on Human Rights (1948, see Part VI), the Millennium Development Goals (2000), the World Summit Outcome Document (2005), and the Sustainable Development Goals (2015). The General Assembly designed many standards and road maps for countries to follow in their efforts to control the spread of weapons of mass destruction, eradicate poverty, protect the global environment, create gender equality, and promote human security.

There have also been moments in time when the General Assembly took on a more robust role. During the Cold War and the conflict between the Soviet Union and the United States, the Security Council faced gridlock as the hope for great power collaboration failed. In response, with U.S. Secretary of State Dean Acheson's initiative, the United States pushed for the General Assembly to assume a greater role in issues of peace and security. In 1950, the General Assembly adopted the "Uniting for Peace" Resolution, holding that if the Security Council is not able to come to agreement on an issue of international peace and security, then the General Assembly may take up the matter.

United Nations General Assembly Special Sessions

Year	Session	Topic
2016	30th	World Drug Problem
2015	29th	Follow-up to the Programme of Action of the International Conference on Population and Development beyond 2014
2005	28th	Commemoration of the 60th Anniversary of the Liberation of the Nazi Concentration Camps
2002	27th	World Summit for Children
2001	26th	Problem of Human Immunodeficiency Virus/Acquired Immunodeficiency Syndrome (HIV/AIDS) in All Its Aspects
2001	25th	Implementation of the Outcome of the UN Conference on Human Settlements (Habitat II)
2000	24th	Social Development
2000	23rd	Women 2000: Gender Equality, Development and Peace for the Twenty-First Century
1999	22nd	Small Island Developing States
1999	21st	Population and Development
1998	20th	World Drug Problem
1997	19th	Review and Appraisal of the Implementation of Agenda 21 (Earth Summit + 5)
1990	18th	International Economic Cooperation
1990	17th	Drug Abuse
1989	16th	Apartheid
1988	15th	Disarmament
1986	14th	Namibia
1986	13th	Africa
1982	12th	Disarmament
1980	11th	New International Economic Order
1978	10th	Disarmament
1978	9th	Namibia
1978	8th	Financing of the UN Interim Force in Lebanon
1975	7th	Development and International Economic Cooperation
1974	6th	Raw Materials and Development
1967	5th	South West Africa (Namibia)
1963	4th	Financial Situation of the UN
1961	3rd	Tunisia
1948	2nd	Palestine
1948	1st	Palestine

Unlike most national legislatures, the General Assembly does not divide based on political party or ideological orientation. However, there are groups that effectively work together and create voting blocs and coalitions. Some of these groups are based on regional associations. Countries in the same geographic area tend to share similar political and economic concerns, and over the past seventy-plus years, many have solidified their consistent alliances. Five distinct groups, which are also used as electoral groups, are immediately recognizable in the General Assembly. These are the African Group (with fifty-four countries as members), Asia-Pacific Group (fifty-five members), Eastern European Group (twenty-three members), Latin American and Caribbean Group (GRULAC; thirty-three members), Western European and Others Group (WEOG; twenty-nine members) that includes Canada and Israel. Some countries present special cases. For instance, Turkey straddles two groups (Asia-Pacific and WEOG, but only WEOG for elections). The United States is not officially a member of any group but does have observer status and election voting privileges in WEOG. Israel was admitted to WEOG in 2000. Broader common interest groups also exist, including the very large developing country bloc known as the Group of 77 (G-77) and the Non-Aligned Movement.

The General Assembly can also create special working groups or ad hoc committees to examine a specific topic and submit a report with policy recommendations. All countries can participate in these committees and working groups. The meetings include formal and informal discussions. Working groups have been created to examine topics ranging from the human rights of the elderly to the biodiversity of the oceans.

CHALLENGES AND REFORM

The agenda of the General Assembly is consistently ambitious and includes climate change, counterterrorism, development, disarmament, drug control, education, health security, humanitarian assistance, human rights, promotion of global justice, and refugee assistance, among many others. The scope of the General Assembly's work can be viewed as a strength or a weakness, as some find the agenda to be too ambitious and even watered down. In response, efforts to reform the General Assembly's approach have been considered for decades. As both the debates and resolutions are often repetitive from year to year, many have called to streamline this process, refocus the meetings, and prioritize the implementation of resolutions and member state compliance.

There was a push during the 2005 World Summit to review and strengthen the General Assembly's program of work, including establishing an ongoing Ad Hoc Working Group on the Revitalization of the General Assembly. Ideas include simplifying and focusing the agenda as well as ending the emphasis on passing consensus resolutions, which critics argue create weak resolutions based on compromise. Other revitalization areas include creating a more effective committee system and enhancing the role of nongovernmental organizations and specialists during deliberations. There is also a focus on enhancing the powers of the General Assembly, specifically from member states representing the developing world. However, more powerful countries are generally reluctant to improve the General Assembly's capacities. As an Ambassador from Pakistan pointed out, revitalization "is a political rather than a procedural matter." Although it is often dismissed as a global "talk shop," the General Assembly is the only institution where representatives from all over the world can meet and have both unofficial and official discussions. Despite criticisms of its effectiveness and ongoing calls for reform, without the General Assembly the logistics of regularly gathering representatives of countries from around the world to address global issues would be extremely difficult.

See also: Arms Control and Disarmament; Charter of the United Nations; Economic and Social Council; Economic Development; Environmental Protection; Human Rights Council; Human Security; International Court of Justice; Membership; Nongovernmental Organizations; Office of Secretary-General; Peacebuilding Commission; President of General Assembly; Refugees and Migration; Security Council; Terrorism; United Nations Budget and Financing; United Nations Environment Programme; Voting and Negotiating Blocs; Women and Gender.

FURTHER READING

Aeschlimann, Johann, and Mary Regan, eds. 2017. *The GA Handbook: A Practical Guide to the United Nations General Assembly.* Second edition. New York: Permanent Mission of Switzerland to the United Nations.

Brazys, Samuel, and Diana Panke. 2017. "Why Do States Change Positions in the United Nations General Assembly?" *International Political Science Review* 38 (1): 70–84.

Panke, Diana. 2013. *Unequal Actors in Equalising Institutions: Negotiations in the United Nations General Assembly.* New York: Palgrave Macmillan.

Peterson, M. J. 2006. *The UN General Assembly.* London: Routledge.

Rauschning, Dietrich, Katja Wiesbrock, and Martin Lailach, eds. 1997. *Key Resolutions of the United Nations General Assembly, 1946–1996.* Cambridge: Cambridge University Press.

Security Council

The Security Council is the principal organ assigned to ensure the maintenance of international peace and security. This charge is ambitious and places the Security Council at the center of global politics, although the record of success in securing global order is mixed. While the Security Council was designed to create a collaborative approach to fostering peace and security, great power politics have overwhelmed the body's capacity in many cases. While some find this principal organ antiquated and ineffective, others point to declining instances of war, the emergence of peacekeeping, and the containment of many local conflicts as indicators of the Security Council's success.

In the ashes of World War I and the return to conflict with World War II, global leaders wanted to find a way to escape the cycle of war by creating an international organization to diminish threats to international peace and security. The balance of power approach had failed, as had the League of Nations. After the outbreak of World War II, the Allied Powers agreed to build on the Concert of Europe model and the idea that powerful military countries could forge an alliance to serve as an international police force. Like the League of Nations before, the UN blueprint included an executive council that would focus on securing global peace, yet the hope was that the revised Security Council approach would escape the gridlock of the League. Negotiations during World War II about the design of a future Security Council created several controversies, especially regarding which countries would be granted membership and voting privileges. Despite criticism, the debate was finally settled at the 1945 San Francisco Conference, where it was decided that permanent membership and veto power would be given to the powerful victors of World War II.

STRUCTURE

The UN Charter gives the Security Council primary authority for maintaining and restoring international peace and security. The UN architects designed the Security Council to be a small and efficient body. The "Permanent Five" (P-5) members are France, the United Kingdom, the United States, the Russian Federation (descendant of the Soviet Union), and the People's Republic of China (which took over the seat in 1971 from the Republic of China). The Charter originally provided for eleven members, but this was expanded to fifteen in 1965 in one of the few amendments to the Charter. In addition to the permanent members, the General Assembly elects the ten non-permanent members (based on regional geographic representation, with five from Africa and Asia, two from Latin America and the Caribbean, two from Western Europe and Others, and one East European) that serve two-year terms. Five of these non-permanent members are elected each year and countries cannot serve consecutive terms, which keeps any non-permanent country from essentially serving as a permanent member through being reelected every time.

A President presides over the Security Council, with the office rotating monthly among all fifteen members (in alphabetical order). Article 29 of the Charter establishes that the Security Council can create "subsidiary organs" to support its work, which includes the Counter-Terrorism Committee set out in Resolutions 1373 (2001) and 1624 (2005), the Non-Proliferation Committee established through Resolutions 1540 (2004) and 2325 (2016), and a number of Sanctions Committees. While the Security Council created the International Criminal Tribunal for the former Yugoslavia in 1993 and the International Criminal Tribunal for Rwanda in 1994 as subsidiary organs, both judicial bodies operated independently. The Security Council also calls upon groups of experts to assist with technical issues and factual information regarding specific situations, as well as working groups examining areas such as children and armed conflict and conflict in Africa.

The Security Council is always in session with an ongoing meeting agenda. Members agree to be "on-call" at any time to respond to potential security threats. The formal meeting space of the Security Council is at UN Headquarters in New

York, although the Council has met in other locations around the globe, including Addis Ababa (1972), Panama City (1973), and Nairobi (2004). Delegates gather around a horseshoe-shaped table for formal procedures, while informal conversations often occur in private meetings, which are considered "off the record" and shielded from the press. Countries contributing troops for Security Council–authorized missions may also participate when a meeting concerns logistics and coordination of operations.

While General Assembly resolutions are not approved by the Security Council (and vice versa), there is some overlap in the relationship between the two organs. The General Assembly chooses the nonpermanent members of the Security Council and coordinates with the Council to elect judges to the International Court of Justice (ICJ). The Security Council takes the lead in the appointment of a Secretary-General, with the General Assembly thus far always approving the Council's recommendation. Under Article 99 of the Charter, the Secretary-General may bring security issues to the Security Council, but this capability is rarely directly invoked.

DECISION-MAKING PROCESS

To pass a Security Council resolution, there must be nine affirmative votes, "including the concurring votes of the permanent members" (Charter, Article 27(3)). A "no" vote by one of the permanent members is termed a "veto" (Latin for "I forbid"), which blocks a resolution regardless of the number of affirmative votes. Yet, permanent members can choose to abstain from a vote and, therefore, allow a resolution to pass without their positive approval. On procedural matters, the veto is not allowed. Article 27(3) requires countries that are parties to a dispute to abstain from the vote, yet this Charter provision is rarely enforced. These two provisions create situations that are labeled the "double veto." Members of the Security Council determine whether an issue is a "dispute" or a simple "situation." By determining if an issue is subject to a vote, the permanent members essentially create a loophole and thus hold "double veto" power. A similar issue arises as members decide whether an issue should be categorized as a "substantive issue" or a "procedural issue."

Unlike other UN institutions, the Security Council's decisions are legally binding. Article 25 of the Charter establishes that all members of the UN will "accept and carry out the decisions of the Security Council." However, implementation of Security Council resolutions is not guaranteed. While any member state of the UN can bring an issue to the Security Council, agreement by the P-5 is essential for the Council to be effective. UN operations are often authorized through a political process where the focus may be on a Security Council member's strategic interest rather than the risk of escalation of violence. In fact, the Security Council was divided, and at times even paralyzed, by the Cold War. For example, by June 1962 the Soviet Union had vetoed a hundred resolutions. This gridlock triggered the adoption of the "Uniting for Peace" Resolution by the General Assembly (1950), which allows the Assembly to bypass the Security Council and pass

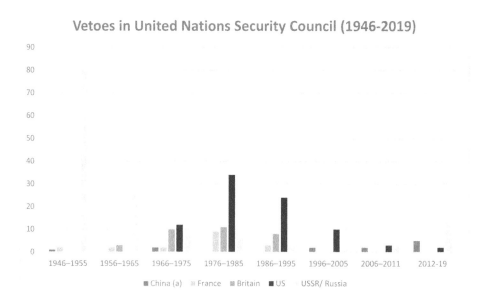

recommendations on the use of force if the Council is not able to act, although this provision is rarely used. With the decrease in Cold War tensions by the late 1980s, the Security Council responded to issues in Afghanistan, Cambodia, Iran, and Iraq. The drop in the number of vetoes created renewed optimism about the Council's abilities, but this enthusiasm was dampened by tragedies such as Somalia (1991–1993), Rwanda (1994), and Bosnia (1995), where the UN was unable to prevent brutal violence. At the same time, Security Council members did authorize operations to reconstruct postconflict Kosovo (1999) and established a transitional government in East Timor (1999). More recently, the conflict in Syria highlights the Security Council's difficulties. Since the start of the conflict in 2011, despite allegations of war crimes and the use of chemical weapons, Russia and China have vetoed multiple resolutions designed to address the threats to peace and security in Syria.

ACTIVITIES

In addressing threats to peace and security, there are several tools the Security Council can use. First, the Security Council is guided to prioritize peaceful approaches and avoid the use of military force. The peaceful settlement tools incorporated under Chapter VI are noncoercive and rely on approaches such as fact-finding, mediation, and negotiation. In some cases, the condemning of an action or the shaming of a contentious party can be effective. The Security Council played a key role in negotiating the 2015 agreement to end Iran's nuclear program. The Council can also refer situations to the ICJ and the International Criminal Court, although there has been relatively limited use of this capability. Article 94 authorizes the Security Council to act in cases of noncompliance with an ICJ ruling, but this provision has also largely not been used although, in one instance in 1986, the United States rejected a resolution calling for its fulfillment of an ICJ ruling on its activities in Nicaragua.

Chapter VII of the Charter expands the Security Council's toolbox to include coercive approaches to end violence. The use of sanctions, the disruption of diplomatic relations, and interrupting communication systems is granted through Article 41. For example, in response to the development of North Korean nuclear and ballistic missile programs, the Security Council imposed multiple targeted sanctions and passed resolutions condemning North Korea and demanding that such actions cease. Article 42 grants the Security Council enforcement powers and allows the UN to "take such action by air, sea, or land forces as may be necessary to maintain or restore international peace and security." Articles 43–47 allow for the command and deployment of military forces, although the UN has no standing army and must rely on member states to contribute troops for such endeavors. Two

---

Use and Misuse of the Security Council: Persian Gulf War versus the Iraq War

The Persian Gulf War (1991) and the Iraq War (2003–2011) present very different outcomes in the Security Council's efforts to address breaches of the peace. In the first case, an international coalition received Security Council authorization to intervene and restore Kuwait's sovereignty. In the second case, there was a small coalition of forces, no Security Council authorization, and the violence extended for years. In August 1990, when Iraqi troops invaded neighboring Kuwait, the Security Council responded to Iraq's aggression by passing multiple resolutions. At the end of November 1990, Resolution 678 authorized the use of "all necessary means" to compel Iraq to withdraw from Kuwait and the military campaign began in mid-January 1991. In a moment of rare consensus, a coalition of thirty-nine countries contributed troops or support. Many proclaimed the UN-authorized intervention as a symbol of the "new world order" with Soviet-U.S. hostilities at an end. The actions invigorated the Security Council and brought renewed optimism about UN capacities to promote international peace and stability.

The controversy over the 2003 Iraq War, one of the most contentious moments within Security Council history, provides a low counter point. After the terrorist attacks on September 11, 2001, the United States focused on removing Saddam Hussein from power in Iraq and halting the country's alleged weapons of mass destruction program. Secretary-General Kofi Annan called for mediation and continued arms inspections. Within the Security Council, there were months of negotiations, resulting in the unanimous passage of Resolution 1441 in November 2002 calling for Iraq's "full, final, and complete disclosure" of its weapons of mass destruction and ballistic missiles programs. However, the provisions set forth by Resolution 1441 did not satisfy the United States, which made a case for military action against Iraq. Within the Security Council, most members did not support the allegations against Iraq. Even close allies of the United States, including the delegations from France and Germany, did not find the evidence of an Iraqi weapons program convincing enough to warrant intervention. Despite facing significant opposition, the United States proceeded without Security Council authorization, launching an air attack against Iraq in March 2003. The Iraq War provoked many to question the UN's relevance and capacity to manage threats to international peace and security.

notable authorizations of use of force under Chapter VII are Korea (1950–1953) and Iraq (1990–1991).

A significant shift in the Security Council approach to maintaining peace and security is the invention of peacekeeping. Since 1948, the Security Council has authorized more than seventy peacekeeping operations. Much of the Security Council's agenda now includes monitoring field operations, holding special meetings on operations, and receiving progress reports from the Secretary-General and others engaged in peacekeeping missions. Peacekeeping is often referred to as "Chapter VI ½" as the approach falls between peaceful settlement and the full use of force. Further blurring the lines between Chapter VI and Chapter VII, many operations authorized since 2010 are "stabilization efforts" and include elements of counterinsurgency and counterterrorism (i.e., Mali, Democratic Republic of Congo, Central African Republic, and South Sudan). In 2013, the Security Council committed an "Intervention Brigade" under the UN Organization Stabilization Mission in the Democratic Republic of Congo to "carry out targeted offensive operations . . . prevent the expansion of all armed groups, neutralize these groups, and disarm them." The Security Council also created the Peacebuilding Commission in 2005 (in conjunction with the General Assembly) and benefits from three regional offices for preventive diplomacy in Central Asia, West Africa, and Central Africa established between 2002 and 2011.

CHALLENGES AND REFORM

The Security Council continues to evolve and change. In terms of process, the Security Council has consistently modified its working methods since the 1990s. Innovations include the creation of "Arria-formula" meetings. These informal and confidential meetings provide an opportunity for direct conversations with government representatives and other relevant stakeholders. Another development is open debate time, where non-Council members may attend and share their viewpoints. One report indicates that the number of hours dedicated to such debate almost doubled between 2013 and 2016 (from 90 hours to over 160), which demonstrates growing transparency and inclusiveness. Yet, some of these changes are controversial, particularly the Security Council's incremental extension of coverage for "peace and security." Since Resolution 688 in 1991, which condemned the political repression of the Iraqi people, the Security Council has passed several resolutions that include the protection of human rights, particularly in cases of mass atrocities, including invoking the norm of the responsibility to protect. Another expansion of scope includes passing Resolution 1325 in 2000 calling for greater understanding and engagement of women in building peace and security through representation, gendered perspectives, and protection (see Part VI).

The Security Council is notable for the lack of action taken regarding several issues. The inability to negotiate the Vietnam conflict in the 1960s, prevent genocide in Rwanda (1994), the failure to stop the Iraq War (2003), and the incapacity to respond to Russia's incursion into Crimea (2014) all highlight the Security Council's inability to address certain threats to peace and security. The

Israeli-Arab/Palestinian conflict is another area where the Security Council has little traction, in part due to the intervention of great powers—in particular, the United States rejecting many resolutions regarding this issue.

One consistent area of critique is representation on the Security Council. As UN membership grew, appeals for expansion of the Security Council increased. In 1965, the Security Council did grow from eleven to fifteen members by adding four additional non-permanent members. Yet, many argue that the membership does not reflect the current power and relevance of countries. There are repeated calls for expanding both permanent and non-permanent members, which tends to trigger clashes between regional powers for representation. Germany, India, Japan, and Brazil frequently make the list of potential new permanent members. While the conversation is often about increasing geographic representation, there

---

Proposed Security Council Reforms

Membership Reforms
  Addition of More Members
  The Annan Plans (proposed by Secretary-General Kofi Annan in 2005)
  - *Plan A:* Add six permanent members (with no veto) and three nonpermanent seats with two-year terms (twenty-four members in total)
  - *Plan B:* Add eight nonpermanent seats with four-year renewable terms and one nonpermanent seat with a two-year nonrenewable term (twenty-four members in total)

G4 Plan
  - Emphasis on adding Brazil, Germany, India, and Japan as permanent members

Uniting for Consensus ("Coffee Club") Plan
  - Change from ten to twenty nonpermanent seats with two-year terms, which would be renewable (twenty-five members in total)

African Group ("Ezulwini Consensus") Plan
  - Emphasis on adding two permanent members, with veto power, and five nonpermanent seats for African countries

Expanded Terms
  - Give nonpermanent members the possibility of immediate re-election
  - Give nonpermanent members extended terms (i.e., six years)

Voting Reforms
  - Add new permanent members with/without veto power
  - Prohibit all veto capacities in cases of mass atrocities
  - Require at least two vetoes to block a resolution
  - Reduce the ability to use a veto in resolutions building on Chapter VII of the UN Charter
  - Remove veto power from the Permanent Five

are concerns that Security Council reforms would decrease efficiency, particularly if new members are granted veto power. There are also proposals to eliminate or restrict the use of the veto in cases of mass atrocities and on those resolutions with Chapter VII authorization. Although a Working Group was established in 1993 by the General Assembly, which was changed to an Intergovernmental Negotiation process in 2008, little progress has been made. In addition, any membership reforms will require amending the Charter. This requires ratification by two-thirds of the General Assembly and all permanent members of the Security Council. The P-5 countries are unlikely to support diluting their power.

The Security Council has been effective in deescalating many situations that had the potential to intensify into significant conflicts. In addition, evidence of Security Council success is found in the remarkable reduction in war between countries over the past seventy-five years. Yet, internal armed conflicts and civil wars remain problematic, many of which are riddled with nonstate actors who no longer operate within the confines of state borders, as well as the rise of transnational terrorism. Furthermore, many conflicts increasingly target civilians and UN staff and are internationalized, with outside states supporting governments and opposition groups, including Syria (2011–), Libya (2011–), Yemen (2015–), and the Democratic Republic of Congo (2008–). Such developments challenge a Security Council crafted to assist countries in navigating conflict and bound to uphold sovereignty as it seeks to maintain international peace and security.

See also: Collective Security; General Assembly; Human Rights; International Court of Justice; International Criminal Court; Office of Secretary-General; Peacebuilding Commission; Peaceful Settlement; Peacekeeping; President of Security Council; Regionalism; Responsibility to Protect; Role of Great Powers; Terrorism; United Nations Headquarters; United Nations Historical Background; United Nations Reform.

FURTHER READING

Bosco, David L. 2009. *Five to Rule Them All: The UN Security Council and the Making of the Modern World.* Oxford: Oxford University Press.

Lowe, Vaughan, Adam Roberts, Jennifer Welsh, and Dominik Zaum, eds. 2010. *The United Nations Security Council and War: The Evolution of Thought and Practice Since 1945.* Oxford: Oxford University Press.

Nadin, Peter. 2016. *UN Security Council Reform.* New York: Routledge.

Sievers, Loraine, and Sam Daws. 2014. *The Procedure of the UN Security Council.* Fourth edition. Oxford: Oxford University Press.

Von Einsiedel, Sebastian, David M. Malone, and Bruno S. Ugarte, eds. 2016. *The UN Security Council in the Twenty-First Century.* Boulder, CO: Lynne Rienner.

Economic and Social Council (ECOSOC)

The Economic and Social Council (ECOSOC) holds a very broad mandate and role in the UN System but is often overlooked compared to the other principal organs. The inclusion of ECOSOC with principal organ status at the founding of the UN was a strong signal that the creators of the organization were committed to more than the maintenance of international peace and security. ECOSOC oversees and assists with coordinating the work of a wide range of UN-related entities and is called upon to promote "international economic, social, cultural, educational, health, and related matters" and "human rights and fundamental freedoms for all" (UN Charter, Article 62). In 2013, ECOSOC underwent reform that included taking on a central position in the UN System–wide promotion of sustainable development. ECOSOC also maintains the formal process for including nongovernmental organizations (NGOs) and describes itself as a "gateway for UN partnership and participation by the rest of the world." During the creation of the UN, NGOs participated in the discussion and their role was formalized in the Charter with ECOSOC established as the channel for NGO representation at the UN. Therefore, ECOSOC serves as an intersection between the interests of member states, UN staff, and global civil society.

MEMBERSHIP AND STRUCTURE

The General Assembly elects the fifty-four members of ECOSOC. The size of ECOSOC grew incrementally as UN membership increased. In 1965, ECOSOC expanded from eighteen members to twenty-seven, and then in 1973 to its current size. Both changes were two of the very few situations where the Charter was amended. Membership is nonpermanent and determined by region, as the African states receive fourteen seats, Western European and Others have thirteen seats, Asia holds eleven, ten are reserved for Latin American and Caribbean countries, and Eastern European member states hold the remaining six. The three-year terms are renewable and are staggered as eighteen members are elected each year. Permanent members of the Security Council are regularly elected as members of ECOSOC.

Leadership within ECOSOC includes a Bureau of one President and four Vice-Presidents, who are elected across geographic regions. Representatives of the UN's specialized agencies can participate in ECOSOC meetings and deliberations, but they do not hold a vote. There is also a subcommittee that reviews consultative status applications by NGOs. ECOSOC directly oversees five Regional Commissions (Africa, Europe, Latin America and the Caribbean, Asia and the Pacific, and Western Asia) and a range of Functional Commissions (including Crime Prevention and Criminal Justice, Social Development, Statistics, and Status of Women). Varied specialized agencies, programmes, and funds also report to ECOSOC.

RELATIONSHIP WITH OTHER ACTORS

Representatives from a wide spectrum of civil society, including academics, foundations, philanthropists, and members of the business community, contribute to the UN. Article 71 of the Charter directly mentions NGOs, noting, "The Economic and Social Council may make suitable arrangements for consultation with non-governmental organizations which are concerned with matters within its competence." Over five thousand NGOs hold such consultative status and, although they cannot vote, they receive documents, participate in meetings and events, and make written and oral statements. The specific level of engagement varies as NGOs are placed into one of three categories of consultative status (General, Special, and Roster) based on their contributions to issues covered by ECOSOC. NGOs with consultative status include Rotary International (status first granted in 1947), International Commission of Jurists (1957), World Federation for Mental Health (1963), Association for World Education (1979), Minority Rights Group (1987), Academic Council on the United Nations System (1996), Global Youth Action Network (2005), and Academy of Dentistry International (2018). The ideas and expertise of NGOs enhance ECOSOC's ability to provide meaningful information and policy directions.

Most of the decisions made in ECOSOC are based on consensus, although resolutions can also pass by simple majority vote. Once adopted, ECOSOC may make recommendations to the General Assembly and other related bodies. Approved resolutions are not binding but can help to highlight the need for action and potentially impact policy-making of member states and inside the UN System. The relationship between ECOSOC and the General Assembly is a major source of confusion and overlap as the Charter (including Articles 13, 60, 62, and 66) outlines that both are tasked with promoting economic and social development.

RESPONSIBILITIES AND OPERATIONS

ECOSOC's mandate traditionally covered two main categories, with one focused on economic development and the other on social development. The social programs are generally viewed as successful, with considerable progress in areas concerning the trafficking of narcotic drugs, protection of children, and the rights of women. ECOSOC also oversaw the functioning of the predecessor to the Human Rights Council, the Commission on Human Rights. After the passage of General Assembly Resolution 68/1 in 2013, ECOSOC emphasizes coordinating and encouraging action across the three dimensions of sustainable development: economic, social, and environmental. ECOSOC continues to explore ways to finance development and raise awareness of the Sustainable Development Goals (SDGs). The creation of an annual theme, which is now coordinated to be the same theme as the session of the High-level Political Forum on Sustainable Development (HLPF), also promotes ECOSOC goals. For example, the 2019 theme was "Empowering People and Ensuring Inclusiveness and Equality."

Prior to the 2013 reforms, ECOSOC held two main meetings every year, the first early in the year as an organizational session and a second substantive session in the summer. After 2013, ECOSOC adjusted its calendar to run from July to July and ceased alternating between Geneva and New York (except for the humanitarian-focused session). ECOSOC shapes the focus and work of other entities within the UN System. This process now begins with the HLPF in July in New York, where government ministers, senior government officials, members from other international organizations, as well as NGOs and other civil society representatives, spend eight days working on an approach to encourage economic and social development that also promotes sustainability. This meeting sets the stage for the year and provides leadership and priorities to define the work of many of the UN commissions, funds, and programmes. Starting in 2007, ECOSOC hosted the Annual Ministerial Review, which included examining the progress made on the Millennium Development Goals, and the biennial Development Cooperation Forum. These have now been linked to the HLPF to monitor the SDGs, encourage operational connections across the UN System, and maintain global partnerships in support of sustainable development.

ECOSOC's main focus is preparing reports, providing recommendations, organizing conferences and events, and attempting to coordinate other UN entities and their programs and policies. ECOSOC is the primary receiver of reports from UN funds and programmes and provides follow-up after UN conferences. For instance, following the International Conferences on Financing for Development (held in Monterrey in 2002, Doha in 2008, and Addis Ababa in 2015), ECOSOC assisted with creating next steps and action plans. This process also includes an annual meeting with the International Monetary Fund, UN Conference on Trade and Development, World Bank, and World Trade Organization (WTO). Since the establishment of the Addis Ababa Action Agenda in 2015, this meeting has been incorporated into the ECOSOC Forum on Financing for Development follow-up.

ECOSOC seeks to adapt and react to changing global circumstances. For example, electronic discussions (e-Discussions) are organized around ECOSOC's annual theme. This open electronic forum is part of an effort to further ideas and gather suggestions from communities not traditionally involved in the UN System. Similarly, the ECOSOC Youth Forum, which began in 2012, provides a platform for future generations to share their ideas on solving global challenges. For instance, the 2017 forum examined "the role of youth in poverty eradication and promoting prosperity in a changing world." Special meetings can also be called to address emergency situations, with past meetings including severe acute respiratory syndrome (SARS) in 2003, food crises (2005 and 2008), avian flu (2005), the Ebola virus (2014), and a number of natural disasters (2000, 2004, 2010, 2013, 2017, and 2019).

CHALLENGES AND REFORM

ECOSOC wrestles with a dizzying spectrum of issues and an ambitious agenda. Given concerns over a lack of clear parameters for ECOSOC's mandate, there have been calls for reform from the start and ongoing efforts to focus the scope of ECOSOC's work. There is also debate over the size of ECOSOC. Many argue that the body is too small and, given the focus on development, the Global South is underrepresented. Others claim that when ECOSOC expanded to fifty-four members, it became too big and cumbersome to be an authentic decision-making body. ECOSOC is often accused of merely serving as a global "talk shop" with little power to implement policies or compel the UN entities it oversees to make changes and reform areas of inefficiency. Yet, calls for reinforcing ECOSOC's principal organ status to have the body operate more as an "Economic Security Council" did not gain traction. Coordinating across member states, commissions, specialized agencies, and thousands of NGOs is no easy task. ECOSOC's coordination mandate is additionally challenging because many of the issue areas under its responsibility overlap with entities that are outside of ECOSOC's direct jurisdiction. Indeed, some, like the WTO, are only loosely affiliated with the UN. ECOSOC's struggles to coordinate a decentralized UN System are further complicated by the overlap with and unclear relationship to the General Assembly, as well as UN System changes that impact its work. This includes sharing oversight of funds, programmes, and other entities (including separate meetings of the HLPF) with the General Assembly, a change in peacebuilding architecture with the establishment of the Peacebuilding Commission, and removal of the Commission of Human Rights with the creation of the Human Rights Council. To resolve such issues, some argue for ECOSOC to be put completely under the authority of General Assembly as a subsidiary body.

During the decolonialization period of the 1960s, ECOSOC became embroiled in the controversies raised as African and Asian countries demanded a greater voice in how the UN addressed economic and social development. Members from the Global South insisted on greater participation in the process that determined policies, as well as a greater commitment to aid and development assistance. The 2005 World Summit Outcome Document called for enhancing ECOSOC's oversight capacities. In response, the General Assembly passed Resolution 61/16 (2006) titled "Strengthening of the Economic and Social Council" and further significant reforms were carried out in 2013 (and reviewed in General Assembly Resolution 72/305 in 2018). Areas addressed include instituting the annual theme to provide more focus and coherence, shifting the meeting schedule, new reporting processes, and encouraging greater visibility and coordination capabilities. There is also an emphasis on better bringing relevant stakeholders, including non-state actors, into the process of promoting and financing sustainable development. ECOSOC's influence on global policy is informational and rests in its ability to produce knowledge, raise awareness, and coordinate agendas across the UN System. However, creating an integrated approach, considering the plethora of UN agencies, remains a demanding task and, despite the recent efforts to overhaul the organization, criticism and calls for further reform persist.

See also: Economic Development; Functional Commissions; General Assembly; High-level Political Forum on Sustainable Development; Human Rights Council; International Monetary Fund; Nongovernmental Organizations; Regional Commissions; Research and Training Institutes; Security Council; Sustainable Development; Sustainable Development Goals; United Nations Children's Fund; United Nations Conference on Trade and Development; United Nations Conferences and Summits; United Nations Development Programme; United Nations Reform; World Bank Group; World Food Programme; World Trade Organization.

FURTHER READING

Alger, Chadwick. 2002. "The Emerging Roles of NGOs in the UN System: From Article 71 to a People's Millennium Assembly." *Global Governance* 8 (1): 93–117.

Alston, Phillip. 1987. "Out of the Abyss: The Challenges Confronting the New U.N. Committee on Economic, Social and Cultural Rights." *Human Rights Quarterly* 9 (3): 332–81.

Breen, Claire. 2007. "The Necessity of a Role for the ECOSOC in the Maintenance of International Peace and Security." *Journal of Conflict and Security Law* 12 (2): 261–94.

Rosenthal, Gert. 2018. "The Economic and Social Council." In *The Oxford Handbook on the United Nations*. Second edition, edited by Thomas G. Weiss and Sam Daws, 165–77. Oxford: Oxford University Press.

Weiss, Thomas G. 2010. "ECOSOC Is Dead: Long Live ECOSOC." *Dialogue on Globalization*, Friedrich-Ebert-Foundation. Available at http://library.fes.de/pdf-files/bueros/usa/07709.pdf.

Secretariat

The Secretariat is staffed by international civil servants who support the everyday functioning of the UN. The establishment of such permanent bureaucratic structures was a key development in the evolution of international organizations. Countries could come together multilaterally as a collective group, but to move beyond such meetings required an ongoing organizational structure and supporting staff. A series of international public administrative unions developed in the nineteenth century to help countries coordinate on functional tasks, such as international post and telegraph communication, with the Universal Postal Union (founded initially as the General Postal Union in 1874 but named the Universal Postal Union in 1878) and the International Telecommunication Union (founded in 1865 as the International Telegraph Union before changing the organization's name in 1934) joining the UN System as specialized agencies in 1948 and 1949, respectively. A universal international civil service was supported by the League of Nations (the precursor to the UN), which instituted the Secretariat as a main organ. The UN followed this model, establishing the Secretariat as one of the six principal organs.

STAFFING THE SECRETARIAT

The UN Secretariat began initial operations with only approximately 300 individuals, although this quickly grew to around 3,000 staff in the first year of operation. Since the UN's inception, the staff has expanded significantly in both size and scope. As of December 2018, the Secretary-General reports that there were 37,505 staff based in the main UN headquarters cities and other offices across the globe. As noted in the UN Charter, Secretariat staff should ensure that they remain removed from outside influence and member states should respect this independence (Article 100). Along with operating independently and resisting political pressure, members of the Secretariat are expected to serve impartially, avoiding taking sides or displaying bias toward a particular group or country. Their priority should be the aims and purposes of the UN. Overall, Secretariat staff are called upon to reflect "the highest standards of efficiency, competence, and integrity" (Article 101(3)). At the same time, the Charter requires that "due regard" should also be given to ensuring that staff are hired "on as wide a geographical basis as possible" (Article 101(3)). The UN closely monitors staffing representation, including detailing staffing levels by "unrepresented," "underrepresented," "within range," and "overrepresented" countries.

STRUCTURE

The Secretary-General is the head of the Secretariat, with the officeholder responsible for, among other duties, appointing staff (Article 101(1)) and shaping the administrative structure of the Secretariat. The post of Deputy Secretary-General was also created in 1997 (with the first officeholder in place in 1998) as part of the broader Executive Office of the Secretary-General. As with any political bureaucracy, there are a range of departments and offices that make up the Secretariat. The exact offices and parameters shift over time as the Secretariat is reformed on a regular basis. However, key organization components include distinct departments responsible for particular issue areas, such as the Department of Peace Operations. Other departments oversee certain services, with the Department of Global Communications working to boost understanding and appreciation of UN work around the world via communications, outreach, and collaboration with media organizations. A range of offices also fall within the Secretariat structure, including high-profile ones such as the Office of the UN High Commissioner for Human Rights, as well as certain special advisers, representatives, and envoys. Secretariat support is also provided for bodies in the UN System, such as the separate Regional Commissions. The distinct departments and offices are expected to coordinate with each other in order to keep UN efforts operating in a coherent manner, including across the main headquarters in New York and the other official headquarters offices in Geneva, Nairobi, and Vienna along with other UN operations spanning the globe, although this often proves to be problematic in practice. The specialized agencies in the UN System have their own bureaucratic structure and staff and are led by a separate executive head.

ROLE AND RESPONSIBILITIES

Secretariat staff perform a range of necessary administrative duties in running the day-to-day affairs of the UN, including preparing and distributing documents, record keeping, organizing and supporting meetings and conferences, and providing language translation for documents and meetings (which is vital in an organization operating with six official languages: Arabic, Chinese, English, French, Russian, and Spanish). The Secretariat also provides important support for budget formulation and financial management and carries out research and analysis. As longstanding participants in the UN System, as opposed to rotating political appointments, staff provide institutional memory and perspective based on their experience. Through preparing formal reports, briefings, and engagement in meetings, along with a range of opportunities for informal interactions, members of the Secretariat can provide information and advice on how to address issues. Secretariat members may influence agendas and policies via carrying out regular duties or may intentionally engage more directly in pressing particular recommendations to affect the positions taken.

In addition, once decisions are made by other UN bodies, the Secretariat is often called upon to assist with the implementation of the adopted action items.

The Secretariat's position provides latitude for guiding and impacting how those decisions are carried out. Overall, what can be an important role in shaping and implementing UN affairs has led some analysts to label the Secretariat as the "Second UN" in the decision-making process (with the member states acting as the "First UN" and nongovernmental organizations [NGOs] viewed as the "Third UN").

DEBATES AND ISSUES

While the Secretariat has the ability to influence UN System affairs, the degree to which this should occur is debated. On the one hand, the Secretariat does have principal organ status with the ability to take on a key role as a political actor in its own right. On the other hand, the Secretariat can be understood as a neutral set of civil servants who are not supposed to insert their views into UN decisions and activities. Instead, they are expected to simply carry out the directives of the member states. The Secretariat must also cope with a decentralized UN System, which makes the expected coordination across offices and organizational components complicated and can prevent actions from being taken efficiently and effectively. The Secretariat's role in implementing programs also provides opportunities for corruption. For example, there were allegations of mishandling funds during the Oil-for-Food Programme, which oversaw the selling of Iraqi oil to meet the needs of the country's citizens.

The hiring process for Secretariat staff can also be controversial. Balancing the "geographical basis" the Charter calls for with the skills needed in the Secretariat is complicated, and the emphasis is often on ensuring geographical representation as countries insist that their nationals are represented. This geographical diversity brings different perspectives to the Secretariat but also creates challenges for integrating staff from varied political and cultural backgrounds. Disagreement over the proper length of appointment also causes complications. Long-term appointments provide stability and institutional memory yet also generate concern over limiting the influx of fresh ideas and energy brought by new staff members. However, short-term appointments raise difficulties in return, with staff members mindful of how their actions might impact future job opportunities outside of the UN. Yet, it is not unusual for some individuals to rotate between positions at the UN, member states, and NGOs across their careers. Member states can insist on short-term contracts via secondment, where national public servants are provided to the UN with the understanding that this will be for a fixed time before the staff return to their home country's bureaucracy. This approach, which was prevalent for acquiring staff from communist countries in the Soviet bloc during the Cold War, raises concerns over whether these staff are able to act independently from the interests of their home countries as they know that they will be returning to the national civil service. Finally, despite a UN commitment to gender equality in staffing, women remain underrepresented in the Secretariat, particularly in positions of leadership.

REFORM

A range of Secretariat structural reforms have been proposed over the years, yielding mixed results. Such reform efforts are continually revisited, both in terms of regular reorganization of the Secretariat offices, which occurs under the Secretary-General, and broader efforts to promote greater efficiency and coordination across a generally decentralized UN System. For example, Secretary-General Kofi Annan, who rose up through the ranks of the Secretariat over several decades, presided over several reports and reform efforts. This included issuing *Renewing the United Nations: A Programme for Reform* in his first year in office, which targeted a new structure for leadership and management along with substantive proposals for policy formulation and issue priorities. Following efforts included Annan's 2002 *Strengthening of the United Nations: An Agenda for Further Change*, an extensive report that sought to build upon previous endeavors as well as to move reform in new dimensions. Hiring practices also remain an enduring area of discussion for improvement, as the organization continues to wrestle with the best way to ensure that the UN is staffed with skilled and committed individuals. The UN remains focused on continuing to improve gender representation in the Secretariat, with UN offices themselves restructured into the UN Entity for Gender Equality and Empowerment of Women (UN Women) in order to better monitor and promote gender equity. The Secretariat deals with a demanding range of issues and institutions, as well trying to balance the priorities of member states within the parameters of the UN.

See also: Deputy Secretary-General; Executive Heads of Specialized Agencies; International Telecommunication Union; Kofi Annan; Nongovernmental Organizations; Office of Secretary-General; Regional Commissions; Special Representatives of the United Nations Secretary-General; United Nations Budget and Financing; United Nations Entity for Gender Equality and the Empowerment of Women; United Nations Headquarters; United Nations Reform; Universal Postal Union.

FURTHER READING

Ameri, Houshang. 1996. *Politics of Staffing the United Nations Secretariat*. New York: Peter Lang.

Cliffe, Sarah, and Alexandra Novosseloff. 2017. *Restructuring the UN Secretariat to Strengthen Preventative Diplomacy and Peace Operations*. New York: Center on International Cooperation, New York University.

Weinlich, Silke. 2014. *The UN Secretariat's Influence on the Evolution of Peacekeeping*. New York: Palgrave Macmillan.

Weiss, Thomas G. 2010. "Reinvigorating the International Civil Service." *Global Governance* 16 (1): 39–57.

Williams, Abiodun. 2010. "Strategic Planning in the Executive Office of the UN Secretary-General." *Global Governance* 16 (4): 435–49.

International Court of Justice (ICJ)

The International Court of Justice (ICJ) serves as a mechanism for the impartial, peaceful resolution of conflict between countries. The powers and jurisdiction of what is often referred to as the "World Court" are established in two places, the UN Charter (Chapter XIV) and the ICJ Statute. The ICJ is identified by Article 92 of the Charter as "the principal judicial organ" of the UN. While classified as a principal organ, the ICJ also operates to a degree as an independent institution. The court's location away from the UN's New York Headquarters in The Hague, Netherlands, enhances its semi-independent status, but funding comes from the UN as approved by the General Assembly.

During the eighteenth and nineteenth centuries, disagreements between countries were often settled diplomatically on a bilateral basis. However, there were times when diplomacy failed and countries sought an outside opinion to help peacefully settle disagreements. This approach was used by the United States and the British in the Jay Treaty of 1794 and the *Alabama* claims arbitration in 1872, where independent commissions addressed questions that arose between the countries that could not be resolved through regular diplomatic discussions. The 1899 Hague Peace Conference led to the creation of the Permanent Court of Arbitration. With a gift from U.S. industrialist Andrew Carnegie, in 1913 the court was headquartered in what became known as the Peace Palace. Today, the ICJ resides in the same building.

The creation of the UN's precursor, the League of Nations, built on this legal tradition and established the Permanent Court of International Justice (PCIJ). The PCIJ also met at the Peace Palace and was authorized to hear cases concerning legal issues between countries as well as offering advisory opinions to questions referred by the League of Nations. However, with the outbreak of World War II, the PCIJ was rendered ineffective. Yet, the countries that designed the UN agreed that the PCIJ was important and wanted to continue the tradition of judicial settlement. The legal jurisdiction of the PCIJ was transferred to the ICJ.

MEMBERSHIP AND JUDGES

All member states of the UN are automatically members of the ICJ. Countries that are not members of the UN are eligible for membership through application (e.g., Switzerland before joining the UN in 2002). The Security Council and the General Assembly jointly elect fifteen judges to serve on the ICJ for renewable nine-year terms. To ensure continuity, five judges are elected every three years. Article 3 of the ICJ Statute bars two judges from a single country from sitting on the court at the same time. Every three years, the members of the ICJ elect a President and a Vice-President, and these officeholders may be reelected. The vote is taken by secret ballot, and the winner is determined by a majority of votes. The President, as well as the Registrar appointed by the court, is required to live in The Hague.

The ICJ Statute states that judges and the legal approach should reflect the "main forms of civilization and of the principal legal systems of the world" (Article 9). Like most institutions within the UN System, elections are based on the regional groups. Traditionally, Africa and Asia are both allocated three judges, Western European and Others (WEOG) holds five seats, and there are two judges from both the Latin America and the Caribbean and the Eastern European regions. All of the permanent members of the Security Council are usually represented on the ICJ. However, this was not the case for China between 1967 and 1985 when a dispute over Chinese representation at the UN led to no Chinese candidates being submitted. In addition, the judge from the United Kingdom was not reelected in November 2017, which also shifted the regional representation to four from WEOG and four from Asia as the winning judge was from India. Unlike most UN entities, once a judge is elected the individual is not acting as a representative of their country. When hearing a case from a country that is not represented on the ICJ, the state parties may select a temporary judge to hear only that case.

CASES AND JUDICIAL PROCESS

As of November 2019, there have been 178 contentious cases between countries submitted to the ICJ and 27 advisory proceedings. A total of 105 countries have been involved in those contentious cases as the applicant or respondent. All of the permanent five powers, except for China, have appeared before the ICJ, with the United States (twenty-five) engaged in the most cases. Other frequent participants include Belgium (seven), Colombia (seven), France (fourteen), Germany (seven), Nicaragua (fifteen), and the United Kingdom (fourteen). A majority vote by the attending judges establishes the ICJ's decision. Written decisions, including dissenting views, are issued in order to verify the legal framework and logic of the rulings. As there are no higher courts, countries cannot appeal a decision or an award. However, a country's sovereignty is a legal priority established in the Charter, and the ICJ does not hold supranational authority above a state. In fact, the jurisdiction of the court is noncompulsory, meaning that the parties to a dispute must agree to be part of the case. If a country chooses not to be part of a case at the ICJ or rejects the court's jurisdiction, their case is not heard unless there are other legal justifications in place for hearing the case. The body of international law that the ICJ applies to cases includes international treaties, international customs, other general principles of law that are recognized by countries, as well as precedents established through previous judicial decisions.

Many of the cases brought to the ICJ fall within the categories of territorial and maritime disputes, with other areas including the use of armed force, diplomatic immunity, and issues concerning property. While the court's rulings are considered final and binding, the ICJ does not have the means to enforce its decisions. Usually compliance with a ruling is voluntary or comes through the coercion from other countries. The Charter authorizes the Security Council to "make recommendations or decide upon measures to be taken to give effect to the judgment" of the ICJ (Article 94). Yet, this tends to be problematic as such actions are vulnerable to veto by the Security Council's five permanent members. One example of noncompliance with a ruling is found in the *Nicaragua v. United States of America* case where the ICJ found that the United States had violated Nicaragua's sovereignty by supporting a government opposition group and supplying military support and use of mines in the country's harbors. The court ruled in favor of Nicaragua in 1986, finding in part that the United States was "in breach of its obligations under customary international law not to . . . interrupt peaceful maritime commerce," and awarded reparations to Nicaragua. The United States argued in

1984 that the ICJ lacked jurisdiction, then refused to participate in the proceedings as they moved forward, and ultimately used its veto to block the Security Council's endorsement of the ruling.

JURISDICTION

Jurisdiction for the ICJ comes in three distinct ways. First, countries can include clauses in the treaties that they negotiate and approve indicating that if a dispute arises regarding the terms of the treaty, then the ICJ has jurisdiction over such matters. Special agreements by countries provide the second source where countries consent to use the ICJ to resolve a dispute. Finally, as set out in Article 36(2) of the ICJ Statute, countries can agree to compulsory jurisdiction. As of January 2018, seventy-four states put declarations in place establishing their willingness to accept the compulsory jurisdiction of the ICJ, although many of these incorporate reservations that limit the extent of the jurisdiction and countries may also withdraw their declaration, as the United States did in 1985 to protest the Nicaragua case. Major countries from every region have deposited declarations, such as: Australia, Canada, Democratic Republic of the Congo, Egypt, Germany, India, Japan, Kenya, Mexico, Netherlands, Nigeria, Pakistan, Poland, and the United Kingdom.

Cases can also come to the ICJ at the request of other UN principal organs. Article 33 of the Charter notes judicial settlement as a means to peacefully settle disputes, with Article 36 explicitly stating that "the Security Council should also take into consideration that legal disputes should as a general rule be referred by the parties to the International Court of Justice." Article 96 of the Charter holds that either the Security Council or the General Assembly may ask the ICJ to provide an advisory opinion. As also specified in Article 96, with General Assembly authorization, other organs and specialized agencies may also submit legal questions to the ICJ for an advisory opinion. Advisory opinions are considered suggestions or clarifications and are, therefore, nonbinding. In addition, the ICJ submits an annual report to the General Assembly. The President of the ICJ also makes a statement to the General Assembly in conjunction with the report and provides a private briefing to the Security Council.

The ICJ faces persistent questions about whether it should hear specific cases, particularly if the case includes issues that are perceived as being political. This was a significant concern when Ethiopia and Liberia brought suit against South Africa when that country was governed through white-minority rule. South Africa was alleged to be exercising colonial administration over South West Africa (contemporary Namibia) and excluding self-determination for black citizens under apartheid policies. In 1962, the ICJ found that Ethiopia and Liberia had a legal interest in the case, yet, after hearing the case, this decision was reversed in 1966. Typically, the ICJ rejects the argument against hearing a case based on political questions in favor of deciding whether it can rule on the legal questions within the case. Other recent notable cases include the 1999 Application of the Convention on the Prevention and Punishment of the Crime of Genocide (*Croatia v. Serbia*) and the 2014 ruling on a Japanese whaling program that was found in violation of the International Convention for the Regulation of Whaling.

CHALLENGES AND POTENTIAL REFORM

The ICJ, like many entities within the UN System, was impacted by Cold War politics and struggles between the great powers. The number of contentious cases increased significantly since then, with 95 of the 178 cases occurring from 1991 onward. However, the ICJ faces greater international legal competition due to the rise in the number of permanent international courts in that same time period. There is also criticism that the court's judges, despite conditions of neutrality, continue to represent the interests of their home countries. While the ICJ usually escapes discussions regarding UN reform, there have been conversations about extending its jurisdiction, the number of judges, and calls for a more gender inclusive bench. Despite such limitations, the ICJ is often viewed as possessing important symbolic value and representing a positive step for those who support strengthening the role of international law.

See also: General Assembly; International Criminal Court; Membership; Peaceful Settlement; Role of Great Powers; Security Council; Self-Determination; United Nations Headquarters; United Nations Historical Background.

FURTHER READING

Cronin-Furman, Kathleen Renée. 2006. "The International Court of Justice and the United Nations Security Council: Rethinking a Complicated Relationship." *Columbia Law Review* 106 (2): 435–63.

Gill, Terry D. 2003. *Rosenne's the World Court: What It Is and How It Works*. Sixth Revised Edition. Leiden, Netherlands: Martinus Nijhoff Publishers.

Johns, Leslie. 2015. *Strengthening International Courts: The Hidden Costs of Legalization*. Ann Arbor: University of Michigan Press.

Mennecke, Martin, and Christian J. Tams. 2007. "The Genocide Case Before the International Court of Justice." *Security and Peace* 25 (2): 71–76.

Schulte, Constanze. 2005. *Compliance with Decisions of the International Court of Justice*. Oxford: Oxford University Press.

Trusteeship Council

Coming out of World War II, which was fought in part to ensure principles of freedom and self-government, there was a strong emphasis at the founding of the UN on the self-determination of peoples. The structure of the UN reinforced this commitment by designating principal organ status to the Trusteeship Council, which was tasked with overseeing trust territories and assisting with guiding these to political self-sufficiency. The last trust territory, Palau, achieved independence (and UN membership) in 1994. Therefore, the Trusteeship Council no longer had an ongoing purpose and suspended operations. Much of the recent discussion of the Trusteeship Council revolves around ideas for eliminating the organ or reforming the body to address new issues.

The focus on supervising territories on the path to self-governance started under the UN's precursor, the League of Nations. Territories taken over by the victors of

World War I were not annexed, as was the usual process after past wars, but instead designated as "mandates" without independence to be administered by the controlling state with oversight by the League of Nations (e.g., territory that was captured from the Germans in Central Africa). Self-determination was stressed by the UN as part of the organization's purposes in Article 1(2) of the Charter and was reinforced with Chapter XI (Declaration regarding Non-Self-Governing Territories) and Chapter XII (International Trusteeship System). This trusteeship system inherited mandates from the League of Nations and added additional "territories . . . detached from enemy states as a result of the Second World War" (Article 77). The areas placed under the trusteeship system, which were considered not yet prepared to govern themselves, were labeled trust territories. The Trusteeship Council was responsible for overseeing eleven trust territories across Africa and the Pacific that fell under the administration of seven different member states (the United States, the United Kingdom, New Zealand, Italy, France, Belgium, and Australia).

MEMBERSHIP

As established in Article 86 of the Charter, membership in the Trusteeship Council was drawn from three categories. First, member states that were administering trust territories. Second, Security Council permanent members that were not administering trust territories. Third, as many additional representatives, which were elected by the General Assembly for a three-year period of service, that were needed to maintain an equal number of members administering trust territories and members which were not administering trust territories. At its largest, the Trusteeship Council comprised seven administering members, two nonadministering members from the Security Council (China and the Soviet Union), and five more elected nonadministering members to balance out the Council. To further offset the economically developed administering powers, the elected members were drawn from developing states (e.g., in 1956, the elected members were Burma, Guatemala, Haiti, India, and Syria). However, the membership shifted and declined over time as trust territories gained independence. By 1965, only Australia, New Zealand, the United Kingdom, and the United States remained as administering states, with French involvement moved to the category of Security Council member along with the Chinese and the Soviets, and Liberia as the lone elected member. Nauru's independence in 1968 left an imbalance of only two administering members (Australia and the United States) and four Security Council nonadministering members (China, France, the Soviet Union, and the United Kingdom) that was impossible to address by electing yet more nonadministering members. At this point, the sole remaining members of the Trusteeship Council are the five permanent members from the Security Council.

VOTING

A President and Vice-President lead the Trusteeship Council. These officeholders are selected by the members of the Council at the start of each regular session, with the positions designed to rotate between administering and nonadministering members. Although the Trusteeship Council no longer operates, the members do still hold a brief session to elect the President and Vice-President. This most recently occurred in November 2019, with the next meeting scheduled for November 2021. Decisions in the Trusteeship Council are made by a simple majority, with each member having one vote. There were no special voting privileges for members administering trust territories to ensure that administering and nonadministering members had an equal voice. The existence of these balanced voting blocs encouraged the members to find ways to cooperate in order to act. However, provisions were in place for tie votes. The members would then vote a second time, either after a recess or at the next meeting, and if still deadlocked, then the proposal at hand was rejected. Thus, the overarching prerogative sat with the administering members who could block any proposed changes to the status quo when they united.

TRUST TERRITORY SUPERVISION AND OUTCOME

The Trusteeship Council provided international supervision of the trust territories. The goal was to help lead these territories to self-governance but also to promote better conditions for the people living in the territories as they moved toward this point. The Trusteeship Council directly monitored the trust territories by undertaking exploratory visits as well as reviewing petitions from the territories. Administering authorities were also expected to submit reports, with the Trusteeship Council tasked with providing a questionnaire to the administering authorities "on the political, economic, social, and educational advancement of the inhabitants of each trust territory" (Article 88). The Trusteeship Council reviewed the material to provide observations and recommendations and reported annually to the General Assembly on its activities and conditions in the trust territories.

All eleven trust territories achieved some form of self-determination. Almost all of the trust territories became fully independent and went on to join the UN through a variety of paths. Some transitioned from a single territory to one independent state, such as Nauru and Western Samoa (as the state of Samoa). Others merged or divided their territory in the process of becoming a state. For example, the Cameroons under French administration joined with the southern part of the Cameroons under British administration to create the state of Cameroon, but the northern section under British control joined Nigeria instead. In another instance, the single Belgian administered Ruanda-Urundi split off to form the separate states of Rwanda and Burundi. The bulk of the Trusteeship Council's work was resolved fairly quickly, with the majority of territories achieving independence by the 1960s. New Guinea followed soon afterward in 1975 (uniting with Papua to form the new state of Papua New Guinea), with only the Trust Territory of the Pacific Islands (made up of the Marshall Islands, Micronesia, Northern Mariana Islands, and Palau) administered by the United States stretching into the early 1990s. The Northern Mariana Islands are the lone area that did not gain UN membership, agreeing instead to remain as a U.S. territory but with commonwealth status (the same political arrangement as Puerto Rico).

> **Trust Territories Addressed by the Trusteeship Council**
>
> 1. Cameroons (British administration)
>   *Southern territory joined Cameroon and northern territory joined Nigeria in 1961*
> 2. Cameroons (French administration)
>   *Independent as Cameroon 1960, UN membership in 1960*
> 3. Nauru (Australian administration on behalf of Australia, New Zealand, and the United Kingdom)
>   *Independent in 1968, UN membership in 1999*
> 4. New Guinea (Australian administration)
>   *United with Papua in 1975 to form Papua New Guinea, UN membership in 1975*
> 5. Ruanda-Urundi (Belgian administration)
>   *Independence as two separate states of Rwanda and Burundi in 1961, UN membership in 1962*
> 6. Somaliland (Italian administration)
>   *United with British Somaliland Protectorate in 1960 to form Somalia, UN membership in 1960*
> 7. Tanganyika (British administration)
>   *Independent in 1961, UN membership in 1961, united with Zanzibar and then UN member under name of United Republic of Tanzania in 1964*
> 8. Togoland (British administration)
>   *United with Gold Coast to form Independent State of Ghana, UN membership in 1957*
> 9. Togoland (French administration)
>   *Independent as Togo in 1960, UN membership in 1960*
> 10. Trust Territory of the Pacific Islands (U.S. administration)
>   Commonwealth of the Northern Mariana Islands
>   *Became fully self-governing as Commonwealth of the United States in 1990, not a UN member*
>
>   Federated States of Micronesia
>   *Fully self-governing in free Association with the United States in 1990, UN membership in 1991*
>
>   Palau
>   *Fully self-governing in free Association with the United States in 1994, UN membership in 1994*
>
>   Republic of the Marshall Islands
>   *Fully self-governing in free Association with the United States in 1990, UN membership in 1991*
> 11. Western Samoa (New Zealand administration)
>   *Independent as Samoa in 1962, UN membership in 1976*

PAST CONCERNS AND FUTURE POSSIBILITIES

While most of the ongoing debate over the Trusteeship Council revolves around reforming or eliminating the Council, other issues have been raised regarding operations of the organ while it was still functioning. Article 77 of the Charter specifies that further territories could be entered into the trusteeship system "by states responsible for their administration." However, despite the hope that this would provide the Trusteeship Council with a wider role in overseeing a number of territorial transitions, no additional territories were designated to the trusteeship system by the colonial powers and the broader decolonization process at the UN took place by other means. The handling of the path to independence for trust territories has been questioned. Critics point to the lack of independence granted for certain territories, which were instead merged into other territories (as in the case of the Southern Cameroons) as a violation of their right of self-determination. Procedural controversies have also been highlighted. Such areas identified include: the format and wording of the questionnaire for administering authorities, whether to allow dissenting opinions in the annual report to the General Assembly, the approach taken to visiting missions, and the handling of petitions. In addition, critics point to the economic exploitation and environmental damage that occurred in territories while they were under the trusteeship system, as seen with the mining of phosphates (used for fertilizer) in Nauru.

The future of the Trusteeship Council remains unclear. As there are only six principal organs, these bodies carry a high status in the UN, so a variety of ideas have been proposed to revive the dormant Council and put the organ to work on new issues. One possibility is to have the Trusteeship Council oversee the so-called failed states, where the state has collapsed to the point that there is a lack of functional political governance. This mission is viewed by some as a natural extension of overseeing trust territories, which were not regarded at the time as capable of self-governance and in need of monitoring and assistance to achieve this status. There have been concerns expressed that the UN is essentially already engaged in "neotrusteeship," such as the state rebuilding efforts in Timor-Leste (East Timor), without the guidance of a body like the Trusteeship Council to provide proper oversight. The UN has been increasingly involved in such postconflict peacebuilding efforts, but instead of assigning this area to a reformed Trusteeship Council, the UN created a separate body in 2005, the Peacebuilding Commission, with the lower status of advisory subsidiary body.

Another area that has been targeted for Trusteeship Council involvement is assisting with self-governance efforts of minority peoples. The situation of indigenous peoples, who consider themselves to be distinct from the country in which they live and often lay sovereign claim to certain territory, has been pointed to as a potentially natural extension of the Trusteeship Council purpose. There is a Permanent Forum on Indigenous Issues under the Economic and Social Council, but shifting indigenous peoples to the level of principal organ would give this work higher status and focus. A very different approach would be to repurpose the Trusteeship Council to oversee the "global commons." Global commons areas, such as the high seas, atmosphere, and outer space, lie beyond states' political boundaries and could be managed by the Trusteeship Council for the greater good and protection of all people. Others do not wish to reform the Trusteeship Council but instead seek to amend the Charter to do away with the Council altogether. Supporters of eliminating the Trusteeship Council believe that it should be officially removed from the organizational structure of the UN as the organ completed its task and no longer functions. Efforts to reform or abolish the Trusteeship Council have thus far not succeeded.

See also: Economic and Social Council; Global Commons; Indigenous Peoples; Peacebuilding Commission; Permanent Forum on Indigenous Issues; Security Council; Self-Determination; United Nations Reform.

FURTHER READING

Butler, Michael J. 2012. "Ten Years After: (Re) Assessing Neo-Trusteeship and UN State-Building in Timor-Leste." *International Studies Perspectives* 13 (1): 85–104.

Mohamed, Saira. 2005. "From Keeping Peace to Building Peace: A Proposal for a Revitalized United Nations Trusteeship Council." *Columbia Law Review* 105 (3): 809–40.

Murray, James N., Jr. 1957. *The United Nations Trusteeship System*. Urbana: University of Illinois Press.

Thullen, George. 1964. *Problems of the Trusteeship System: A Study of Political Behavior in the United Nations*. Geneva: Droz.

Wilde, Ralph. 2018. "Trusteeship Council." In *The Oxford Handbook on the United Nations*. Second edition, edited by Thomas G. Weiss and Sam Daws, 178–89. Oxford: Oxford University Press.

PART III

The United Nations System

INTRODUCTION

While central to the operations of the United Nations (UN), the principal organs (covered in Part II) are only a part of the broader organizational structure known as the UN System. As detailed in the UN System organizational chart, the UN operates as a family of interconnected institutions. The UN System has evolved over time in response to changing needs and shifts in global issues, including adding a number of additional bodies. Understanding the different components of the UN System, which is the focus of Part III (organized by sections on specialized agencies, programmes and funds, other subsidiary bodies, and related organizations), is necessary in order to fully grasp the functioning of the UN in the international arena.

The *specialized agencies* are autonomous international organizations that have signed agreements to be a part of the UN System, as allowed by the Charter in Articles 57 and 63. The specialized agencies are coordinated by the Economic and Social Council (ECOSOC) but remain legally independent and operate distinctly in terms of their structure, leadership, organizational rules, members, funding, and institutional culture. Although all specialized agencies now operate under the umbrella of the UN System, some actually predate the creation of the UN (such as the International Labour Organization, which was founded in 1919), while others emerged around the same time as the UN in 1945 (e.g., the Food and Agriculture Organization) or even afterward (illustrated by the UN Industrial Development Organization, established in 1966). The relative history and operations often impact the interaction of the specialized agencies as a part of the broader UN System. There are also several institutions labeled by the UN as "*related organizations*" (e.g., the International Atomic Energy Agency). These organizations cooperate with the UN, but without formal reference to Articles 57 and 63 or reporting under ECOSOC, so they are distinct from the specialized agencies.

Programmes and funds are another type of bodies in the UN System. As specified in Article 22 of the Charter, the General Assembly "may establish such subsidiary organs as it deems necessary for the performance of its functions," which

Date When Specialized Agencies Joined the United Nations System

Specialized Agency	Date Joined UN
Food and Agriculture Organization	1946
International Labour Organization	1946
UN Educational, Scientific and Cultural Organization	1946
International Civil Aviation Organization	1947
International Monetary Fund	1947
World Bank Group	1947
Universal Postal Union	1948
World Health Organization	1948
International Telecommunications Union	1949
World Meteorological Organization	1951
International Maritime Organization	1959
World Intellectual Property Organization	1974
International Fund for Agricultural Development	1977
UN Industrial Development Organization	1985
UN World Tourism Organization	2003

led to the creation of institutions such as the UN Development Programme. Although not legally distinct from the UN and guided by UN administrative guidelines, in practical terms many of the programmes and funds function along the lines of specialized agencies. This includes operating under the direction of an executive head, engaging in activities in the field, and receiving most of their financing from outside of the regular UN budget (via voluntary funding sources). The UN System is also made up of a range of *other subsidiary bodies*, which are generally more directly embedded in the administrative structure of the UN compared to the programmes and funds, although some (such as the Regional Commissions) provide UN support across different areas of the globe.

With the range of bodies present in the UN System, this provides the means to address a great array of international issues. At the same time, there are concerns about overlap in responsibilities across different institutions. In addition, coordinating across the various components of the UN System is a major challenge. This calls into question the degree to which the UN System can act effectively as a centralized system versus a decentralized set of bodies operating separately. Ideas for improving coordination and coherence across the UN System are often a key dimension of UN reform plans.

SPECIALIZED AGENCIES

Food and Agriculture Organization (FAO)

Food is an essential resource for all of humanity. Starting in the mid-1800s, there was an increasing recognition of the interdependence of agricultural production and markets and initial moves to build cooperation. Notably, the International Institute of Agriculture (IIA), which collected and studied international data and provided a forum for discussing agricultural issues, was founded in Rome, Italy, in 1905. Efforts in the League of Nations focused on nutrition set further groundwork for engagement with food issues, but ongoing concerns during World War II made food and agriculture even more of a focus for the international community. The planning process began while the war was still in progress, with the key event the 1943 Conference on Food and Agriculture held in Hot Springs, Virginia. An interim commission was established at this conference to draft a constitution and framework for the planned Food and Agriculture Organization (FAO). The agreement founding the FAO was signed on October 16, 1945, the date now celebrated as "World Food Day," and the organization was situated in the UN System as a specialized agency in 1946. The FAO was temporarily headquartered in Washington, DC, before moving to Rome in 1951, a city that also now hosts the later founded UN food agencies the World Food Programme (WFP) and International Fund for Agricultural Development, where the organization absorbed the IIA library and resources.

RESPONSIBILITIES

Focused on the overarching goal to create "freedom from hunger," the FAO's central mandate points are to raise nutrition levels along with standards of living, advance food and agricultural productivity and distribution, and improve conditions for rural populations. Areas of food and agriculture addressed include aquaculture, crops, fisheries, forestry, land use, livestock, and water systems for agriculture, along with emergency situations tied to drought, famine, pests, and plant disease. The FAO is responsible for collecting, analyzing, and distributing a wide array of data and carrying out research related to food and agriculture. The organization is also designed to promote and spread knowledge regarding food and agriculture as well as recommend actions and policies for making improvements. FAO-designated functions also include providing technical and field assistance to ensure that the organization is working toward meeting its mandate.

STRUCTURE

The FAO is a large and complex organization, with offices based around the globe. The Conference, which first met in October 1945 directly following the founding of the FAO, is the highest governing body and convenes every two years to establish overall policy and the work program as well as to approve the budget. Regional conferences, which are supported by regional offices, are held in the year in between the full Conference session. Supervision of ongoing work is provided by the Council, which is designated to normally meet five times in between Conference sessions. The forty-nine Council members are elected by the Conference on a regional basis for three-year terms with staggered terms of office so that one-third of the members rotate in a given year. The Council is supported by three elected committees: Programme, Finance, and Constitutional and Legal Matters. The FAO is also assisted by technical committees (Agriculture, Commodity Problems, Fisheries, and Forestry) and the Committee on World Food Security. The head of the organization, the Director-General, has often played a notable, and at times controversial, role in shaping FAO affairs. The work of the FAO is organized into six departments: Agriculture and Consumer Protection; Climate, Biodiversity, Land and Water; Economic and Social Development; Fisheries and Aquaculture; Forestry; and Programme Support and Technical Cooperation.

As of early 2020, the FAO has near universal membership, with only one UN member, Liechtenstein, not in the FAO and the member state total at 194 due to the participation of non-UN members Cook Islands and Niue. Associate members, most recently Faroe Islands and Tokelau, are allowed to participate in deliberations but may not hold office or vote. In addition, the FAO was the first to allow membership by a regional economic organization with the European Union, which had developed important powers in the agricultural realm due to the common agricultural policy, joining in 1991. The FAO's regular budget is funded by members' assessed contributions, but voluntary contributions also support technical assistance programs along with core functions of the organization. For the 2018–2019 cycle, 61 percent of the budget came from voluntary funds, while the remaining 39 percent was based on assessed contributions.

ACTIVITIES

Given the breadth of the FAO's mandate, there are a great number of food and agriculture areas addressed through the organization's wide-ranging activities. The FAO promotes and seeks to provide proper nutrition and food security. Programs dedicated to improving sustainable agriculture and food production span across animals, crops, fisheries, and forestry, and the organization is linked to each stage of distributing the goods produced. Feeding the world is connected to overcoming poverty through applying resources, investment, and rural development projects. Emergency assistance is provided during human-made and natural disasters, and early warning systems and response analysis seek to better address such situations. The FAO is a central depository and knowledge sharing hub, making the organization a central authority for food and agricultural data and this information underpins policy recommendations.

In recent years, the FAO has emphasized the organization's contributions toward meeting the UN's Sustainable Development Goals (SDGs). SDG 2 on zero hunger, which seeks to "end hunger, achieve food security and improved nutrition and promote sustainable agriculture," closely mirrors the organization's mission. However, the FAO is engaged with issues across all of the SDGs, including water for agriculture tied to SDG 6 ("ensure availability and sustainable management of water and sanitation for all") and fisheries linked to SDG 14 ("conserve and sustainably use the oceans, seas and marine resources"). Since food issues cross into many areas, the FAO engages with different organizations ranging from the International Atomic Energy Agency on food irradiation standards to the World Trade

Organization (WTO) on food trade laws. One organizational connection often emphasized is the joint effort with the World Health Organization on the Codex Alimentarius ("Food Code" in Latin) to set international food standards in order to protect consumer health.

CHALLENGES AND REFORM

Since the FAO's creation, there has been an ongoing debate over whether the organization should serve as an activist body with strong capabilities to guide food and agricultural affairs or play a more limited role as a technical body providing a forum for consultation and data collection. Over time the FAO has struggled to balance the tension between these two positions, which are often connected to conflicting interests between food exporting and food importing countries. For example, it has been argued that the FAO position on food security and trade has shifted from an emphasis on agricultural development to highlighting the importance of trade liberalization as promoted by the WTO. In the FAO's first decades of operation, the organization was largely recognized as a prestigious organization whose work was supported by large budget and personnel levels. However, the agency's influence and status began to diminish starting in the 1970s era of food crises and continued to erode in the face of accusations of poor management, politicized leadership, and ineffectiveness. In response, the organization faced cutbacks, including in funding and staffing support.

The FAO faces competing institutional frameworks working on food issues and operating as a more marginal part of the international food network, including the rise of the Consultative Group in International Agricultural Research. The WFP was initiated as an experiment under joint UN and FAO control but has since separated and largely operates independently. The FAO has undergone detailed independent external evaluation, with transformative restructuring and organizational shifts in response, but it remains to be seen whether this process will alter the views of those concerned about FAO performance. The reform effort also faces the historical split over the proper role of the FAO, with concerns raised that the emphasis will tilt away from active assistance to less developed areas. Food and agriculture is always a major issue area in the global arena, and a revitalized FAO can play an important part in assisting those in need.

See also: Environmental Protection; Executive Heads of Specialized Agencies; International Atomic Energy Agency; International Fund for Agricultural Development; Sustainable Development Goals; United Nations Development Programme; United Nations Entity for Gender Equality and the Empowerment of Women; United Nations Industrial Development Organization; World Food Programme; World Health Organization; World Trade Organization.

FURTHER READING

Farsund, Arild Aurvåg, Carsten Daugbjerg, and Oluf Langhelle. 2015. "Food Security and Trade: Reconciling Discourses in the Food and Agriculture Organization and the World Trade Organization." *Food Security* 7 (2): 383–91.

Jarosz, Lucy. 2009. "The Political Economy of Global Governance and the World Food Crisis: The Case of the FAO." *Review* 32 (1): 37–60.
Shaw, D. John. 2007. *World Food Security: A History Since 1945*. New York: Palgrave Macmillan.
Staples, Amy L. S. 2006. *The Birth of Development: How the World Bank, Food and Agriculture Organization, and World Health Organization Changed the World, 1945–1965*. Kent, OH: Kent State University Press.
Talbot, Ross B. 1994. *Historical Dictionary of the International Food Agencies: FAO, WFP, WFC, IFAD*. Metuchen, NJ: Scarecrow Press.

International Civil Aviation Organization (ICAO)

The new capacity for air travel in the twentieth century created a need for countries to cooperate as flights transcended national lines and required standardized equipment and operations. By the time of the League of Nations in 1919, several international bodies, including the International Commission on Aerial Navigation (ICAN), were being established. Then, in late 1944, fifty-two countries met in Chicago and agreed to the Convention on International Civil Aviation, which set out the International Civil Aviation Organization (ICAO). These negotiations and the agreement, referred to as the Chicago Convention, predated the establishment of the UN Charter. The Provisional International Civil Aviation Organization (PICAO) was established as an interim body to provide preparatory work in anticipation of the ratification of the Chicago Convention to formally create ICAO. ICAO took over from PICAO in April 1947 and officially entered the UN System as a specialized agency that year.

The Chicago Convention strengthened global civil aviation management, with ICAO absorbing some of its organizational predecessors, including ICAN. While there was some debate over where to locate ICAO's headquarters, Montreal, Canada, won out over other candidates. The organization moved into a new headquarters building in 1996, where it works alongside other aviation-related organizations based in Montreal—including the nongovernmental International Air Transport Association created in 1945 to support cooperation between airlines.

RESPONSIBILITIES

Civil aviation covers a wide range of civilian aircraft operations, excluding military flights, so ICAO's areas of responsibility encompass an extensive mandate to encourage safe and effective civil aviation across the globe. The Preamble to the Chicago Convention stresses promoting cooperation and peace via "principles and arrangements" that ensure the "safe and orderly" development of civil aviation. The specific objectives are set out in Article 44, which include a further emphasis on safety and "orderly growth" of operations "for peaceful purposes," the development of all aspects of international civil aviation, and fair opportunities without discrimination across countries. These objectives cover both air navigation (which addresses the movement of aircraft) and air transport (which comprises passengers, baggage, and other cargo). ICAO ensures the safety of flights, focusing on operational and technical details, as well as countering unlawful interference that undermines flight security. The standardization of civil aviation, with guiding regulations, best practices, and principles for cooperative relations, sit at the heart of ICAO's directive. A key exclusion to ICAO's oversight is guidance of airlines' commercial rights. Countries, or more recently blocs of countries, typically maintain air service agreements established on a county-to-country basis that regulate the carriers and the number of flights between countries.

STRUCTURE

All member states, 193 as of 2019, are represented on ICAO's Assembly, which, unless an "extraordinary meeting" is called, normally only meets every three years. The Assembly's powers and duties are set out in Article 49 of the Chicago Convention, which includes approving the budget, reviewing reports, requesting that other bodies take action on an issue, and addressing issues "not specifically assigned to the Council." The thirty-six member Council, whose members are elected by the Assembly to three-year terms, holds regular sessions across the year. Membership is divided between countries with "chief importance in air transport," countries that contribute the most facilities, and a set of countries to ensure balanced geographic representation. ICAO's Council is noted for the breadth of powers and functions assigned, including playing a legislative role and taking on administrative duties, along with investigatory and dispute settlement capabilities. Decision-making in ICAO is also guided by subsidiary bodies, in particular the Air Navigation Commission (ANC). The Council elects a President for a three-year term, but in practice the Presidents have been reelected and served much longer tenures. The Secretariat is headed by a Secretary-General appointed by the Council. Secretariat staff are largely technical specialists. ICAO's budget is supported by the member states, whose expected contribution is based on a formula which takes into account the relative wealth of a country along with their level of aviation services.

ACTIVITIES

ICAO operates as both a service organization, providing technical assistance and establishing civil aviation standards, and a forum for member states to come together to coordinate their policies. The organization has created extensive technical assistance programs to support countries with developing their civil aviation sector, including airport facilities, civil aviation manufacturing, and aviation training. ICAO provides countries with planning assistance, direct engagement with civil aviation experts, means to improve security measures, and processes for obtaining equipment. ICAO's technical expertise also leads the organization to work alongside other specialized agencies. For example, in conjunction with the Universal Post Union, ICAO assists with air mail regulation and coordinates with the World Health Organization on preventing diseases spreading via commercial flights. ICAO collects and integrates statistical data, for example tracking air transport and air carrier economics, provides forecasts on the future of civil aviation, and plays a key role in providing civil aviation information to the international community through its documentation and publications.

ICAO is noted for its legal activities, with the organization creating a great array of international conventions and agreements. Areas covered include air traffic control and communications, noise management, safety protocols, search and rescue processes, transport of dangerous goods, meteorological services, taxation policies for air transport, and security measures for airlines and their facilities. Compared to many specialized agencies, ICAO has strong regulatory capability. Air transport and navigation in the modern world is closely directed by guidelines developed under ICAO, including the addition of technical annexes to the Chicago Convention that provide standards and recommended practices (SARPs). Nineteen Annexes setting out SARPs are in place, starting with Annex 1 on personnel licensing, moving through areas such as rules of the air, aircraft nationality and registration, environmental protection, and most recently targeting safety management in Annex 19. However, ICAO's member states have many opportunities to shape the content and to press ICAO on the body's response to global issues. For example, the European Union used discussions in ICAO to push for progress on environmental protections. ICAO also provides the space for countries to settle civil aviation disputes, as in the instance of assisting Greece and Turkey, which clash on territorial claims over Cyprus.

CHALLENGES AND REFORM

International civil aviation cooperation positively impacts national practices, yet the role of ICAO relative to the member states does provide some challenges. While there is largely freedom of air transport under ICAO's guidance, country concerns about preserving sovereign control over their airspace limits the full freedom of the skies. Member state disagreements over how to handle issues also impact ICAO's efforts. The organization has faced criticism for not making enough progress on addressing the negative environmental impact of civil aviation emissions, which is a flashpoint for discord between members. Other unforeseen issues, including technological developments such as satellite navigation systems and rising security threats to civil aviation, have created calls for the organization to undergo a full review of its activities to best engage in twenty-first century civil aviation concerns. The Council has expanded on several occasions, most recently to thirty-six members in 2002, although concerns over underrepresentation from Africa and Asia remain. The ANC shifted to nineteen members in 2005. Reform proposals include altering the power of the Assembly relative to the Council and modifying the role of the President of the Council.

In response to technological innovations and an increasingly interconnected world, ICAO's engagement with civil aviation issues continues to evolve. A series of new international regulations and agreements were devised to address shifts in international civil aviation. As part of this, ICAO consistently reshapes the

Chicago Convention, which by 2006 was in its ninth revised edition. In response to the changing world, the organization reevaluated its own activities, including initiating a general strategic action plan in 1997, with follow-up strategic objectives, and a plan of action for enhanced aviation security after the events of September 11, 2001, where planes themselves were employed as the means of a terrorist attack. Civil aviation benefits from the careful international guidance provided by ICAO as global aviation issues and capabilities continue to advance and expand.

See also: Environmental Protection; International Maritime Organization; International Telecommunication Union; Secretariat; Terrorism; United Nations Historical Background; Universal Postal Union; World Health Organization; World Meteorological Organization; World Tourism Organization.

FURTHER READING

Lindenthal, Alexandra. 2014. "Aviation and Climate Protection: EU Leadership within the International Civil Aviation Organization." *Environmental Politics* 23 (6): 1064–81.

MacKenzie, David. 2010. *ICAO: A History of the International Civil Aviation Organization*. Toronto: University of Toronto Press.

Milde, Michael. 2008. *International Air Law and ICAO*. Utrecht, Netherlands: Eleven International Publishing.

Sochor, Eugene. 1989. "Decision-Making in the International Civil Aviation Organization: Politics, Processes, and Personalities." *International Review of Administrative Sciences* 55: 241–59.

Weber, Ludwig. 2007. *International Civil Aviation Organization: An Introduction*. Alphen aan den Rijn, Netherlands: Kluwer Law International.

International Fund for Agricultural Development (IFAD)

Agriculture is a mainstay economic activity for many of the world's poorest people and is a key part of economic growth in underdeveloped areas. Food insecurity and areas of famine in the early 1970s, exacerbated by rising prices due to the oil crisis at the time, led to the 1974 World Food Conference. A key outcome of the conference was a resolution to establish an International Fund for Agricultural Development (IFAD) to bolster the international community's organizational capability to address global food concerns. Several years of negotiations regarding the founding of IFAD followed, including the commitment of $1 billion in starting funds, before the first official meeting of the organization in December 1977 and the first project funding was approved in April 1978. Although there was debate over where IFAD should be placed in the UN System, with some arguing it should serve as a subsidiary agency under UN programmes and funds, ultimately the organization was situated along with the International Monetary Fund (IMF) and the World Bank as an independent international financial specialized agency. Following the path of the other previously established UN food organizations, the Food and Agriculture Organization (FAO) and World Food Programme, IFAD is headquartered in Rome, Italy.

RESPONSIBILITIES

There are other international organizations that finance agricultural development, but such funding is just a portion of those institutions' broader purposes. IFAD is unique since agricultural development is the organization's sole mandate. IFAD is built on the idea that hunger and malnutrition are problems grounded in the underlying level of poverty and underdevelopment. Since they are usually reliant on agriculture, the organization focuses on helping the poorest rural populations in developing countries. According to Article 2 of the Agreement Establishing IFAD, "the objective of the Fund shall be to mobilize additional resources to be made available on concessional terms for agricultural development in developing Member States. In fulfilling this objective the Fund shall provide financing primarily for projects and programmes specifically designed to introduce, expand or improve food production systems and to strengthen related policies and institutions." Thus, IFAD is responsible for gathering financial support and distributing these funds to ventures serving those in need primarily via low-interest loans and grants.

STRUCTURE

IFAD's historical roots impact how the organization's structural dimensions compare to other parts of the UN System. Financing is at the heart of the organization, with significant funding provided by both developed countries and oil-exporting countries. This reflects the financial commitment made by the Organization of the Petroleum Exporting Countries (OPEC) when IFAD was founded at a time of oil revenue windfall. Additional resources are drawn from investment income and loan repayments, along with some supplementary funds for programming and cofinancing with other institutions. The financing provided by countries comes from voluntary contributions instead of assessed organizational dues. In order to maintain funding capability, countries need to make additional payments over time to replenish the funds available. Initially divided into three categories (developed, oil-exporting, and other developing countries), membership is now labeled as List A made up of developed countries, List B consisting of contributing developing countries (primarily from OPEC), and List C representing a list of potential recipient countries (further broken down into three geographic subgroups of Africa; Europe, Asia, and the Pacific; and Latin America and the Caribbean).

Votes were originally distributed equally across the three main categories of member states, but under the current system a set portion of votes are divided equally across each member. The remaining votes are distributed based on the level of contribution. Membership in IFAD is not fully universal, with the organization's 177 member states missing 18 UN members as of early 2020 (non-UN members Cook Islands and Niue make up the difference). If more countries join, then the membership votes will be redistributed to take this into account and votes connected to contributions will also shift depending on the amount paid by the new member. This complex voting system is a hybrid between the usual one-member one-vote approach used in most of the UN System and voting rights based on member contributions that dictate other international financial institutions like the IMF. The Executive Board, which meets three times a year to oversee operations and determine the program of work, consists of eighteen members and eighteen alternate members elected for three-year terms with eight seats allocated for List A, four for List B, and six for List C (two from each geographic subgroup). Executive Board members are approved by the Governing Council, the highest body in IFAD that brings together all members at an annual meeting. The President of IFAD, who is also elected by the Governing Council, manages the organization, which is supported by a small staff, and serves as chair at the Executive Board meetings.

ACTIVITIES

IFAD's activities are focused on resource mobilization and allocation. The Governing Council is responsible for reviewing IFAD's resources and setting in motion a consultation process on replenishment, which extends over multiple sessions, on a regular basis. IFAD launched the twelfth replenishment cycle in 2020. The Executive Council approves funding for projects and programs but does so under the guidance of policies and criteria set by the Governing Council. Many loans are interest-free and repaid over forty years, with a grace period of ten years, with service charges as low as 0.75 percent. IFAD focuses on rural poverty engagement to bolster economic opportunities in areas where agricultural resources are often underutilized due to difficult circumstances. In the IFAD Strategic Framework for 2016–2025, the organization points to three key objectives: increasing poor rural people's productive capacities and their benefits from market participation as well as strengthening the environmental and climate dimensions of their economic activities. IFAD also emphasizes support of the UN's Sustainable Development Goals (SDGs) for 2030, including interagency collaboration with the FAO and WFP to address the SDGs. Along with the FAO, Article 8 of the Agreement Establishing IFAD indicates that IFAD is expected to cooperate closely with other organizations connected to agricultural development. IFAD has a range of national and international partnerships and often engages in cofinancing of projects. In contrast to other international financial institutions that guide the entire life cycle of a project, IFAD is set up to approve and fund projects but otherwise mainly ensures that other institutions are responsible for implementation.

CHALLENGES AND REFORM

IFAD is recognized as acting early to evaluate the organization and reform institutional processes, which is acknowledged as lowering administrative costs while increasing project delivery capability. Legal controversies connected to mandate limitations have also been addressed, including whether funds could be provided to nongovernmental organizations, how to handle migrant remittances, the potential for direct supervision of projects, and project engagement in nonmember territories, such as the Palestinians. However, difficult challenges remain for the organization. Reliance on voluntary donor contributions through replenishment, which has often been a politically contentious and extended process, limits IFAD's ability to implement its objectives. Alternative funding options continue to be explored but require support from the member states.

IFAD was created to address the gap in devoted agricultural funding, but questions linger from the debate over the body's creation whether an independent institution is the best mechanism. This is not an empty consideration since operations of the World Food Council, a UN body also established out of the 1974 World Food Conference, were ended in 1992. At the same time, decreased funding for agricultural development for the rural poor from other sources makes IFAD's relatively limited resources further stretched. IFAD relies on significant levels of cofinancing with other organizations and cross-institutional collaboration, but this can be difficult to effectively coordinate. Relations with FAO have been problematic and unproductive at times, despite both organizations being based in Rome. Finally, IFAD is challenged by the very nature of its work, with the organization involved in projects in poor rural areas often lacking economic infrastructure and good governance. As long as these underserved populations require agricultural and development assistance, IFAD's central purpose and role in the international community remains important.

See also: Economic Development; Food and Agriculture Organization; Indigenous Peoples; International Monetary Fund; Sustainable Development Goals; United Nations Conferences and Summits; United Nations Industrial Development Organization; World Bank Group; World Food Programme.

FURTHER READING

Haudry de Soucy, Roberto. 2011. "Investing in the Development of South American Campesino Camelid Economies: The Experience of the International Fund for Agricultural Development (IFAD)." In *Fibre Production in South American Camelids and Other Fibre Animals*, edited by Ma Ángeles Pérez-Cabal, Juan Pablo Gutiérrez, Isabel Cervantes, and Ma Jesús Alcalde, 195–99. Wageningen: Wageningen Academic Publishers.

Kamau, Faith, and Marieclaire Colaiacomo. 2012. "Financing for Development: Examining the Concept of Resource Mobilization for International Organizations, a Case Study of the International Fund for Agricultural Development (IFAD)." *International Organizations Law Review* 9 (2): 467–96.

Shaw, D. John. 2009. *Global Food and Agricultural Institutions*. London: Routledge.

Talbot, Ross B. 1990. *The Four World Food Agencies in Rome: FAO, WFP, WFC, IFAD*. Ames: Iowa State University Press.

International Labour Organization (ILO)

In the nineteenth century, labor and social reform movements advocated for basic standards to protect workers and promote better labor conditions. An international institution focused on labor was part of the 1919 Treaty of Versailles, which drew

World War I to a close and founded the League of Nations. The International Labour Organization (ILO) was established as an autonomous organization alongside the League based in Geneva, Switzerland, where the ILO is still headquartered. Labor was viewed as a pressing social justice issue that needed to be addressed in order to ensure a lasting peace, with Western countries also concerned about the 1917 Bolshevik Revolution in Russia and the rising demands of organized labor movements in their own countries. In order to incorporate the voices of all parties involved with labor, the ILO was not set up as a traditional international governmental organization with only member states but instead also included representation from workers and employers.

To escape the renewed violence in Europe during World War II, the ILO temporarily relocated to Montreal, Canada, in 1940. The organization began preparations for transitioning to working with the planned replacement of the League of Nations, including a key 1944 conference held in Philadelphia. The ILO sent representatives to the 1945 San Francisco Conference that created the UN and became a specialized agency in the UN System in 1946. The organization's work was recognized when it was awarded the Nobel Peace Prize on the fiftieth anniversary of its founding in 1969.

RESPONSIBILITIES

Three central documents set out the principles and purposes that guide the ILO's work. The 1919 Constitution reflects the organization's roots in ensuring social justice to promote peace. Thus, the ILO was founded to address unjust and discriminatory labor conditions that could lead to unrest, including ensuring the right of collective labor associations, reasonable and equitable work hours and wages, and the abolition of child labor. The 1944 Declaration Concerning the Aims and Purposes of the International Labour Organization, set out in Philadelphia, reinforced the previously established principles and additionally stressed that labor should not be treated as a commodity; progress is based on freedom of expression and association; workers, employers, and governments must operate as equals to promote the common welfare of all; and "poverty anywhere constitutes a danger to prosperity everywhere." The 1998 Declaration on Fundamental Principles and Rights at Work reinforced the members' commitment to follow the guiding principles of the ILO and the conventions established by the organization.

STRUCTURE

The tripartite member representation in the ILO is unique among the UN's specialized agencies. Each member delegation is made up of four people: two from the government and one each representing that country's workers and employers. These individuals operate separately and have their own votes in the two decision-making bodies of the ILO, the International Labour Conference and the Governing Body, with members of the three groups from different countries often holding separate meetings. The International Labour Conference meets annually in Geneva to discuss labor issues, adopt labor standards, set general policies, and approve the budget. The Governing Body convenes three times a year to keep the work of the ILO underway by preparing the budget, establishing the Conference agenda, and making decisions for carrying out ILO policies. This smaller executive council consists of "titular members" distributed across twenty-eight government, fourteen worker, and fourteen employer representatives, as well as sixty-six "deputy members" similarly distributed, who serve three-year terms after being elected by the group of delegates from their category at the International Labour Conference. While the representatives are selected to represent diverse geographical locations, ten of the government seats are reserved for members of "chief industrial importance," such as Brazil, Japan, and the United States. A range of committees, also with tripartite representation, focus on key industries or particular labor issues. The secretariat of the organization, the International Labour Office, is headed by a Director-General elected by the Governing Body. The ILO also founded the International Institute for Labour Studies in Geneva to assist with research and the International Training Centre in Turin, Italy.

At 187 member states as of 2019, the ILO has near universal membership with all regular UN members represented, except Andorra, Bhutan, Lichtenstein, Micronesia, Monaco, Nauru, and North Korea. The Cook Islands is also a member. However, membership has fluctuated across time as members have withdrawn from the ILO. This was more of an issue during the time of the League of Nations and World War II as countries such as Germany withdrew, but in another key instance the United States left the ILO in 1977 only to return shortly thereafter in 1980. Worker and employer representation is controversial at times, with the independent credentials of delegates being challenged. This has particularly been an issue for representatives from fascist and communist countries where the line between government worker and employer is blurred. The budget of the ILO is primarily supported by assessed dues from the member states, although technical assistance programs also benefit from voluntary contribution support.

ACTIVITIES

The activities of the ILO are carried out across three main areas: international labor standards, research and education, and technical assistance. A central function is formulating international labor standards in the form of binding conventions and guideline recommendations. Before the ILO, there were very few agreed upon labor standards across countries, but the organization has created a great number that encompass all dimensions of labor. As of 2019, there are 190 conventions and 206 recommendations, with eight "fundamental" conventions recognized by the ILO that address areas such as forced labor, the right to organize, child labor, and equal remuneration. The ILO also closely monitors the satisfactory implementation of standards, including reviewing required government progress reports. The agency engages in extensive research, including maintaining labor statistics databases, and publishes a variety of materials to raise awareness and inform the global community about labor issues.

A major growth area for the ILO since the agency joined the UN System has been the development of technical assistance programs for the private sector and member governments. The ILO is also actively engaged with the Global Compact, which builds relationships between the UN and private companies, and in promoting the Sustainable Development Goals (SDGs), in particular SDG 8 on decent work and economic growth. The ILO's work on labor conditions leads to coordination with a number of UN bodies, especially to address the needs of particular workplaces. For example, the ILO works with the International Maritime Organization to assist maritime workers and addresses industrial conditions with the UN Industrial Development Organization. Labor issues that arise for specific populations have also led to interorganizational collaboration. For instance, the ILO holds a memorandum of understanding with the UN High Commissioner for Refugees and addresses migrant workers with the International Organization for Migration.

CHALLENGES AND REFORM

Members with different political systems, in particular capitalism and communism, have clashed within the ILO. The tripartism ideal relies on countries having independent worker and employer bodies, and when these are not clearly distinguishable from the government representatives, this leads to disagreements. Yet, the unique structure of tripartism perseveres and provides a central focus to the ILO's work. At the same time, challenges remain for the tripartism model, including whether the largely European-based model of labor organization that the ILO was set up on translates to developing areas of the world. Another issue is how social progress in the informal labor sector can be promoted. Globalization also presents challenges for maintaining fair and equitable labor conditions and raises questions regarding how to represent all workers and forms of employer in the modern, interdependent economy at the ILO. Issues such as these are being addressed via ILO institutional arrangements that were established 100 years ago, raising the issue of how the agency can adapt to shifting economic situations. Other areas of possible reform include building greater coherence with existing institutional partners, better engaging with civil society actors outside of the traditional worker and employer organizations, and devising a more coherent strategy that links together all three categories of ILO activities. The ILO continues to play a positive role in promoting and supporting labor, and ongoing institutional developments will help to ensure that the organization maintains labor issues as an important part of the global agenda.

See also: Economic Development; Executive Heads of Specialized Agencies; Human Rights; Indigenous Peoples; International Maritime Organization; International Organization for Migration; Joint United Nations Programme on HIV/AIDS; United Nations High Commissioner for Refugees; United Nations Historical Background; United Nations Industrial Development Organization; World Health Organization.

FURTHER READING

Hughes, Stephen, and Nigel Haworth. 2011. *The International Labour Organization (ILO): Coming in from the Cold*. New York: Routledge.

La Hovary, Claire. 2015. "A Challenging Ménage à Trois?: Tripartism in the International Labour Organization." *International Organizations Law Review* 12 (1): 204–36.

Maupain, Francis. 2013. *The Future of the International Labour Organization in the Global Economy*. Portland, OR: Hart Publishing.

Rodgers, Gerry, Eddy Lee, Lee Swepston, and Jasmien Van Daele. 2009. *The International Labour Organization and the Quest for Social Justice, 1919–2009*. Ithaca, NY: Cornell University Press.

Ryder, Guy. 2015. "The International Labour Organization: The Next 100 Years." *Journal of Industrial Relations* 57 (5): 748–57.

International Maritime Organization (IMO)

International merchant shipping has an age-old history across the globe. However, despite the many years of maritime engagement between different societies, the effort to regularize shipping via an international organization is a relatively new development. Compared to earlier efforts to regulate communication, such as the Universal Postal Union, the basis of what would become the International Maritime Organization (IMO) did not fully emerge until after the establishment of the UN System in 1945 because, up to that point, countries stressed maintaining national-level regulations instead. The Provisional Maritime Consultative Council was agreed upon in 1946 and began operations in 1947 as a temporary effort before the Inter-Governmental Maritime Consultative Organization (IMCO) was created in 1948. However, another ten years passed before enough countries ratified the convention, and the organization started functioning in 1959 as a UN specialized agency. Reflecting the shift in organizational capabilities, "intergovernmental" was changed to "international" and "consultative" was dropped from the name altogether in 1982. Given the historically central place in global maritime affairs, London serves as the headquarters for the IMO—the only part of the UN System based in this city.

RESPONSIBILITIES

The IMO promotes cooperation on shipping to ensure maritime security and safety and to prevent pollution of the marine environment from shipping activities. From the organization's inception, the IMO has been responsible for encouraging safe and efficient international navigation. Issues of maritime safety include congested shipping traffic and avoiding collisions, search and rescue, transport of dangerous goods, container and ship regulations, overloading, and crew training. As threats to shipping emerged, such as hijacking, terrorist attacks, and modern piracy, the IMO has also incorporated addressing security dimensions as part of its agenda. As concern over environmental protection increased, the IMO began tackling the marine dimension of this global problem as well. Environmental areas to address include intentional as well as accidental dumping and discharge into the water, emissions impacting air and atmosphere quality, ship construction and recycling, and harmful aquatic organisms spreading via marine transport.

STRUCTURE

The Assembly, the IMO's supreme governing body, includes representatives from all member states and regularly meets every two years. The Council serves as the executive organ of the IMO and undertakes all functions of the organization in between meetings of the Assembly. The forty members of the Council are elected by the Assembly for two-year terms and represent ten countries with the largest interest in international shipping services, ten with the largest interest in seaborne trade, and twenty more who have special interests in maritime transport or navigation in a manner that ensures that all geographic areas are represented. The Secretariat, headed by the Secretary-General, carries out administrative duties. Much of the work of the organization is undertaken in committees. The Maritime Safety Committee is the original committee of the organization and, along with the Marine Environment Protection Committee, is assisted by seven subcommittees focused on particular areas, such as ship design and construction. The IMO is also supported by the Legal Committee, Technical Cooperation Committee, and Facilitation Committee.

Membership greatly increased from the original 28 member states, which were primarily northern hemisphere–based traditional maritime countries, to 174 (as of early 2020). There are also three members that hold associate status since they do not currently possess full independence (Faroe Islands, Hong Kong, and Macao). A range of nongovernmental organizations possess consultative status and contribute to the work of the IMO. The IMO also grants observer status to a significant number of international governmental organizations from outside of the UN System and coordinates with (and at times gains some financial support from) other parts of the UN System. The expected contribution provided by member states to the IMO's budget is based mainly on the tonnage of the country's merchant fleet, thereby making the top five contributors relatively small countries with large shipping interests, with Panama the highest contributor.

ACTIVITIES

IMO activities are based around two main categories: standard setting and technical assistance. While not possessing the level of legislative regulatory authority that specialized agency compatriot International Civil Aviation Authority has over the airlines, the IMO plays a central role in convening meetings and formulating agreements to protect maritime affairs. The IMO helps to develop binding treaties as well as providing rules and recommendations for states to carry out. The IMO can coordinate regulations with other bodies when there is overlap, such as ship scrapping labor issues with the International Labour Organization. The standard-setting process is often extended and complicated. For example, the

Legal Committee can provide a forum for debate and setting of priorities, scope, and principles before moving into drafting the actual legal text to serve as the basis for full diplomatic conference negotiations. Along with liability and compensation, the other two main areas covered by IMO conventions are the prevention of marine pollution and maritime safety and security. Although the IMO lists thirty different treaties, the organization identifies three key conventions: International Convention for the Safety of Life at Sea, International Convention for the Prevention of Pollution from Ships, and International Convention on Standards of Training, Certification and Watchkeeping for Seafarers. Each of these has been modified and updated over time.

Legal guidelines must be properly carried out to be useful, and the IMO is noted for being the first UN agency to create a Technical Cooperation Committee in order to help countries implement conventions. Developing countries have particular technical assistance shipping needs, and the IMO at times coordinates this work with other bodies such as the UN Development Programme. Since pollution cuts across different areas of the globe, the work carried out by the IMO for marine environmental protection also connects with the mandates of other environmentally focused parts of the UN System, such as the UN Environment Programme. The emphasis on training and implementation also led to the establishment of the World Maritime University in Malmö, Sweden, and the International Maritime Law Institute based in Malta.

CHALLENGES AND REFORM

While the IMO can provide technical assistance and guidance for carrying out international maritime standards, implementation ultimately relies on the cooperation of all parties involved—from government agencies to the shipping industry to the seafarers themselves. Coordinating these diverse actors is complicated by the complexity of global shipping, where the country of origin for a ship may be different from the management and the transportation route often goes to a further set of countries. The convention ratification record of IMO member states greatly differs, along with the political will to accept and enforce established rules and regulations. "Flag states" (countries where ships are registered) have posed particular concerns over an inability or unwillingness to properly comply with maritime conventions. The IMO must also handle different financial and technical issues facing developing and developed countries, as well as the tensions between these sets of countries over conflicting shipping needs and concerns by developing countries that developed members of the IMO have tended to dictate the affairs of the organization. Countries also emphasize different priorities, which can impede efficient agenda planning at the IMO. Even when the agenda becomes clear, there can be further debate over whether agenda items should be addressed via a new convention or a protocol addition.

In an era of increased globalization, the need for effective and efficient global shipping standards becomes ever more pressing. The IMO has historically adapted well to shifting global maritime needs. A widely cited instance is the oil pollution and legal protections instituted following the 1967 Torrey Canyon tanker accident, which created the largest oil spill ever seen at that point. In the realm of maritime security, the IMO is noted for the response following the 1985 hijacking of the cruise ship *Achille Lauro*. The organization also evolved following the passing of the 1982 UN Convention on the Law of the Sea. As new shipping concerns arise, the IMO is likely to continue to adapt in reaction. At the same time, there have been calls for the IMO to be more proactive in pursuing potential solutions to problems before they arise or worsen, including seeking to address root causes of issues not just their negative outcomes. Other reform proposed includes improving participation of developing countries, in particular coastal members of the IMO, in the decision-making process.

See also: Environmental Protection; Global Commons; International Civil Aviation Organization; International Labour Organization; International Seabed Authority; International Telecommunication Union; Nongovernmental Organizations; Terrorism; United Nations Development Programme; United Nations Environment Programme; Universal Postal Union.

FURTHER READING

Basaran, Ilker. 2016. "The Evolution of the International Maritime Organization's Role in Shipping." *Journal of Maritime Law and Commerce* 47 (1): 101–17.

Gaskell, Nicholas. 2003. "Decision Making and the Legal Committee of the International Maritime Organization." *The International Journal of Marine and Coastal Law* 18 (2): 155–214.

Karim, Md Saiful. 2015. *Prevention of Pollution of the Marine Environment from Vessels: The Potential and Limits of the International Maritime Organisation*. New York: Springer.

Nordquist, Myron H., and John Norton Moore, eds. 1999. *Current Maritime Issues and the International Maritime Organization*. The Hague: Martinus Nijhoff Publishers.

Simmonds, Kenneth R. 1994. *The International Maritime Organization*. London: Simmonds and Hill.

International Monetary Fund (IMF)

The 1930s were a time of great political and economic turmoil. Near the end of World War II, countries came together to plan new international economic institutions. The intent was to build institutions that would foster global economic cooperation and stability and eliminate the nationalistic economic policies that fed the Great Depression and fascism leading up to the war. The Bretton Woods Conference was held in the United States from July 1 to 22, 1944. At the end of the conference, delegates signed the Articles of Agreement for both the International Monetary Fund (IMF) and the International Bank for Reconstruction and Development (IBRD), the organizational center of the modern World Bank Group. These two institutions, both headquartered in Washington, DC, remain closely connected, along with the more recently created World Trade Organization, in

> **Bretton Woods**
>
> Many observers view economic nationalism and protectionism between the two world wars (1919–1939) as a contributing factor to economic downturn and the outbreak of World War II. Therefore, before World War II was even over, world leaders began planning for a different approach to the international economic system. The United Nations Monetary and Financial Conference was held in Bretton Woods, New Hampshire, from July 1 to 22, 1944. The meeting is commonly referred to as the Bretton Woods Conference. The conference was sponsored by the United States, whose economy at that time encompassed over half of global industrial production. The revised global economic system was designed to promote economic growth by encouraging steady and secure economic relations between countries based on removing barriers to free trade, providing support to stabilize currencies and monetary management, and providing the capital needed for economic development. Articles of Agreement were drafted at the conference for creating the International Monetary Fund and the International Bank for Reconstruction (now a central part of the World Bank Group). To further encourage free trade, an International Trade Organization was planned to follow shortly afterward. However, this was not put into place until 1995 with the creation of the World Trade Organization. Instead, the General Agreement on Tariffs and Trade (GATT) guided free trade relations between 1948 and 1995. The three international financial institutions serve as organizational pillars of liberal economic global governance and together are referred to as the "Bretton Woods Institutions." The Bretton Woods system remains a guiding force of modern economic relations across the globe.

promoting global economic prosperity. With the commitment of countries providing 80 percent of required funding, the IMF officially came into existence in December 1945 and began financial operations in March 1947. In November 1947, the IMF became a specialized agency in the UN System.

RESPONSIBILITIES

The IMF supports economic growth and international cooperation to reduce the risk of instability in the global financial system through consultation, recommendations, and the collection of funds for distribution to provide assistance to members in times of financial adversity. The Articles of Agreement list six purposes: to promote international monetary cooperation, to facilitate positive economic growth and policy, to promote stable and orderly exchange rates, to assist with establishing a multilateral system of payments between members and eliminating foreign exchange restrictions, to make resources available to members to correct balance of payments difficulties, and to shorten the length and degree of disequilibrium in the international balance of payments between members. The Articles of Agreement have been amended seven times, with the most recent amendment coming into effect in January 2016.

Over time, the IMF's mission has evolved based on the changing needs of the global community. Initially, the IMF was responsible for providing short-term finances to address temporary imbalances in the exchange rate network. However, this changed in the early 1970s as floating exchange rates were adopted in place of pegged rates and less developed members joined the organization. The IMF then focused more on financial crises connected to areas such as banking and sovereign debt, which often require longer-term support. The debt repayment needs of countries, particularly in Latin America, drew IMF attention in the 1980s and then communist country transitions following the collapse of the Soviet Union in the early 1990s. The 2008 global financial crisis greatly impacted IMF responsibilities. In particular, the organization reengaged in Western Europe (notably in Greece) with expanded resources to counter the repercussions of the crisis.

STRUCTURE

Decision-making authority rests with the IMF's Board of Governors. Every member state is represented by a governor (and an alternative governor for when the governor is not available), usually a high-ranking economic official appointed by the member state. An Executive Board, made up of twenty-four Executive Directors (and the same number of alternates), carries out the regular operations. While the Board of Governors usually convenes once a year, the Executive Board meets in an ongoing manner—often multiple times a week. There are two advisory ministerial committees (which work jointly with the World Bank): the International Monetary and Financial Committee and the Development Committee. The Managing Director is selected by the Executive Directors for a five-year term, serving as Chair of the Executive Board and guiding the staff of the organization. Most of the staff are based at the Washington, DC, headquarters, although the IMF does have over eighty country and seven regional offices. The Managing Director has always been a European, while an individual from the United States has always held the World Bank Presidency. As of early 2020, except for Andorra, Cuba (which withdrew in 1964), Liechtenstein, Monaco, and North Korea, all regular UN members are also members of the IMF. However, unlike other specialized agencies, Kosovo is a member of the IMF (as well as the IBRD), bringing total IMF membership to 189.

The IMF's funds are contributed by member states. The amount provided, referred to as the member's quota, is based on an economic formula that is reviewed and adjusted on a regular basis. The IMF can also increase its resources through borrowing. Following the 2008 crisis, the amount that the fund could borrow and lend to members in need was greatly increased. The quota is tied to voting power. All members get the same number of starting votes, but additional votes are added based on the member's quota contribution. As of early 2020, the United States controls 16.5 percent of the votes, and because amendments to the Articles of Agreement require 85 percent approval, the United States essentially has a veto over such alterations. The Executive Directors also make decisions based on weighted voting. Most of the Executive Directors represent a block of member-state votes, but economically powerful countries possessing a large number of votes can have an Executive Director solely committed to their interests. However, the Articles of Agreement changes approved in January 2016 increased the quotas for members and tied this to Executive Board reform. Where previously the top five quota member states had an Executive Director appointed, now all of the Executive Board is elected.

ACTIVITIES

The IMF is involved in three main areas of activities: providing funds to members for addressing serious monetary problems, surveillance and analysis, and technical assistance. Having contributed to the IMF, members may draw back on those funds to address financial imbalances. In times of greater need, countries may require a higher level of support and the IMF can arrange loans. Over time, the IMF has developed a range of lending "facilities," which vary by goal, quota limit, and repayment period. However, when countries borrow at levels higher than their quota, they are subject to conditionality, which often requires economic policies and structural adjustment conditions set out by the IMF.

The IMF engages in extensive surveillance activities of the international financial system and specific country policies in order to prevent economic crises and monitor improvements. The IMF consults with members and requires the submission of national economic data, which is used to track trends, distribute research analysis, and provide strategic policy advice. The IMF also provides technical assistance and uses its expertise to help with policy and structural reforms and financial training.

CHALLENGES AND REFORM

The terms placed on countries receiving funds from the IMF are framed by the organization as necessary to counter the fiscal policy that brought about a country's economic difficulties. This conditionality is often challenged by those who argue that IMF prescriptions may cause economic and social harm to a population. Governments receiving IMF benefits can also be destabilized in the face of frustrated citizens reacting to policies such as cutbacks in public spending and price controls. Some critique the IMF's "lender of last resort" role as encouraging countries to pursue careless economic policies knowing that the IMF safety net is there. These measures can also damage the organization's reputation in cases when the IMF is entangled in a country with ongoing financial mismanagement and unsustainable levels of debt. IMF decision-making is also challenged. With the economic powers dictating IMF actions, questions are often raised about who the IMF helps, in what manner, and how quickly.

In an era of increased globalization and concerns regarding economic inequality, some accuse the IMF of reinforcing development inequity by insisting that an open, globalized system works for all while actually serving the wealthiest. Beyond how the IMF handles economic crises, there are also critics of its surveillance capabilities. Most recently, some point out that the IMF did not forecast the 2008 global crisis. The scale of economic disruption caused by this crisis has encouraged IMF reforms; however, the length of the reform process has been criticized, with the December 2010 plans not reaching the needed 85 percent approval until January 2016. Still others encourage the IMF to engage in broader reforms and develop more customized planning for different countries. Before the 2008 crisis, the IMF was in a period of relatively limited activity, leading some to believe the organization was less relevant in guiding global economic relations in the twenty-first century, but engagement since 2008 has demonstrated the IMF's important ongoing role in international financial affairs.

See also: Economic and Social Council; Economic Development; Executive Heads of Specialized Agencies; International Fund for Agricultural Development; Peacebuilding; Sustainable Development Goals; United Nations Conference on Trade and Development; United Nations Development Programme; World Bank Group; World Trade Organization.

FURTHER READING

Ban, Cornel, and Kevin Gallagher. 2015. "Recalibrating Policy Orthodoxy: The IMF Since the Great Recession: IMF, Great Recession, Policy Change." *Governance* 28 (2): 131–46.
Bird, Graham R., and Dane Rowlands. 2016. *The International Monetary Fund: Distinguishing Reality from Rhetoric*. Cheltenham, UK: Edward Elgar Publishing.
Reinhart, Carmen M., and Christoph Trebesch. 2016. "The International Monetary Fund: 70 Years of Reinvention." *Journal of Economic Perspectives* 30 (1): 3–28.
Tenney, Sarah, and Norman K. Humphreys. 2011. *Historical Dictionary of the International Monetary Fund*. Third edition. Lanham, MD: Scarecrow Press.
Vreeland, James Raymond. 2007. *The International Monetary Fund: Politics of Conditional Lending*. New York: Routledge.

International Telecommunication Union (ITU)

In the modern telecommunication era, the International Telecommunication Union (ITU) oversees a wide array of wired and wireless communication systems. At the same time, the organization is the oldest body to join the UN System because the original institution, the International Telegraph Union, was founded in 1865 to standardize equipment, frequencies, and operation protocols following the invention of the telegraph. May 17 is celebrated as World Telecommunication and Information Society Day, marking the date in 1865 when the original International Telegraph Convention was signed in Paris. The International Radiotelegraph Union (established in 1906) and the ITU held simultaneous Conferences in 1932 to formulate the International Telecommunication Convention and then merged together to form the renamed ITU in 1934. Originally based in Berne, which allowed the organization to maintain routine operations in neutral Switzerland during World War II, ITU headquarters moved to Geneva in 1948 after the organization agreed in 1947 to become a UN specialized agency. The ITU has operated as a part of the UN System since January 1949.

RESPONSIBILITIES

The international electrical communication subjects overseen by the ITU have greatly expanded over time, but the overarching responsibility remains to coordinate agreement by the organization's members to regulate communication networks and services. Universal standards ensure the proper interconnection of telecommunication systems to maintain the efficient and effective exchange of information. Communication interference is avoided through the allocation and registration of areas such as radio frequencies and satellite orbits. In addition, the ITU is tasked with promoting development of telecommunication capabilities and providing assistance and access for less technologically capable areas of the world.

STRUCTURE

The ITU lacked other international governmental organization precursors to serve as models for its original structure. The structure evolved across the ITU's long history, with particularly notable changes after the 1934 merger, when the organization joined the UN System, and a major reform set out in 1992. Today, the ITU operates with a very complex governance structure. The supreme authority is the Plenipotentiary Conference, which now meets every four years in order to ensure greater stability in amending the rules to address telecommunication changes compared to the previously varied meeting schedule. The administrative secretariat, originally set up as the Bureau by the first regular ITU Conference in 1868 and now titled the General Secretariat, provides management support. This body is headed by the Secretary-General, with the assistance of a Deputy Secretary-General, a position which was internationalized beyond Swiss control via election by the Plenipotentiary Conference in conjunction with the move to Geneva. The Council is a newer body, created in 1947 to oversee the ITU's work in between Conferences. A set of Consultative Committees and the International Frequency Registration Board were replaced by three Sectors as part of the 1992 reform process, each with its own governance structure: Radiocommunication Sector (ITU-R), Telecommunication Standardization Sector (ITU-T), and Telecommunication Development Sector (ITU-D).

Membership in the ITU is also linked to the Sectors. Dating back to the early years of the ITU, private telegraph companies engaged as advisory members. In the modern era, over seven hundred telecommunication companies and organizations participate as full or associate members in the relevant Sectors, creating a mixed membership approach that is unique in the UN System. The ITU was founded with twenty European member states. Shortly thereafter, the ITU opened up on a wider scale as these countries could vote on behalf of their overseas territories (a practice ended in 1973), and representatives from colonial administrations were allowed. The ITU now maintains a universal presence with 193 member states (as of early 2020). Nonstate membership also impacts financing of the ITU. Private sector members provide an important source of funding, along with cost recovery for services such as the sale of publications. ITU financing is also unusual in the UN System since members have free choice to select their class of contribution based on the number of contributory units they will provide, although the Universal Postal Union uses a similar system.

ACTIVITIES

Reflective of the complex organizational structure, the activities of the ITU are complicated and often involve highly technical work across a range of meetings, exhibitions, studies, publications, standard setting, policy coordination, and technical assistance. The original International Telecommunication Convention that governed the ITU had a difficult revision process. In 1992, two documents, a Constitution and Convention, which are complemented by other regulations, were established to make this more efficient. However, substantial activity has still been required since then to address many amendments to both. The three Sectors are central for carrying out substantive work, with each tackling issues in their domain via a Conference or Assembly along with other preparatory meetings and a range of subgroups. Technical standardization has long been a focus of the ITU, even as, for example, the debate over what constitutes a "word" for telegraph use shifted to counting "bits" for tracking modern telecommunications traffic. Regulation of the radio frequency spectrum was also extended to outer space to ensure that the transmission of satellite data is not disrupted along with coordinating access to geostationary satellite orbit slots.

The ITU has increasingly concentrated on development assistance, shifting the organization from facilitating the technical dimensions of telecommunications to improving affordable access to telecommunications infrastructure and technological advancements. An extension of this emphasis is found in the World Summit on the Information Society (WSIS) to address the inadequate levels of communication and information technology in the developing world. The first phase of WSIS was held in Geneva in 2003 and concentrated on more inclusive internet access. The second phase took place in Tunis in 2005, with a particular stress on internet governance. Other areas of technical assistance include bolstering administrative capabilities, specialized training, and planning support. The ITU's common focus on the needs of developing countries leads to engagement with bodies such as the UN Development Programme, while work on liberalizing telecommunications also builds connections with organizations like the World Trade Organization. The ITU also coordinates with other specialized agencies that oversee actors that rely on communications, like ships in the International Maritime Organization and airplanes in the International Civil Aviation Organization.

CHALLENGES AND REFORM

Although a technical organization, the ITU faces political challenges. From the ITU's formative years, national interests and a focus on maintaining the status quo infused organizational affairs. From the early days of the telegraph, there were issues with members' willingness to have the ITU adapt to and incorporate the telephone and then radio, and pressures and political disputes continue as new telecommunications areas arise, such as satellites, electronic communication, and the internet. The ITU seeks to promote the most effective technical regulations and ways to engage the private sector. At the same time, the organization must also wrestle with the digital divide between developed and developing countries and the related emphasis on telecommunication development for areas in need. Maintaining the balance between ensuring efficiency while maintaining equity can be difficult. Providing greater avenues for participation in the ITU by not-for-profit dimensions of civil society is another area to explore. The financing model of the ITU has come under question; reforms could provide more secure and stable funding. At the same time, there are other concerns regarding cost recovery charges impacting access for less developed members.

With ever-changing telecommunication technology, the ITU faces a particularly challenging environment in which to operate and adapt. Given the telecommunication developments from the 1940s through the 1980s, the major reform effort established in 1992 was relatively slow in coming. The complex governance structure also raises challenges for coordination and coherence across the ITU. Reform proposals range from restructuring the existing institution to more radical plans to transform the ITU under a new structure. The ITU has a long history and foundation of engagement with telecommunication to build upon as the organization addresses ongoing demands and considers the best path forward.

See also: Cybersecurity; Executive Heads of Specialized Agencies; Global Commons; International Civil Aviation Organization; International Maritime Organization; United Nations Conferences and Summits; United Nations Development Programme; United Nations Educational, Scientific and Cultural Organization; Universal Postal Union; World Trade Organization.

FURTHER READING

Allison, Audrey L. 2014. *The ITU and Managing Satellite Orbital and Spectrum Resources in the 21st Century.* New York: Springer.

Codding, George A., and Anthony M. Rutkowski. 1982. *The International Telecommunication Union in a Changing World.* Dedham, MA: Artech House.

Fari, Simone. 2015. *The Formative Years of the Telegraph Union.* Newcastle upon Tyne, UK: Cambridge Scholars Publisher.

Lyall, Francis. 2011. *International Communications: The International Telecommunication Union and the Universal Postal Union.* Burlington, VT: Ashgate.

MacLean, Don. 2008. "Sovereign Right and the Dynamics of Power in the ITU: Lessons in the Quest for Inclusive Governance." In *Governing Global Electronic Networks: International Perspectives on Policy and Power*, edited by William J. Drake and Ernest J. Wilson, 85–126. Cambridge, MA: MIT Press.

United Nations Educational, Scientific and Cultural Organization (UNESCO)

During the ravages of World War II, a vision of a more peaceful future supported by international organizations began to emerge. As enshrined in the Constitution of the UN Educational, Scientific and Cultural Organization (UNESCO), the central idea of the founders was, "That since wars begin in the minds of men, it is in the minds of men that the defences of peace must be constructed." Education was the initial focus for building an international institution to better inform "the minds of men" and encourage them to relate in a more peaceful manner. The process got underway in late 1942 with a Conference of Allied Ministers, although organizational precursors the International Bureau of Education (IBE) based in

Geneva and the International Institute of Intellectual Cooperation (IIIC) setup in Paris already existed. The early emphasis on education expanded to include building a culture of peace, so the intended organization was originally referred to as UNECO. However, late in the process, an additional focus on science was added, so by the time the Constitution was adopted at the end of a conference held in London in November 1945 the body was known as UNESCO. The organization formally came into existence in November 1946 when enough countries ratified the Constitution, and UNESCO joined the UN as a specialized agency headquartered in Paris shortly thereafter.

RESPONSIBILITIES

As established in the Constitution, UNESCO's ultimate responsibility is to promote the development of a more peaceful world. The underlying logic of the organization is that conflict and violence can be overcome through improving educational, cultural, and scientific capabilities. Responsibilities in the area of science are divided between the natural sciences and social and human sciences. In addition, although not listed in the name of the organization, a further area of responsibility is communication and information. UNESCO translates this broad mandate into a "medium-term strategy," with the 2014–2021 iteration emphasizing nine strategic objectives ranging from developing education systems to foster high quality and inclusive lifelong learning for all to promoting freedom of expression, media development, and access to information and knowledge.

STRUCTURE

Usually meeting in Paris every two years, UNESCO's supreme governing body is the General Conference, which sets UNESCO's policies and general program, along with overseeing a range of commissions and committees, and approves the budget. The fifty-eight-member Executive Board, selected by the General Conference for four-year terms on the basis of ensuring a breadth of geographical and cultural representation, meets twice a year to prepare and implement UNESCO's program of work. The Secretariat is headed by a Director-General, nominated by the Executive Board and approved by the General Conference, who serves for a four-year term. Compared to more technical UN agencies focused on placing staff in the field, the majority of Secretariat staff are based in the Paris headquarters office although there are also over fifty field offices based across the globe. UNESCO is also supported by a number of institutes and centers operating in various countries, primarily in the area of education, including incorporating the IBE still based in Geneva.

A distinctive feature of UNESCO is the inclusion of National Commissions, which are established at the country level to bring together a network of civil society actors and governmental agencies working on UNESCO-related issues. The National Commissions can consult with UNESCO and advise delegations to the General Conference, coordinate activities within a country, and encourage the following of UNESCO policies. In part, these bodies grew out of French pressure during the negotiations to establish UNESCO for maintaining the IIIC emphasis on the role of intellectual and civil society engagement. This also led to a high level of UNESCO involvement with nongovernmental organizations (NGOs) from the start. UNESCO recognizes a large number of NGOs as formal consulting partners and works with an even wider array when implementing programs. In addition, UNESCO maintains a think-tank-like quality, drawing in expert groups and intellectuals to discuss and report on topics related to the organization's mandate.

UNESCO's regular budget is funded by countries paying assessed membership dues, although there has been an increase in the percentage of the overall finances being supported from voluntary extra-budgetary sources. Given the reliance on member state funding, fluctuating membership over time has greatly impacted UNESCO's budgetary capabilities. Members have left and then returned to UNESCO at various times in the organization's history, often citing concerns that the agency was acting in a politically biased manner. For example, the Soviet Union initially refused to join UNESCO, and several Eastern European countries suspended their participation in 1952, but all became active members in 1954. The United States and United Kingdom departed in the mid-1980s but returned in 2003 and 1997, respectively. The United States—the largest contributor to UNESCO's budget—withdrew again at the end of 2018, along with Israel, as part of a protest against a perceived anti-Israel stance in UNESCO, which included member states in the General Conference voting to given the Palestinians membership in 2011. These most recent withdrawals leave UNESCO with 193 member states. UN member Liechtenstein does not participate, but the Cook Islands and Niue are members. There are also 11 associate members, which are territories that lack independent control over their international affairs, such as the British Virgin Islands.

ACTIVITIES

UNESCO's activities, as well as the related budget allocation, are largely designed around the agency's five central themes: education, natural sciences, social and human sciences, culture, and communication and information. Across all sectors UNESCO is known for working to set international standards through legally binding treaties, such as the 2005 Convention for the Protection and Promotion of the Diversity of Cultural Expressions, as well as recommendations and declarations. International conferences, either convened solely by UNESCO, or in partnership with other organizations, are used to discuss issues and establish global commitments for action. The agency is also extensively involved in data collection, studies, and publications. UNESCO was closely engaged with the Millennium Development Goals, particularly with the goal of achieving universal primary education. This has extended to involvement with the Sustainable Development Goals, including promoting the specific Goal 4 on quality education and more broadly linking in UNESCO's other sectors, such as the value of science and technology for making progress.

The original emphasis in developing UNESCO, education, is also the largest and best funded sector, with a wide range of efforts to improve the quality of and access to education for the world's population. As the only UN agency with a specific science mandate, UNESCO works to build scientific cooperation. This work is divided into two categories: the natural sciences, with a key focus on sustainable environmental and development practices, and the much smaller social and human sciences, which include research, training, and exchange programs. UNESCO's efforts to promote and protect culture are often the organization's best

---

UNESCO World Heritage Sites Added in 2019

Ancient Ferrous Metallurgy Sites (Burkina Faso)

Archaeological Ruins of Liangzhu City (China)

Babylon (Iraq)

Bagan (Myanmar)

Budj Bim Cultural Landscape (Australia)

Churches of the Pskov School of Architecture (Russia)

Dilmun Burial Mounds (Bahrain)

Erzgebirge/Krušnohorˇí Mining Region (Czechia/Germany)

French Austral Lands and Seas (France)

Historic Centre of Sheki with the Khan's Palace (Azerbaijan)

Hyrcanian Forests (Iran)

Jaipur City, Rajasthan (India)

Jodrell Bank Observatory (United Kingdom)

Krzemionki Prehistoric Striped Flint Mining Region (Poland)

Landscape for Breeding and Training of Ceremonial Carriage Horses at Kladruby nad Labem (Czechia)

Le Colline del Prosecco di Conegliano e Valdobbiadene (Italy)

Megalithic Jar Sites in Xiengkhuang—Plain of Jars (Laos)

Migratory Bird Sanctuaries along the Coast of Yellow Sea-Bohai Gulf of China (China)

Mozu-Furuichi Kofun Group: Mounded Tombs of Ancient Japan (Japan)

Ombilin Coal Mining Heritage of Sawahlunto (Indonesia)

Paraty and Ilha Grande—Culture and Biodiversity (Brazil)

Risco Caido and the Sacred Mountains of Gran Canaria Cultural Landscape (Spain)

Royal Building of *Mafra*—Palace, Basilica, Convent, *Cerco* Garden and Hunting Park (Portugal)

Sanctuary of Bom Jesus do Monte in Braga (Portugal)

Seowon, Korean Neo-Confucian Academies (Republic of Korea)

The 20th-Century Architecture of Frank Lloyd Wright (United States)

Vatnajökull National Park (Iceland)

Water Management System of Augsburg (Germany)

Writing-on-Stone / Áísínai'pi (Canada)

known among the general public, in particular via the World Heritage List that now indicates over one thousand sites designated as worthy of protection and preservation. Communication and information activities involve the smallest budget allocation of the five sectors but have often been the most contentious for UNESCO. Illustrative of this is the clash during the 1970s and 1980s over the idea of a New World Information and Communication Order (NWICO) to make global information flows more equitable. This clash was an important factor in the first withdrawal of the United States from UNESCO as it perceived NWICO as an attack against Western, developed countries. Given the breadth of UNESCO's activities, the organization often coordinates with other UN bodies, such as the World Health Organization for health education, the UN Population Fund for social science examination of demographic changes, and the International Telecommunication Union for communication issues.

CHALLENGES AND REFORM

UNESCO oversees a wide-ranging mandate and related activities, which creates a complicated landscape for the organization to manage. This is exacerbated by power struggles between members over what UNESCO should prioritize and how the agency should carry out its work. These clashes have led to claims of politicization, accusing the agency of operating in a biased manner, even extending to how decisions are made to add sites to the World Heritage List. At times members have become so aggrieved that they have withdrawn from UNESCO, taking with them much needed resource support. Despite operating with one of the larger specialized agency budgets, considering the scope of UNESCO's activities the organization is generally viewed as operating with a limited budget compared to programmatic requirements. Yet, some donors have questioned the budget needs of UNESCO in light of so much programming and have called for a more focused set of priorities. This has been difficult to establish as the organization tries to address varied member state priorities. The division of resources across sectors is tied to issues with the structure of the organization. Instead of integrating its themes in the pursuit of peace, UNESCO has maintained a rigid, compartmentalized structure that limits interdisciplinary engagement across themes. Critiques of how the organization functions have intensified due to claims of managerial and staff mismanagement, impacting UNESCO's ability to deliver more positive results using its existing resources. In addition, questions have been raised regarding the intellectual think-tank approach of UNESCO, which often promotes a top-down intellectual emphasis over methods that could better engage the world's population. The ideals of UNESCO set a positive moral tone for building world peace, but the practicalities of pursing the organization's mandate remain challenging.

See also: Environmental Protection; Executive Heads of Specialized Agencies; Goodwill Ambassadors and Messengers of Peace; Human Rights; International Seabed Authority; International Telecommunication Union; Joint United Nations Programme on HIV/AIDS; Nongovernmental Organizations; Sustainable Development Goals; United Nations Population Fund; World Health Organization; World Meteorological Organization.

FURTHER READING

Bertacchini, Enrico, Claudia Liuzza, Lynn Meskell, and Donatella Saccone. 2016. "The Politicization of UNESCO World Heritage Decision Making." *Public Choice* 167 (1–2): 95–129.

Duedahl, Poul, ed. 2016. *A History of UNESCO: Global Actions and Impacts*. New York: Palgrave Macmillan.

Hüfner, Klaus. 2017. "The Financial Crisis of UNESCO after 2011: Political Reactions and Organizational Consequences." *Global Policy* 8 (5): 96–101.

Kozymka, Irena. 2014. *The Diplomacy of Culture: The Role of UNESCO in Sustaining Cultural Diversity*. New York: Palgrave Macmillan.

Singh, J. P. 2011. *United Nations Educational, Scientific and Cultural Organization (UNESCO): Creating Norms for a Complex World*. New York: Routledge.

United Nations Industrial Development Organization (UNIDO)

Production through manufacturing is a driving component of economic development. Yet, developing countries often lack the needed support to improve their level of industrialization. The effort to institutionalize industrialization assistance was an extended process with several stages and one often disrupted by competing views between already industrialized countries and those seeking to industrialize. While pressure from developing countries (organized through the Group of 77 [G-77]) in the 1960s led to the establishment of the UN Conference on Trade and Development (UNCTAD), the call for institutional commitment to focus on industrialization initially only led to the Industrial Development Centre based in the UN Secretariat. Further progress was made in November 1966 when the General Assembly passed a resolution creating the UN Industrial Development Organization (UNIDO) as an autonomous organ, which became operational at the start of 1967. This outcome was a compromise between developing countries, which wanted a fully independent UNIDO established, and developed countries, which sought to limit the organizational scope. Due to the organization's focus, there was discussion of the organization being hosted in a developing country, but ultimately UNIDO's headquarters was established in Vienna, Austria. The 1975 meeting of UNIDO's Second General Conference in Lima, Peru, advised that the organization be transformed into a specialized agency, which was then endorsed by the General Assembly and the process of writing a constitution for the body began. By 1979, the UNIDO Constitution was adopted, but this did not take effect until the required eighty countries ratified the document in June 1985. UNIDO's new General Conference session met in August and full operations as a specialized agency got underway at the start of 1986.

RESPONSIBILITIES

UNIDO is the only agency in the UN System to solely focus on promoting development through industrialization. The organization's Constitution linked increased industrial progress for developing countries to the effort to create "a new international economic order." As UNIDO evolved, the organization's mandate shifted to emphasize supporting inclusive and sustainable industrial development, with industrialization still targeted to overcome poverty but in an environmentally sustainable manner. The overarching areas of focus set out by the organization are creating shared prosperity, advancing economic competitiveness, safeguarding the environment, strengthening knowledge and institutions, and cross-cutting services. UNIDO serves as one of four implementing agencies, along with the UN Development Programme (UNDP), the UN Environment Programme (UNEP), and the World Bank, for the Montreal Protocol on Substances that Deplete the Ozone Layer.

STRUCTURE

UNIDO first held a General Conference in Vienna in 1971. Since becoming a specialized agency, the General Conference, which sets the policy and program of work along with approving the budget, meets every two years, almost exclusively in Vienna. The General Conference also elects the fifty-three members of the Industrial Development Board, which meets once a year to maintain organizational business (a change instituted in 2011 as a cost-cutting move as the Board used to meet twice in the year that the General Conference did not assemble), for four-year terms and the twenty-seven members of the Programme and Budget Committee, which meets once a year and operates as a subsidiary body to the Board, to two-year terms. In order to ensure that representation on both bodies is balanced, a set number of countries are selected from predivided lists: List A made up of African and Asian developing countries, List B European developed countries, List C developing countries in the Americas, and List D East European countries. No other permanent organs or committees have been put into place. UNIDO also has country and regional offices, but its field presence is relatively limited compared to other institutions although efforts to expand this include setting up UNIDO desks in UNDP country offices. UNIDO used to be headed by an Executive Director selected by the UN Secretary-General, but as a specialized agency the General Conference, based on the recommendation of the Board, is now able to appoint the holder of the renamed office of Director-General.

As of April 2019, UNIDO has 170 member states, but this number has fluctuated. The organization falls short of universal membership as some countries choose not to join because they have limited industrial concerns (e.g., small islands like Palau and some developed countries including Iceland and Singapore). However, eleven industrialized countries have withdrawn from UNIDO. This exodus includes Australia, Canada, and the United States in the 1990s, but also more recently the United Kingdom and Lithuania in 2012 followed by five other European countries and New Zealand since then. Before the United States withdrew, it provided around a quarter of UNIDO's budget. UNIDO's shift to being a specialized agency provided the organization with greater control over its budget and the ability to fund the regular budget through member state assessed contributions instead of relying on funding as a UN subsidiary body. Extra-budgetary resources for carrying out particular projects are provided through voluntary funding sources. A significant portion of this is devoted to assisting developing countries with phasing out ozone-depleting substances and other environmentally focused projects, for which UNIDO receives funding support from the Multilateral Fund for the Implementation of the Montreal Protocol and the Global Environment Facility.

ACTIVITIES

UNIDO serves as a global forum for encouraging and discussing industrialization. The organization collects statistics and supports research on industrialization, which are distributed and used to support policy recommendations. A central publication is the *Industrial Development Report*. Developing countries are provided with technical assistance across a range of industrial development needs. UNIDO works broadly across sectors to encourage industrialization efforts to be more competitive and conform to the standards of global markets. UNIDO emphasizes its commitment for working toward Sustainable Development Goal 9 to "build resilient infrastructure, promote inclusive and sustainable industrialization and foster innovation." As UNIDO has extended activities connected to the environment, the organization has built its relationship with UNEP. Other areas of coordination include agricultural industry with the Food and Agriculture Organization and the International Fund for Agricultural Development and industrial dimensions of trade with the World Trade Organization, as well as connections with related nongovernmental organizations and partnerships with universities and academic networks. UNIDO is also engaged with private sector partnerships sector via the UN Global Compact.

CHALLENGES AND REFORM

From the start, there was division between developed and developing countries over the creation and role for UNIDO. Developed countries often viewed UNIDO as an organizational pressure point to be used against them and a move away from an international political economy perspective based on nonintervention in government policies. Developed countries also faced the threat of losing their existing industrial advantage over developing countries. In relation to UNIDO's activities, the argument was made by many developing countries that UNIDO was inefficiently and ineffectively operated, and funding for development purposes should be funneled to other bodies that would do the work better. The Canadians were the first to act on their concerns, withdrawing in 1993, followed by the United States in 1996 and Australia in 1997, which greatly damaged UNIDO's funding support. The organization underwent extensive reform in the 1990s to cut back and determine the best path forward for rebuilding.

UNIDO continues to face challenges from deficient levels of support. The General Conference has lacked full attendance, and there have been vacant seats on the Board and the Programme and Budget Committee. Despite reform efforts, there has been another wave of membership withdrawal starting in 2012. This creates further funding stress on the organization. Loss of members' contributions that support the regular budget has shifted organizational reliance to voluntary funding connected to technical assistance activities, which impacts the organizational proficiency and ability to address the other areas of UNIDO's mandate. The multiple and ongoing organizational restructuring impact workflow and staff morale. Field network support and level of presence are also further negatively affected. UNIDO continues to reform in an attempt to improve organizational performance and maintain relevance through building around existing resources and areas of potential strength. In an era focused on climate change impacts, the organization's work to support sustainable development in industrialization provides one such path. With fewer industrialized members, the future of the organization will rely on engaged developing country members. As UNIDO builds networking capabilities, the organization's work may connect it more closely with the private sector that can be linked to bolster developing-to-developing country connections and partnerships.

See also: Economic Development; Executive Heads of Specialized Agencies; Food and Agriculture Organization; International Labour Organization; Nongovernmental Organizations; Secretariat; Sustainable Development Goals; United Nations Conference on Trade and Development; United Nations Development Programme; United Nations Environment Programme; World Bank Group.

FURTHER READING

Bredel, Ralf. 2003. *Long-Term Conflict Prevention and Industrial Development: The United Nations and its Specialized Agency, UNIDO.* Leiden, Netherlands: Martinus Nijhoff.

Browne, Stephen. 2012. *United Nations Industrial Development Organization: Industrial Solutions for a Sustainable Future.* New York: Routledge.

Campbell, Persia. 1967. "The Birth of UNIDO." *Ekistics* 24 (141): 227–30.

Lambert, Youry. 1993. *The United Nations Industrial Development Organization: UNIDO and Problems of International Economic Cooperation.* Westport, CT: Praeger.

Luken, Ralph A. 2009. "Greening an International Organization: UNIDO's Strategic Responses." *Review of International Organizations* 4 (2): 159–84.

Universal Postal Union (UPU)

People have been sending messages to each other across the span of human history. However, in a preelectronic age when communication by physical post was essential, countries recognized the need to manage postal flows across different national systems and began establishing a range of bilateral agreements to cooperate on postal affairs. The move toward universal postal oversight culminated in the Treaty of Berne, signed on October 9, 1874, and entered into force in 1875, which established the General Postal Union and is celebrated today as World Post Day. Still headquartered in Berne, Switzerland, the organization shifted to its current name, the Universal Postal Union (UPU), in 1878. The UPU is the second oldest organization in the UN System after the International Telecommunications Union, and is recognized as a key organizational precursor to twentieth-century universal organization developments in the League of Nations and the UN. While the UPU deferred from being a part of the League of Nations, the organization quickly became a specialized agency following the establishment of the UN System, signing an agreement in 1947 that took effect in 1948.

RESPONSIBILITIES

From the UPU's establishment, the organization has operated in a nonpolitical, technical manner to ensure efficient international postal operations. The UPU does not provide mail service. Instead, the members of the UPU operate as a single postal territory with the national postal services responsible for delivery. Reciprocal collaboration and exchange across national systems, along with the promotion of effective technical cooperation, guarantees that mail freely, reliably, and securely travels between and across territorial boundaries. The UPU coordinates the guidelines that harmonize a universal postal system by providing uniform regulations in all sectors—including rates and charges collected, stamp, letter, and parcel standards, prohibited items, and service quality.

STRUCTURE

Across the history of the UPU, there have been important changes in organizational structure. The UPU does not have a standing plenary body, but instead the supreme authority is the Universal Postal Congress. The Treaty of Berne also created the International Bureau (originally called the International Office, but changed in 1878), which started operations in 1875 and was overseen by the Swiss government until 1972. The International Bureau provides institutional support and is headed by the Director General with support from a Deputy Director General. To join the UN, the organization needed to create a permanent organ to provide oversight in between meetings of the Congress, so the Executive and Liaison Committee was established at the 1947 Paris Congress. In 1964, this body became the Executive Committee and then the current Council of Administration structure was established in 1994. Also emerging from the 1994 Seoul Congress was the newly framed Postal Operations Council, replacing the Consultative Council for Postal Studies that was based on the previous Consultative Committee for Postal Studies and its Management Council, which is responsible for technical and operational dimensions of the post. Most recently, the Consultative Committee, a hybrid body to include nongovernmental organizations and the ideas and interests of a fuller range of postal stakeholders, was put into place in 2004.

Membership in the UPU has evolved in interesting ways. The organization started with twenty-two members, including entities like Egypt that were not fully independent at the time. With the services becoming increasingly popular, the membership base quickly expanded. Colonies were allowed to join, with the first new additions being British India and the French colonies in 1876. The UPU did not view this as a political statement on territorial control, merely as a technical postal question of whether or not a territory had viable postal services. Although expulsion is not technically allowed, the UPU did block South Africa from participation during the apartheid period. The approach to membership had to shift when joining the UN System, so approval of two-thirds of the existing members is now required for new member states to join. From 1964 onward, any UN member could unilaterally join the UPU with only non-UN countries still requiring the two-thirds approval. The UPU lives up to its "universal" name with 192 members (as of early 2020), although the membership list diverges from the UN. Andorra, Marshall Islands, Micronesia, and Palau are not members of the UPU, but the UPU does have members not in the UN with Aruba, Curacao, and Sint Maarten as a group, as well as Overseas Territories of the United Kingdom and the Vatican. The UPU does allow, and maintains relations with, separate Restricted Unions with limited membership, such as the Caribbean Postal Union. In addition, the UN Postal Administration operates as a separate body in the UN System but is bound by UPU rules. The UPU's approach to funding, via differentiated membership dues with countries divided into contribution classes, provided a model followed by later international organizations.

ACTIVITIES

The UPU oversees the documentation of standardized principles and practices to ensure the efficient flow of international mail. The UPU held eleven regular Congresses, with each iteration adjusting and extending postal regulations, before joining the UN System. Congresses then met every five years, before shifting to a four-year schedule following Bucharest 2004. One notable Congress occurred at Vienna 1964, which is viewed as a watershed event marking the shift to the modern UPU with the reorganization of the binding documents that encompass the Acts of the Union into the following: the Constitution with the fundamental rules along with General Regulations for the application of the Constitution and UPU operations that do not need to be renewed, the Convention covering basic rules for letters and parcel post and Regulations connected to these, along with special Agreements for particular services. This structure was adjusted at the 1999 Beijing Conference and 2004 Bucharest Conference, and specific details are amended in an ongoing process.

The UPU has also shifted to providing technical assistance in a range of areas, particularly after the 1964 Vienna Congress as the organization sought to adapt to the gap between the postal operations of developing and developed members. Although the UPU initially had limited engagement with other parts of the UN System, the UPU has connected more with other specialized agencies, especially those involved with social and communication areas, such as the UN Educational, Scientific and Cultural Organization and the World Intellectual Property Organization, as well as organizations with linked responsibilities such as the transport of perishable biological materials (World Health Organization) and air mail (International Civil Aviation Organization). Data collected by the UPU provide useful records, for instance helping with the mapping of the international postal network and tracking security trends. The Postal Security Group also provides valuable expertise and strategies for fighting fraud and other mail security concerns.

CHALLENGES AND REFORM

The UPU has faced some challenges adapting from the organization's historical roots. From the founding in Berne, French remains the only official language of the UPU, but there are longstanding pressures to expand the languages employed. As of 1994, English is a working language, other languages with interpretation are used at meetings, and documents are available across core languages. The UPU also faces varied disputes over international postal regulations. For example, contentious stamp designs have at times pushed the boundaries of what is acceptable. While the original assumption was that mail volume between countries would be fairly equal, this is not the case and terminal dues, payment that the receiving post office is due for delivering inbound mail, are an ongoing area of debate. The modern era shift to electronic communication also poses challenges. The UPU supports philately (stamp collecting), but as the use of stamps declines this has a carry-over effect to collecting. The organization also faces financial challenges in maintaining funding levels and long-term sustainability.

To address the financial stresses and structural inefficiencies, the UPU is exploring reform options. Along with reviewing the UPU World Postal Strategy established at the 2016 Universal Postal Congress held in Istanbul, the Extraordinary Congress in September 2018 in Ethiopia considered possible structural changes to streamline the work of the UPU. Other reform suggestions include integrating private commercial carriers into the work of the UPU. Yet, the new era of communication also provides opportunities for the UPU to offer advice based on its experience, and the organization can continue to serve as a hub for coordination, data gathering, and standard setting. The UPU has a long history of adapting to shifting postal circumstances and remains a central organization in ensuring efficient services for people around the globe.

See also: Executive Heads of Specialized Agencies; International Civil Aviation Organization; International Telecommunication Union; Nongovernmental Organizations; United Nations Educational, Scientific and Cultural Organization; World Health Organization; World Intellectual Property Organization.

FURTHER READING

Akzin, Benjamin. 1933. "Membership in the Universal Postal Union." *The American Journal of International Law* 27 (4): 651–74.

Campbell, James I., Jr. 2016. "Quantifying the Distortive Effects of UPU Terminal Dues." In *The Future of the Postal Sector in a Digital World*, edited by Michael A. Crew and Timothy J. Brennan, 313–30. New York: Springer.

Codding, George A. 1964. *The Universal Postal Union: Coordinator of the International Mails*. New York: New York University Press.

Lyall, Francis. 2011. *International Communications: The International Telecommunication Union and the Universal Postal Union*. Burlington, VT: Ashgate.

Vial, Virginie. 2008. "The Universal Postal Union's Strategy for Fighting 'Snail Mail' Fraud May Be the Key to Making e-Commerce Safer." *Global Business and Organizational Excellence* 27 (4): 32–39.

World Bank Group

The original organizational development of the World Bank Group built out of the 1944 Bretton Woods Conference, where the International Bank for Reconstruction and Development (IBRD) was initiated alongside the International Monetary Fund (IMF). Along with the later established World Trade Organization, these three bodies sit at the heart of international financial institution efforts to promote global economic prosperity. Unlike the other UN specialized agencies, the modern World Bank Group is not a single organizational entity. While all of the World Bank Group is headquartered in Washington, DC, each component part has a particular focus in promoting the overarching goal of reducing poverty. The IBRD began operations in 1946 and was joined in 1960 by the International Development Association (IDA). The two linked institutions are now usually referred to as the World Bank, although some uses of the term "World Bank" will only indicate the IBRD. The broader World Bank Group encompasses the International Finance Corporation (IFC, founded in 1956), the International Centre for Settlement and Investment Disputes (ICSID, founded in 1966), and the Multilateral Investment Guarantee Agency (MIGA, founded in 1988). After contentious negotiations, the agreement for the IBRD to join the UN System as a specialized agency was approved by the General Assembly in November 1947, but, along with IMF, the organization often acts more independently from the UN System than other specialized agencies. As noted in the official UN System organizational chart, ICSID and MIGA do not have specialized agency status, unlike the other parts of the World Bank Group.

RESPONSIBILITIES

The World Bank Group as a whole encourages economic growth and development, with an emphasis on addressing poverty and improving the economic capabilities of developing countries. The original mandate of the IBRD was set out in the founding Articles of Agreement. Coming out of the ravages of World War II, the focus was on reconstruction as well as building development across the globe. As reflected in the organizational expansion, responsibilities evolved over time in reaction to the needs of less developed countries to emphasize addressing poverty. Both the IBRD and IDA provide loans targeted at poverty alleviation, but the IDA focuses on assisting the poorest developing countries with more accessible financial terms. The IFC supplements this work by encouraging private enterprise in developing countries. The most recent addition to the World Bank Group, MIGA, promotes foreign investment for developing countries through providing guarantees to the investors. ICSID also supports foreign investment by serving as an independent body to settle disputes between international investors and developing country governments.

STRUCTURE

The World Bank Group is overseen by a Board of Governors, which meets once a year in conjunction with the IMF. Two ministerial committees, also in coordination with the IMF, provide support: International Monetary and Financial Committee and the Development Committee. The twenty-five Executive Directors of the Board of Directors are engaged full time to carry out the work of the institution. The President oversees all five bodies within the World Bank Group, although IFC and MIGA have their own independent executive officers who report to the President. The President, who has always been from the United States (with the IMF head selected from a European country), chairs the Executive Director meetings and oversees a vast bureaucratic staff based mainly in Washington, DC.

The exact funding process varies across the different parts of the World Bank Group. For instance, member states in the IBRD, which operates as a global financial cooperative, subscribe to shares in the organization through a financial commitment where a portion is paid up front, while the remainder is to be made available as needed. An increase in the level of funding authorized, known as a replenishment, also occurs. Additionally, funds flow back into the IBRD from loan repayments and fees. At the same time, given the large scale of IBRD lending, most capital for loans is drawn from international financial markets. The amount contributed by member states has important implications for voting. The exact approach for allocating votes varies across IBRD, IDA, IFC, and MIGA, but across all of the institutions a central principle is that voting power is tied to the level of financial contribution. Membership levels fluctuate across the five institutions in the World Bank Group. Membership in the IMF is required to become a member of the IBRD, so the two organizations have the same 189 member states. This includes Kosovo, which is not a member of any other specialized agencies. The IDA is slightly smaller, with 173 members, while the IFC and MIGA have 185 and 181 members, respectively. The smallest body is ICSID, with 154 members (all membership numbers listed current as of 2019).

ACTIVITIES

Although the exact responsibilities differ according to institutional areas, overall the World Bank Group is an extremely influential actor in global development through providing loans, technical assistance, and policy advice. The form and focus of financial support vary across the different institutions. IBRD loans must be repaid at market rates, so the institution works to support projects in middle- and low-income countries with good credit records. By contrast, the IDA was created to undertake higher risk, providing poorer developing countries with long-term, interest-free loans with a small administrative fee. Overall, for fiscal year 2018, the four lending institutions financed almost $64 billion to support country and private sector operations via grants, loans, investments, and guarantees. The IBRD and IDA approved just under four hundred new operations for fiscal year 2017, which brought their overall lifetime lending numbers to $681 billion and $345 billion, respectively. The amount of technical assistance provided greatly expanded over the past several decades, with a particular emphasis on establishing strong institutions and management capabilities that allow developing countries to use financial resources most effectively when undertaking projects.

The World Bank Group has a major impact through accumulating knowledge and providing policy advice. An enormous amount of data is collected and analyzed across a range of research projects, which culminates in a wide array of influential publications that guide the global dialogue on poverty reduction and development. The organization shapes policies for both donors and countries receiving assistance across many sectors. For example, strategies are designed to bolster education in developing countries, which is an important component of overcoming poverty. Due to the scope of the work undertaken in the World Bank Group, there is a high degree of coordination with many parts of the UN System, including other development agencies such as the UN Development Programme and the International Fund for Agricultural Development. In addition, the World Bank often interacts with civil society, including local organizations and communities impacted by projects, and nongovernmental organizations, including those working in traditional development areas as well as wider areas such as religious and environmental issues.

CHALLENGES AND REFORM

Given the major role that the World Bank Group plays in the international arena, there is an extensive amount written on challenges faced by, and efforts to reform, the organization. General themes include evaluating the degree to which the loan strategies employed have been successful in lessening poverty and whether practices fail to live up to the organization's principles of promoting good governance and prioritizing the needs of the world's poor. The governance structure is viewed by some as biased toward the interests of the wealthy countries and foreign investors. As a supporter of a globalized economy, the organization is tied to broader concerns over the potential inequity between the benefits of this system for the wealthy over the poor. Since the work of the World Bank Group impacts an array of issues beyond economics, critics also note how the organization does not fully consider other perspectives, such as environmental and gendered. The World Bank Group is under constant pressure from multiple constituencies, with many claiming that the organization is still not doing enough to help the world's poor, yet the organization also gets criticized by some who perceive it as trying to do too much by adding so many areas of responsibility. While new institutional challengers are emerging, such as China's Asian Infrastructure Investment Bank, the ongoing level of financial resources and policy influence will likely ensure that the World Bank Group will remain at the center of promoting development and fighting poverty.

See also: Economic and Social Council; Economic Development; Executive Heads of Specialized Agencies; Indigenous Peoples; International Fund for Agricultural Development; International Monetary Fund; Joint United Nations Programme on HIV/AIDS; Nongovernmental Organizations; Peacebuilding; Sustainable Development Goals; United Nations Development Programme; United Nations Industrial Development Organization; Women and Gender.

FURTHER READING

Clemens, Michael A., and Michael Kremer. 2016. "The New Role for the World Bank." *The Journal of Economic Perspectives* 30 (1): 53–76.

Ferguson, Lucy, and Sophie Harman. 2015. "Gender and Infrastructure in the World Bank." *Development Policy Review* 33 (5): 653–71.

Marshall, Katherine. 2008. *The World Bank: From Reconstruction to Development to Equity*. New York: Routledge.

Toussaint, Eric. 2008. "Difficult Beginnings between the UN and the World Bank." In *The World Bank: A Critical Primer*, edited by Sylvain Dropsy, 30–35. London: Pluto Press.

Weaver, Catherine. 2008. *Hypocrisy Trap: The World Bank and the Poverty of Reform*. Princeton, NJ: Princeton University Press.

World Health Organization (WHO)

Health is an essential issue for people around the globe. International efforts to coordinate the promotion and protection of health have a relatively complicated history that informed the founding and ongoing operations of the World Health Organization (WHO) as part of the UN System. In particular, the establishment of the new agency had to address three precursor organizations: Pan American Sanitary Bureau, Office International d'Hygiène Publique, and the League of Nations' Health Organization. A series of international sanitary conventions also had to be built in as part of the WHO's current International Health Regulations. At the founding of the UN in 1945, there was a push to establish a universal health agency to serve the UN System. This led to an International Health Conference in 1946, which culminated in the creation of the Constitution of the World Health Organization on July 22, 1946. An interim commission addressed health concerns until the Constitution received enough signatures on April 7, 1948, to come into force, with this date now celebrated as World Health Day. The first World Health Assembly meeting was held and formal UN specialized agency status was established later that year. WHO took over from two of the preceding health organizations and remains headquartered in Geneva, Switzerland, where the League body was based, but the now named Pan American Health Organization retains autonomous organizational status while working within WHO as a regional office for the Americas.

RESPONSIBILITIES

As succinctly stated in WHO's Constitution, the objective of the organization is "the attainment by all peoples of the highest possible level of health." In order to meet this objective, the functions mandated to WHO are wide ranging, with twenty-two separate function entries listed in the constitution alone. However, the proper scope of WHO's mandate has been debated over time. From the start, some members pushed for narrower responsibilities focused on technical issues related to disease control, while others encouraged a social medicine approach to address the broader social and economic conditions that impact people's health. This debate was reflected in the comprehensive "Health for All" approach launched in the late 1970s and pushback from those who wanted a disease control emphasis with limited governmental intervention in health-related areas. WHO is also described as shifting from a focus on "international health," built on health concerns of member countries, to "global health," which takes into account a wider range of stakeholders engaged in health governance. In addition, a "global health security" approach expands WHO's agenda for addressing public health emergencies, but this is criticized by some as pushing the boundaries of WHO's mission too far.

STRUCTURE

WHO is one of the bigger and more complex specialized agencies, although the central organizational components remain as established in 1948. The World Health Assembly meets annually in Geneva with each member sending up to three delegates, usually selected for their technical expertise, to set policies, programs, and regulations along with approving the organization's budget. An Executive Board, made up of thirty-four members that serve three-year terms, prepares the agenda each January for the yearly Health Assembly meetings and convenes again after this gathering to follow up and guide implementation of the outcome of this meeting. There are a range of expert advisory panels and technical committees working on both long-term and more specific health problems. A Director-General, appointed for a five-year term by the Health Assembly based on the nomination from the Board, sits at the head of the Secretariat's administrative and technical staff.

The Director-General must cope with the highly regionalized structure of WHO led by Regional Directors, which decentralizes authority across the organization to a much greater degree than in other specialized agencies. The overarching structure of WHO is often explained as having three tiers, made up of the Geneva headquarters, six regional offices, and around 150 country offices (run by heads appointed by the Regional Directors) that advise governments on health matters. The 194 member states (as of early 2020) are drawn from across all regions, with the Cook Islands and Niue serving as members and Liechtenstein the only full UN member not participating. Puerto Rico and Tokelau hold associate member status. The source of WHO's extensive budget has shifted significantly over time. Traditionally, most of the organization's financial support came from required assessed contributions paid by member states, but recent finances have shifted with over 75 percent of the budget relying on voluntary funding.

ACTIVITIES

The extensive health challenges facing the global population means that WHO is engaged in a wide array of activities. The organization is active in preventing and controlling communicable diseases, such as the effort to eradicate smallpox, as well as responding to the contagious spread of global outbreaks, as in the case of SARS (severe acute respiratory syndrome). WHO also tackles noncommunicable diseases, including cardiovascular ailments, cancer, and substance abuse. More broadly, the agency promotes a healthy living environment covering diverse areas of economic and social conditions that impact health. Across all areas, WHO plays a normative role in setting rules and standards through conferences, conventions, and regulations, including in relation to pharmaceuticals. WHO's efforts are backed by extensive research, surveillance, and information sharing, which allows the organization to warn of rising health problems, raise global awareness, and promote solutions. National health services are strengthened and health professionals trained by WHO, which is a particularly valuable service for developing countries in need of such technical assistance.

While Sustainable Development Goal 3 on good health and well-being connects directly with WHO's work, health dimensions embedded in the other goals (with fourteen of the seventeen goals including targets related to health) widely engage WHO in this UN effort to make measurable progress by 2030. Given the centrality of health to other issue areas, WHO works with a variety of bodies within the UN System, such as the Food and Agriculture Organization to improve nutrition and the International Labour Organization to address working conditions. WHO also coordinates through bodies such as the Global Alliance for Vaccines and Immunization and the Global Fund to Fight HIV/AIDS, Tuberculosis, and Malaria. Furthermore, WHO collaborates with a wide range of other actors connected to health, including business partners, nonprofit nongovernmental organizations, philanthropic foundations, and the medical community.

CHALLENGES AND REFORM

WHO has generally been viewed as an effective and well-managed specialized agency, making great inroads into countering serious health problems and promoting best health practices. However, WHO's status was shaken by criticism of its handling of the H1N1 flu epidemic in 2009 and the Ebola outbreak in 2014, and the organization continues to face new global outbreaks, such as the coronavirus pandemic in 2020. Concerns have been raised that WHO is undermined by political interests that keep the body from undertaking what is best for global health needs. The organization also faces ongoing difficulties with balancing its operational program activities with normative guideline setting, with some critics arguing that WHO should prioritize and focus on providing standards, leaving operations to other actors who are better suited for this task. Operations are also complicated by the decentralized, autonomous regional office structure and the related tensions and lack of cohesion that exist between different components of the organization. WHO is greatly reliant on voluntary contributions, and a major budget shortfall in 2011 resulted in an organizational crisis that led to cutbacks and undermined staff morale.

The funding setback pressed reform efforts forward, with WHO adopting a new emphasis on improving health outcomes, seeking excellence as an efficient and effective body, and encouraging greater coherence for addressing global health issues. WHO faces many new organizational competitors in health governance, which undermines its authoritative place as the central health body in the global arena. WHO wrestles with how to cooperate with these new institutions without being co-opted into them, or left aside, as new health institutions and networks are created that operate on their own independent basis but also address dimensions of WHO's mandate. For example, funding for health programs increasingly comes from other parts of the UN System, such as the World Bank, or outside private actors like the significant contributions provided by the Bill and Melinda Gates Foundation. WHO must carefully define its role in the shifting landscape of global health governance and determine the best organizational priorities in light of so many dimensions of and approaches to health concerns. In doing so, WHO can work to ensure that it is able to continue to hold an important position in addressing health for peoples across the globe.

See also: Food and Agriculture Organization; Health; International Civil Aviation Organization; International Labour Organization; Joint United Nations Programme on HIV/AIDS; Nongovernmental Organizations; United Nations Children's Fund; United Nations Development Programme; United Nations Educational, Scientific and Cultural Organization; United Nations Human Settlements Programme; United Nations Relief and Works Agency for Palestine Refugees in the Near East; Sustainable Development Goals; Universal Postal Union; World Bank Group; World Intellectual Property Organization; World Tourism Organization.

FURTHER READING

Abeysinghe, Sudeepa. 2015. *Pandemics, Science and Policy: H1N1 and the World Health Organization.* New York: Palgrave Macmillan.

Beigbeder, Yves. 2018. *The World Health Organization: Achievements and Failures.* New York: Routledge.

Chorev, Nitsan. 2012. *The World Health Organization between North and South.* Ithaca, NY: Cornell University Press.

Gostin, Lawrence O. 2014. "Fulfilling the Promise of the World Health Organization." In *Global Health Law*, 89–128. Cambridge, MA: Harvard University Press.

Kamradt-Scott, Adam. 2015. *Managing Global Health Security: The World Health Organization and Disease Outbreak Control.* New York: Palgrave Macmillan.

World Intellectual Property Organization (WIPO)

Intellectual property rights provide protection for new applications of knowledge and ideas, with patents for industrial property and copyrights for artistic creations the two most prominent categories. Such rights were traditionally granted within a country, but as the connections between countries grew in the nineteenth century, there was a move to internationalize protection to ensure that creations could not be copied and reproduced in another country without recognition or compensation. The 1883 Paris Convention for the Protection of Industrial Policy and the 1886 Berne Convention for the Protection of Literary and Artistic Works were established, each overseen by a public international union. The Paris Union and Berne Union were combined in 1893 to form the United International Bureaux for the Protection of Intellectual Property (BIRPI), which moved within Switzerland from Berne to Geneva in 1960. In light of technological advances and rising global production in the 1960s, the system of protection was bolstered in 1967 through the signing of a new convention establishing the World Intellectual Property Organization (WIPO). This convention came into effect in 1970, at which point WIPO formally absorbed BIRPI and its functions. In 1974, WIPO became a UN specialized agency, with the organization's headquarters remaining in Geneva.

RESPONSIBILITIES

According to the WIPO Convention, the organization has two primary objectives: "to promote the protection of intellectual property throughout the world through cooperation among States and, where appropriate, in collaboration with any other international organization" and "to ensure administrative cooperation among the Unions." Since taking on BIRPI responsibilities, WIPO continues to administer the Berne, Paris, and other related unions. Protecting intellectual property rights, and the economic rewards for this ownership, is designed to provide incentives for further investment and creativity. WIPO's adoption of the Development Agenda in 2007, which emphasizes recognizing the needs of developing countries, has important implications for the organization's mandate. WIPO is called upon to balance its traditional role in promotion and protection with ensuring that people across the globe can benefit from and share new developments.

STRUCTURE

Three primary organs were established in the WIPO Convention: General Assembly, Conference, and Coordination Committee. The General Assembly does not have representatives from all member states, only those that are members of related Unions, yet is designated as the highest-level decision-making organ. All members are represented in the Conference, which technically is the second highest legislative body, but in practice the two organs usually meet at the same time and place on identical agenda items. The Coordination Committee, composed of members from the Executive Committees of the Paris and Berne Unions, provides advice to other bodies in WIPO, prepares the agenda and budget for General Assembly and Conference, and nominates the Director General for General Assembly approval. There are also six external offices (four in Asia, one in Algeria, and one in Brazil) that provide support in those areas.

The organizational structure is complicated by the administration of various governing bodies created by intellectual property treaties. The collective meeting of all WIPO bodies, which occurs each fall, is known as the Assemblies of the Member States. Adding to the decision-making complexity are a number of subsidiary committees working on governance and technical issues, as well as high-level diplomatic conferences held to finalize treaties. Several hundred nongovernmental organizations, along with other international governmental organizations, also have observer status for WIPO meetings. The International Bureau operates as the bureaucratic Secretariat of the organization, headed by the Director General and subdivided into seven sectors guided by a Deputy or Assistant Director General: development; brands and designs; global issues; patents and technology; global infrastructure; administration and management; and copyright and creative industries.

Compared to other specialized agencies, which often rely significantly on member state contributions, WIPO has an unusual funding arrangement where such contributions represent less than 5 percent of the organization's financing. Around 95 percent of the WIPO's funding is income derived from fees paid by those using the registration and protection systems, with the small remainder of the budget supported by minor areas such as fees for arbitration and publication sales. WIPO inherited member states from the Berne and Paris Unions and grew as more countries joined these bodies, but the organization's membership also includes other member states from the UN System. As of early 2020, the organization encompasses 193 members in total, with regular UN members Micronesia, Palau, and South Sudan not participating, but Cook Islands, Holy See, and Niue acting as full members.

ACTIVITIES

WIPO acts as a central forum for discussion and international lawmaking to set the rules and practices governing international property. Along with the WIPO Convention, the organization administers twenty-five additional treaties that are organized into three broad categories: intellectual property protection (which still includes the Berne and Paris Conventions along with the most recent addition of the 2013 Marrakesh Treaty to Facilitate Access to Published Works for Persons Who Are Blind, Visually Impaired or Otherwise Print Disabled), classification (such as the 1971 Strasbourg Agreement that founded the International Patent Classification system), and global protection system (including the largest fee-generating area, the Patent Cooperation Treaty, which was established in 1970 and has been modified since then). WIPO also provides services to protect intellectual property, including registration for international patents, trademarks, and designs, and systems to support patent offices. In addition, the Arbitration and Mediation Center was established in 1994 (with an office added in Singapore in 2010) to assist with resolving disputes.

Especially since the initiation of the Development Agenda, WIPO has been involved in providing technical assistance to developing countries, which includes training, documentation, and equipment, to help establish the institutions and expertise needed to effectively monitor and implement intellectual property standards. The WIPO Academy was set up in 1998 as an avenue to provide such training. WIPO's sphere of cooperation expanded with the creation of the Agreement on Trade-Related Intellectual Property Rights (TRIPS), which came into force in 1995 and connects intellectual property into the international trading system governed by the World Trade Organization (WTO). WIPO also cooperates with other specialized agencies, which address areas of intellectual property rights, including the Food and Agricultural Organization, World Health Organization, and United Nations Educational, Scientific and Cultural Organization. Public-private partnerships are also encouraged by WIPO.

CHALLENGES AND REFORM

Technological advancements, including the evolution of digital, genetic, and internet capabilities, push the boundaries of intellectual property. This challenges WIPO to adapt and modify what is considered intellectual property and to develop protections for new technologies. Coping with new areas adds a further burden to the existing difficulties of enforcing the extensive intellectual property rights regime, which already encompasses a wide range of international treaties and efforts to coordinate across sometimes conflicting national laws. Embedding dimensions of intellectual property rights within the WTO with TRIPS is viewed by some as overriding WIPO's jurisdiction and raises coordination issues. WIPO also faces the ongoing challenge of integrating the Development Agenda into its work. The debate continues over how to best balance the interests of those producing intellectual property and those in need of affordable access, particularly in developing countries. An illustrative example is pharmaceutical patent rights. The member states in WIPO are often encouraged to develop a shared vision of the organization's role and activities that best meet the needs of all. This also reflects WIPO's place as a specialized agency in the UN System designed to meet the UN's overarching goals and not just narrowly focused on the benefits of protecting intellectual property rights.

Although WIPO regularly benefits from a budget surplus generated by fees, there are concerns that private sector actors paying for these services will use their financial leverage to influence the organization's policies and activities. The organization's particularly complex governance structure is viewed by critics as unwieldy and limiting effectiveness. WIPO has pursued governance reform, including a Working Group on Constitutional Reform (1999–2002), but implementation has been relatively limited (e.g., the WIPO Conference was designated to be abolished in 2003, but this is still awaiting ratification by enough member states), and there are ongoing recommendations to further address internal management and decision-making processes. Such reform is viewed as bolstering WIPO's ability to adapt and improve its important work promoting and protecting intellectual property in order to encourage creativity and progress across the globe.

See also: Food and Agriculture Organization; Nongovernmental Organizations; United Nations Educational, Scientific and Cultural Organization; United Nations Purposes; World Health Organization; World Trade Organization.

FURTHER READING

De Beer, Jeremy, ed. 2009. *Implementing the World Intellectual Property Organization's Development Agenda*. Ottawa: Wilfrid Laurier University Press.

Deere Birkbeck, Carolyn. 2016. *The World Intellectual Property Organization (WIPO): A Reference Guide*. Cheltenham, UK: Edward Elgar Publishing.

Haugen, Hans Morten. 2010. "Access Versus Incentives: Analysing Intellectual Property Policies in Four UN Specialized Agencies by Emphasizing the Role of the World Intellectual Property Organization and Human Rights." *The Journal of World Intellectual Property* 13 (6): 697–728.

May, Christopher. 2007. *The World Intellectual Property Organization: Resurgence and the Development Agenda*. New York: Routledge.

Stack, Alexander. 2011. *International Patent Law: Cooperation, Harmonization, and an Institutional Analysis of WIPO and the WTO*. Cheltenham, UK: Edward Elgar.

World Meteorological Organization (WMO)

The modern World Meteorological Organization (WMO), headquartered in Geneva, Switzerland, monitors weather-related information with an array of technology, but the ideas and processes have deep historical roots. Humanity shares the global climate and weather patterns cross borders, so separate national efforts cannot properly track trends. Early recognition of the need to cooperate on collecting, analyzing, and quickly distributing meteorological data was spurred on by advancements in shipping and the ability to share information with the invention of the telegraph. A central development in international organization for meteorology was the First International Meteorological Congress held in Vienna in 1873, which is widely recognized as the main starting point for what would become known as the International Meteorological Organization (IMO). However, after the Second International Meteorological Congress in 1879, the IMO cooperative efforts focused on the nongovernmental expert gatherings of the Conference of Directors of Meteorological Services and the related organizational structures. The debate over whether international meteorological efforts should be governmental or nongovernmental continued over the years, including declining the opportunity to join with the intergovernmental League of Nations, but the tide turned to an intergovernmental focus following the establishment of the UN System. In 1947, the World Meteorological Convention was signed, coming into effect on March 23, 1950, and that date is now celebrated as World Meteorological Day. In 1951, the final Conference of Directors of Meteorological Services met in Paris to dissolve the IMO and transition to the WMO with the holding of the First WMO Congress. That same year, the WMO joined the UN System as a specialized agency.

RESPONSIBILITIES

Since the WMO's creation, the organization has played a predominant role in facilitating cooperation on the gathering and sharing of weather information. The sectors addressed have been extended to hydrology and climate as well as moving into space weather. The scientific and technological approaches have expanded beyond ship logbooks and telegraph communication with computerized capabilities and observations from satellites. However, the central responsibility remains the same. The WMO is the authoritative body that ensures that data reporting methods are standardized to allow for comparability. The organization enables the coordination of collecting, processing, and rapidly distributing these data on a global scale, as well as improving meteorological analysis capabilities and activities. All of this is aimed at providing accurate meteorological forecasting for tracking weather patterns, determining atmospheric trends and climate shifts, and tracing the impact on the distribution of water resources.

STRUCTURE

The World Meteorological Congress, held every four years, is the highest level of governance for the organization. Important meteorological work has long been carried out by technical bodies, and the WMO maintained this through eight Technical Commissions meeting at least every four years. These commissions carry out studies and provide recommendations in their areas of focus, including aeronautics, agriculture, climatology, and hydrology. However, the WMO started shifting to only two Technical Commissions (Service Commission and Infrastructure Commission) following the reforms passed by the Congress in June 2019. A new Scientific Advisory Panel was added as well. Another carryover from the historical roots of the WMO is the Regional Associations, which provide coordination for members who are based in the region or whose meteorological activities extend into that area. For example, France, Portugal, Spain, and the United Kingdom are also included in the African region. These bodies, which also meet at least every four years, started as Regional Commissions and were established across time as: Africa (Region I), Asia (Region II), South America (Region III), North America, Central America and the Caribbean (Region IV), South-West Pacific (Region V), and Europe (Region VI). An Executive Council meets each year to supervise the organization in between Congresses. The historically important role of the heads of national meteorological services can still be seen in the makeup of the Executive Council, which has such representatives from twenty-seven member states along with a President, three Vice-Presidents, and the Presidents of the Regional Associations. The WMO enlarged and enhanced the organization's Secretariat from the days of the IMO, which is now headed by a Secretary-General instead of a Chief of the Secretariat.

Almost all WMO members are fully independent countries, but territories that are responsible for their own meteorological services, although not their foreign affairs, are also allowed to apply to join with the permission of the country in charge of external relations. Member territories' voting privileges are not allowed for certain important subjects, such as amending the World Meteorological Convention. As of early 2020, there are six member territories (British Caribbean Territories, Curacao and Sint Maarten, French Polynesia, Hong Kong, Macao, and New Caledonia), with non-UN members Cook Islands and Niue serving as full member states along with 185 other member states that are also UN members (making 187 member states overall). The permanent representatives of members are usually the heads of the national meteorological services. They focus on technical issues and maintain communication between the WMO, members, and other bodies connected to the WMO's work in between Congresses. Detailing the level of funding committed to meteorological observations drawn upon by the WMO is complicated as many such activities are based on national services funded by the host country. However, direct WMO funding is primarily provided through member assessments at a level set at the Congress, but some voluntary extra-budgetary resources, such as support for technical assistance, are available.

ACTIVITIES

Along with seeking to improve WMO governance, the Strategic Plan for 2020–2023 focuses on four other overarching objectives: better serving the needs of society, strengthening technical capabilities for observations and predictions, enhancing services through advanced targeted scientific research, and ensuring information and services for developing countries. The significant majority of WMO's work is built around a series of different technical and scientific programs. A central program most often associated with the WMO is the World Weather Watch, which encompasses several systems and support programs for the observation and exchange of meteorological information. The World Climate Programme—which is made up of the World Climate Research Programme, the Global Climate Observing System, the World Climate Services Programme, and the Global Programme of Research on Climate Change Vulnerability, Impacts and Adaptation—has taken on increasing prominence. Building out of the June 2019 reforms, the World Climate Research Programme will combine with the Commission for Atmospheric Sciences to establish the Research Board on Weather, Climate, Water, and the Environment, which will connect with the Intergovernmental Panel on Climate Change (IPCC).

Other programs include focusing on the atmosphere and environment, hydrology and water resources, and applications of meteorology. The WMO also provides education and training programs along with technical cooperation. As meteorological matters impact the issues addressed by many other organizations, the WMO coordinates with a diverse set of international bodies working in areas of common interest, from aeronautical meteorology with the International Civil Aviation Organization to technical assistance needs with the UN Development Programme. A Joint Technical Commission for Oceanography and Marine Meteorology was established with the Intergovernmental Oceanographic Commission of the UN Educational, Scientific and Cultural Organization in 1999. With the 2019 structural reforms, this will shift to become a Joint Collaborative Board. The work of the WMO with the UN Environment Programme to establish the IPCC is also frequently noted.

CHALLENGES AND REFORM

Given the advanced technology involved in WMO data collection, an ongoing challenge is ensuring that this technology is supported as well as updated to meet new requirements. For example, satellites have become a critical part of the WMO measuring system so maintaining access and operations of geostationary and polar satellite capabilities is essential. These systems are expensive and as new related challenges emerge, such as space weather, the organization's funding availability and prioritization must continue to evolve. With the increasingly volatile climate and high-impact weather events, there are a pressing range of costs involved in coping with the impact and seeking measures to address the underlying problems. Efforts to tackle the technical challenges of environmental stresses are exacerbated by political impediments in the global community, particularly in the area of climate change.

The WMO has a long and respected history of emphasizing a scientific focus on data collection and analysis that serves the organization well in the international political situation. As the global community continues to engage with pressing meteorological issues, one reform recommendation, as with the few other specialized agencies where there is a longer four-year gap between supreme body meetings such as the International Telecommunications Union, is to have the Congress meet every two years. Financial and scientific concerns limit the likelihood of such a move, which meant focusing the reforms launched in 2019 on bolstering more efficient and effective governance mechanisms in between meetings of the Congress. According to the WMO, the reform "will be an evolving process which requires flexibility and readjustment." Collaboration between the WMO and a range of other actors connected to the organization's work is a central part of its operations and also needs to be carefully managed moving forward. International cooperation on meteorology has a long history and remains an ever-pressing issue area. The WMO's model work on knowledge and information sharing remains central to global coordination efforts.

See also: Environmental Protection; Executive Heads of Specialized Agencies; International Civil Aviation Organization; International Telecommunication Union; Nongovernmental Organizations; Preparatory Commission for the Comprehensive Nuclear-Test-Ban Treaty Organization; United Nations Development Programme; United Nations Educational, Scientific and Cultural Organization; United Nations Environment Programme; World Tourism Organization.

FURTHER READING

Albert, Steven. 2000. "Information and Knowledge Exchange: The Cases of the World Meteorological Organization and the World Health Organization." *Knowledge and Process Management* 7 (2): 66–75.

Bogdan, Thomas J., and Terrance G. Onsager. 2010. "New Space Weather Activities in the World Meteorological Organization." *Space Weather* 8 (10): 1–2.

Daniel, Howard. 1973. *One Hundred Years of International Cooperation in Meteorology (1873–1973): A Historical Review*. Geneva: World Meteorological Organization.

Edwards, Paul N. 2006. "Meteorology as Infrastructural Globalism." *Osiris* 21 (1): 229–50.

World Tourism Organization (UNWTO)

Tourism is an important element of the international economy and benefits from the coordination of promotion and best practices. The first efforts to provide a central organization for national tourism actors were nongovernmental. Building upon several versions dating back to 1925, the nongovernmental precursor to the World Tourism Organization (WTO) was the International Union of Official Travel Organizations from 1947. World Tourism Day is celebrated on September 27, the day in 1970 that the statutes founding the international governmental World Tourism Organization were adopted. The first World Tourism Organization General Assembly met in Madrid, Spain, in 1975 and decided to move its headquarters from Geneva, Switzerland, to Madrid at the start of the following year. The World Tourism Organization initially remained outside of the UN System. While the UN General Assembly noted in 1969 that an agreement should be entered into with the forthcoming World Tourism Organization, and shortly after the move to Madrid linked to the organization as an executing agency for the UN Development Programme, the body was not allowed to join the UN as a specialized agency until 2003. In 2005, the organization officially adopted the acronym UNWTO in order to distinguish from the World Trade Organization, which uses the acronym WTO (although the UNWTO remains known by the abbreviation OMT in French and Spanish).

RESPONSIBILITIES

As the only overarching international governmental organization engaged with tourism, the UNWTO has a pivotal responsibility for helping to guide tourism across the globe. The organization seeks to ensure that tourism is maintained as an important part of the global agenda. Tourism is promoted as a path for economic development, although in an environmentally sustainable manner that also respects the ethics and social responsibility of tourism. UNWTO builds partnerships across all sectors of tourism. Members are provided with knowledge and training, as well as assistance with improving tourism abilities.

STRUCTURE

The UNWTO structure is made up of five main parts. The members gather every two years at the General Assembly in order to debate tourism topics and approve the work program, as well as to set the budget. A smaller Executive Council, made up of one member for every five full members, meets at least twice a year and oversees the work of the organization. The Executive Council is elected by the General Assembly, although Spain as the UNWTO host has a permanent seat. The Secretariat, headed by a Secretary-General, implements the organization's activities. The General Assembly also has six subsidiary Regional Commissions (Africa, Americas, East Asia and the Pacific, Europe, Middle East, and South Asia), which gather at least once a year to discuss issues of regional concern and maintain contact in between General Assembly meetings. Finally, a series of specialized committees provide advice for their areas of focus, including tourism competitiveness, ethics, sustainability, statistics, and budget.

The UNWTO expanded to 159 member states with the 2019 addition of Palau. However, this membership falls short of the full UN membership with notable missing countries including Australia, Canada, and the United States, although the UNWTO also allows Aruba, Flanders, Hong Kong, Macao, Madeira, Netherlands Antilles, and Puerto Rico to serve as Associate Members alongside observers the Holy See and Palestine. While some countries never joined the UNWTO, Australia, Canada, and the United States are examples of countries that were members but withdrew from the organization. The nongovernmental historical roots of the UNWTO are reflected in the additional category of Affiliate Member, with over five hundred private and public sector actors connected to a wide range of tourism areas represented in the organization. A lack of member state status does not block participation by Affiliate Members from that country. All members contribute to the financing of the UNWTO, with approximately 90 percent of the organization's budget funded by the country members.

ACTIVITIES

The advancement of development through tourism is at the heart of many UNWTO initiatives and projects, and the organization directly engages with developing areas through providing technical assistance and consultation on tourism planning. One dimension of this work is assisting small and medium tourist enterprises with information and training, such as improving energy use through the Hotel Energy Solutions project. The expansion of tourism is encouraged and promoted. For example, the ongoing Silk Road program and action plan was launched to foster tourism along this historically significant route. The Affiliate Members are drawn upon to support the exchange of expertise, generation and dissemination of knowledge, and the development of talent. Positive engagement is encouraged through the presentation of Awards for Excellence and Innovation in tourism. The UNWTO is a vital source for research and comprehensive statistics on tourism, including establishing indicators and monitoring tourism developments, which can influence tourism policies.

The UNWTO stresses the connection between tourism and the UN's Sustainable Development Goals (SDGs) and was named as the lead organization for the 2017 International Year of Sustainable Tourism declared by the UN General Assembly. With its emphasis on tourism and development, the UNWTO networks with development organizations but also other specialized agencies with tourism-related coverage, including the International Civil Aviation Organization (air travel), the World Health Organization (transmittable diseases), and the World Meteorological Organization (weather impacts). The UNWTO occasionally engages with developing international standards for tourism, most notably the Global Code of Ethics for Tourism that was drafted between 1997 and 1999, approved at the UNWTO General Assembly in 1999, and recognized by the UN General Assembly in 2001. While a nonbinding document that relies on voluntary compliance, the Global Code is designed to ensure that the positive effects of tourism are maximized, while the negative effects are minimized. This goal is

> *Global Code of Ethics for Tourism*
>
> 1. Tourism should contribute to enhanced respect and understanding for both societies and the people that live within them.
> 2. Tourism should serve as a mechanism for the fulfillment of both individuals and societies.
> 3. Tourism should enhance and promote sustainable development.
> 4. Tourism should enhance and promote cultural heritage.
> 5. Tourism should support the overall well-being of both the host country and the communities within.
> 6. The promoters of tourism have an obligation to uphold these principles.
> 7. All people have a right of tourism.
> 8. All tourist movements should be free.
> 9. The workers and entrepreneurs within the tourism sector are provided rights and privileges.
> 10. All parties should promote the essential values of the Global Code of Ethics for Tourism.
>
> Source: Adapted from the Global Code of Ethics for Tourism, World Tourism Organization.

supported by the World Committee on Tourism Ethics established in 2004. In order to encourage tourists to follow the principles encompassed in the Global Code, in 2005 the UNWTO released "The Responsible Tourist and Traveller" with highlights in the 2017 brochure "Tips for a Responsible Traveller" linked to the International Year of Sustainable Tourism for Development.

CHALLENGES AND REFORM

Membership remains a challenge for the UNWTO. The organization lacks universal member state involvement and must seek to add new member states and keep existing member states from withdrawing. Some withdrawals are connected to concerns over UNWTO policies, for example Canada withdrew in 2012 to protest when Robert Mugabe, President of Zimbabwe at the time, was identified as a global leader for tourism. The wider issue for some developed countries is that the UNWTO is not viewed as providing essential benefits worth the price of membership. However, the United States, after withdrawing in 1995, announced in June 2019 that it was "exploring the possibility" of rejoining the organization. The lack of full membership has financial implications as the UNWTO budget relies primarily on member states, and several key tourism-connected countries are not members. With the tourism development emphasis of the UNWTO, a gap between developed country and developing country engagement is problematic. At the same time, the organization faces criticism for what some label an emphasis on liberalization and global tourism market forces. This view runs counter to tourism mechanisms focused on local services and elevating human needs. More broadly, some question the degree to which tourism provides for development and poverty reduction.

Climate change and shifting weather patterns impact tourism flows and susceptibility to catastrophic events. Yet, tourism itself can feed into this cycle through pollution and greenhouse gas emissions created by international travel. An increase in tourists to a particular area, such as UN Educational, Scientific and Cultural Organization World Heritage Sites, can stress local resources and cause damage. The UNWTO is also working to adapt to the threat terrorism poses to tourist safety and destabilization of the tourism industry in impacted areas. In addressing international travel crises, the UNWTO implemented a more anticipatory approach for notifying tourists. The UNWTO is at the forefront of developing sustainable tourism indicators and is well placed to engage with the UN System emphasis on the SDGs for 2030. Further reform will ensure that sustainable tourism development responds to environmental risks, better incorporates local grassroots perspectives on tourism planning and practices, and more fully considers varying perspectives on the proper code of ethics and principles for responsible travelling. As a relatively new specialized agency, the UNWTO can continue to progress in its role addressing tourism for the UN System.

See also: Environmental Protection; International Civil Aviation Organization; Nongovernmental Organizations; Sustainable Development Goals; Terrorism; United Nations Development Programme; United Nations Educational, Scientific and Cultural Organization; World Health Organization; World Meteorological Organization; World Trade Organization.

FURTHER READING

Afifi, Galal M.H. 2015. "Benchmarking the UNWTO Practical Tips for the Global Traveller: An Islamic Preview." *Almatourism* 6 (12): 18–34.

Castañeda, Quetzil. 2012. "The Neoliberal Imperative of Tourism: Rights and Legitimization in the UNWTO Global Code of Ethics for Tourism." *Practicing Anthropology* 34 (3): 47–51.

Ferguson, Lucy. 2007. "The United Nations World Tourism Organisation." *New Political Economy* 12 (4): 557–68.

Miller, Graham, and Louise Twining-Ward. 2005. "The World Tourism Organization." In *Monitoring for a Sustainable Tourism Transition: The Challenge of Developing and Using Indicators*, 177–200. Cambridge, MA: CABI.

PROGRAMMES AND FUNDS

United Nations Children's Fund (UNICEF)

The UN Children's Fund (UNICEF), one of the most predominant and well-regarded organizations within the UN System, is known for humanitarian work with children and innovative outreach. UNICEF's accomplishments include earning a Nobel Peace Prize in 1965 in recognition of the body's efforts and "promotion of brotherhood among the nations." Created by the General Assembly in December 1946 as the UN International Children's Emergency Fund, the first UN development fund, UNICEF was originally intended as a temporary response to the mass displacement and needs of children after World War II. The organization's initial work focused on providing food, clothing, and short-term healthcare. At the time, the United States and Canada made significant financial contributions, with further funding from forty-six additional countries following afterward. In 1950, the General Assembly extended UNICEF's mandate to include relief efforts for children in other areas of the world. In 1953, the organization was added as a permanent UN body and, although "international" and "emergency" were removed from the organization's name, it continues to operate under the original acronym of UNICEF. UNICEF is a pioneering organization, both in creating funding sources as well as the ability to appeal to the global spotlight. The agency's high profile is enhanced by a long list of celebrity Goodwill Ambassadors, starting with Danny Kaye in 1954, including Audrey Hepburn, Queen Rania of Jordan, Richard Attenborough, David Beckham, and Jackie Chan.

RESPONSIBILITIES

UNICEF's mandate and scope of responsibility has evolved since the organization's founding. The initial mandate of emergency assistance has grown to an extensive range of information gathering, monitoring, data collection, advocacy, and services that include raising awareness about human rights, education initiatives, and child advocacy programs. In 1959, with the innovative Declaration of the Rights of the Child, the agency's mandate expanded from ensuring that children had the food and related supplies needed to address malnutrition and disease to include areas such as the physical and emotional development of children. Although health concerns continue to serve as the foundation of UNICEF's guiding principles, with the 1989 passage of the Convention on the Rights of the Child the organization began a focused campaign to advance global awareness about children's rights. As UNICEF increasingly adopted a human rights–based approach advocating for children's rights, this focus expanded to include gender-equitable campaigns for women, adolescents, and children.

STRUCTURE

An Executive Director, appointed by the Secretary-General, oversees UNICEF. Seven people (four men and three women) have served in that position since 1947, and all have been citizens of the United States. The agency's work is carried out through a thirty-six-member Executive Board of member state representatives, elected by the Economic and Social Council to serve three years terms with regional group representation set as: twelve from Western Europe and Others, eight Africa, seven Asia, five Latin America and the Caribbean, and four Eastern Europe. Most of UNICEF's policies are initiated out of the headquarters office in

New York, where the Executive Board meets three times a year. As the governing body of UNICEF, the Executive Board provides oversight of the organization's activities, programs and budgets, and is supported by a Bureau made up of a President and four Vice-Presidents drawn from across the five regional groups. UNICEF's focus on children in low- and middle-income countries is facilitated by regional offices based in Jordan, Kenya, Nepal, Panama, Senegal, Switzerland, and Thailand. A large supply warehouse is maintained in Copenhagen, Denmark, which includes providing field offices with medical, education and sanitation kits, and UNICEF also oversees a research center in Florence, Italy.

A decentralized institutional structure promotes UNICEF's ideals across multiple levels and encourages creative initiatives to further the aims of the institution. UNICEF runs field offices in countries across the globe, which allows for a rapid response in crisis situations. These offices support UNICEF's ability to be a "provider of last resort," enabling the organization to step in if government services at the local or national level are incapacitated. The agency's work is also supported by thirty-three National Committees that hold nongovernmental organization status and concentrate on fundraising and nurturing relationships with civil society and the business community.

ACTIVITIES

UNICEF focuses on high impact areas to assist children, with extensive immunization, nutrition, and health care programs. Consistent with the organization's original mandate, UNICEF provides significant emergency response assistance. Notable relief efforts were provided after the 2004 tsunami in the Indian Ocean, the 2010 earthquake in Haiti, and the flooding in Pakistan the same year. When the Ebola virus emerged in West Africa in 2014, UNICEF teams provided staff and supplies in Guinea, Liberia, and Sierra Leone. According to the organization's 2018 annual report, in just one year UNICEF tended to 337 emergency situations in 102 countries. UNICEF is known for mass immunization efforts and campaigns for universal childhood vaccinations. The agency also trains local health care providers and focuses on preventative maternal and child healthcare. These efforts are credited with contributing to the global drop in polio, maternal and neonatal tetanus, and malaria.

UNICEF's status was enhanced during the 1979 UN International Year of the Child. Three years later, UNICEF launched the child survival revolution, or GOBI ("G" for growth monitoring, "O" for oral rehydration therapy, "B" for breastfeeding and "I" for immunizations). The agency was also instrumental when the leaders of seventy-one countries and eighty-eight senior officials attended the 1990 World Summit for Children to create a plan of action to ensure the survival, protection, and development of children. UNICEF was influential during the General Assembly's 2002 Special Session on Children, which centered on improving the lives of children across the globe. UNICEF also brought focus to the needs of children addressed in the Millennium Development Goals (MDGs), with MDG 4 specifically targeting the reduction of child mortality, and continues to emphasize the importance of children in the implementation of the UN's 2030 Agenda articulated in the Sustainable Development Goals.

UNICEF operates with a large annual budget, funded exclusively by voluntary contributions from both governmental and private sources. The agency is known for taking a creative approach to fundraising that includes iconic greeting cards, annual Trick for Treat for UNICEF campaigns, hosting benefit concerts, and sponsoring sporting events. The organization also maintains an online retail outlet where supporters can purchase items such as handmade crafts and humanitarian gifts. UNICEF has received several significant grants from private foundations, including those established by philanthropists Ted Turner and Bill Gates. UNICEF works to strengthen collaboration with the private sector and actively promotes the integration of technology for information sharing and rapid response. The organization also partners with businesses to develop corporate social responsibility guidelines. UNICEF often collaborates with other UN bodies, such as the World Health Organization to enhance local healthcare services and the Food and Agriculture Organization to address youth malnutrition, as well as the UN Development Programme, UN Entity for Gender Equality and the Empowerment of Women (UN Women), and UN High Commissioner for Refugees.

CHALLENGES AND REFORM

With the expansion of UNICEF's work, the organization faces accusations that it has lost focus. There are concerns raised that the growing emphasis on education competes with the agency's capacities to address health issues like infant mortality, and critics argue that undertaking more areas dilutes UNICEF's overall impact. The organization has also faced criticism over education campaigns regarding family planning. Despite such issues, UNICEF remains one of the most popular and respected agencies in the UN System. Markers of UNICEF's success between 2000 and 2015 include declining child and maternal mortality rates, a notable increase internationally in children attending school, and the incremental adoption of human rights for children. Many point to UNICEF as a model UN agency and, in 2006, UNICEF received the Prince of Asturias Award.

See also: Food and Agriculture Organization; General Assembly; Goodwill Ambassadors and Messengers of Peace; Health; Human Rights; Joint United Nations Programme on HIV/AIDS; Nongovernmental Organizations; Sustainable Development Goals; United Nations Development Programme; United Nations Entity for Gender Equality and the Empowerment of Women; United Nations High Commissioner for Refugees; Women and Gender; World Food Programme; World Health Organization.

FURTHER READING

Banerji, Debabar. 2003. "Reflections on the Twenty-Fifth Anniversary of the Alma-Ata Declaration." *International Journal of Health Services* 33 (4): 813–18.

Black, Maggie. 1996. *Children First: The Story of UNICEF, Past and Present.* Oxford: Oxford University Press.

Jolly, Richard. 2014. *UNICEF (United Nations Children's Fund): Global Governance That Works*. New York: Routledge.

Jones, Phillip W. 2006. "Elusive Mandate: UNICEF and Educational Development." *International Journal of Educational Development* 26 (6): 591–604.

Oestreich, Joel E. 1998. "UNICEF and the Implementation of the Convention on the Rights of the Child." *Global Governance* 4 (2): 183–98.

United Nations Conference on Trade and Development (UNCTAD)

The UN Conference on Trade and Development (UNCTAD) was designed to assist countries that are often labelled the "developing world" or the "Global South." As UN membership expanded, many of the new members looked to the UN for assistance with economic development. Poorer countries wanted a forum to help adjust the imbalances of trade and development. Many claimed that the organizations originally set up to address economic development, specifically the World Bank and International Monetary Fund (IMF), were not properly focused on the needs of developing countries. Indeed, some even maintained that these organizations intensified the inequalities between rich and poor countries.

UNCTAD's origins begin in 1962 at the Conference on the Problems of Economic Development, which took place in Cairo, Egypt. While this meeting was not associated with the UN, it did trigger an appeal for the creation of an organization within the UN framework. A coalition of developing countries in General Assembly (known as the Group of 77 [G-77]) advocated for the creation of a permanent organization with a staff, budget, and location outside of New York. Although several years would pass before the UN created such an organization, in 1962 the Economic and Social Council and the General Assembly did pass resolutions authorizing a UN-sponsored conference on the topic of trade and development. The first gathering (UNCTAD I) met in Geneva, Switzerland, in 1964 from March to June. Issues on the agenda included commodities, manufacturing, finance, and regional difficulties. The need for a permanent organ within the UN was emphasized, with the structure and functions of this body debated and developed. This goal was met when the General Assembly established UNCTAD in December 1964 as a permanent intergovernmental body headquartered in Geneva, with offices in New York and Addis Ababa, Ethiopia.

RESPONSIBILITIES

The primary mandate of UNCTAD is to promote international trade and reduce poverty for developing countries by integrating these countries into the global economy in an equitable manner. As expressed in UNCTAD I's outcome document, the organization seeks to promote "a better and more effective system of international economic cooperation, whereby the division of the world into areas of poverty and plenty may be banished and prosperity achieved by all." UNCTAD serves two central purposes: a forum for intergovernmental debate and dialogue and a practical organization for research, technical assistance, and policy formation.

STRUCTURE

UNCTAD acts under the purview of the General Assembly and is overseen by its 195 members (all 193 UN member states, as well as UN nonmember states the Holy See and Palestine). The highlight of UNCTAD's activities is the conference meeting held every four years, where organizational policy and priorities are set. Every member gets one vote, with a two-thirds majority needed to pass resolutions and a simple majority required for procedural decisions. UNCTAD has hosted fourteen conference sessions, with the fifteenth scheduled for October 2020. During the conference, several side-meeting forums include nongovernmental organizations, academic institutions, and representatives from the private sector. These include a Ministerial Forum, a Civil Society Forum, a Youth Forum, and a World Investment Forum. A Secretary-General, appointed by the UN Secretary-General and confirmed by the General Assembly, heads the organization and rotates between Africa, Asia, and Latin America. Raul Prebisch, a renowned economist and advocate for the developing world, served as the first Secretary-General. The Secretary-General oversees five divisions: Africa, Least Developed Countries, and Special Programmes; Globalization and Development Strategies; Investment and Enterprise; International Trade and Commodities; and Technology and Logistics.

A Trade and Development Board, made up of those members who are willing to participate (157 in 2019), serves as the permanent governing body and meets in Geneva. Each year the body submits an annual report to the General Assembly and is responsible for most of the organization's management between UNCTAD's conferences. Within UNCTAD, there are several standing committees addressing areas such as commodities, poverty alleviation, economic cooperation among poorer countries, the development of service sectors, international investment, and multinational corporations. These committees are supplemented by several ad hoc working groups examining issues including trade, environment, development, and the role of enterprises in development. UNCTAD runs with a small operational budget funded by the UN and additional extra-budgetary technical assistance. The organization also relies on voluntary contributions to support its activities from member states and other outside donors, including international organizations (such as the European Union, nongovernmental organizations, and the private sector).

ACTIVITIES

UNCTAD is noted as the venue for the creation of the Declaration on the Establishment of a New International Economic Order (NIEO) in 1974. The NIEO called for several reforms of the global capitalist system, including improved terms of trade, debt relief for poorer states, and IMF restructuring to enhance the influence of developing countries. While many of these ideas were branded as radical and never implemented, some went on to inform both the Millennium Development Goals and the Sustainable Development Goals. At the Doha, Qatar, conference session in 2012, participants called for the establishment of action plans to create socioeconomic benchmarks and financial and technical assistance

Principles of the New International Economic Order

1. Sovereign equality of all countries
2. Cooperation of all countries based on equity to banish disparities and secure prosperity
3. Ensure the accelerated development of all developing countries
4. Right of every country to adopt the economic and social system that it deems the most appropriate
5. Full permanent sovereignty of every country over its natural resources and economic activities
6. Right of all peoples under foreign occupation to restitution and full compensation for exploitation and depletion of resources
7. Regulation and supervision of the activities of transnational corporations
8. Right of territories under colonial and racial domination to achieve liberation and to regain effective control over their natural resources and economic activities
9. Extending of assistance to areas subjected to economic, political, or any other coercive measures
10. Just and equitable relationship between the prices of raw materials, primary commodities, manufactured and semimanufactured goods exported by developing countries and the prices of raw materials, primary commodities, manufactures, capital goods, and equipment imported by them to improve unsatisfactory terms of trade
11. Extension of active assistance to developing countries by the whole international community, free of any political or military conditions
12. Ensuring that one of the main aims of the reformed international monetary system is the promotion of the development of developing countries and the adequate flow of real resources to them
13. Improving the competitiveness of natural materials facing competition from synthetic substitutes
14. Preferential and nonreciprocal treatment for developing countries in all fields of international economic cooperation whenever possible
15. Securing favorable conditions for the transfer of financial resources to developing countries
16. Giving developing countries access to modern science and technology and the creation of indigenous technology in forms and in accordance with procedures that are suited to their economies
17. The need for all countries to put an end to the waste of natural resources, including food products
18. The need for developing countries to concentrate all their resources for the cause of development
19. The strengthening of mutual economic, trade, financial, and technical cooperation among the developing countries
20. Facilitating the role of producers' associations and assisting in the promotion of sustained growth of the world economy and accelerating the development of developing countries

Source: Adapted from the 1974 General Assembly Resolution 3201 (S-VI): Declaration on the Establishment of a New International Economic Order.

programs. UNCTAD also works with other UN-affiliated organizations including the UN Development Programme, the World Bank, the IMF, and the World Trade Organization (WTO) on issues regarding capacity building and technical assistance to least developed countries.

Today, much of UNCTAD's work focuses on data collection and analysis to provide key information about trade and investment patterns and approaches to sustainable development. Another major undertaking includes policy analysis to help countries decrease economic vulnerabilities and poverty. The organization offers technical assistance designed for countries with special challenges including the least developed countries, small island states, and landlocked countries. The Secretariat spearheads efforts to provide both data and analysis as well as training programs on trade for government officials of developing countries. Recent work includes supporting innovations in technology, standardized accounting practices, and sustainable agriculture practices.

CHALLENGES AND REFORM

Views on UNCTAD's record are mixed. Although some find progress, others are more critical and believe that the organization has not lived up to its mandate. The organization's notable successes include raising issue awareness and bringing consensus, at times, to the challenges faced by the developing world. UNCTAD, unlike the IMF and World Bank, has provided an alternative framework that highlights the perceived unfair advantages of the wealthy countries and the unevenness of economic growth. In addition, the organization has brought attention to discriminatory trade practices and the need for further evenhanded integration of developing countries into the world economy. At the same time, UNCTAD faces criticism that its work is redundant with the IMF and the WTO. On several of UNCTAD's goals, like having wealthier countries dedicate 0.7 percent of their gross national product for foreign development aid, efforts remain halfhearted. Furthermore, many countries in the industrialized world are reluctant to give weight to a one-state one-vote forum where developing countries hold a clear majority.

Another challenge area UNCTAD faces is creating consensus. Unity among developing countries was a key factor in UNCTAD's early success. However, this consensus has faded as the challenges facing different regions grow more diverse. Some observers also note the waning strength of UNCTAD as the BRICS (Brazil, Russia, India, China and South Africa) are no longer acting as central voices for the developing world due to their increasing focus on relations with the industrialized world. The organization's goals are evolving and now include a commitment to sustainable development in their policy recommendations on trade, finance, investment, and technology. UNCTAD's work on poverty reduction and parity of economic development continues and is now enhanced by a vision of using clean energy and sustainable practices to grow the economies of developing countries and foster financial equalities at the global level.

See also: Economic and Social Council; Economic Development; Functional Commissions; International Monetary Fund; Membership; Nongovernmental Organizations; Sustainable Development Goals; United Nations Conferences and Summits; United Nations

Development Programme; United Nations Industrial Development Organization; World Bank Group; World Trade Organization.

FURTHER READING

Karshenas, Massoud. 2016. "Power, Ideology and Global Development: On the Origins, Evolution and Achievements of UNCTAD." *Development and Change* 47 (4): 664–85.

Rothstein, Robert L. 1979. *Global Bargaining: UNCTAD and the Quest for a New International Economic Order*. Princeton, NJ: Princeton University Press.

Taylor, Ian, and Karen Smith. 2007. *United Nations Conference on Trade and Development (UNCTAD)*. New York: Routledge.

Toye, John. 2014. "Assessing the G77: 50 Years after UNCTAD and 40 Years after the NIEO." *Third World Quarterly* 35 (10): 1759–74.

United Nations Development Programme (UNDP)

The history of the UN Development Programme (UNDP) begins with both UN and U.S. efforts to promote economic development following the end of World War II. At the time, many reasoned that promoting economic security was essential to maintaining international peace and security. This pledge was expressed in Article 55 of the UN Charter, which promised to work for "higher standards of living, full employment, and conditions of economic and social progress and development." This initiative was promoted by U.S. President Harry S. Truman in his 1949 Inaugural Address, who wanted "a bold new program for making the benefits of our scientific advances and industrial progress available for the improvement and growth of underdeveloped nations."

Toward such goals, the General Assembly created the UN Expanded Programme of Technical Assistance (EPTA) in 1949 to coordinate the efforts of UN agencies that were working to promote economic growth. The program was funded by voluntary contributions separate from the UN's general budget. EPTA assisted countries with the creation of economic development plans and also provided training programs, expertise, and grants. These efforts also incorporated the idea that development aid should be administered multilaterally, with many countries working together, to avoid the chance of coercion and the appearance of neocolonialism. In late 1958, the General Assembly formed the UN Special Fund to encourage financing and technical assistance programs for "preinvestment" projects to foster the conditions necessary to start large development projects such as those funded by EPTA. In 1965, in the midst of what was labeled the "Development Decade," the General Assembly decided to consolidate the two programs to create the UNDP.

RESPONSIBILITIES

UNDP proclaims two primary goals: "eradication of poverty, and the reduction of inequalities and exclusion." To promote this agenda, UNDP helps determine what a country's development needs are, creates priorities, and then designs programs and policies. The organization's original responsibilities of providing technical assistance by supplying expertise, training, and development aid have expanded to include working toward sustainable development, fostering democratic governance, peacebuilding, and environmental disaster resistance. UNDP's 2018–2021 Strategic Plan is built around accomplishing the UN's 2030 Agenda for Sustainable Development in relation to removing poverty, encouraging innovative structural transformations, and bolstering resistance to crises to protect development advances already in place. The organization serves as a hub for managing the work of many other UN organizations. Beyond the coordination of programs, UNDP is often described as an incubator organization that cultivated several new entities, some of which, like the UN Population Fund (UNFPA) and the UN Development Fund for Women (now a part of the UN Entity for Gender Equality and the Empowerment of Women [UN Women]), went on to become separate bodies in the UN System.

STRUCTURE

UNDP is headquartered in New York but also has field offices around the globe. Originally overseen by a forty-eight-member Governing Council, UNDP now shares a thirty-six-member Executive Board with UNFPA and the UN Office for Project Services to oversee operations (as established by General Assembly Resolution 48/162 in December 1993). Members of the Executive Board are elected for three-year terms by the Economic and Social Council, with representatives from eight African countries, seven Asian, four Eastern European, five Latin America and the Caribbean, and twelve from the Western European and Others Group. A five-person Bureau of the Executive Board, with one from each regional group, consists of a President and four Vice-Presidents. UN member states that do not serve on the board may attend meetings and participate in discussions but do not hold voting privileges.

The organization is headed by an Administrator, who is appointed by the Secretary-General and then confirmed by the General Assembly. This individual holds a four-year term and serves as Vice-Chair of the UN Sustainable Development Group (UNDSG), which was created to foster coherence in planning and the UN's work within countries between the many agencies and funds that focus on economic and sustainable development. The Vice-Chair also oversees the inter-agency meetings of the UNDSG Core Group, which includes the UN Department of Economic and Social Affairs, Food and Agriculture Organization, UN High Commissioner for Refugees, and World Health Organization among other entities. UNDP also has Regional Bureaus for Africa, Asia and the Pacific, Arab States, Europe and the Commonwealth of Independent States, and Latin America and the Caribbean. In 2018, UNDP, which is funded solely by voluntary contributions, reported receiving over $5 billion in contributions from member states, other international organizations, and private sector donations. The top five individual state donors that year were Germany, Japan, the United States, Sweden, and the United Kingdom. Some governments pledge funds for a single year, whereas others make multiyear commitments.

ACTIVITIES

UNDP acts as a central network that coordinates the work of the entire UN System. While the organization's reports provide a global perspective, this effort is combined with work at country and regional levels. At the country level, UNDP plays a key role in the Resident Coordinator System and oversees thousands of development projects in approximately 170 different countries. UNDP also administers areas such as UN Volunteers and the UN Capital Development Fund. UNDP is well-known for the creation of the yearly progress statement published since 1990 known as the *Human Development Report*. This report provides key development indicators, analysis, and policy recommendations. The organization is also noted for the creation of the Human Development Index, which includes measures of income, education, and life expectancy to offer an alternative understanding of development measures. UNDP has given particular focus to promoting gender equality, including working with the UN Conference on Trade and Development (UNCTAD) to highlight issues associated with gender and trade. UNDP's 2018–2021 Strategic Plan emphasizes collaboration with UN Women, UNFPA, and UN Children's Fund. UNDP is also credited with innovation and advocacy in areas like postconflict development and sustainable development policies. The organization serves as a voice for promoting the concerns of marginalized people and the origin of many ideas to support development progress. Such programs include promoting South-South cooperation, addressing sanitation, and working for the diffusion of technology to address climate mitigation in developing countries.

CHALLENGES AND REFORM

Methods and approaches to promote development are not without controversy. Some have criticized the traditional "development" goal itself for being modeled on the idea that increased industrialization will lead to greater levels of economic prosperity. This approach may not be sustainable and focuses on country development rather than human development and also has environmental implications. In addition, some analysts find that financial assistance does not always produce development progress as some international lending efforts create cycles of poverty rather than end them. Some critics claim that UNDP sits largely on the sidelines and is less relevant in comparison to efforts by major international financial institutions, like the International Monetary Fund and World Bank, to address the developing world and fault UNDP for the organization's lack of capacity to serve a centralized funding role. At the same time, other observers counter that UNDP offers a better way to promote development with the focus on local empowerment since the priority should be assisting people, rather than governments.

UNDP has undergone several reform efforts, including taking on a comprehensive program review after a 1969 study (often referred to as the Jackson Report) called for more coordination and centralized coherence. After the 1992 UN Conference on Environment and Development, UNDP expanded to coordinate sustainable development efforts from several other UN agencies, including in the World Bank, UNCTAD, and the UN Environment Programme. The organization's mission broadened further in the 1990s to include social development, human empowerment, and humanitarian assistance as its focus moved beyond development of a country's economy to emphasize poverty reduction and human development. In 2000, the Millennium Development Goals redefined the UNDP's long list of objectives to include poverty eradication, environmental sustainability, enhancing the capacities of local health care systems, and promoting gender equality. In October 2014, UNDP undertook significant restructuring as staff was cut by 10 percent and reorganized. Prior to the reforms, 60 percent of staff worked at UNDP headquarters in New York with 40 percent in regional offices. Post-restructuring, 44 percent were in New York and 56 percent in regional offices. This ongoing reform process also tries to address and eliminate redundant groups and offices. At the same time, UNDP continues to find new agendas through its work on implementation of the Sustainable Development Goals for 2030.

See also: Economic Development; Food and Agriculture Organization; Human Security; International Maritime Organization; International Monetary Fund; International Telecommunication Union; Joint United Nations Programme on HIV/AIDS; Membership; Peacebuilding; Preparatory Commission for the Comprehensive Nuclear-Test-Ban Treaty Organization; Sustainable Development; Sustainable Development Goals; United Nations Conference on Trade and Development; United Nations Children's Fund; United Nations Entity for Gender Equality and the Empowerment of Women; United Nations Environment Programme; United Nations High Commissioner for Refugees; United Nations Industrial Development Organization; United Nations Population Fund; United Nations Reform; World Bank Group; World Health Organization; World Meteorological Organization; World Tourism Organization.

FURTHER READING

Browne, Stephen. 2011. *The United Nations Development Programme and System.* New York: Routledge.

Murphy, Craig N. 2006. *The United Nations Development Programme: A Better Way?* Cambridge: Cambridge University Press.

Santiso, Carlos. 2002. "Promoting Democratic Governance and Preventing the Recurrence of Conflict: The Role of the United Nations Development Programme in Post-Conflict Peace-Building." *Journal of Latin American Studies* 34 (3): 555–86.

Stokke, Olav. 2009. *The UN and Development: From Aid to Cooperation.* Bloomington: Indiana University Press.

United Nations Entity for Gender Equality and the Empowerment of Women (UN Women)

The UN Entity for Gender Equality and the Empowerment of Women (UN Women) was created by General Assembly Resolution 64/289 in July 2010 to consolidate and coordinate the UN System's existing mechanisms for gender equality and female empowerment. UN Women is comprised of the former Division for the Advancement of Women, International Research and Training Institute for the Advancement of Women, Office of the Special Adviser on Gender Issues and Advancement of Women, and the UN Development Fund for Women, each of which aimed to reduce gender inequality through various social, financial, or institutional initiatives. UN Women's mission builds on the tradition of the first UN body to handle gender-related issues, the Commission on the Status of Women (CSW), an Economic and Social Council (ECOSOC) Functional Commission formed in 1946 to bring consciousness to women's issues and address discriminatory regulations and laws. The CSW first met in Lake Success, New York, with all fifteen original member states represented by female delegates. The CSW's work proved instrumental early in the history of the UN, with the body's notable inclusion of gender-sensitive language in the Universal Declaration of Human Rights (see Part VI). The CSW later drafted landmark international agreements on women's rights, such as the Convention on the Elimination of Discrimination against Women, and prepared the Fourth World Conference on Women that led to the Beijing Declaration and Platform for Action. UN Women provides instrumental efforts toward achieving the UN goal of female empowerment through both internal efforts within the UN System addressing gender parity and external operations in a broad range of areas regarding gender equality.

RESPONSIBILITIES

UN Women is the only UN entity that solely focuses on women's equality across a range of priority areas. UN Women has a wide spectrum of responsibilities relative to its mandate for the development of women's rights. Primarily, UN Women works to increase the political engagement and representation of women, end gender-based violence and discrimination, and generally seeks to improve peace, security, and quality of living for women. Encouraging economic growth and eradicating poverty for women is another key target area for UN Women, as economic difficulties disproportionally affect women. The range of agenda items stems from the bodies that were integrated into UN Women. Many of their old functions and aims were transferred to the work of UN Women, ensuring a multifaceted approach toward advancing gender equity and empowerment.

STRUCTURE

UN Women has a distinct organizational structure. The body is governed by a joint multitiered structure as well as an Executive Director and internal directorate. The first half of UN Women's governance structure is guided by the General Assembly, ECOSOC, and an Executive Board. The Executive Board directs UN Women's activities and operational policy affairs and is composed of representatives from forty-one member states, each of which is elected to serve a three-year term by ECOSOC. The seat distribution of the Executive Board is allocated regionally: with the African bloc holding ten positions, the Asian bloc also ten, Eastern Europe with four, Latin America and the Caribbean with six, Western Europe and Others with five, and an additional six seats for the highest contributing countries. The Executive Board also includes a group of officers, known as the Bureau, elected by their peers on the Board. The Bureau is tasked with facilitating the Executive Board's work. The Bureau consists of one President and four Vice Presidents, in order to provide representation for all regional groups. The presidency rotates by regional representation each year to ensure fairness across all geographical blocs.

The second half of UN Women's multitiered governance structure is composed of the General Assembly, ECOSOC, and the CSW. This half is structured to offer norm-based policy input and support. The CSW provides ideas, suggestions, and policy guidance for UN Women. In order to coordinate between these two governance structures, ECOSOC creates connections to ensure consistent policy and action for UN Women. Finally, the Executive Director is part of a directorate that facilitates the operations of the Executive Board and the entity as a whole. In both tiers, the General Assembly receives reports from UN Women, manages policy oversight, and collaborates with the directorate. Voluntary funding comprises the vast majority (around 98 percent) of UN Women's budget as most financial support is provided by sources outside of the UN's regular budget (the remaining 2 percent, which supports the normative intergovernmental processes). Voluntary contributions come from member states, with Sweden standing out as the top contributor in 2018, as well as individuals, foundations, and the private sector.

ACTIVITIES

UN Women implements programming to advance women's rights. In order to advocate for women, this includes educational platforms, support networks for women, and increasing recognition and compensation for women's domestic labor. The body also works directly with member states to develop and strengthen existing legal and normative frameworks for gender equality. UN Women aids in the political participation of women to integrate gendered perspectives into public policy across developing countries by training female candidates in conjunction with offering civic engagement. UN Women runs the UN Trust Fund to End Violence against Women, which empowers women vulnerable to violence, improves their access to services, and strengthens the implementation of regulations to protect women. Other priority areas include public awareness, achieved through initiatives like the launch of the #HeForShe campaign in 2014, which aims to increase the participation of men and boys in fighting for gender equality. The appointment of Goodwill Ambassadors, such as actress Nicole Kidman, to UN Women also provides a highly visible public voice for the entity's work.

UN Women holds meetings and issues research reports. The agency frequently works with other UN bodies to accomplish shared goals, including the Food and Agriculture Organization, UN Children's Fund, UN Population Fund, UN Development Programme, and World Food Programme. In addition, UN Women collaborates with a wide range of nongovernmental organizations to end violence against women, ensure protective measures for women during conflict, provide specialized humanitarian relief for women, and advocate for equality through female representation in governance, national planning, and sustainable development. UN Women also institutes internal efforts to achieve gender parity, such as measures to promote gender mainstreaming and accountability throughout the UN System. This includes the integration of gender-specific policies and programs that aim to involve women into all levels of decision-making.

CHALLENGES AND REFORM

The large breadth of UN Women's work and its complex governance structure has led to criticism of its effectiveness. A lack of gender parity persists within the UN. Similar to other components of the UN System, coordination also remains challenging. Much responsibility falls on ECOSOC to execute and ensure proper coordination between the various components of the entity. Critics argue that because UN Women advocates for global development of women's rights, appointing states to oversight positions that fail to comply with such goals undermines the body's work and mission. Therefore, controversy has emerged over the selection of member states to the CSW that hold questionable records on women's rights (i.e., the appointment of Saudi Arabia to a position on the CSW in 2017). The issue of the wide mandate and priority areas for the entity's work also creates difficulty regarding agenda setting. Finally, another challenge faced by UN Women is the need for additional funding, as programming and operational work is limited by the entity's financial means.

Through its involvement across other entities within the UN and complex governance structure, UN Women is deeply embedded within the UN System. However, given that UN Women is a relatively new fixture within the UN System, there has been limited discussion of its potential reform thus far. There has been debate regarding future directions for UN Women to pursue, including working in greater conjunction with governments to implement gender-sensitive programming and to elevate the status of women throughout the UN's member states. UN Women follows in its predecessors' footsteps and empowers women throughout the international community. UN Women has made significant strides in the fight for gender equality, and through its ongoing development is poised to be a strong advocate for a more equal world.

See also: Ban Ki-moon; Economic Development; Economic and Social Council; Food and Agriculture Organization; Functional Commissions; Goodwill Ambassadors and Messengers of Peace; Human Rights; Human Security; Joint United Nations Programme on HIV/AIDS; Research and Training Institutes; Secretariat; Sustainable Development Goals; United Nations Children's Fund; United Nations Development Programme; United Nations Population Fund; Women and Gender; World Food Programme.

FURTHER READING

Burki, Talha. 2010. "UN Women Spearheading Drive for Gender Equality." *The Lancet* 376 (9739): 405–6.

Charlesworth, Hilary, and Christine Chinkin. 2013. "The New United Nations 'Gender Architecture': A Room with a View?" *Max Planck Yearbook of United Nations Law* 17: 2–60.

Defies, Elizabeth F. 2011. "The United Nations and Women—A Critique." *William & Mary Journal of Women and the Law* 17 (2): 395–433.
Menon, Sawaswathi. 2015. "UN Women: Prospects and Challenges." *Future United Nations Development System* 30 (June): 1–4.
Roberts, Fleur. 2011. "Understanding the Need for UN Women: Notes for New Zealand Civil Society." *Women's Studies Journal* 25 (1): 31–46.

United Nations Environment Programme (UNEP)

The UN Environment Programme (UNEP) was established by General Assembly Resolution 2997 following the 1972 UN Conference on the Human Environment held in Stockholm, Sweden. Since debuting in 1973, UNEP serves as an information-gathering organization that raises awareness and encourages countries to mitigate pollution and protect local resources. The organization promotes inclusiveness and holds that developing countries are central partners in environmental issues. In fact, UNEP was the first UN agency based in the so-called Global South, with the organization's headquarters deliberately placed in Nairobi, Kenya. This commitment carries over into staffing practices as UNEP hires many individuals from the developing world. Over time, the organization has seen significant growth and increasing relevance, rising from what some have described as a minor body to a leading global institution with a full agenda.

RESPONSIBILITIES

UNEP's original mandate included assessing and monitoring the environment, promoting international cooperation and coordination of environmental policies, and enhancing the contribution of scientific communities and other experts. The organization is also tasked with acting as a facilitator for policy creation. UNEP operates as a hub organization that plays a centralizing role in coordinating other programs and is a partner in establishing policy recommendations for other agencies, setting national goals and indicators, as well as tracking changes and reporting about environmental threats at the global level. UNEP works to set the global environmental agenda and is often referred to as a "catalyst" for international environmental laws, treaties, and agreements.

STRUCTURE

UNEP was originally led by a geographically apportioned fifty-eight-member Governing Council. As the global scope of environmental issues became more pressing, advocates called for an organization with a broader mandate, universal membership, and more robust legal capacities. Following the June 2012 UN Conference on Sustainable Development (often referred to as Rio+20), the Governing Council was replaced with the enhanced UN Environment Assembly (UNEA). This move was the result of decades of advocacy that called for prioritizing environmental issues. As the primary governing body of UNEP, UNEA establishes policies, develops legal mechanisms, oversees programs, and organizes representatives from all 193 UN member states. UNEA is designed to meet every two years (thus far meetings occurred in June 2014, May 2016, December 2017, and March 2019, with the next scheduled for February 2021) and is headed by a Bureau, consisting of Ministers of the Environment from member states, made up of a President, eight Vice Presidents, and a Rapporteur.

UNEA meetings include many side events that bring together the private sector and nongovernmental organizations. Discussions often focus on a range of topics, such as climate change and human rights, coral reefs, environmental refugees, green chemistry, and marine pollution. In between meetings, a Committee of Permanent Representatives (with 122 accredited members as of January 2020) coordinates the agenda, sets up policies for approval, and ensures implementation. The Executive Director, who holds the rank of UN Under-Secretary-General, along with a Deputy Secretary-General oversees UNEP's Secretariat, which is composed of a set of divisions: communication, corporate services, economy, ecosystems, law, science, and policy and programme. UNEP also operates regionally and subregionally through a set of additional offices. UNEP's budget is relatively modest, and voluntary contributions from countries and other stakeholders make up around 95 percent of UNEP's funding.

ACTIVITIES

UNEP defines its work according to seven main categories: climate change, disasters and conflicts, ecosystem management, environmental governance, chemicals and waste, resource efficiency, and keeping the environment under review. The challenges for each area are tackled through environmental assessment, environmental management, and supporting measures with sustainability. Since UNEP's creation, the scope of activities has grown significantly. In 1988, together with World Meteorological Organization (WMO), UNEP established the Intergovernmental Panel on Climate Change (IPCC). The IPCC, which won the Nobel Prize (shared with former U.S. Vice President Al Gore) in 2007, draws upon scientific expertise to assess the research on climate change and produce a "Summary for Policymakers," which is subsequently reviewed by all participating governments. In addition, UNEP produces reports on the environment, including *Global Environmental Outlook*. The 1992 UN Conference on Environment and Development, also known as the Earth Summit, moved the focus of global initiatives from environmental protection to sustainable development. This gathering is considered one of the most impactful for UNEP. UNEP is one of eighteen agencies that collaborate as part of the Global Environmental Facility.

UNEP plays a key role in the Multilateral Environmental Agreements (MEAs) registered with the UN, which include accords on biodiversity, endangered species, hazardous waste, mercury pollution, and ozone layer protection. The agency directly manages several of these important accords (eleven as of early 2020), including the Convention on International Trade in Endangered Species of Wild Fauna and Flora, the Montreal Protocol on Substances that Deplete the Ozone

Layer, and the Convention on the Conservation of Migratory Species of Wild Animals, as well as six regional seas conventions. Each MEA has its own secretariat to oversee the implementation of the agreement. While much of UNEP's work is focused on global environmental challenges, the organization also has many regional initiatives. For example, it spearheaded the regional program Mainstreaming Environment and Sustainability in Africa Universities Partnership. During the UN Decade of Education for Sustainable Development (2005–2014), UNEP created educational programs for policy makers, educators, and youth that highlighted the challenges and opportunities surrounding environmental issues. UNEP is also active in other international governmental organizations, such as observer status at the Arctic Council and supporting the Council's scientific and technical working groups.

CHALLENGES AND REFORM

The UNEA meetings in Kenya often become venues for airing differences between the developed and developing world. For instance, there is criticism over the very concept of sustainable development as some claim this privileges western ideas regarding conservation and neglects local cultural perspectives and voices. UNEP itself is critical of progress in addressing environmental threats. Some blame this lack of improvement on weak and piecemeal approaches that do not have robust centralized efficiency and suffer from significant underfunding and missing enforcement capacities. While the creation of the UNEA has increased the visibility and scope of UNEP's work and was a deliberate attempt to enhance the agency's capacities, it also makes UNEP's work more political, cumbersome, and time consuming. Critics find that the UNEA's universal membership results in more contentious and unwieldy meetings, where numerous resolutions clog the intergovernmental process. There are also concerns expressed by some that UNEP's location in Nairobi isolates the body from other UN agencies and makes both staffing and outreach more challenging.

While many observers still point to institutional weaknesses, UNEP has found considerable success and is credited with helping to create national ministries of environment. The organization is also effective in folding environmental policies and activism into the work of many other UN agencies, including the UN Educational, Scientific and Cultural Organization, the WMO, and the UN Development Programme. UNEP is often praised for promoting global awareness about environmental issues and serving as hub for countries to coordinate environmental policy. The *Global Environmental Outlook* reports play an essential role in summarizing knowledge from the scientific community. UNEP was also a central player in the development of the Sustainability Development Goals (SDGs) for the UN's 2030 Agenda and contributed to drafting the goals in such a way that environmental sustainability was an essential element that crosscut each issue in the goals themselves, the targets, and the monitoring process. Furthermore, the organization's work on the 2030 Agenda helped to connect environmental protection with economic and social development, and UNEP is now one of the primary agencies tasked with monitoring the ambitious indicators within the SDGs.

UNEP continues to pursue several enhancement goals, including raising the credibility of science-based information to inform both global and national environmental policies. In terms of reform, there are recommendations that UNEP should strengthen its regional presence and persistent calls to increase the organization's budget. UNEP remains a subsidiary body of the General Assembly, but with growing environmental threats there are proposals to elevate UNEP's standing in the UN System. Some states (such as European Union members, including France and Germany) propose that UNEP should be made a specialized agency, yet others (particularly the United States and China) reject this idea. Another idea is to replace the now outdated Trusteeship Council, which would give UNEP the same principal organ status as the Economic and Social Council. UNEP continues to work toward streamlining coordination efforts with other UN agencies, increasing responsiveness to individual country needs, and elevating efforts to provide a livable planet for future inhabitants. Overall, UNEP is progressively influential as the organization raises awareness about environmental issues and helps create international agreements that protect, preserve, and sustain the Earth's natural systems.

See also: Environmental Protection; General Assembly; Global Commons; International Maritime Organization; Nongovernmental Organizations; Sustainable Development Goals; Trusteeship Council; United Nations Conferences and Summits; United Nations Development Programme; United Nations Educational, Scientific and Cultural Organization; United Nations Human Settlements Programme; United Nations Industrial Development Organization; United Nations Reform; World Meteorological Organization.

FURTHER READING

Andresen, Steinar. 2007. "The Effectiveness of UN Environmental Institutions." *International Environmental Agreements* 7 (4): 317–36.

Desai, Bharat H. 2012. "The Quest for a United Nations Specialised Agency for the Environment." *The Round Table* 101 (2): 167–79.

DeSombre, Elizabeth R. 2017. *Global Environmental Institutions*. Second edition. London: Routledge.

Ivanova, Maria. 2012. "Institutional Design and UNEP Reform: Historical Insights on Form, Function and Financing." *International Affairs* 88 (3): 565–84.

Young, Oran R. 2010. *Institutional Dynamics: Emergent Patterns of Change in International Environmental Governance*. Cambridge, MA: MIT Press.

United Nations High Commissioner for Refugees (UNHCR)

The UN has worked extensively to shelter and provide relief to people during times of crisis. War and political violence often force people to flee their homes, and after both world wars international organizations were created to help refugees. This work assists both people and governments since refugees are vulnerable to exploitation, health threats, human rights violations, and strain economic and political systems. While originally created as a temporary solution, the Office of the UN High Commissioner for Refugees' (UNHCR) scope of work has grown extensively and the organization now works at the forefront of what many label as a global crisis. In recognition of its work, UNHCR has been awarded two Nobel Peace Prizes, one in 1954 for its efforts in restoring people to their homes in Europe and a second in 1981 for service in Asia, Africa, and Latin America during the 1970s. In the twenty-first century, UNHCR faces the daunting task of assisting millions of displaced persons and aiding people who are increasingly forced to leave their homes due to new threats, such as climate change and natural disasters.

The origins of UNCHR are rooted in other organizations working with refugees. The League of Nations assisted over two million persons displaced during and after World War I, providing legal and political protections, such as the Nansen Passport, as well as resettlement. The League made Fridtjof Nansen the High Commissioner for Refugees in 1921. Following Nansen's death in 1930, the League established the Nansen International Office for Refugees in 1931. A separate High Commissioner for Refugees from Germany was appointed in 1933, but the two were merged together in 1939 after Germany withdrew from the League. During World War II, forty-four countries came together to create the United Nations Relief and Rehabilitation Administration (UNRRA). Starting in late 1943, this agency distributed relief aid, including food, shelter, and clothing to civilians and repatriated millions of displaced persons. UNRRA disbanded in 1947 and was succeeded by the International Refugee Organization, created as a special UN body. Like the UNRRA, the organization had a limited scope and was discharged in 1952. In December 1949, the General Assembly passed Resolution 319 to create a High Commissioner's Office for Refugees. The General Assembly adopted the Statute of the Office of the UN High Commissioner for Refugees in December 1950 under Resolution 428, with work getting underway January 1, 1951. UNHCR had humble beginnings as it was initially designed with a limited mandate and only a three-year authorization. When the refugee problem proved not to be temporary and solely European, as was originally assumed, the General Assembly saw UNHCR's ongoing value. By 1956, the organization was called on to assist refugees outside of its originally assigned area. The UNHCR is headquartered in Geneva, Switzerland.

RESPONSIBILITIES

UNHCR is responsible for serving two constituencies. First, the organization advocates for refugees through its work with governments and is a central player in the development of international law regarding refugees. The foundation for this effort was established with the 1951 Convention Relating to the Status of Refugees, which included the range of refugee rights. This was enhanced by the 1967 Protocol, which extended the time frame and geographical range for applying the Convention beyond occurrences in Europe before January 1951. The second aspect of UNHCR's focus relates to the organization's fieldwork, as outlined in Resolution 428, which provides assistance to refugees, stateless persons, asylum seekers, and returnees.

STRUCTURE

The organization is composed of an Executive Committee and a High Commissioner. UNHCR began with a temporary Advisory Committee in 1951 that included fourteen countries and the Holy See, which was followed from 1955 to 1958 by the Executive Committee of the UN Refugee Fund. Starting in 1959, governance is provided by the Executive Committee of the Programme of the UN High Commissioner for Refugees, which is made up of 102 member states (as of 2018). Members of the Executive Committee are elected by ECOSOC and must have an interest in resolution of refugee issues. The Executive Committee acts under the purview of the General Assembly, and an annual report is submitted to the Assembly. The Executive Committee officers are a Chairperson, two Vice-Chairpersons, and a Rapporteur. Representatives from specialized agencies can observe at public meetings of the Executive Committee, and nongovernmental organizations with consultative status can submit statements. The responsibilities of the Executive Committee, which meets every fall in Geneva, involve advising the High Commissioner, approving programs, and authorizing the budget. Within the Executive Committee, a Standing Committee (established in 1995 in place of other subcommittees) usually convenes three times a year.

The General Assembly selects the High Commissioner, who serves a five-year term. In 2016, Filippo Grandi started his term as the eleventh High Commissioner. The previous High Commissioner, António Guterres, completed his ten years in office at the end of 2015 and was subsequently elected to the post of UN Secretary-General, taking office at the start of 2017. The General Assembly and Economic and Social Council (ECOSOC) provide a direct line of oversight to the High Commissioner, who receives policy directives from both principal organs. The organization's budget has grown from $300,000 in 1950 to $8.6 billion in 2019. UNHCR's primary source of funding comes through voluntary contributions, with the United States and European Union being the two largest donors in 2019. The remaining budget is supported by other UN member states, as well as private sector donations from corporations, individuals, and foundations. Approximately 90 percent of UNHCR staff work in field operations.

ACTIVITIES

UNHCR's primary activities include serving communities that are forcibly displaced as well as stateless people. While UNHCR is reluctant to create refugee camps in lieu of permanent housing, a central element of its work is providing adequate shelter in humanitarian emergencies, including tents and emergency assistance. The organization also works to promote voluntary repatriation, integration into host states and, occasionally, relocation to a third state. The agency has extensive field experience and is often the lead organization when working with over 900 partners, including other UN agencies and nongovernmental organizations. These include the UN High Commissioner for Human Rights, the UN Development Programme, the UN Population Fund, the UN Children's Fund, the World Food Programme, and the World Health Organization. There are also close partnerships with many humanitarian organizations, which receive around 40 percent of UNHCR's annual spending, including holding an Annual Consultation with Nongovernmental Organizations. UNHCR also engages with celebrity advocates like Goodwill Ambassador Ben Stiller and Special Envoy Angelina Jolie.

UNHCR maps refugee flows and generates important information on trends and statistics. The organization's annual *Statistical Yearbook* and databases are important tools for countries, relief agencies, and the UN. Recently, UNHCR adopted an initiative on the sources of displacement to address the political, economic, and social causes that force people to leave their homes. This program remains controversial as it skirts what may be sensitive issues within member states.

CHALLENGES AND REFORM

UNHCR's directives, mandate, and budget have expanded as international efforts to assist people who are forced to leave their homes grew over time. In 1985, UNHCR served nine million people, but by 1992 that number had grown to seventeen million. As of 2019, UNHCR reports over seventy million forcibly displaced people across the globe as local violence and regional warfare created a sharp escalation in dislocation. Environmental changes, including sea level rise, drought, flooding, and desertification also contribute to this crisis. At the same time, the agency's resources, both in terms of financial and personnel, have not grown at the same rate to keep up.

UNHCR also faces challenges with emerging anti-immigrant sentiments by UN member states. This results in political leaders rejecting international obligations to grant political asylum and increasing cases of refoulement, where refugees or asylum seekers are forced to return to their home state where they face a high likelihood of persecution. In addition, people who are forced to leave due to climate change are typically considered economic migrants and, therefore, are not under the protections of the Refugee Convention. Recent discussions within the UN led to the 2018 Global Compact on Refugees, which seeks to protect, and even empower, refugees while addressing the pressures that host countries encounter and building shared, cooperative global responses. UNHCR faces several daunting tasks as it works in many of the most difficult and dangerous places to serve some of the most vulnerable people on the planet.

See also: António Guterres; Environmental Protection; International Labour Organization; Goodwill Ambassadors and Messengers of Peace; Joint United Nations Programme on HIV/AIDS; Nongovernmental Organizations; Refugees and Migration; United Nations Children's Fund; United Nations Development Programme; United Nations Population Fund; World Food Programme; World Health Organization.

FURTHER READING

Barnett, Michael. 2001. "Humanitarianism with a Sovereign Face: UNHCR in the Global Undertow." *International Migration Review* 35 (1): 244–77.

Betts, Alexander, Gil Loescher, and James Milner. 2012. *The United Nations High Commissioner for Refugees (UNHCR): The Politics and Practice of Refugee Protection*. Second edition. New York: Routledge.

Gilbert, Goeff. 2009. "The UNHCR and the New Geopolitics of Refugees." *Harvard International Review* 31 (3): 56–59.

Loescher, Gil. 2009. *The UNHCR and World Politics: A Perilous Path*. Oxford: Oxford University Press.

United Nations Human Settlements Programme (UN-Habitat)

The origins of the UN Human Settlements Programme (UN-Habitat) date back to 1975, when the General Assembly created the UN Habitat and Human Settlements Foundation (UNHHSF) to address the growing issues of urbanization and housing. This early agency operated under the parameters of the UN Environment Programme (UNEP) and was organized to channel technical assistance and resources to urban area resettlement programs. UNHHSF was given a modest budget to cover the first four years. In 1976, the UN Conference on Human Settlements (Habitat I) held in Vancouver, Canada, called for a focus on problems created due to rapid urbanization. The conference established the Vancouver Declaration on Human Settlements and a list of recommendations in the Vancouver Action Plan. This prompted the establishment of the UN Centre for Human Settlements (Habitat) in 1977, with the intergovernmental governing body the Commission for Human Settlements created by transforming the Economic and Social Council's Committee on Housing, Building and Planning.

As issues concerning urban management continued to grow, in 1996 the UN hosted the Second UN Conference on Human Settlements (Habitat II) in Istanbul, Turkey, which produced the Habitat Agenda and the Istanbul Declaration on Human Settlements. Since Habitat I, the world population continued to grow, with an increased percentage living in cities, and there was immense urban expansion, particularly in the developing world. With a limited mandate and resources, existing UN institutions could not address the growing difficulties of urban poverty. The General Assembly held a special session in 2001 to review the implementation of outcomes from Habitat II and issued the UN Declaration on Cities and Other Human Settlements in the New Millennium. Building upon this, with the passage of Resolution 56/206, the General Assembly combined the existing bodies to forge UN-Habitat, with a broadened mandate and enhanced organizational status, which began operations on January 1, 2002.

RESPONSIBILITIES

The goals of UN-Habitat, as stated in its Results Framework 2014–2019, include promoting "environmentally, economically, and socially sustainable, gender sensitive and inclusive urban development policies implemented by national, regional and local authorities" and improving "the standard of living of the urban poor." In

2015, the adoption of the UN Sustainable Development Goals (SDGs) in the UN's Agenda for 2030 provided momentum and a specific directive for the organization's efforts. SDG 11, which pledges to "make cities and human settlements inclusive, safe, resilient and sustainable," provides UN-Habitat with a broad charge.

In 2016, the organization's responsibilities were magnified by the UN Conference on Housing and Sustainable Urban Development (Habitat III) held in Quito, Ecuador. This was the first major UN conference after the approval of the SDGs. The conference established the New Urban Agenda to address how humanity builds, governs, and even thinks about life in cities. Habitat III brought a more inclusive approach as the conference tackled issues associated with the management of megacities and the importance of sustainable urbanization in controlling climate change. The conference specifically called on UN-Habitat to secure adequate shelter for people living within cities, promote a healthy social environment, encourage inclusive human settlements in urban settings, urban planning, waste management, and participatory slum upgrading. Combined, these directives called on UN-Habitat to help create safe, healthy, and sustainable urban environments across the world. These ideas helped to structure UN-Habitat's Strategic Plan for 2020–2023.

STRUCTURE

UN-Habitat is headquartered in Nairobi, Kenya. Until recently, the organization was overseen by a fifty-eight-member Governing Council. Governance of UN-Habitat was altered in 2019 following the passage of General Assembly Resolution 73/239. The limited membership Governing Council was replaced by the UN-Habitat Assembly bringing together all 193 UN member states every four years. The first Assembly session was held in May 2019 with the theme "Innovation for Better Quality of Life in Cities and Communities" and connected member states, UN specialized agencies, and a range of nonstate actors. A thirty-six-member Executive Board, elected by the Assembly, guides the organization in between Assembly meetings. Membership on the Board is based on regional distribution, with ten African seats, eight Asian, eight Western European and Others, six Latin America and the Caribbean, and four Eastern Europe. The Board is supported by a Bureau made up of a Chair, three Vice-Chairs, and a Rapporteur. Member states not on the Board, as well as representatives from specialized agencies, are allowed to participate at meetings as observers. Finally, the Committee of Permanent Representatives gathers every two years, once to prepare for the Assembly meeting and once to review the outcome at the mid-way point between the meetings. UN-Habitat also includes a Secretariat supervised by an Executive Director, whose position is at the level of Under-Secretary-General, who is supported by a Deputy Executive Director. The UN Secretary-General nominates the Executive Director, and the General Assembly then approves the selection. UN-Habitat, which oversees the UNHHSF, is mostly funded by voluntary contributions. The great majority of UN-Habitat's funding comes from the member states, with additional funding from other UN agencies and the rest made up by contributions from other international organizations, local governments, civil society, and the private sector.

ACTIVITIES

UN-Habitat's primary activities include providing basic services in urban areas (such as housing, water, sanitation, and health services) as well as consulting on development programs, infrastructure enhancement, environmental planning, disaster management, and advising municipal governments. At the same time, UN-Habitat is a hub organization that coordinates and acts as a centralizing venue for many UN activities and programs that address urban issues. For example, UN-Habitat frequently works with UNEP and collaborates with the World Health Organization on urban health. The organization also provides policy recommendations to city planners and local governments on managing slums, financing for housing, developing sustainable infrastructure, and managing migration influx. The research and publications produced by UN-Habitat are important for policy makers as well as nongovernmental organizations and the private sector. A key example is the *World Cities Report*, which provides a wealth of statistics on employment rates, education, access to clean water, shelter, sanitation, and health services. UN-Habitat is also known for the creation of the City Prosperity Index, which is based on measures of productivity, infrastructure, quality of life, equity and inclusion, environmental sustainability, and governance.

CHALLENGES AND REFORM

Between 1997 and 2002, UN-Habitat engaged in a noteworthy revitalization effort. This involved structural changes, as well as a refocusing of priorities. However, in 2017 a report by the High-Level Independent Panel to Assess and Enhance the Effectiveness of UN-Habitat found that the organization still faced significant challenges in meeting its goals. The report identified a need for increased accountability, efficiency, and transparency. The assessment offered several suggestions, although many are controversial. One recommendation that was carried out was to make UN-Habitat a universal body (similar to UNEP), although critics of the report claim that this will actually make the organization less efficient. Another suggestion includes creating a Committee of Stakeholders that would be composed of ten members from nongovernmental representatives, five members representing the private sector, and five urban experts, along with a separate Committee of Local Governments. In addition, the report proposed the creation of "UN-Urban" (in similar fashion to UN-Energy and UN-Water) that would be housed within the New York–based Department of Economic and Social Affairs.

UN-Habitat must cope with a flat, and even declining, budget. To remedy this, there are suggestions that a sustainable urbanization fund should be developed to assist with fundraising for a more stable financing stream. UN-Habitat itself has called for more member state participation and greater efficiency, as well as better coordination with UN Regional Commissions, more robust country teams, improved communication with local authorities, and increased focus on the urban-rural relationship. Other suggestions include expanding the CPI indicators to incorporate dimensions such as the amount of public spaces, green spaces, and quality of social bonds in urban areas. UN-Habitat is noted for its generation of ideas and consulting role. The organization is central to conversations about how the 2015 Paris Agreement on climate change and the SDGs can be integrated into urban management. With a projected global population of 9.7 billion by 2050 and potentially two-thirds of the world inhabitants living in cities (up from 55 percent in 2018), UN-Habitat is increasingly indispensable. In the face of the pressure from climate change, sustainability, and urban migration, UN-Habitat will continue to play a role mapping the prospects for a future that meets the growing needs of humans in urban environments.

See also: Environmental Protection; General Assembly; Health; Nongovernmental Organizations; Regional Commissions; Sustainable Development Goals; United Nations Conferences and Summits; United Nations Environment Programme; World Health Organization.

FURTHER READING

Acioly, Claudio, Jr. 2015. "A Conversation with Claudio Acioly Jr. on UN-Habitat." *Georgetown Journal of International Affairs* 16 (2): 61–66.

Aerni, Philipp. 2016 "Coping with Migration-Induced Urban Growth: Addressing the Blind Spot of UN Habitat." *Sustainability* 8 (8): 1–21.

Carter, Donald K. 2016. *Remaking Post-Industrial Cities: Lessons from North America and Europe*. London: Routledge.

Croese, Sylvia, Liza Rose Cirolia, and Nick Graham. 2016. "Towards Habitat III: Confronting the Disjuncture between Global Policy and Local Practice on Africa's 'Challenge of Slums.'" *Habitat International* 53 (April): 237–42.

United Nations Population Fund (UNFPA)

The global human population reached an estimated 7.8 billion in early 2020 and is expected to continue to climb to around 9.7 billion by 2050. This worrying trend has become a leading global issue. Population growth is important at several levels. Most prominently, the increase in population raises questions about planetary and country capacities to effectively care for and maintain healthy populations. Second, this also engages issues of human security and access to reproductive services, as well as gender equality and economic development. UN efforts to deal with the rise in population often align with efforts to reduce poverty and advocate for reproductive health. Global efforts to address the challenges of population have expanded and the UN Population Fund (UNFPA) sits at the forefront of policy and programs, as well as debate and controversy surrounding this issue. The fund was initially created to serve as a channel to make resources available to developing countries who sought to moderate population growth. Since UNFPA's creation, the organization has taken on many new roles, including field operations that promote education, the distribution of family planning materials, and advocacy for the rights of women and girls.

The UN began gathering population data shortly after the organization's creation, with the establishment of the Population Commission as a Functional Commission under the Economic and Social Council (ECOSOC) in 1946 (renamed the Commission on Population and Development in 1994). The World Population Conference, held in Rome, was organized by the UN in 1954, with the Second World Population Conference meeting in 1965 in Belgrade. At the same time, the United States created a global initiative for family planning through the U.S. Agency for International Development (USAID) and advocated for the UN's partnership in this undertaking. Under Secretary-General U Thant, the UN established a Trust Fund for Population Activities in 1967 to help developing countries with research and training. This fund began functioning in 1969 as the UN Fund for Population Activities, operating under the UN Development Programme (UNDP) before becoming a General Assembly fund in 1972. In 1987, the fund was renamed the UN Population Fund (although the original acronym of UNFPA remains).

RESPONSIBILITIES

UNFPA's early mandate emphasized fostering knowledge and capacity on family planning. The organization was also called on to enhance awareness about and develop strategies for population problems, as well as to provide coordination in the UN System. Over the years, the agenda of UNFPA evolved and expanded. For instance, the 1994 International Conference on Population and Development (ICPD) held in Cairo, Egypt, called for a more comprehensive approach to include gender rights and the Programme of Action adopted guides much of UNFPA's work. To support the 2000 Millennium Development Goals, UNFPA began a more systematic approach to integrating education and economic development. With the adoption of the Sustainable Development Goals (SDGs), in 2015 UNFPA refocused its agenda in relation to the goals, especially SDG 3 on good health and well-being, SDG 4 on quality education, and SDG 5 on gender equality. The Nairobi Summit on ICPD25 was held in November 2019, and the Nairobi Statement concluded at this meeting also shapes UNFPA's focus moving forward.

STRUCTURE

UNFPA is headquartered in New York but administers programs through over 120 country offices and 6 regional offices. UNFPA's original governing body was the Governing Council of UNDP, but this was replaced at the beginning of 1994 with an Executive Board consisting of thirty-six member states to oversee UNDP, UNFPA, and the UN Office for Project Services. A Bureau of the Executive Board consists of one President and four Vice-Presidents, with each officeholder coming from a different regional group. Executive Board membership is also apportioned by region: the African states have eight members, Asian states have seven,

Eastern European states hold four seats, Latin American and the Caribbean states have five, and Western European and Other states have twelve. Executive Board members are elected by ECOSOC and serve three-year terms. Within UNFPA, there is an Executive Director appointed by the Secretary-General. This position was most recently filled in October 2017, when Dr. Natalia Kanem was selected by Secretary-General António Guterres. UNFPA operates primarily on voluntary contributions from governments, as well as funds provided by individuals, foundations, and the private sector. In 1973, the fund ran with a modest budget of $52 million, but by 2018 total contributions reached over $1.2 billion.

ACTIVITIES

UNFPA promotes reproductive health care for women and youth in countries across the globe. The organization reported in 2018 that it "procured the equivalent of a year's worth of contraception for about 68 million couples in developing countries." To realize the agency's mission statement "to deliver a world where every pregnancy is wanted, every childbirth is safe and every young person's potential is fulfilled," UNFPA seeks to provide universal access to reproductive health services, reduce maternal mortality, and assist with family planning and reproductive education. In recent years, these issues have dovetailed to a greater degree with efforts toward development, the protection of human rights, and a public health-based approach. UNFPA assists governments, at their request, with formulating policies and strategies to reduce poverty and support sustainable development. Furthermore, the fund supports countries as they collect and analyze population data and assess information on population trends. These government-level activities include education campaigns and training of birth attendants. Field operations promote voluntary family planning, sexuality education, maternal health, health care support, and training for midwives to assist with pre- and postnatal care. These activities include supplying clean delivery kits, supporting programs to keep girls in school, preventing child marriages, and discouraging female genital mutilation.

After the World Population Conferences of 1954 and 1965, UNFPA played a central role in the 1974 World Population Conference in Bucharest, Romania; the International Conference on Population in Mexico City, Mexico; and the 1994 ICPD and 2019 ICPD follow-up summit. This has included raising funds to hold the conferences, providing planning guidance, and having the Executive Director serve as Secretary-General of the conference. UNFPA is also designed to work collaboratively and engage with many nongovernmental organizations, as well as other UN bodies, including the Joint United Nations Programme on HIV/AIDS (UNAIDS), UN Children's Fund, UN Entity for Gender Equality and the Empowerment of Women (UN Women), and World Health Organization. UNFPA's activities are promoted by Goodwill Ambassadors, such as actress Ashley Judd and Queen Mother Ashi Sangay Choden Wangchuck of Bhutan. Within the UN System itself, UNFPA contributes to the policy-making process by participating in deliberations, providing technical information to the General Assembly, and engaging with other parts of ECOSOC like the Regional Commissions. UNFPA is a founding member of the UN Development Group (now the UN Sustainable Development Group), which was established in 1997 to improve the coordination and consistency of UN development programs.

CHALLENGES AND REFORM

The issues surrounding family planning are often controversial as they include contraception, abortion, and women's reproductive rights. Thus, for much of UNFPA's existence, the organization has been the focus of political controversy over its mandate, field operations, and policies. UNFPA's assistance to countries that allow abortions created political backlash in the United States during the 1980s and resulted in the cutting of all financial support under the Reagan administration. This move was repeated in 2002 under George W. Bush administration due to concerns regarding UNFPA's relationship with China and its "One-Child Policy," yet it was reversed under the Obama administration, only to be cut again in 2017 under the Trump administration. Family planning also creates tensions with the Catholic Church and the government of Iran. UNFPA's ongoing work with faith-based organizations is an effort to ensure cultural sensitivity and create partnerships in family planning and educational programs. UNFPA also faces jurisdictional issues with other UN agencies, such as UNAIDS. Regardless of administrative and funding challenges, UNFPA is well-known for its advocacy, country programs, and monitoring of population issues and will continue to lead global efforts to address population growth, reproduction, and gender rights.

See also: António Guterres; Economic and Social Council; Economic Development; Functional Commissions; General Assembly; Goodwill Ambassadors and Messengers of Peace; Human Security; Joint United Nations Programme on HIV/AIDS; Regional Commissions; Sustainable Development Goals; U Thant; United Nations Children's Fund; United Nations Conferences and Summits; United Nations Development Programme; United Nations Educational, Scientific and Cultural Organization; United Nations Entity for Gender Equality and the Empowerment of Women; Women and Gender; World Health Organization.

FURTHER READING

Farkas, Rachel. 2003. "The Bush Administration's Decision to Defund the United Nations Population Fund and Its Implications for Women in Developing Nations." *Berkeley Women's Law Journal* 18 (1): 237–53.

Karam, Azza. 2010. "The United Nations Population Fund's (UNFPA's) Legacy of Engaging Faith-Based Organizations as Cultural Agents of Change." *CrossCurrents* 60 (3): 432–50.

Larson, Heidi, and Michael R. Reich. 2009. "The Political Limits of the United Nations in Advancing Reproductive Health and Rights." In *Reproductive Health and Human Rights: The Way Forward*, edited by Laura Reichenbach and Mindy Jane Roseman, 196–210. Philadelphia: University of Pennsylvania Press.

Sadik, Nafis. 2002. *An Agenda for People: The UNFPA through Three Decades*. New York: New York University Press.

United Nations Relief and Works Agency for Palestine Refugees in the Near East (UNRWA)

Since the early days of the UN, the organization has worked to provide relief for victims of war and conflict. In December 1949, the General Assembly adopted Resolution 302 to assist Palestinians displaced due to the 1948 Arab-Israeli conflict. This created the UN Relief and Works Agency for Palestine Refugees in the Near East (UNRWA), which started operations in May 1950. While the agency was originally designed to serve 750,000 refugees, that number has since increased to around 5.5 million. Years of failed peace agreements undermined UNRWA's initial goal of repatriation and resettlement as most refugees did not want to be resettled in different countries and Israel refused repatriation. Making operations more difficult, UNRWA has faced repeated waves of violence, including the 1967 Arab-Israeli War, the 1973 Yom Kippur War, two Palestinian intifadas (uprisings), conflict in the Gaza Strip, a civil war in Lebanon, and the three-week Gaza War that started at the end of 2008. Most recently, the conflict in Syria (2011–) has impacted refugee camps that UNRWA supports. This wave of violence destroyed thousands of Palestinian homes and damaged the local economy and infrastructure. Such ongoing vulnerabilities undermine both long-term stability for the region and security for the Palestinian refugees and present strenuous challenges to UNRWA's ability to carry out its mandate.

RESPONSIBILITIES

UNRWA was set up as a temporary approach to address the immediate needs of the Palestinian refugees who fled in 1948. The agency's original mandate set by the General Assembly was "to prevent starvation and distress and to further the conditions for peace and stability." Furthermore, the original jurisdiction covered "persons whose normal place of residence was Palestine during the period 1 June 1946 to 15 May 1948, and who lost both home and means of livelihood as a result of the 1948 conflict." Today, this authority covers the descendants of the displaced, which means that UNRWA now serves four generations. UNRWA's annual report declares the organization's mission as to "help Palestine refugees in Jordan, Lebanon, Syria, West Bank and the Gaza Strip achieve their full human development potential pending a just solution to their plight." UNRWA holds an unusual position as it has evolved from a temporary relief agency to a quasi-governmental human development agency with a variety of programs that provide education, health care, economic development, and human rights advocacy. UNRWA remains a temporary organization, with its mandate continually renewed (most recently in December 2019, with the mandate extended to 2023).

STRUCTURE

UNRWA reports directly to the General Assembly and is headed by a Commissioner-General, who is appointed by the Secretary-General in consultation with the UNRWA Advisory Commission. This position is supported by a Deputy Commissioner-General. They oversee several substantive departments, including the Departments of Education, Health, Relief and Social Services, and Infrastructure and Camp Improvement. The General Assembly established the Advisory Commission, often referred to as AdCom, whose primary directive is to advise and assist the Commissioner-General. As of early 2020, this body includes twenty-eight members and four observers (European Union, League of Arab States, Organization of Islamic Cooperation, and Palestine) and is guided by a Chair and Vice-Chair, with one officer from a host country and one from a donor country. AdCom holds meetings twice a year, typically in June and November, in Amman, Jordan, and is supported by a Sub-Committee, which has a Bureau made up of the Chair of the Sub-Committee and two Vice-Chairs.

The organization has two headquarters, one in Amman and the other in the Gaza Strip. Field offices are supported in Gaza, Jordan, Lebanon, Syria, the West Bank, as well as liaison offices in New York, Washington, DC, Brussels (Belgium), and Cairo (Egypt). There are also a Spokesperson Office and Department of Microfinance in Jerusalem. Within Jordan, UNRWA assists with ten refugee camps. With over 30,000 staff members, many of which are Palestinians, UNRWA's operation is one of the biggest in the UN System. UNRWA reports that around 93 percent of the agency's funds come through voluntary contributions from member states, regional bodies like the European Union, foundations, non-governmental organizations, and private donors. In 2017, UNRWA reported total contributions of just over $1.1 billion, with the largest financier being the United States as it pledged $364 million. However, U.S. President Donald Trump's administration announced in 2018 that funding to the organization would be cut. UNRWA's end of 2018 financial report indicates that the agency still brought in almost $1.3 billion due to a positive response by other donors to provide additional contributions (the United States ranked sixth for the year with the $60 million donated before funds were suspended). The loss of U.S. support makes reaching UNRWA's funding targets in future years more difficult.

ACTIVITIES

UNRWA has altered and changed its program focus to address the variable and complex needs of Palestine refugees. A previous Commissioner-General, Georgio Giacomelli, highlights this adaptability: "UNRWA's mandate is flexible, not explicit. We provide the refugees with the help they need, when they need it." Although UNRWA began as a relief operation to address the immediate needs of a displaced community, the agency's mission grew from temporary food and shelter assistance to offering educational, health, and social services. Unlike many other programmes and funds, UNRWA provides services directly to its population of concern, operating schools and a program that oversees health clinics. UNRWA also runs a microfinance operation that provides loans and emergency financial assistance to Palestine refugees. Beyond this, the agency runs and maintains refugee camp infrastructure as well as some protective services. UNRWA reports educating around 530,000 children and providing health care services to 3.1 million people each year. In addition, the agency has distributed almost 476,000 micro loans, equaling over $530 million, since 1991. These services are provided to a community that often has limited access to electricity, fuel, food, and health care. UNRWA often works with the World Health Organization and the UN Educational, Scientific and Cultural Organization to provide services. Controversially, the agency has raised concerns regarding alleged Palestinian human rights violations, such as detentions, land confiscation, violations during riot control, and discrimination in the judicial system.

CHALLENGES AND REFORM

Unlike other refugee agencies and UN programmes and funds, UNRWA has seen little success with long-term solutions and operates under significant political, financial, and operational uncertainty. As the agency's work is ultimately tied to the prolonged Israeli-Palestinian conflict, UNRWA faces significant challenges in realizing permanent solutions. Thus, the organization's efforts remain highly relevant yet continually thwarted. UNRWA has come under significant criticism as the Israeli-Palestinian conflict has progressed. There are those that promote a limited role for UNRWA that avoids political advocacy and claim the organization should only focus on providing relief assistance. At the same time, there are others who view UNRWA as an appropriate venue for the promotion of a permanent solution to the refugee issue, advocacy of human rights, and even the mediation of the overall conflict. Another area of controversy concerns the right of descendants of Palestinian women to be recognized as refugees. Currently, only descendants of Palestinian men are given such status, which results in accusations against UNRWA of not promoting gender parity.

UNRWA also faces a lack of sustained and reliable funding, and the funding the agency does receive has not kept pace with growth in the Palestinian population. These financial challenges produce overcrowded classrooms, inadequate health care access, and crumbling infrastructure. UNRWA also faces mixed messages from Israel. The agency operates at the request and permission of the host states in which it operates and must work with governments, particularly Israel, to carry out the directives of the General Assembly. This is most challenging in the case of Israel, which has most often been supportive of UNRWA's presence but also critical in the face of UNRWA's accusations of human rights violations on the part of Israel. Aggravating these difficulties, when the United States cut funding to UNRWA in 2018 this move was supported by Israeli Prime Minister Benjamin Netanyahu. The implications of this development are contested within Israel as security agencies express concern that a sharp decrease in UNRWA's services may lead to a governance vacuum that will cause a humanitarian crisis. This could enhance opportunities for groups like Hamas and potentially destabilize the region. UNRWA's harshest critics claim that the agency perpetuates the Palestinian identity and their ongoing refugee status, which, in turn, creates incentives against long-term repatriation. Despite these and other challenges, UNRWA continues working with a population facing chronic challenges and uncertainty in a resilient and adaptive manner.

See also: General Assembly; Human Rights; Refugees and Migration; Self-Determination; United Nations Educational, Scientific and Cultural Organization; United Nations High Commissioner for Refugees; World Health Organization.

FURTHER READING

Bartholomeusz, Lance. 2010. "The Mandate of UNRWA at Sixty." *Refugee Survey Quarterly* 28 (2–3): 452–74.

Bocco, Riccardo. 2010. "UNRWA and the Palestinian Refugees: A History within History." *Refugee Survey Quarterly* 28 (2–3): 229–52.

Brooks-Rubin, Liana, 2014. "Whither UNRWA?" In *The Palestinian Refugee Problem*, edited by Rex Brynen and Roula El-Rifai, 54–75. London: Pluto Press.

Feldman, Ilana. 2012. "The Challenge of Categories: UNRWA and the Definition of a 'Palestine Refugee.'" *Journal of Refugee Studies* 25 (3): 387–406.

Hanafi, Sari, Leila Hilal, and Lex Takkenberg, eds. 2014. *UNRWA and Palestinian Refugees: From Relief and Works to Human Development*. New York: Routledge.

World Food Programme (WFP)

In a world divided by those who have enough to eat and those who do not, the ability to guide food aid and development projects to areas of need is a vital dimension of global food support. John Boyd Orr, the first Director-General of the Food and Agriculture Organization (FAO), put forth an initial plan in 1946 to create a World Food Board. This body was designed, in part, to ensure that agricultural surplus would be distributed to countries lacking in food, but this effort did not come to fruition. In a time when U.S. surpluses continued to expand, the General Assembly passed a resolution in 1960 inviting the FAO to explore new arrangements for the distribution of food aid. In 1961, the FAO produced an expert group report, which received U.S. support, especially from George McGovern (Director of the US Office for Food and Peace at the time), at an advisory committee meeting review of the report. That same year, the General Assembly and FAO jointly approved the creation of the World Food Programme (WFP). Basic bureaucratic functions began in 1962, with a three-year experimental probationary period of operations from 1963 to 1965. The organization's mandate was extended from the end of 1965 by another set of parallel General Assembly and FAO resolutions for "a continuing basis for as long as multilateral food aid is found feasible and desirable." The WFP continues operations from its headquarters in Rome, Italy, where the FAO and the International Food and Agricultural Fund are also based.

RESPONSIBILITIES

The WFP guides international food distribution and assistance. The WFP's General Regulations specify that the organization's purposes are to support development through the use of food aid, address emergency relief food needs, and promote food security in the world. Food aid is employed to assist with economic and social development programs. Emergency food relief covers refugees and other populations lacking food due to natural or human-made disasters in the immediate aftermath and during the postdisaster recovery period. From the WFP's modest roots, the scope of the organization's responsibilities greatly expanded. Today, the WFP is the largest multilateral humanitarian agency addressing food needs in the world.

STRUCTURE

The structural capabilities of the WFP have shifted dramatically since the organization's creation as a joint UN-FAO program. While the WFP was supervised by both the UN and the FAO, the FAO predominantly dictated WFP affairs, including taking responsibility for technical assistance and approving emergency aid. The FAO-WFP structural connection became problematic as the WFP developed, especially during the time of difficult relations between WFP Executive Director James Ingram (1982–1992) and FAO Director-General Edouard Saouma (1976–1993). The outcome of this clash favored the WFP, with the body separating from the FAO and gaining significant managerial and operational independence. The WFP still reports to the UN and the FAO, and both play a role in selecting the WFP representatives. The WFP's governing body, the Executive Board, consists of thirty-six members, half elected by the Economic and Social Council and half by the FAO, with twenty-one from developing countries (eight Africa, seven Asia/Middle East, five Latin America and the Caribbean, and one rotating seat across the regions), twelve from Western developed countries, and three from Eastern Europe.

The WFP Executive Director is appointed by the UN Secretary-General and the FAO Director-General. The position has been held by a U.S. national ever since Catherine Bertini (1992–2002) took over the now more independent WFP from the Australian Ingram. Further leadership support is provided by a Deputy Executive Director and three Assistant Executive Directors. While the WFP started as a small organization, there are now thousands of staff based around the world in various country field offices. The WFP's membership is drawn from the countries participating in the UN or the FAO, so the body's 195 members is more than the UN due to the additional members of Cook Islands and Niue. The WFP operates with one of the largest resource bases in the UN System. The member states are the primary contributors to the WFP, although some support also comes from the private sector and individual personal donations. All contributions are voluntary and include food supplies, services such as shipping and storage, and financial resources, with the United States the largest donor.

ACTIVITIES

For approximately the first thirty years, the WFP committed the majority of its resources to development projects, but in the face of the rising number and increased scale of disasters the emphasis flipped with up to 90 percent of the operational budget committed to emergency food aid assistance. WFP development programs are designed to address food deficiencies and to remove the population's need for food aid by bolstering nutritional progress and sustainable livelihoods, especially via support for women and children. Humanitarian relief requires careful logistical planning and implementation to ensure the efficient delivery of food aid. In reaction to a disaster, the WFP determines a thorough plan of action for the level of needed assistance and the best method of delivery. Longer-term assistance is also provided for populations requiring protracted relief. Potential emergency situations are monitored using vulnerability analysis to ensure being properly prepared and able to act to limit the impact of a crisis and to promote the best ability of the population to recover.

The WFP's role, as explained in the General Regulations, is "to provide services" to other entities "for operations which are consistent with the purposes of the WFP and which complement WFP's operations." In the early years, WFP's coordination with other organizations was focused around the FAO. As the WFP extended its abilities and gained independence, the agency increasingly connected with other institutions. A notable example is an agreement with the UN High Commissioner for Refugees, where the WFP takes on the central role in providing food to refugees in times of humanitarian crisis. As part of the WFP's emphasis on the hunger and nutrition needs of women and children, the agency coordinates with organizations such as the UN Children's Fund. The WFP also works closely with a range of nongovernmental organizations for food aid delivery and supervision.

CHALLENGES AND REFORM

A challenge for the WFP is meeting short-term food needs while encouraging long-term development. In general, the shift from an emphasis on development to emergency activities limits the organization's focus on more extended programmatic planning. Another concern is that dependence on food aid may impede funding and planning by receiving governments to improve food production and access. Some critics argue that the WFP is too focused on donor demands over recipient interests. This includes distributing food surpluses from economically developed countries in a manner that can undermine local food prices and pursuing policies that normalize a cycle of food insecurity instead of providing for the means to avoid disasters. Given the WFP's reliance on voluntary contributions, the organization must balance operating in a manner that maintains and widens donor support with recipient requirements. Despite an extensive budget, given the scope of food emergencies around the globe a major challenge for the WFP is ensuring the needed level of resources. Spikes in food prices affect the WFP's purchasing power and exacerbate financing issues. The WFP's financing model is based primarily on responding to crises, so the organization could benefit from more stable resource provision and financial management.

The WFP wrestles with corruption that disrupts and diverts food aid distribution, which the organization seeks to counter by more directly implementing distribution.

This level of local control also allows the WFP to use greater gender-based programming, including at times by excluding men from distribution centers to limit the possibility of corruption although critics of this approach argue that this can lead to young, single men facing higher levels of hunger and malnutrition. Overall, the WFP is viewed as one of the most successful and effective UN programs with a high level of support. The organization started small but adapted and expanded over time to take on a central position in providing humanitarian assistance. The WFP's food aid mandate is in place for as long as it is "feasible and desirable," so all signs point to the agency continuing to deliver essential assistance.

See also: Economic and Social Council; Economic Development; Executive Heads of Specialized Agencies; Food and Agriculture Organization; General Assembly; International Fund for Agricultural Development; Joint United Nations Programme on HIV/AIDS; Nongovernmental Organizations; Refugees and Migration; United Nations Children's Fund; United Nations High Commissioner for Refugees.

FURTHER READING

Charlton, Mark W. 1992. "Innovation and Inter-Organizational Politics: The Case of the World Food Programme." *International Journal* 47 (3): 630–65.

Ingram, James C. 2007. *Bread and Stones: Leadership and the Struggle to Reform the United Nations World Food Programme.* Charleston, SC: BookSurge.

O'Connor, Daniel, Philip Boyle, Suzan Ilcan, and Marcia Oliver. 2017. "Living with Insecurity: Food Security, Resilience, and the World Food Programme (WFP)." *Global Social Policy* 17 (1): 3–20.

Ramachandran, Vijaya, Benjamin Leo, and Owen McCarthy. 2013. "Strategies to Improve the World Food Programme's Revenue Mobilisation and Procurement Practices." *Development Policy Review* 31 (3): 321–41.

Shaw, D. John. 2011. *The World's Largest Humanitarian Agency: The Transformation of the UN World Food Programme and of Food Aid.* New York: Palgrave Macmillan.

OTHER SUBSIDIARY BODIES

Disarmament Commission

Tasked with maintaining international peace and security, from the early days of its operations the UN sought to establish institutional mechanisms to promote the elimination of weapons. In 1946, the General Assembly set up the Atomic Energy Commission and the next year the Security Council instituted a Commission for Conventional Armaments. After little progress was made, these two bodies were merged into a single Disarmament Commission by the General Assembly in 1952. Work within this eleven-member body was undermined by the Cold War clash and competing propaganda efforts between Western countries and the Soviet Union, leading to the creation of a subcommittee for focusing on discussions between Canada, France, the Soviet Union, the United Kingdom, and the United States. By 1957, the Soviets, claiming in part that they were outnumbered, refused to participate in either body. The Disarmament Commission was expanded to twenty-five members, and then to all members of the UN. Nonetheless, the body still barely managed to convene a meeting. Following the first Special Session of the General Assembly on Disarmament (SSOD-I) in 1978, a renewed Disarmament Commission with representatives from all UN members was launched. The Disarmament Commission remains the sole distinct body within the UN System, which provides a universal forum for all members to come together to discuss limiting and removing arms from the global arena.

RESPONSIBILITIES

The Disarmament Commission is a subsidiary body of the General Assembly responsible for further consideration of outcomes of Special Sessions of the General Assembly on Disarmament. A second special session was held in 1982 and a third in 1988, although a substantive outcome document was only generated at the end of the SSOD-I. Further direction on the work of the Disarmament Commission comes from additional General Assembly resolutions. Such mandates emerge from the work of the First Committee, which focuses on disarmament and international security. As a deliberative body, the Disarmament Commission provides a venue for open discussion of disarmament issues, but the body only provides recommendations, it cannot create resolutions or binding actions.

STRUCTURE

The Disarmament Commission usually meets at UN Headquarters in New York for a three-week period in the spring and then reports to the General Assembly. The meeting includes plenary gatherings and working groups, the number of which varies depending on the agenda, and is chaired on a rotating geographical basis. As part of the broader disarmament structure of the UN, the Disarmament Commission is supported by the Office for Disarmament Affairs in the Secretariat. Also emerging from SSOD-I, the sixty-five-member Conference on Disarmament (a successor to previous, smaller committees on disarmament) was established in 1979 in Geneva, Switzerland. The Disarmament Commission is set up to provide a universal discussion forum to debate the normative approach to disarmament, while the smaller Conference on Disarmament operates to negotiate specific multilateral disarmament agreements. The Conference on Disarmament is an autonomous body that meets three times a year but maintains a close relationship with the UN, including reporting to the General Assembly. The UN Institute for Disarmament Research, which opened in 1980, is also based in Geneva and provides data, analysis, and support for disarmament negotiations.

ACTIVITIES

The Disarmament Commission's deliberations on disarmament issues are built around a focused agenda in order to provide in-depth discussion on those items. For example, the 2018 agenda had two main items: nuclear disarmament and nonproliferation of nuclear weapons and preventing an arms race in outer space. Recommendations, guidelines, and principles that emerge can then be approved by the General Assembly. In recent years, providing this outcome document has been a challenge, with a large gap between the 1999 guidelines issued on conventional arms control/limitations and disarmament and the 2017 recommendations on practical confidence-building measures in the field of conventional weapons. There has been an even longer delay in convening SSOD-IV, which was called for by the General Assembly in 1995, due to the member states' inability to agree upon the central objectives and related agenda for this special session. The General Assembly created a series of Working Groups since 2003 (with subsequent efforts in 2007 and 2016) for examining possible goals and agenda items, as well as forming a full preparatory committee for SSOD-IV, but this effort is ongoing.

CHALLENGES AND REFORM

The work of the Disarmament Commission is mostly viewed as drawn-out and relatively ineffective. From the Commission's early iteration to its current form, the body is often undermined by distrust and competing political agendas between the participating member states. Disputes over the agenda have impeded the ability for the body to provide concrete ideas for periods of time. While disarmament is a difficult global issue to address in the best of circumstances, the body is critiqued for its internal organizational issues, working methods, and rules of procedure. Any progress on global disarmament measures largely occurs through other means. The limitations present in the Disarmament Commission have led to calls for reform, including in Secretary-General Kofi Annan's 1997 *Renewing the United Nations: A Programme for Reform*. Ongoing recommendations for reform emphasize improving communication and agenda coordination across the Disarmament Commission, General Assembly First Committee, and the Conference for Disarmament. If such reforms cannot be successfully implemented to strengthen the Disarmament Commission, then some are calling for an end to its work and transferring the deliberations of this body to other venues. For now, the Disarmament Commission remains the universal meeting place for discussion and reinforcement of the international community's commitment to pursuing disarmament.

See also: Arms Control and Disarmament; General Assembly; International Atomic Energy Agency; Kofi Annan; Organization for the Prohibition of Chemical Weapons; Research and Training Institutes; United Nations Purposes.

FURTHER READING

Bourantonis, Dimitris. 1993. *The United Nations and the Quest for Nuclear Disarmament*. Brookfield, VT: Dartmouth College Press.

Gillis, Melissa. 2017. *Disarmament: A Basic Guide*. Fourth edition. New York: United Nations Office for Disarmament Affairs.

Godsberg, Alicia. 2011. "Nuclear Disarmament and the United Nations Disarmament Machinery." *ILSA Journal of International and Comparative Law* 18 (2): 581–95.

Morales Pedraza, Jorge. 2016. "The Reform of the United Nations Disarmament Machinery." *Public Organization Review* 16 (3): 319–34.

Functional Commissions

Article 68 of the UN Charter authorizes the Economic and Social Council (ECOSOC) to "set up commissions in economic and social fields and for the promotion of human rights, and such other commissions as may be required for the performance of its functions." ECOSOC quickly took advantage of this power to set up a range of commissions in 1946. These include the Commission for Social Development (CSD, renamed in 1966 from Social Commission), Commission on Narcotic Drugs (CND), Commission on the Status of Women (CSW), and the Statistical Commission. That same year the Population Commission was established, which was renamed with an expanded focus as Commission on Population and Development (CPD) in 1994. Various groups and committees of experts working on the prevention of crime date back to 1948, with the current Commission on Crime Prevention and Criminal Justice (CCPCJ) beginning operations in 1992. The Commission on Science and Technology for Development (CSTD) also started in 1992, building upon the 1979 intergovernmental committee working on this topic. The UN Forum on Forests (UNFF), put into place in 2000, is not explicitly labeled as a Commission. Although the UN itself often lists UNFF as one of the Functional Commissions, others classify UNFF instead as a separate expert body advising ECOSOC similar to the Permanent Forum on Indigenous Issues.

RESPONSIBILITIES

The Commissions serve as deliberative bodies to examine and make recommendations to ECOSOC on the issues that fall under their mandate. By providing expertise in particular fields, the Commissions are designed to serve as authoritative bodies to inform policy prescriptions to ECOSOC. For example, the CPD tracks population trends, develops strategies to counter population issues, and addresses questions and provides advice on integrating population and development policies and programs.

STRUCTURE

The Functional Commissions are important subsidiary units that report directly to ECOSOC but do not have as much autonomy compared to ECOSOC's Regional Commissions. All of the Functional Commissions are guided under a shared set of rules of procedure, but each developed distinct structures and operations to match their area of focus. This leads some Commissions to serve a wider structural role in the UN System. In one example, the CND and CCPCJ act as governing bodies in the broader UN Office on Drugs and Crime. The Commissions are often supported by other parts of the UN System. For instance, given the shared development emphasis, the UN Conference on Trade and Development provides administrative support to the CSTD. Membership levels vary slightly across the Commissions, and the size of each Commission can shift across time, with the number of members (as of 2019) ranging from Statistical Commission (twenty-four) to CND (fifty-three) and in between with CCPCJ (forty), CSTD (forty-three), CSW (forty-five), CSD (forty-six), and CPD (forty-seven). Terms of membership are usually for four years. UNFF is different, operating as a universal forum for all UN member states along with representatives from specialized agencies and other related organizations. "Major groups" of forest-related stakeholders are also welcome to participate in sessions and meetings, and the UNFF also has a Collaborative Partnership of Forests with other international institutions from within the UN System, such as the UN Environment Programme, and outside the UN, including the International Tropical Timber Organization.

ACTIVITIES

In their role as expert bodies, the Commissions collect and study a range of information within their area of responsibility. The Commissions disseminate this information and use it to formulate priorities, recommendations, and strategies. Where there are related standards and conventions, some of which emerge from global conferences, the Commissions can assess progress and adherence to these agreements. For example, the CSD monitors the implementation of the Copenhagen Declaration and Programme of Action from the 1995 World Summit for Social Development. Each Commission concentrates on distinct issues areas, although coordination, mainly in the form of participation in meetings and the sharing of documents, can occur where there is overlap. While most Commissions focus on substantive issues, the Statistical Commission provides guidance for standards, methods, compilation, and dissemination of international statistics.

CHALLENGES AND REFORM

Compared to more independent institutions in the UN System, the Functional Commissions are often perceived as possessing a relatively marginalized status, which leads to calls for upgrading the institutional status of some Commissions. This shift did occur in 2006 when the Human Rights Council replaced the Commission on Human Rights and again in 2013 when the High-level Political Forum on Sustainable Development replaced the Commission on Sustainable Development. There are also questions raised regarding the potential overlap and duplication of work by the Commissions and other bodies in the UN System. For example, the long-standing CSW now shares institutional space with the UN Entity for Gender Equality and the Empowerment of Women (UN Women) and other gender focused activities in the UN, although some argue that the discussion and policy focus of Commissions differentiate their work from the bodies focused on implementing programs. The Commissions are called upon to better coordinate and collaborate between themselves and other actors working on similar themes in the UN System. As central forums for debate and discussion, there are concerns that the interests of developing countries are at times not well represented. Dating back to the first year of UN operations, the Functional Commissions are a longstanding part of the work of the UN within ECOSOC.

See also: Economic and Social Council; High-level Political Forum on Sustainable Development; Human Rights Council; Permanent Forum on Indigenous Issues; Regional Commissions; United Nations Conference on Trade and Development; United Nations Entity for Gender Equality and the Empowerment of Women; United Nations Environment Programme; United Nations Population Fund; Women and Gender.

FURTHER READING

Clark, Roger S. 2011. "The Role of the United Nations." In *International Crime and Justice*, edited by Mangai Natarajan, 337–42. Cambridge: Cambridge University Press.

Farrior, Stephanie. 2009. "United Nations Commission on the Status of Women." In *Encyclopedia of Human Rights*, edited by David P. Forsythe. Oxford: Oxford University Press. Available at www.oxfordreference.com.

Fazey, Cindy S. J. 2003. "The Commission on Narcotic Drugs and the United Nations International Drug Control Programme: Politics, Policies and Prospect for Change." *International Journal of Drug Policy* 14 (2): 155–69.

Humphreys, David. 2001. "The Creation of the United Nations Forum on Forests." *Environmental Politics* 10 (1): 160–66.

High-level Political Forum on Sustainable Development (HLPF)

In 2012, the UN Conference on Sustainable Development (Rio+20) undertook an ambitious effort to craft an integrated approach to sustainable development. The conference built on the Millennium Development Goals (MDGs) of 2000 and brought together the priorities of economic and social development with environmental protection. The delegates drafted an outcome document (anticipating the expiration of the MDGs in 2015) titled "The Future We Want" and called for the creation of a set of goals with priorities and benchmarks, which led to the Sustainable Development Goals (SDGs) adopted in 2015. The second objective was to secure voluntary commitments from governments and other stakeholders to implement those goals. The High-level Political Forum on Sustainable Development (HLPF) supplanted the Commission on Sustainable Development (CSD), which had been meeting since 1993. Critics found that the CSD did not include high-level political officials or key players in the economic sector and lacked the prestige to encourage the robust commitments necessary for achieving the SDGs. While proposals were made to reform the CSD, others wanted to create a Council on Sustainable Development. Delegates at Rio+20 compromised and created a hybrid organization to provide a forum with different levels of meetings. In

July 2013, the General Assembly adopted Resolution 67/290, formally replacing the CSD with the HLPF.

RESPONSIBILITIES

HLPF's mandate is ambitious as the forum is directed to serve as the center for political leadership and management of the SDGs. Within this context, the HLPF is supposed to "provide a dynamic platform for regular dialogue," along with "stocktaking" and "agenda-setting." The forum is also called upon to act as an accountability venue and to follow up and review SDG implementation. The body also promotes coherent and coordinated sustainable development policies and integration across the three different aspects of sustainable development (economic, environmental, and social).

STRUCTURE

As a hybrid body, the HLPF serves under the sponsorships of both the General Assembly and the Economic and Social Council (ECOSOC). Every UN member state is eligible for membership in the HLPF, although participation is voluntary. The HLPF convenes every four years under the General Assembly as an intergovernmental forum where Heads of State and Government are the primary participants and the meeting is chaired by the President of the General Assembly. In contrast, the HLPF meets annually under ECOSOC, where the body is convened and chaired by the President of ECOSOC and the primary attendees are at the ministerial level. Thus, following the approval of the SDGs in 2015, there was a meeting (referred to as the SDG Summit) at the General Assembly in September 2019, which was preceded by a separate meeting in July 2019 under ECOSOC's guidance. All relevant organizations within the UN System are provided access and allowed to contribute at meetings. There is also an open invitation to representatives of business, industry, and nongovernmental organizations to encourage engagement by all sustainable development stakeholders. Such civil society actors have access to official documents, can attend HLPF meetings, and submit documents and recommendations. The Office for Intergovernmental Support and Coordination for Sustainable Development of the UN Department of Economic and Social Affairs acts as the Secretariat of the HLPF.

ACTIVITIES

The HLPF is not a distinct organization, but instead a forum that brings together actors within the UN System. Thus, activities center on the meetings. In September 2013, the HLPF convened its first meeting at the beginning of the General Assembly's 68th session. In 2018, more than 2,200 participants attended the ECOSOC-led session, including over 125 Heads and Deputy Heads of State and Government, Ministers, Vice-Ministers, and other officials. The eight days of meetings (which includes a three-day ministerial session) under ECOSOC are the annual high point of HLPF activities, where priorities and best practices are highlighted. For both meetings, HLPF's primary activities include "orchestration" as the forum directs and assists governments and other stakeholders in the coordination of implementing the SDGs. As a hub organization, the HLPF links civil society, institutions, and member states and offers leadership in the form of goal setting and innovation. A wide array of side events explore particular areas and provide avenues for interaction between the actors attending. The HLPF serves as an accountability mechanism when countries present their Voluntary National Reviews (VNR) of progress in fulfilling the SDGs. Each forum produces a declaration to be presented to the General Assembly for consideration. Each year, the HLPF focuses on a theme and set of goals. For example, the 2017 theme was "Eradicating Poverty and Promoting Prosperity in a Changing World" with a focus on SDGs 1, 2, 3, 5, 9, and 14 compared to the 2019 theme of "Empowering People and Ensuring Inclusiveness and Equality" and SDGs 4, 8, 10, 13, and 16.

CHALLENGES AND REFORM

One mark of HLPF success is the increase in VNR reporting countries. In 2016, there were only twenty-two, but the following three years saw forty-three, forty-six, and then forty-seven countries (including seven reporting for the second time) presenting. Observers point out that the countries at Rio+20 did not provide significant resources to HLPF to meet the ambitious agenda. Some find public presentations of VRNs to be a weak accountability mechanism and point to varying levels of quality in the reports. Furthermore, questioning of the VRNs is not usually robust, although there is progress toward reporting both advancements and challenge areas. Finally, while there are accountability mechanisms, there is no verification system. General Assembly Resolution 70/299 specified that the HLPF format and operations were to be reviewed during the Assembly's 74th session (2019–2020) to assess if changes should be implemented. Despite HLPF's weak points, many find success in the creation of goals, a public forum for communication, and multiple stakeholder engagement in support of the SDGs.

See also: Economic and Social Council; Functional Commissions; General Assembly; Nongovernmental Organizations; President of General Assembly; Sustainable Development; Sustainable Development Goals; United Nations Conferences and Summits.

FURTHER READING

Abbott, Kenneth W., and Steven Bernstein. 2015. "The High-level Political Forum on Sustainable Development: Orchestration by Default and Design." *Global Policy* 6 (3): 222–33.

Bernstein, Steven. 2017. "The United Nations and the Governance of Sustainable Development Goals." In *Governing through Goals: Sustainable Development Goals as Governance Innovation*, edited by Norichika Kanie and Frank Biermann, 213–39. Cambridge, MA: MIT Press.

Dodds, Felix, Jorge Laguna-Celis, and Liz Thompson. 2014. *From Rio+ 20 to a New Development Agenda: Building a Bridge to a Sustainable Future.* London: Routledge.

Strandenaes, Jan-Gustav. 2014. "Participatory Democracy—HLPF Laying the Basis for Sustainable Development Governance in the 21st Century." New York: UN Department of Economic and Social Affairs. Available at https://sustainabledevelopment.un.org/majorgroups/hlpfresources.

Human Rights Council

One of the UN's primary objectives is to promote respect for human rights. In 1946, the UN Commission on Human Rights was designed to carry out this work. However, by the early 2000s, many countries and nongovernmental organizations found the Commission to be ineffective. In response, Secretary-General Kofi Annan advocated for replacing the Commission. At the September 2005 UN World Summit plans to create a new organization were discussed, although there were controversies concerning size, membership, how members would be elected, and whether or not the body would be a major organ within the UN System. UN member states ultimately agreed to replace the Commission with a Human Rights Council. In March 2006, General Assembly Resolution 60/251 created the Human Rights Council as a subsidiary organ, with 170 votes in favor, 4 against (Israel, the United States, Palau, and Marshall Islands) and 3 abstentions (Belarus, Iran, and Venezuela). The Human Rights Council convened its first session in June 2006 and is headquartered in Geneva, Switzerland.

RESPONSIBILITIES

Resolution 60/251 states that the Human Rights Council is "responsible for promoting universal respect for the protection of all human rights and fundamental freedoms for all." The Human Rights Council focuses on the promotion and protection of the full range of human rights around the world and addresses instances of human rights violations. This includes evaluations of member states' human rights progress. The Human Rights Council provides a venue for dialogue on human rights issues, develops additional international human rights legal protections, and encourages coordination and incorporation of human rights across the UN System.

STRUCTURE

The Human Rights Council is comprised of forty-seven member states elected annually by the General Assembly via secret ballot. Members serve three-year staggered terms and represent geographic regions, with thirteen African states members, thirteen from Asian states, eight from Latin American and the Caribbean states, seven from the Western European and Others Group, and six representing Eastern Europe. As of April 2019, 114 of the 193 member states have been selected. States cannot serve more than two consecutive terms, and the General

Assembly may suspend a country's membership for committing "gross and systematic violations of human rights," as in the case of Libya in 2011.

The Human Rights Council includes a Bureau of the Council, composed of a President and four Vice-Presidents chosen from each of the five regional groups to serve for one year. The Office of the UN High Commissioner for Human Rights serves as the Secretariat. The Human Rights Council includes several subsidiary bodies. The Universal Periodic Review (UPR) Working Group reviews human rights conditions within all UN member states, the Advisory Committee lends expertise, and a Complaint Procedure hears allegations from individuals and organizations. The Human Rights Council also created "subsidiary expert mechanisms," which includes five expert forums to research and make recommendations: Expert Mechanism on the Rights of Indigenous People, Forum on Minority Issues, Social Forum, Forum on Business and Human Rights, and Forum on Human Rights, Democracy and the Rule of Law. Open-ended working groups examine means to better implement existing international legal protections and work on creating such protections for new human rights areas. Finally, independent experts are appointed via "Special Procedures" to examine thematic issues on a global scale or problems within a particular country.

ACTIVITIES

The Human Rights Council holds sessions at least three times per year, convening the 42nd session in September 2019. The main session runs across four weeks each February and March and, in accordance with its mandate, the Council must meet for a minimum of ten weeks per year. The Human Rights Council also convenes special sessions on particular topics, with the 28th special session held in May 2018 on "Violations of international law in the context of large-scale civilian protests in the Occupied Palestinian Territory, including East Jerusalem." One significant Human Rights Council innovation is the UPR process, where all member states are evaluated on their compliance with international human rights obligations across each UPR cycle (with the most recent third cycle running from 2017 to 2021). This process is intended to be supportive, with states not bound to accept each recommendation, and to encourage the overall improvement of human rights across the globe. In addition, the Human Rights Council reviews recommendations from a complaint procedure, reflecting the previous Commission on Human Rights 1503 procedure, which further brings awareness to potential human rights violations. In addition, the Human Rights Council carries out a wide range of independent investigations. The Human Rights Council also endorsed the Guiding Principles on Business and Human Rights as well as highlighted the importance of a human rights approach to disaster response, recovery, and reconstruction.

CHALLENGES AND REFORM

While the Human Rights Council does not hold enforcement power, the body can wield influence through "naming and shaming" a country. Yet, this can lead to

> **Human Rights Council Special Sessions**
>
> 2006—Human rights situation in the Occupied Palestinian Territories
>
> 2006—Human rights situation in Lebanon caused by Israeli military operations
>
> 2006—Israeli military incursions in Occupied Palestinian Territories
>
> 2006—Human rights situation in Darfur
>
> 2007—Human rights situation in Myanmar
>
> 2008—Human rights violations emanating from Israeli military incursions in the Occupied Palestinian Territories
>
> 2008—Impact of the world food crisis caused by soaring food prices on the right to food
>
> 2008—Human rights situation in the east of the Democratic Republic of the Congo
>
> 2009—The grave violations of human rights in the Occupied Palestinian Territory
>
> 2009—The impact of the global economic and financial crises on human rights
>
> 2009—Human rights situation in Sri Lanka
>
> 2009—Human rights situation in the Occupied Palestinian Territory
>
> 2010—Support to recovery process after earthquake in Haiti
>
> 2010—Human rights situation in Côte d'Ivoire
>
> 2011—Human rights situation in Libya
>
> 2011—Human rights situation in Syria
>
> 2011—Human rights situation in Syria
>
> 2011—Human rights situation in Syria
>
> 2012—Human rights situation in Syria
>
> 2014—Human rights situation in the Central African Republic
>
> 2014—Human rights situation in the Occupied Palestinian Territory
>
> 2014—Human rights situation in Iraq
>
> 2015—Terrorist attacks and human rights abuses and violations committed by the terrorist group Boko Haram
>
> 2015—Preventing further deterioration of the human rights situation in Burundi
>
> 2016—The deteriorating situation of human rights in Syria
>
> 2016—Human rights situation in South Sudan
>
> 2017—Human Rights situation of the minority Rohingya Muslim population and other minorities in the Rakhine State of Myanmar
>
> 2018—The deteriorating situation of human rights in the Occupied Palestinian Territory

backlash as several countries have either withdrawn from the Council or boycotted the UPR. While the UPR is a major innovation and mark of progress, it can be problematic since some reports are deliberately vague and countries under scrutiny can undermine the intended robust review process. The Human Rights Council faces similar criticism as its predecessor and, in June 2018, the United States withdrew, citing concerns with countries being elected to the Council with poor human rights records and a persistent anti-Israel bias. Yet, many of the more powerful countries are reluctant to impose membership criteria (i.e., China, Russia and even the United States) as they may fail to meet their own standards. The Human Rights Council is also highly politicized, with a clear divide between developed and developing countries, and the body is commonly criticized for selectivity. For instance, special sessions have been dominated by scrutiny of Israel and Syria, but not Yemen. The Human Rights Council is impactful through promoting new standards and procedures to highlight and inspire respect for human rights.

See also: Functional Commissions; General Assembly; Human Rights; Indigenous Peoples; Kofi Annan; Nongovernmental Organizations; United Nations Conferences and Summits; United Nations Headquarters; United Nations Purposes; United Nations Reform.

FURTHER READING

Boyle, Kevin. 2009. "The United Nations Human Rights Council: Origins, Antecedents, and Prospects." In *New Institutions for Human Rights Protection*, edited by Kevin Boyle, 11–47. Oxford: Oxford University Press.

Carraro, Valentina. 2017. "The United Nations Treaty Bodies and Universal Periodic Review: Advancing Human Rights by Preventing Politicization?" *Human Rights Quarterly* 39 (4): 943–70.

Cox, Eric. 2010. "State Interests and the Creation and Functioning of the United Nations Human Rights Council." *Journal of International Law and International Relations* 6 (1): 87–117.

Freedman, Rosa. 2013. *The United Nations Human Rights Council: A Critique and Early Assessment*. London: Routledge.

Joint United Nations Programme on HIV/AIDS (UNAIDS)

As an increasing number of cases of HIV/AIDS (human immunodeficiency virus that leads to acquired immunodeficiency syndrome) emerged in the 1980s, the UN realized that it faced a dangerous new threat to health on a global scale. Initially, HIV/AIDS was addressed through the World Health Organization (WHO), with the first programme launched in 1986 culminating in the renamed Global Programme on AIDS (GPA) in 1988. However, as the scope of the disease and the related need to coordinate across sectors engaged in working on HIV/AIDS-related issues became clear, the UN undertook an innovative form of institutional development designed to provide a coordinating mechanism. The Joint United Nations Programme on HIV/AIDS (UNAIDS) was established by the Economic and Social Council in 1994 and began operations in January 1996, with its headquarters based in Geneva, Switzerland.

RESPONSIBILITIES

UNAIDS is designed to advocate for a concentrated and engaged global response to the HIV/AIDS epidemic. A central role of UNAIDS is to coordinate the contributing agencies (listed below) in order to ensure that the capacities of each body are connected and focused effectively on countering the HIV/AIDS. UNAIDS is responsible for assisting individuals and communities coping with the disease, preventing the spread of HIV/AIDS, and addressing the socioeconomic dimensions of the disease such as the unequal impact on the poor.

STRUCTURE

UNAIDS brings together eleven cosponsors from agencies working on HIV/AIDS issues across the UN System. The original six institutions are WHO, UN Children's Fund, UN Development Programme, UN Educational, Scientific and Cultural Organization, UN Population Fund, and the World Bank. Since the founding of UNAIDS, five more bodies have joined: International Labour Organization, UN High Commissioner for Refugees, UN Office on Drugs and Crime, UN Entity for Gender Equality and the Empowerment of Women, and World Food Programme. The heads of these institutions work together through the Committee of Cosponsoring Organizations, which also includes the UNAIDS Executive Director, and report into the broader Programme Coordinating Board (PCB). The PCB is a unique governing structure in the UN System. The body consists of the cosponsors along with twenty-two government representatives selected from across all regions and five nongovernmental organization (NGO) representatives (three from developing and two from developed countries). However, the cosponsors and NGOs can participate but cannot vote. UNAIDS is supported through voluntary funding and also coordinates with the Global Fund to Fight AIDS, Tuberculosis, and Malaria (commonly known as the Global Fund), a much larger separate funding source established in 2002.

ACTIVITIES

Along with coordinating at the UN System level through its structure, UNAIDS works across and within countries to promote coordinated government agency responses as well as working with NGOs engaged with issues related to HIV/AIDS. A key activity is serving as a source for compiling and distributing data and information on the current status of infections and progress of efforts to counter the disease. UNAIDS also continues to advocate for addressing HIV/AIDS on the global agenda, maintaining and raising awareness, and pressing for needed action. For example, UNAIDS lobbies to decrease the cost of medications needed to treat the disease. While early on the institution was focused on such advocacy work, UNAIDS has extended its activities regarding the implementation of programs within countries. Now the organization addresses very diverse issues, including the impact of HIV/AIDS on children, gender equality, and social protection, to ensure equality of treatment and safety from exposure. UNAIDS stresses the need to "fast track" addressing HIV/AIDS. This includes setting the 90–90–90 targets in 2014, to be reached by 2020, which would ensure that 90 percent of people are aware that they are infected, 90 percent of the diagnosed are receiving the needed antiretroviral therapy, and 90 percent under treatment can suppress the virus. These targets are designed to set the necessary groundwork for ending the HIV/AIDS outbreak by 2030 (at a 95 percent level for each target). UNAIDS has also linked its strategic planning with the UN's 2030 Agenda and related Sustainable Development Goals.

CHALLENGES AND REFORM

A key challenge for UNAIDS remains the scope of the ongoing HIV/AIDS epidemic and its impacts. While the organization set ambitious targets for countering the disease, UNAIDS' core funding has declined. The organization signed a cooperation agreement with the Global Fund. However, UNAIDS does not connect to the same degree with other major funders in the global health landscape, in particular the Bill and Melinda Gates Foundation. While UNAIDS has more capability as a separate component in the UN System compared to the GPA operating within WHO, the lack of full authority over the cosponsoring institutions limits its independent impact. UNAIDS represents an important test of UN reform in general, as the UN sought to create a new institutional model to establish coordinating capabilities on a focused issue. Competition between the cosponsors creates challenges to this approach and points to the need for strong leadership to manage the coordination effort. The first UNAIDS Executive Director, Peter Piot, was largely viewed as providing effective leadership. However, his successor, Michel Sidibé, was critiqued for his leadership style and ultimately resigned under pressure. UNAIDS is recognized as playing an important role in raising awareness and managing HIV/AIDS and will require strong leadership. Many hope that Winnie Byanyima, who took office in November 2019, will continue this supportive role.

See also: Health; International Labour Organization; Nongovernmental Organizations; Sustainable Development Goals; United Nations Children's Fund; United Nations Development Programme; United Nations Educational, Scientific and Cultural Organization; United Nations Entity for Gender Equality and the Empowerment of Women; United Nations High Commissioner for Refugees; United Nations Population Fund; United Nations Reform; World Bank Group; World Food Programme; World Health Organization.

FURTHER READING

Harman, Sophie. 2011. "Searching for an Executive Head? Leadership and UNAIDS." *Global Governance* 17 (4): 429–46.

Leon, Joshua K. 2011. "Confronting Catastrophe: Norms, Efficiency and the Evolution of the AIDS Battle in the UN." *Cambridge Review of International Affairs* 24 (3): 471–91.

McRobie, Ellen, et al. 2018. "National Responses to Global Health Targets: Exploring Policy Transfer in the Context of the UNAIDS '90–90–90' Treatment Targets in Ghana and Uganda." *Health Policy and Planning* 33 (1): 17–33.

Sridhar, Devi. 2013. "Coordinating the UN System: Lessons from UNAIDS." *Social Science & Medicine* 76 (January): 21–23.

Peacebuilding Commission

Sixty years after the UN committed to promoting international peace and security, the organization expanded this goal to assisting countries in rebuilding after violent times and preventing countries from relapsing into conflict. The idea of a Peacebuilding Commission (PBC) originated in 2004 with the report of the UN Secretary-General's High-level Panel on Threats, Challenges and Change and gained support from Secretary-General Kofi Annan in his 2005 report *In Larger Freedom: Towards Development, Security and Human Rights for All*. The 2005 World Summit Outcome document recognized that the UN needed a "coordinated, coherent and integrated approach to post-conflict peacebuilding" and called for the PBC arrangements to be in place by the end of the year. Two different resolutions, one by the General Assembly (60/180) and the other by the Security Council (1645), created the PBC. The resolutions passed concurrently, with widespread support, on December 20, 2005. The PBC became operational in June 2006 and is headquartered in New York City.

RESPONSIBILITIES

The resolutions call on the PBC to support a country's ability to recover after a conflict and prevent the need for recurring peacekeeping operations. The PBC's mandate is to coordinate with "all relevant actors within and outside of the United Nations" to create and support a strategy for postconflict peacebuilding and recovery. This includes pooling resources and finances for postconflict countries to support their reconstruction. In April 2016, additional concurrent resolutions by the General Assembly (70/62) and Security Council (2282) reviewing the UN's peacebuilding architecture expanded the PBC's mandate, calling for an "integrated, strategic and coherent approach to peacebuilding, noting that security, development and human rights are closely interlinked and mutually reinforcing."

STRUCTURE

The PBC is unique in two ways. First, the PBC is an advisory body to both the General Assembly and the Security Council, including submitting its annual report to both bodies. Second, the body's work brings together the UN's security agenda and development goals. The PBC includes two primary forums, the Organizational Committee and country-specific configurations. The Organizational Committee is made up of thirty-one member states selected for renewable two-year terms, with seven members chosen from the Security Council (including all five permanent members) and seven members from the General Assembly (elected to promote geographic equity and include those with experience in postconflict operations). In addition, the Economic and Social Council (ECOSOC) selects seven members, five members are from the top ten financial contributors to the UN budget, and five members are from the top ten contributors of UN military and police forces.

The Organizational Committee, guided by a Chair and two Vice-Chairs, meets annually and determines which cases to address. The agenda is based on requests submitted by member states, the Security Council, the General Assembly, ECOSOC, or the Secretary-General. The country-specific meetings, which bring together members of the Organizational Committee along with the countries involved (including the country undergoing peacebuilding) and other related actors, convene as necessary and are often described as "the engine rooms" driving peacebuilding efforts in those areas. PBC meetings can include international organizations (particularly the European Union, International Monetary Fund, Organization of Islamic Cooperation, and the World Bank), along with invited additional member states, representatives from other parts of the UN System, and nongovernmental organizations (NGOs). A final mechanism is the Peacebuilding Fund, which was created in 2006 to provide financial support for peacebuilding. The Peacebuilding Support Office assists the PBC and manages the Peacebuilding Fund. As the PBC is subordinate to the Security Council and General Assembly, it cannot bind actors or enforce its recommendations.

ACTIVITIES

As an intergovernmental advisory body, the PBC supports peace efforts in countries affected by conflict through policy recommendations and establishing strategies for postconflict recovery and reconstruction. The PBC is often referred to as a "debate panel," with an emphasis on coherence in creating short-, medium-, and long-term goals. Postconflict peacebuilding includes anything that is needed to transition a country from war to peace. The PBC can only engage in cases after the violence has ended. In this regard, the body connects UN peacekeeping and postconflict operations. In each case, the country-specific meeting creates an integrated peacebuilding strategy, which first defines the relationship between UN agencies and the country and tailors a unique strategy. For instance, in Sierra Leone the PBC worked to address illegal diamond extraction and external meddling from Liberia. The plan of action includes priorities, objectives, and sequences to achieve the country's objectives.

Some locations incorporate multidimensional peacebuilding, which can include peacemaking, peacekeeping, establishing public order and citizen security, governance, protecting human rights, and supporting socioeconomic development. In other areas, peacebuilding is more securitized and includes counterterrorism and counterinsurgency interventions. The PBC works with neighboring states and regional organizations and provides a hub function for coordination between the UN's principal organs and other relevant UN bodies, member states, and country teams. In addition, the PBC emphasizes engagement by NGOs and the private sector. The PBC has a fairly narrow set of countries on its country-specific agenda: Burundi, Central African Republic, Guinea, Guinea-Bissau, Liberia, and Sierra Leone. The Peacebuilding Fund serves as the international assistance network for financial donors across a wider array of countries, committing $772 million across forty-one countries as of 2017. Along with country-specific engagement, the PBC emphasizes enhancing thematic areas of peacebuilding, such as building institutions and encouraging women's participation.

CHALLENGES AND REFORM

Building peace is a challenging endeavor, and observers point to the limited number of countries on the PBC's country-specific agenda as making the body's direct impact more modest compared to the UN's broader peacebuilding work. The PBC is also critiqued as being riddled with turf battles, divergent expectations, and as too state centered in serving the interests of countries over people. The PBC is also prone to long-standing debates about whether the peacebuilding is imposing Western models of security and economic development. Suggested reforms of the PBC include creating a rapid-response civilian team, more emphasis on postconflict countries taking ownership of their peacebuilding process, and less state politicization. The 2015 Advisory Group of Experts on the Review of the UN Peacebuilding Architecture emphasized improving the functioning of the PBC through means such as shifting its working methods, bolstering relationships with organs like the Security Council, and better structuring consultation with civil society. The PBC creates important connections between political and security sectors and engages financial and development actors in transitioning a country to peace. In addition, the PBC attracts long-term attention to postconflict states and highlights customized strategies and goals. The PBC's capacity to bring key players together is essential and can be impactful. Overall, the PBC reflects an innovative approach by the UN to promote lasting peace.

See also: Economic and Social Council; Economic Development; General Assembly; Human Rights; International Monetary Fund; Kofi Annan; Nongovernmental Organizations; Peacebuilding; Peacekeeping; Security Council; United Nations Conferences and Summits; United Nations Reform; World Bank Group.

FURTHER READING

Del Castillo, Graciana. 2017. *Obstacles to Peacebuilding.* London: Routledge.

Jenkins, Robert. 2013. *Peacebuilding: From Concept to Commission.* London: Routledge.

Leite, Alexandre Cesar Cunha, Renally Késsia Paiva Nascimento, and Catarina Rose Bezerra. 2018. "Is Peacebuilding Coordinated and Coherent?" *Peace Review* 30 (4): 554–62.

Van Beijnum, Mariska. 2016. "Achievements of the UN Peacebuilding Commission and Challenges Ahead." In *UN Peacebuilding Architecture: The First 10 Years*, edited by Cedric de Congin and Eli Stamnes, 77–94. London: Routledge.

Permanent Forum on Indigenous Issues

Indigenous peoples have worked together to press for institutional representation within the UN in order to address the shared displacement and marginalization they face in the countries where they live. While indigenous groups prefer to be treated as sovereign entities at a level equal to that of the UN member states, they primarily access the UN System as nongovernmental actors. Indigenous matters have traditionally been treated as a human rights issue within the UN System, and indigenous peoples have struggled to have their collective rights treated as distinct from other disadvantaged groups. The push for separate institutional recognition initially paid off in 1982 with the establishment of the Working Group on Indigenous Populations (WGIP) in the Sub-Commission on the Promotion and Protection of Human Rights within the UN Commission on Human Rights. WGIP was replaced by the Expert Mechanism on the Rights of Indigenous Peoples, which first met in 2008, as part of the transition from the Commission on Human Rights to the new Human Rights Council in 2006. The Permanent Forum on Indigenous Issues, established by Economic and Social Council Resolution 2000/22 and started operations in 2002, was the culmination of efforts to establish a distinct UN body dedicated to the full array of indigenous concerns.

RESPONSIBILITIES

As a subsidiary body of ECOSOC, the Permanent Forum serves in an advisory capacity to provide advice and recommendations. More broadly, across the UN System the Permanent Forum is tasked to "raise awareness and promote the integration and coordination of activities relating to indigenous issues." The Permanent Forum is also responsible for collecting and distributing information on indigenous matters and, following the approval in 2007 of the UN Declaration on the Rights of Indigenous Peoples, works to encourage compliance with the Declaration's provisions. The mandate of the Permanent Forum encompasses six substantive areas: culture, economic and social development, education, environment, health, and human rights.

STRUCTURE

The Permanent Forum is a sixteen-member expert body, with indigenous peoples and member states equally represented. Eight individual indigenous experts are selected in consultation with regional indigenous organizations, with the remaining eight members nominated for ECOSOC approval by member state governments, to serve three-year terms. Funding for the Permanent Forum was originally designated to derive from the UN regular budget along with other voluntary contributions. However, in 1985 an additional Voluntary Fund for Indigenous Populations was established by the General Assembly, and subsequently expanded several times, to help support indigenous representatives' participation in relevant UN meetings, including the Permanent Forum. The Trust Fund on Indigenous Issues was also established to support the work and activities of the Permanent Forum and is managed along with other Permanent Forum affairs by a small secretariat in the Department of Economic and Social Affairs. The Permanent Forum is part of the broader institutional support for indigenous matters in the UN System, along with the human rights–focused Expert Mechanism and the Special

Rapporteur on the Rights of Indigenous Peoples. The work of the Permanent Forum is also assisted by an Inter-Agency Support Group on Indigenous Issues.

ACTIVITIES

The Permanent Forum meets each spring across two weeks at UN Headquarters in New York. Along with addressing issues under the six mandated areas, the meeting usually includes a thematic focus on a particular subject. For example, the 2019 session special theme was "Traditional Knowledge: Generation, Transmission and Protection." While the Permanent Forum does not have enforcement mechanisms, the body does play a key information gathering and advisory role, which includes submitting an annual report to ECOSOC. The key activity at the Permanent Forum is hearings where member states and UN agencies are questioned on their policies and indigenous representatives may deliver brief (three to five minute) statements. Some UN agencies, such as the International Fund for Agricultural Development, are acknowledged for collaborative engagement. In addition, with over two thousand indigenous actors in attendance, the meeting provides a central site for indigenous groups to lobby member states and UN officials and for networking to develop strategies to best advocate for their interests.

CHALLENGES AND REFORM

The power dynamics of indigenous engagement at the UN System remains a point of contention at the Permanent Forum. Participation by indigenous peoples who lack sovereign self-determination and full representation can lead to frustration and the perception of cooptation and ongoing marginalization through a neocolonial institutional process. Such concerns have led some indigenous groups to stop engaging at the Permanent Forum and to focus their efforts instead at the national or local levels. At the same time, the Permanent Forum provides an avenue for the voices of indigenous peoples to press for justice on the international stage and serves as a central location for advocacy work and building the global indigenous movement. Those supporting the Permanent Forum still point to the limited mandate and lack of formal enforcement capabilities, which leads to difficulties in implementing and monitoring recommendations. Reforms to provide a stronger venue for indigenous perspectives could include greater equity for opportunities to speak before the Permanent Forum, allowing more input into the final report and bolstering the body's political profile.

See also: Economic and Social Council; Human Rights Council; Indigenous Peoples; International Fund for Agricultural Development; Membership; Nongovernmental Organizations; Self-Determination.

FURTHER READING

Lindroth, Marjo. 2006. "Indigenous-State Relations in the UN: Establishing the Indigenous Forum." *Polar Record* 42 (3): 239–48.

Pineda, Baron. 2013. "Cuando Nos Internacionalizamos: Human Rights and Other Universals at the United Nations Permanent Forum on Indigenous Issues." In *Central*

America in the New Millennium: Living Transition and Reimagining Democracy, edited by Jennifer L. Burrell and Ellen Moodie, 115–30. New York: Berghahn Books.

Schulte-Tenckhoff, Isabelle, and Adil Hasan Khan. 2011. "The Permanent Quest for a Mandate: Assessing the UN Permanent Forum on Indigenous Issues." *Griffith Law Review* 20 (3): 673–701.

Regional Commissions

Although the UN is a universal institution, the organization recognizes that certain issues can benefit from a regional approach. The economically focused Regional Commissions are an institutional reflection of this idea. These bodies were established by the Economic and Social Council (ECOSOC) starting in 1947 with the Economic Commission for Europe (ECE) and the Economic Commission for Asia and the Far East (renamed Economic and Social Commission for Asia and the Pacific [ESCAP] in 1974) to assist with reconstruction after World War II. In recognition of the economic development needs of Latin America, the Economic Commission for Latin America was founded immediately afterward in 1948 (with the Caribbean added in 1984, creating the current acronym ECLAC). The Economic Commission for Africa (ECA, established in 1958) and the Economic Commission for Western Asia (established in 1973, referred to as ESCWA after the word social was added to the name in 1985) followed. Each Regional Commission is headquartered in its region: with ECA in Addis Ababa, Ethiopia, ECE in Geneva, Switzerland, ECLAC in Santiago, Chile, ESCAP in Bangkok, Thailand, and ESCWA in Beirut, Lebanon.

RESPONSIBILITIES

The Regional Commissions are designed to encourage cohesive, integrated regional approaches to economic cooperation and development. They provide a regional arm to coordinate UN projects and adapt globally established UN goals to regional contexts. Given that regional needs differ, which was the thinking behind establishing separate Regional Commissions, the particular priorities and approaches used when addressing these overarching objectives evolved according to regional circumstances.

STRUCTURE

Compared to other UN System bodies within ECOSOC, like the Functional Commissions, the Regional Commissions are more independent institutions that engage directly with countries and then report to ECOSOC. Each Regional Commission has a Secretariat headed by an Executive Secretary, who is designated under the authority of the UN Secretary-General. The exact structure of each Regional Commission varies but consistently includes a ministerial level body to govern (which meets annually or biennially depending on the region) and special committees to work on areas of expertise. Since 1981, a small New York–based Regional Commissions Office represents the Commissions at UN Headquarters.

The Regional Commissions are funded out of the regular UN budget, which requires approval by the General Assembly, but the budget levels across the bodies differ widely, with ECA receiving the highest level of financial resources and ESCWA the lowest. Similarly, staffing levels at ECA are much higher than the others, with ECE possessing the smallest number of posts. Membership size also varies across regions: ECE (fifty-six), ESCAP (fifty-three and nine associate members), ECA (fifty-three), ECLAC (forty-six and fourteen associate members), and ESCWA (eighteen). Membership in each Commission is not strictly regional, as countries with interests outside of their geographical region may join a commission, and there are countries that are members of more than one commission. For example, only thirty-three of ECLAC's forty-six members are from Latin America and the Caribbean, with the remaining members drawn from Asia, Europe, and North America.

ACTIVITIES

The programmatic focus differs across regions, but there is consistent engagement with gathering statistics, trade and investment, environment and sustainable energy, and technical cooperation in the form of training. Annual economic surveys are published by the Regional Commissions as part of data gathering and trend projections across each country in the region. Economic assessments are employed to develop ideas and regulations, some of which extend to impact global debates. For example, the Latin American region under the leadership of Raúl Prebisch (the second Executive Secretary of ECLA, 1950–1963) is noted for challenging liberal economic thinking in relation to developing countries. ECE is acknowledged for innovations in environmental protections, including a series of conventions. Regional connections are promoted through conferences and information exchanges, as well as supporting regional institution-building. For instance, ECA promoted the creation of other regional bodies like the African Development Bank. The Regional Commissions also provide a conduit for global objectives and ideals to countries within their regions, including the 2030 Agenda for meeting the Sustainable Development Goals.

CHALLENGES AND REFORM

Given regional differences, the particular challenges faced by a Commission depends upon the situation. For example, ESCWA has wrestled with disputes between members and warfare in the region that required moving organizational headquarters from Beirut to Baghdad to Amman and then back to Beirut. There are some challenges that the Regional Commissions share, including the fact that other regional organizations have often reduced the Commissions to secondary status in that region. For instance, with the formation of the Association of Southeast Asian Nations, ESCAP has found itself playing a more marginal role. The interconnections created by globalization undermines the rationale of the Commissions based on regional separation and distinctiveness. Important interactions between the Regional Commissions already exist, but their relative strengths and areas addressed provide even greater avenues for sharing knowledge and best practices as well as building stronger cross-regional cooperation. The Regional Commissions are not as well-known or recognized as other bodies in the UN System, yet they remain significant actors for promoting regional cooperation within the universal organization.

See also: Economic and Social Council; Economic Development; Functional Commissions; Regionalism; Sustainable Development Goals; United Nations Headquarters.

FURTHER READING

Berthelot, Yves, ed. 2004. *Unity and Diversity in Development Ideas: Perspectives from the UN Regional Commissions.* Bloomington: Indiana University Press.

Dahi, Omar. 2017. "The UN, the Economic and Social Commission for West Asia, and Development in the Arab World." In *Land of Blue Helmets: The United Nations and the Arab World,* edited by Karim Makdisi and Vijay Prashad, 389–408. Oakland: University of California Press.

Gala, Paulo, Jhean Camargo, and Elton Freitas. 2018. "The Economic Commission for Latin America and the Caribbean (ECLAC) Was Right: Scale-Free Complex Networks and Core-Periphery Patterns in World Trade." *Cambridge Journal of Economics* 42 (3): 633–51.

Shaw, Timothy M. 1989. "The UN Economic Commission for Africa: Continental Development and Self-Reliance." In *The United Nations in the World Political Economy: Essays in Honour of Leon Gordenker,* edited by David P. Forsythe, 98–111. New York: St. Martin's Press.

Sidjanski, Dusan. 1998. *The Economic Commission for Europe in the Age of Change.* Geneva: United Nations.

Research and Training Institutes

The UN System benefits from a set of independent institutes that provide research and analysis on international issues, as well as scholarly and human resources training to bolster staff capabilities. Two early research institutes were established within the Economic and Social Council (ECOSOC), starting with the UN Research Institute for Social Development (UNRISD) in 1963, which is headquartered in Geneva, Switzerland. The UN Social Defense Research Institute (UNSDRI) in Rome, Italy, followed several years later and was renamed the UN Interregional Crime and Justice Research Institute (UNICRI) in 1989 and moved to Turin, Italy, in 2000. The General Assembly created additional research and training bodies. The statute for the UN Institute for Training and Research (UNITAR), based in Geneva, was approved in 1965. The United Nations University (UNU), with primary headquarters based in Tokyo, Japan, was created in 1973 and became operational in 1975. The UN Institute for Disarmament Research (UNIDIR), housed in Geneva, celebrated its thirty-fifth anniversary in 2015. Most recently, the UN System Staff College (UNSCC) started operations in 2002 in Turin (with a second campus in Bonn, Germany). There are additional research and training–related bodies operating within other parts of the UN System, but these six are the primary ones dedicated to furthering the research and training needs of the organization as a whole.

RESPONSIBILITIES

The research and training institutes are designed to improve understanding of global problems and provide vital training to provide the knowledge and skills to better address these challenges. The emphasis and areas of responsibility differ across the institutes. For example, UNIDIR is mandated to provide research to improve disarmament practices and policies. Alternatively, UNSCC is tasked with improving international civil servants' management effectiveness and technical knowledge.

STRUCTURE

The structure for each institute varies but generally includes a Board governing the institute, which often contains related ex officio members, and an executive head (most often titled Director). For example, UNITAR is currently overseen by a Board of Trustees, selected for three-year terms by the UN Secretary-General after consultation with the Presidents of the General Assembly and ECOSOC, along with the Executive Director appointed by the Secretary-General (all four of whom serve as ex officio members of the Board). All six institutes provide regular reports on their activities, with the two solely ECOSOC-based institutes reporting through the related Functional Commission: UNICRI via the Commission on Crime Prevention and Criminal Justice and UNRISD to the Commission for Social Development. Several institutes are embedded in broader structures, for instance, UNICRI and several functional commissions are based in the UN Office on Drugs and Crime. UNICRI also shares a headquarters campus with UNSCC at the International Labour Organization's International Training Center in Turin. The institutes are supported through voluntary funding. For example, UNRISD reports Sweden, Switzerland, and Finland as the highest state funders. Several research foundations, like the Centre for Social Entrepreneurship Studies (one of the largest foundation funders), and UN bodies (e.g., the UN Development Programme) also provide financial support.

ACTIVITIES

The institutes provide networks between the UN and experts from other research communities. The UNU is particularly wide reaching. Coordinated by UNU Centre, the UNU System as a whole has thirteen programs and institutes located in twelve different countries. There are also more than forty other entities with which the UNU collaborates. The specific activities vary by institute, as some focus on research while others provide training. UNICRI carries out studies to promote crime prevention and criminal justice, while UNRISD focuses on social development research. As indicated in its name, UNITAR was designed to provide professional development training and conduct research to support UN objectives, but the organization is best known for providing a range of multilateral diplomatic training and supporting country-level program implementation. The UNU has served for years as a central think tank in the UN System, as well as researching specific global issues, and recently added postgraduate master's and PhD programs. Since 2015, the institutes have emphasized research and training support for the UN's 2030 Agenda for Sustainable Development.

CHALLENGES AND REFORM

The research and training institutes are designed to operate in an autonomous manner. This allows them to research politically sensitive topics that might be controversial in other UN bodies. However, not all of the institutes remain independent. In 2011, the International Research and Training Institute for the Advancement of Women (INSTRAW) was merged into the new UN Entity for Gender Equality and the Empowerment of Women (UN Women) body in the UN System. Reliance on voluntary funding is designed to reinforce the independence of the institutes but can distract the Directors' focus due to the time spent fund raising, which is essential to prevent budget difficulties. Financial limitations have slowed the establishment of needed training facilities. For example, UNSCC was first approved by the General Assembly in 1971, but funding concerns delayed final statute approval until 2001. Financing also comes from richer, more developed areas of the world, which exacerbates the perception that the institutes' activities do not reflect developing world priorities. Pressure by developing countries to ensure that the institutes better consider their needs can be seen in the shift of UNSDRI to UNICRI. With the recent emphasis on the Sustainable Development Goals, the institutes continue to evolve to provide support to vital areas of research and training needs in the UN System.

See also: Arms Control and Disarmament; Economic and Social Council; International Labour Organization; President of General Assembly; Regional Commissions; Sustainable Development Goals; United Nations Development Programme; United Nations Entity for Gender Equality and the Empowerment of Women.

FURTHER READING

El-Ayouty, Yassin. 1972. "Peace Research and the United Nations: A Role for the World Organization." *The Journal of Conflict Resolution* 16 (4): 539–53.

Jordan, Robert S. 1976. "UNITAR and UN Research." *International Organization* 30 (1): 163–71.

Kester, Kevin. 2017. "The Case of Educational Peacebuilding Inside the United Nations Universities: A Review and Critique." *Journal of Transformative Education* 15 (1): 59–78.

Newland, Kathleen. 1984. *The UNU in the Mid-Eighties.* Tokyo: The United Nations University.

RELATED ORGANIZATIONS

International Atomic Energy Agency (IAEA)

The United Nations' (UN) pledge in the Preamble to the UN Charter to "save succeeding generations from the scourge of war" extends to the possibility of nuclear war. In the wake of the 1945 U.S. atomic attack on Japan and Soviet development of nuclear capacity in 1949, there was a clear need for international regulation. The very first General Assembly resolution in 1946 called for the "control of atomic energy . . . to ensure its use only for peaceful purposes" and promoted "the elimination from national armaments of atomic weapons and all other major weapons adaptable to mass destruction." This resolution established a Commission to review and report on atomic energy, but this made little progress and, in 1952, was merged with the Commission for Conventional Armaments to create the Disarmament Commission. U.S. President Dwight D. Eisenhower's "Atoms for Peace" speech in 1953 called for the creation of an "international atomic energy agency." In 1954, the United States proposed a draft statute and cooperated with other countries on a blueprint for the organizational setup. In fall of 1954, the General Assembly passed Resolution 810 calling for the creation of an organization. Two years later, the Statute of the International Atomic Energy Agency (IAEA) was adopted, which came into force in July 1957 and has since been amended three times (1963, 1973, and 1989; with two additional amendments established in 1999 that have not yet been ratified to take effect as of early 2020). The IAEA is headquartered in Vienna, Austria.

RESPONSIBILITIES

The IAEA acts as a global multilateral venue to build cooperation on nuclear issues and is designed to encourage the use of nuclear technology in a safe and peaceful manner. The overarching dual mission of the agency is to "promote and control the Atom." As specified in the Statute, the IAEA is to support "the contribution of atomic energy to peace, health and prosperity throughout the world" as well as to inhibit atomic power from use "in such a way as to further any military purposes." The IAEA's responsibilities revolve around supporting three main areas: safeguards and verification, safety and security, and science and technology. The agency's mandate has been enhanced by member states in the wake of new developments and nuclear accidents, including Three Mile Island (1979), Chernobyl (1986), and Fukushima Daiichi (2011).

STRUCTURE

The IAEA is considered part of the "UN family," having signed an agreement establishing a relationship with the UN in 1959 and participating on Chief Executives Board for Coordination, yet is an independent organization. As set out in this agreement, the agency submits reports to the General Assembly, the Economic and Social Council, and "when appropriate" to the Security Council. The IAEA has a two-part governing and policy-making structure: General Conference and Board of Governors. The General Conference is comprised of all IAEA member states (171 as of 2019) and meets annually in Vienna. This body elects a President and a General Committee to guide the session. The thirty-five-member Board of Governors typically meets five times per year and is tasked with making policy and budgetary recommendations to the General Conference, overseeing ongoing operations, and appointing the Director General (who is then approved by the General Conference). The Director General oversees five offices: Director General's Office, Secretariat of the Policy-Making Organs, Internal Oversight Services, Legal Affairs, and Public Information and Communication. Additionally, there are six IAEA departments headed by a Deputy Director General: Management, Nuclear Energy, Nuclear Safety and Security, Nuclear Sciences and Applications, Safeguards, and Technical Cooperation. The agency has two separate budgets, approved by the General Conference: the regular budget covering operations and infrastructure investments (with the largest budget item being nuclear verification) and technical cooperation activities (which draws on the Technical Cooperation Fund). IAEA's work is also supplemented by voluntary member state contributions and third-party donors.

ACTIVITIES

The IAEA's primary activities involve safeguarding the use of nuclear science and technology for peaceful purposes. These efforts focus on monitoring compliance with the Nuclear Nonproliferation Treaty to regulate declared and nondeclared nuclear materials as well as the potential diversions of peaceful nuclear material to weapons programs. Yet, the IAEA also works to support nuclear energy and provides educational programs about nuclear fuel, uranium mining, and radioactive waste management. The use of nuclear techniques and radiation technologies in health care is also supported. The IAEA's work connects it with a wide array of other organizations. This includes signing relationship agreements with eight of the specialized agencies, such as the Food and Agricultural Organization, the World Health Organization, and the World Meteorological Organization. The agency also hosts conferences and seminars each year to promote the advancement of scientific and technical information on nuclear materials.

CHALLENGES AND REFORM

The IAEA's successes include the creation of regional nuclear weapon free zones, and many identify the agency as central to the nuclear nonproliferation regime, which has limited the spread of nuclear weapons and provided enhanced safeguards for the use of nuclear materials. There are critical voices that claim the IAEA failed to accurately detect Iraqi nuclear program advancement in the 1990s and did not prevent North Korea and Iran from expanding their weapons programs. There are reoccurring tensions in IAEA's work between serving as a promoter of nuclear materials for peace and development and functioning as a restrictor of nuclear materials for military use. While often viewed as a technical organization, the agency was politicized during the Cold War East-West clash and the North-South conflict over development and economic inequalities. The IAEA faces growing resource constraints as states make more requests, including demands for new programs (both technical and monitoring), which strains the agency's human and financial resources and points to the need for enhanced budget and staffing levels. Additional reforms could include strengthening safeguard measures and verification tools, as well as resolving tensions between the effort to sustain transparency and confidentiality. Overall, the IAEA is regarded as a significant organization working to ensure international peace and security and was recognized in 2005 with the Nobel Peace Prize.

See also: Arms Control and Disarmament; Disarmament Commission; Economic and Social Council; Food and Agriculture Organization; General Assembly; Security Council; World Health Organization; World Meteorological Organization.

FURTHER READING

Findlay, Trevor. 2012. *Unleashing the Nuclear Watchdog: Strengthening and Reform of the IAEA.* Waterloo, Ontario: The Centre for International Governance Innovation.

Fischer, David. 1997. *History of the International Atomic Energy Agency. The First Forty Years.* Vienna: International Atomic Energy Agency.

Glavind, Johanne Grøndahl. 2014. "Effective Multilateralism in the IAEA." In *The EU and Effective Multilateralism: Internal and External Reform Practices,* edited by Edith Drieskens and Louise G. van Schaik, 101–17. New York: Routledge.

Pedraza, Jorge Morales. 2015. "A New Organizational Structure for the International Atomic Energy Agency (IAEA): A Proposal for the Future." *Public Organization Review* 15 (3): 353–64.

International Criminal Court (ICC)

The twentieth century was tragically marked by cases of genocide, war crimes, and mass atrocities. Following World War II, there was discussion over creating an international court to hold individual leaders accountable, but the idea did not come to fruition. Instead, the international community relied on a series of temporary tribunals (i.e., the Nuremburg and Tokyo trials and the International Criminal Tribunals for Rwanda and the Former Yugoslavia). Many of the rulings from these ad hoc tribunals pointed to the need for a more permanent international court, and their rigorous processes provided a model that reassured skeptics. In addition, in 1989, the General Assembly passed a resolution requesting that the International Law Commission draft a proposed statute. The International Law Commission submitted its document in 1994, and the General Assembly created committees to work in 1995 and then 1996–1998 on the draft statute to establish the court. A month-long conference held in Rome, Italy, finalized the text and, at the conference's completion on July 17, 1998, 120 countries voted to adopt the Rome Statute, while 7 countries voted against (including major powers the United States and China), with 21 abstentions. After sixty countries ratified the statute, the International Criminal Court (ICC) came into existence on July 1, 2002. The ICC is located in a city known for international law, The Hague, in the Netherlands.

RESPONSIBILITIES

The Rome Statute identified four main categories of jurisdiction for the court to investigate and, when appropriate, prosecute. These include genocide (intent to destroy a group), crimes against humanity (a wide range of acts connected to attacks against a civilian population), war crimes (as defined by the Geneva conventions), and crimes of aggression ("using armed force by a state against the sovereignty, territorial integrity or political independence of another state"). Cases can be referred to the court by the Security Council, when a citizen of a State Party (a country that has ratified the Rome Statute) is accused, or at the request of another State Party. The ICC addresses individuals who have committed crimes and should not to be confused with the International Court of Justice (ICJ), a principal organ of the UN, which is a legal forum for countries.

STRUCTURE

As of the end of 2019, there were 137 signatories to the Rome Statute, of which 122 countries were formal State Parties who accept the jurisdiction of the ICC. The ICC is made up of three parts: the Assembly of State Parties, the Court (comprised of four organs: Presidency, Office of the Prosecutor, Registry, and the Judicial Divisions), and the Trust Fund for Victims. The Assembly of State Parties, which convenes at least once a year, is the oversight and legislative body of the ICC whose members are all State Parties. Within the Assembly, there is a Bureau with twenty-one members (elected by the Assembly for three-year terms), which includes a President and two Vice-Presidents. The Assembly elects eighteen judges (which are divided into the three Judicial Divisions: Pre-Trial, Trial, and Appeals) and the Prosecutor for nine-year terms. Bureau membership and judge selection is based on geographic distribution and diverse legal systems and should provide fair gender representation of the judges.

The court's Presidency, which administers the affairs of the Court, encompasses a President and two Vice-Presidents who are elected for three-year terms by the judges of the Court. The Registry, which is overseen by the Presidency, is the principal administrative office and provides judicial support (including interpretation services), management of finances and human resources, and external outreach and public information. The Office of the Prosecutor operates independently to oversee investigations and the prosecution of defendants. The Rome Statute also called for a Trust Fund for Victims (established by the Assembly in 2004), which provides for Court-ordered reparations and "physical, psychological, and material support to victims and their families." The ICC can also establish field offices in countries where investigations are being carried out. Funding for the ICC comes from State Parties and voluntary contributions by nonmember states and other organizations.

ACTIVITIES

The ICC investigates crimes committed after July 1, 2002, and lists twenty-seven cases, twelve situations under investigation, and nine preliminary examinations as of the end of 2019. Court activities include pretrials, trials, appeals, issuing arrest warrants, summons, and verdicts. The ICC acts as a complementary court to the legal systems at the domestic level and does not have supranational authority, it only engages when national courts are "unable" or "unwilling" to prosecute offenders. The court cannot enforce verdicts and relies on countries to carry out arrests, detentions, and transportation of defendants, although there is a detention center in The Hague for housing defendants during trial. After conviction, individuals are moved to detention facilities of State Parties. Unlike the ICJ, the ICC operates as an independent judiciary body separate from the UN System, although the court does have a "cooperation agreement" with the UN.

CHALLENGES AND REFORM

The court faces several challenges. Lack of full membership, in particular the United States, remains a point of weakness. Within the United States, there is opposition to the court, which includes concerns that U.S. military personnel will come under its jurisdiction. The notion that the court brings justice to the victims is also contested as, particularly in African cases, the victims may be geographically removed from the process. Because prosecutions have been focused on African cases, there are accusations that the court is biased and that its notions of justice are Western without consideration for local cultures and customs. Many African states call for the inclusion of more non-African cases to ensure the credibility and fairness of the court. The African Union issued a nonbinding resolution in 2017 encouraging its members to leave the ICC. In 2016, Burundi announced its intention to withdraw and, in 2017, was the first country to officially withdraw following the required year-long waiting period. Gambia and South Africa also submitted their notice of withdrawal in 2016 but stopped the process the following year. In 2019, the Philippines became the second country to formally withdraw. Despite these accusations and withdrawals, many find that the court has brought a new era where individuals who commit mass crimes no longer have legal impunity and can be brought to justice.

See also: Human Rights; International Court of Justice; Peaceful Settlement; Security Council.

FURTHER READING

Arsanjani, Mahnoush H. 1999. "The Rome Statute of the International Criminal Court." *American Journal of International Law* 93 (1): 22–43.

Cummings-John, Tamara. 2013. "Cooperation between the United Nations and the International Criminal Court: Recent Developments in Information Sharing and

Contact with Persons Subject to Warrants or Summonses." *International Organizations Law Review* 10 (1): 223–46.

Jalloh, Charles Chernor, and Ilias Bantekas, eds. 2017. *The International Criminal Court and Africa*. Oxford: Oxford University Press.

Schabas, William A. 2017. *An Introduction to the International Criminal Court*. Fifth edition. Cambridge: Cambridge University Press.

International Organization for Migration (IOM)

The International Organization for Migration (IOM) is a key organization working across the globe to assist migrants. The organization's roots date back to 1951 with the establishment of the Provisional Intergovernmental Committee for the Movement of Migrants from Europe, which started operations as the Intergovernmental Committee for European Migration several months later. In 1980, the body was renamed Intergovernmental Committee for Migration due to the organization's work shifting beyond Europe and then transformed into the IOM in 1989. In the past, the IOM connected with the UN in various capacities, including achieving permanent observer status in the General Assembly in 1992 and signing cooperation agreements in 1996 and 2013. In 2016, the two organizations approved an agreement to formalize IOM's status as a related organization in the UN System, which includes IOM participation on the Chief Executives Board for Coordination.

RESPONSIBILITIES

As set out in the organization's Constitution, the IOM is designed to assist with arrangements for the transfer and repatriation of migrants, refugees, and other displaced persons and a wide range of services for migrants including processing, language training, medical examination, and advising on migration questions. In addition, the organization is supposed to encourage coordination, studies, and sharing of views on international migration. The IOM's operational mandate does not explicitly include the protection of migrant rights or a normative role for setting guidelines for the proper treatment of migrants. However, the IOM largely interprets its responsibilities as covering humanitarian dimensions of migration.

STRUCTURE

The Council is the IOM's central organ. This body holds a regular annual session, as well as special sessions when requested, where all members come together to review reports, set policy, and approve the budget. The work of the Council is bolstered by a Standing Committee on Programmes and Finance, with participation open to any member, which usually meets twice a year. The other major IOM organ is the Administration, which comprises the institution's staff and is headed by a Director General and Deputy Director General elected by the Council. Activities are supported by a Department of Operations and Emergencies and a Department of Migration Management, as well as a Department of International Cooperation and Partnerships.

Although IOM headquarters is based in Geneva, Switzerland, the organization is very decentralized and based primarily in the field. This includes nine regional offices and offices in over one hundred countries as well as administrative centers in Panama and the Philippines. The basic administrative budget is supported by the member states. However, given IOM's focus in the field, the vast majority of the organization's funds are voluntary contributions designated to support particular projects, which makes the IOM a donor-driven institution. IOM's membership has grown significantly, reaching 173 member states as of 2019 (and 8 states with observer status) compared to just 79 member states in 2000.

ACTIVITIES

IOM activities are built around four overarching migration management issues: migration and development, facilitating migration, regulating migration, and forced migration. As a project-based organization, the IOM shifts from area and issue emphasis depending on migration circumstances. Broadly, operational activities tend to reflect two main categories: providing needed assistance during emergencies and the traditional role connected to coordinating transfers, resettlement, and reintegration. Along with work in the field, the IOM gathers, analyzes, and publishes a range of data and information on migration, including the *World Migration Report*. IOM's Constitution explicitly instructs the institution to "cooperate closely with international organizations, governmental and nongovernmental," and such cooperation is a regular part of IOM engagement. At the same time, the IOM has a long history of a complicated, at times tense, relationship with the UN High Commissioner for Refugees (UNHCR) due to overlapping responsibilities and competition. In principle, UNHCR should focus more on emergencies while the IOM should be engaged over the longer term, but in practice the IOM works with displaced peoples of all kinds at many stages, including refugees and internally displaced people along with migrants. The two organizations have entered into agreements in order to better differentiate and coordinate their activities.

CHALLENGES AND REFORM

With the IOM now connected to the UN System as a related organization, the institution faces increased scrutiny. The IOM is critiqued by some, including humanitarian nongovernmental organizations, for acting more to meet the interests of the organization's member states than migrants' needs. Because the IOM lacks an explicit human rights protection mandate and is reliant on government funding to maintain operations, the organization has difficulties responding to such critiques. The IOM also faces ongoing questions regarding activities relative to other actors, in particular the UNHCR. The organization must also cope with rising migration pressure caused by developments like climate change that extend beyond the institution's traditional mandate. By linking the IOM to the UN System as a related organization instead of as a full specialized agency, the UN still lacks a lead agency to address migration and, in return, this limits the IOM's policy-making impact. The IOM has expanded its membership, budget, staffing levels, and number of field operations over the past several decades in a manner that increased its capabilities and visibility. The institution's new status in the UN System presents avenues to continue to grow and evolve in its mission to address migration issues. A key illustration of this is the establishment of a UN Network on Migration in support of the 2018 Global Compact for Safe, Orderly and Regular Migration. The IOM sits on the Network's eight-agency Executive Committee, staffs the Secretariat, and the Director General acts as the Network Coordinator.

See also: International Labour Organization; Membership; Nongovernmental Organizations; Refugees and Migration; United Nations High Commissioner for Refugees.

FURTHER READING

Bradley, Megan. 2020. *The International Organization for Migration: Challenges, Commitments, Complexities.* London: Routledge.

Ducasse-Rogier, Marianne. 2001. *The International Organization for Migration, 1951–2001.* Geneva, Switzerland: International Organization for Migration.

Elie, Jerome. 2010. "The Historical Roots of Cooperation Between the UN High Commissioner for Refugees and the International Organization for Migration." *Global Governance* 16 (3): 345–60.

Pécoud, Antoine. 2018. "What Do We Know about the International Organization for Migration?" *Journal of Ethnic and Migration Studies* 44 (10): 1621–38.

International Seabed Authority (ISA)

The Earth's oceans hold significant resources that are part of the global commons. Like outer space and Antarctica, marine resources need to be regulated for both public and private benefit. The UN began addressing issues of ocean exploration, fishing, shipping, and resource extraction at the 1958 Conference on the Law of the Sea in Geneva, which led to four separate Conventions covering: Territorial Sea and Contiguous Zone (entered into force 1964), Continental Shelf (entered into force 1964), High Seas (entered into force 1962), and Fishing and Conservation of the Living Resources of the High Seas (entered into force 1966). This framework was last updated in 1982 when the Third Conference on the Law of the Sea (held 1973–1982) crafted the comprehensive UN Convention on the Law of the Sea (UNCLOS), which called for the creation of three international institutions: International Seabed Authority (ISA), International Tribunal for Law of the Sea (ITLOS), and Commission on the Limits of the Continental Shelf (CLCS). In 1994, ISA was created as an independent international organization headquartered in Kingston, Jamaica.

RESPONSIBILITIES

ISA's primary role is the implementation of UNCLOS, with a specific focus on the seabed and mineral resources. The body's mandate is to regulate the mining of deep-sea minerals in areas of the ocean beyond member states' jurisdiction, as

> **Law of the Sea**
>
> The international law of the sea addresses legal issues of jurisdiction over maritime resources. Marine environments that extend beyond a twelve-nautical-mile coastline are considered international waters and recognized as "global commons." With 71 percent of the planet's surface covered by oceans, regulations are essential for international peace and security, shipping, global commerce, international energy supplies, food, communications, and many natural resources. Starting in 1958, there have been three UN Conferences on the Law of the Sea (1958, 1960, and 1973–1982). Pressures from overfishing, competing sovereignty claims, and increasing competition over resource extraction led to the most recent updated regulations when the Third UN Conference on the Law of the Sea was convened from 1973 to 1982. The process lasted so long because many issues addressed were controversial, including coastal versus landlocked resources, developed versus developing state access, and public versus private regulations. The result, which updated the 1958 Conventions (the 1960 Conference did not produce any new agreements), was a comprehensive treaty, the UN Convention on the Law of the Sea, with 320 articles and nine annexes that include regulations on the high seas, fishing and live resources, and exploration and extraction of the seabed. This updated Convention recognized freedom-of-navigation rights, established territorial boundaries, created Exclusive Economic Zones, continental shelf rights, and founded the International Seabed Authority. The treaty entered into force in 1994 with the sixtieth ratification (as of early 2020, this has reached 168 parties). The United States has not yet ratified the treaty as some claim it will impede sovereignty and impose environmental standards. With melting sea ice in the Artic and increased awareness that protecting oceans and marine environments are directly related to the conservation of the global environment, the Law of the Sea is increasingly relevant.

well as to develop rules and regulations to ensure that the marine environment is not harmed by the effects of such mining. The body also promotes and coordinates the dissemination of marine research in the seabed area.

STRUCTURE

ISA has three principal organs: Assembly, Council, and Secretariat. There are 168 members (as of July 2017), all of whom receive one vote in the Assembly, which is guided by a President and four Vice-Presidents for each annual session. There are also thirty countries, thirty-two international or UN-based organizations, and thirty nongovernmental organizations that hold observer status. The Council holds executive authority and has thirty-six members elected by the Assembly for four-year terms. Membership in the Council is determined by geographic location and state interest in areas of operation. The Council has a President and four Vice-Presidents, elected each year by the Council. The Secretariat, which includes Offices of Administrative Services, Environmental Management and Mineral Resources, and Legal Affairs, provides administrative support and is overseen by a Secretary-General who is elected for a four-year term by the Assembly after being proposed by the Council.

ISA also includes a Legal and Technical Commission to provide expert advice and a Finance Committee focused on budgetary issues. The UN and ISA hold an agreement to "consult and cooperate, whenever appropriate, on matters of mutual concern." ITLOS operates as an independent judicial body to hear disputes connected to UNCLOS, while CLCS provides scientific and technical advice and makes recommendations regarding the boundaries of the continental shelf control when this extends beyond 200 nautical miles.

ACTIVITIES

Much of ISA's work involves issuing survey and mining contracts to both countries and private corporations. ISA contracts hold fifteen-year terms for exploration of minerals. ISA also created a "parallel system" whereby any application for deep-sea mining rights requires the selected mining area to be divided into two halves of "equal estimated commercial value," with one half given to the applicant and the other reserved for use by either ISA or developing countries. ISA's focus evolved to incorporate conservation efforts and protecting marine environments from harm caused by resource extraction. This includes protecting flora and fauna from damage, the conservation of biodiversity, and safeguards against pollution of the seabed.

ISA also implements UNCLOS Article 82, which stipulates that developing states, "particularly the least developed and the land-locked amongst them," should receive some payments for the extraction of resources within the continental shelf beyond two hundred nautical miles. To fulfill this mandate, ISA established the Voluntary Trust Fund for developing countries in 2002. This was enhanced with the 2006 creation of the Endowment Fund for collaborative marine scientific research in the international seabed area. This program recruits scientists and technical personnel from developing countries and provides financial support and technical training to support their marine research. ISA has cooperation agreements with other international organizations, including the International Maritime Organization and the UN Educational, Scientific and Cultural Organization.

CHALLENGES AND REFORM

ISA faces challenges in regulating new activities and extraction methods as science and technology evolve. In addition, to support sustainable practices, scientists have called on ISA to establish no-mining zones and robust protective measures. Others note a need for enhanced regulatory frameworks to adapt to increased demands for mineral resources, which have shifted from exploration to extraction. The adoption of the 2012 Environmental Management Plan for the central Pacific Clarion-Clipperton Zone is viewed as a positive step as it closed parts of the Pacific Ocean to new mining activities to preserve biodiversity and unique ecosystems. Specific reforms call for modification and reviews of existing contracts to ensure that the marine environments are not harmed by mining activities.

Many developing countries view UNCLOS as only benefiting developed countries. ISA is called on to assist with transfer of technology from developed to developing states, which is controversial since this may infringe on intellectual property rights in developed states. In addition, there is debate over the scope of ISA's work as some regulations fall under the purview of national jurisdiction areas that are claimed as Exclusive Economic Zones, or regulated through bilateral agreements. Critics see ISA as not realizing its full potential and call for a more active role in balancing the demands of countries, private industry, and the future of ocean life. Yet, many find UNCLOS to be one of the UN's preeminent successes, as over half of the world's seabed now falls under international jurisdiction with protections against exploitation.

See also: Economic Development; Environmental Protection; Global Commons; International Maritime Organization; Sustainable Development; United Nations Conferences and Summits; United Nations Educational, Scientific and Cultural Organization.

FURTHER READING

Anderson, David. 2008. *Modern Law of the Sea: Selected Essays.* Leiden, Netherlands: Martinus Nijhoff.

Jaeckel, Aline. 2016. "Deep Seabed Mining and Adaptive Management: The Procedural Challenges for the International Seabed Authority." *Marine Policy* 70 (August): 205–11.

Lodge, Michael W. 2006. "The International Seabed Authority and Article 82 of the UN Convention on the Law of the Sea." *The International Journal of Marine and Coastal Law* 21 (3): 323–33.

Wedding, L. M., et al. 2015. "Managing Mining of the Deep Seabed." *Science* 349 (6244): 144–45.

Organization for the Prohibition of Chemical Weapons (OPCW)

Efforts to outlaw the use of chemical weapons in warfare date back several centuries. In 1899, at the Hague Peace Conference, countries pledged to ban weapons with "asphyxiating or deleterious gases." Yet, the agreement failed to prevent a horrific number of deaths resulting from the use of mustard gas during World War I. In response, the 1925 Geneva Protocol banned the use of chemical weapons but did not outlaw their development. Efforts continued, but the introduction of chemical weapons to the agenda of the Eighteen-Nation Disarmament Committee in Geneva in 1968 (a precursor to the current Conference on Disarmament) met with little success. While the Biological Weapons Convention entered into force in 1975, chemical weapons were not addressed. In 1988, a chemical attack on the Kurdish people in northern Iraq elevated the issue. With the end of the Cold War, the United States (a holdout that wanted the right to stockpile and retaliate) became more amenable to a complete ban. In 1992, the draft of the Convention on the Prohibition of the Development, Production, Stockpiling and Use of Chemical

Weapons and on their Destruction, commonly known as the Chemical Weapons Convention (CWC), was put into place, approved by the General Assembly in Resolution 47/39 (November 1992) and then signed in January 1993. The CWC entered into force in April 1997. The Organization for the Prohibition of Chemical Weapons (OPCW) was created as the implementing body for the CWC. The OPCW is headquartered in The Hague, Netherlands. In 2001, the organization's relationship with the General Assembly was formalized as an "independent, autonomous international organization."

RESPONSIBILITIES

The OPCW's mission includes the elimination of all chemical weapons and the promotion of the peaceful use of technology and economic development in the chemical sciences. The OPCW has a strong mandate with significant capacity to implement through a robust verification system. The organization is called upon to assist CWC signatory states with destroying all chemical weapons, eliminating production facilities, and forgoing any acquisitions. In addition to routine inspections and responding to the alleged use of chemical weapons, the OPCW is authorized to perform a surprise review of facilities under the "challenge inspection" process to address possible noncompliance.

STRUCTURE

The OPCW's three main bodies are the Conference of the States Parties (CSP), the Executive Council, and the Technical Secretariat. The CSP is the primary organ with oversight capacity where each member state holds one vote. OPCW membership is based on being a State Party to the Convention, with 193 member states (as of early 2020). Israel has signed, but not ratified, the Convention, while Egypt, North Korea, and South Sudan are not signatories. The CSP was first convened in May 1997 and holds an annual session at The Hague, where it reviews compliance with the CWC, considers the impact of technological advances, adopts the annual budget, and approves the annual report. A Chairperson, elected by the CSP for each session, oversees the proceedings.

The Executive Council, guided by a Chair and four Vice-Chairs, is made up of forty-one member states elected by the CSP for two-year terms and serves as the governing body with executive power for implementing the CWC and ensuring compliance. Membership is allocated to balance geographical representation, the significance of a country's chemical industry, and specific political and security concerns and includes five Eastern European countries, nine African states, ten Western Europe and Others, nine Asia, seven Latin America and the Caribbean (GRULAC), and a rotating seat between GRULAC and Asia. The Executive Council usually meets three times annually, although emergency sessions can be convened. The Technical Secretariat is headed by a Director General appointed by the CSP (on the recommendation of the Executive Council) who serves a four-year term and is supported by a Deputy Director General. The Technical Secretariat oversees on-site inspections, drafts the annual budgets and reports, provides technical training, and raises awareness through seminars and public engagement. This division also sets the number of inspections, coordinates chemical weapon destruction, and performs state and industry inspections. Within the Technical Secretariat, there are five divisions: Verification, Inspectorate, International Cooperation and Assistance, External Relations, and Administration. The 2020 OPCW budget was just under €71 million, with inspections costing almost €31 million.

ACTIVITIES

Much of OPCW's work focuses on inspections and compliance with the elimination of chemical weapons. A recent notable OPCW activity was overseeing a multilateral Joint Mission in Syria and UN partnership (2013–2014) to remove and destroy Syria's declared chemical weapons. The OPCW also works to ensure that, following their destruction, chemical weapons do not return by verifying that toxic chemicals are being used in a proper manner. While encouraging the free trade of many chemicals, the OPCW also monitors the international trade of restricted chemicals and works to ensure that dangerous chemicals do not fall into the hands of terrorists or other criminal actors. Additional programs encourage international cooperation, sharing of knowledge, developing laboratory facilities, and other forms of technical assistance to promote the positive and peaceful use of chemicals across the globe.

CHALLENGES AND REFORMS

The OPCW faces implementation challenges as many sites that produce industrial products, such as chlorine bleach, can be easily modified to produce chemical weapons. In addition, the OPCW is undermined by the threat of chemical use by nonstate actors, such as the 1995 Tokyo sarin gas attack. Overall, the OPCW represents an innovative treaty-based arrangement that is regarded as a model international organization. The institution's impartial and science-based approach provides neutral monitoring and offers punitive measures in cases of noncompliance. With almost all UN states as members of the OPCW and 97 percent of declared chemical weapons destroyed, the organization is viewed as highly effective. In light of these successes, the OPCW was awarded the Nobel Peace Prize in 2013.

See also: Arms Control and Disarmament; Disarmament Commission; General Assembly; International Atomic Energy Agency.

FURTHER READING

Hendrikse, Jeanet. 2005. "A Comprehensive Review of the Official OPCW Proficiency Test" In *Chemical Weapons Convention Chemicals Analysis: Sample Collection, Preparation, and Analytical Methods*, edited by Markku Mesilaakso, 89–132. Hoboken, NJ: John Wiley.

Kenyon, Iran R., and Daniel Feakes. 2007. *The Creation of the Organisation for the Prohibition of Chemical Weapons: A Case Study in the Birth of an Intergovernmental Organisation*. The Hague: TMC Asser Press.

Makdisi, Karim, and Coralie Pison Hindawi. 2019. "Exploring the UN and OPCW Partnership in Syrian Chemical Weapons Disarmament: Inter-organizational Cooperation and Autonomy." *Global Governance* 25 (4): 535–62.

Trapp, Ralf. 2014. "Elimination of the Chemical Weapons Stockpile of Syria." *Journal of Conflict and Security Law* 19 (1): 7–23.

Preparatory Commission for the Comprehensive Nuclear-Test-Ban Treaty Organization (CTBTO)

The idea to restrict the testing of nuclear devices, and thereby limit their development, was introduced in 1954 by Indian Prime Minister Jawaharlal Nehru and progressed in the late 1950s and early 1960s in talks between the United States and Soviet Union. In 1963, the Partial Test Ban Treaty prohibiting nuclear testing in the atmosphere, space, and underwater was adopted, but underground tests were still allowed. Following the end of the Cold War, negotiations at the Conference on Disarmament between 1994 and 1996 led to the Comprehensive Nuclear-Test-Ban Treaty (CTBT). In September 1996, the General Assembly adopted the document through Resolution 50/245 and the Preparatory Commission was established in November 1996. The treaty prohibits all nuclear weapon test explosions, and 184 countries have signed the agreement, with 168 of those ratifying the treaty (as of November 2019). Yet, the treaty remains in limbo and has not entered into force as it requires ratification from all forty-four states that have nuclear power and/or research reactors. Eight of these countries are still needed. China, Egypt, Iran, Israel, and the United States have not ratified the treaty and three others are not yet signatories (India, North Korea, and Pakistan). Pending the needed ratifications, the treaty will enter into force and the Comprehensive Nuclear-Test-Ban Treaty Organization (CTBTO) will be created, with headquarters in Vienna, Austria.

RESPONSIBILITIES

The CTBT bans all nuclear explosions in any location, including the Earth's surface, the atmosphere, underwater, and underground. The ban applies to tests for both civilian and military purposes. As indicated in Article II of the treaty, the CTBTO will be the implementation organization. In addition to creating a monitoring and verification system, the organization will also provide a forum to encourage consultation between member states. As the CTBT is not in force, the Preparatory Commission of the CTBTO was created as an interim body headquartered in Vienna to prepare for implementing the treaty, including establishing verification mechanisms to have these in place when the full organization takes effect. The Preparatory Commission also promotes the CTBT, encouraging further signatures and ratifications.

STRUCTURE

The Preparatory Commission contains two primary organs. The Preparatory Commission plenary body (also referred to as the Preparatory Commission) is composed of all treaty signatories. The plenary body is supported by three subsidiary bodies: one on administrative and financial matters, one on verification-related issues, and an advisory group. The Provisional Technical Secretariat (PTS) is comprised of three technical divisions (International Monitoring System [IMS], International Data Centre [IDC], and On-Site Inspection), as well as divisions addressing administration and legal and external relations, and is headed by an Executive Secretary appointed by the Preparatory Commission for a four-year term. In 2000, the Preparatory Commission agreed to a formal relationship agreement with the UN where both parties agreed to mutual exchange of information and shared participation in relevant meetings. Similar agreements were negotiated with the UN Development Programme in 2000 for operational support and the World Meteorological Organization in 2001 for meteorological observations. The annual budget of around $130 million is financed by state signatories, primarily through assessed contributions, with most of that funding earmarked for the creation of the global verification regime. Voluntary contributions (both financial and equipment) for particular projects are also provided.

When the treaty officially enters into force, the temporary arrangements will be converted to permanent organizational structures. The plenary Preparatory Commission will become the Conference of the State Parties, the Preparatory Commission groups will turn into a fifty-one-member Executive Council elected by the Conference, the PTS will become the Technical Secretariat, and the Executive Secretary will convert to Director General. The verification regime will be supported by the IMS, IDC, and Global Communications Infrastructure (GCI).

ACTIVITIES

The Preparatory Commission, even before the treaty's entry into force, is an active organization involved in building the structures needed for robust nuclear detection systems and the successful implementation of the CTBT. The centerpiece of its activities includes monitoring, data collection, and inspections. The IMS, a worldwide network of monitoring stations, detects any nuclear explosions through monitoring seismic activity, low-frequency acoustic waves, sound waves in the oceans, and the presence of radioactivity. Together, these can identify surface and atmospheric explosions as well as underwater or underground tests. The IMS also includes radionuclide laboratories to process station samples. The IDC in Vienna processes data collected by the IMS, and communicated via the GCI, including explosion magnitude and location. Once the CTBT is in place, then on-site inspections can be carried out, with member state approval, if data suggest a nuclear explosion. The Preparatory Commission has conducted a number of exercises in locations such as Jordan and Kazakhstan to prepare for such inspections and is also called upon to create training activities and clear procedures to ensure that the inspectors will be well prepared.

CHALLENGES AND REFORMS

The primary challenge for the CTBTO is uncertainty surrounding the lack of full ratification. Many argue that the treaty's provisions are too strict, yet without key nuclear powers' ratification, the CTBTO is in a holding pattern. As called for under Article XIV of the CTBT, to encourage the treaty's entry into force the UN Secretary-General, with support from the UN Office for Disarmament Affairs, convenes the Conference on Facilitating Entry into Force of the CTBT. The first conference was held in 1999 in Vienna, with recent conferences convening every two years in New York. Secretary-General António Guterres' 2018 *Securing Our Common Future: An Agenda for Disarmament* also emphasizes the need for final approval of the CTBT. The effectiveness of the CTBTO is indicated by significant state compliance with the treaty. Another remarkable accomplishment is implementing the detection infrastructure. This includes the near completion of over 300 monitoring facilities in eighty-nine countries. Overall, the CTBTO's success is found in both a highly supported global norm against testing and an extensive international detection system already in place.

See also: António Guterres; Arms Control and Disarmament; Ban Ki-moon; Disarmament Commission; General Assembly; Office of Secretary-General; United Nations Development Programme; World Meteorological Organization.

FURTHER READING

Hansen, Keith A. 2006. *The Comprehensive Nuclear Test Ban Treaty: An Insider's Perspective*. Stanford, CA: Stanford University Press.

Kimball, Daryl G. 2016. "The Enduring Nonproliferation Value of the Comprehensive Nuclear Test-Ban Treaty." *The Nonproliferation Review* 23 (3–4): 397–408.

Rietiker, Daniel. 2018. *Humanization of Arms Control: Paving the Way for a World Free of Nuclear Weapons*. New York: Routledge.

Zartman, I. William, Mordechai Melamud, and Paul Meerts, eds. 2014. *Banning the Bang Or the Bomb? Negotiating the Nuclear Test Ban Regime*. Cambridge: Cambridge University Press.

World Trade Organization (WTO)

While the World Trade Organization (WTO) is a relatively new organization, it is part of a continued effort to craft a robust international trade system. In 1941, U.S. President Franklin D. Roosevelt and UK Prime Minister Winston Churchill included this priority in the Atlantic Charter. Clause 4 of this agreement noted that trade is "needed for . . . economic prosperity" and Clause 5 called for "the fullest collaboration between all nations in the economic field." At the 1944 Bretton Woods Conference, the International Monetary Fund (IMF) and the International Bank for Reconstruction and Development (now the center of the modern World Bank Group) were established and plans were put in place for an International Trade Organization (ITO). While a charter for the ITO was agreed upon, due to a lack of U.S. Senate support for ratification, the institution was never formed. Thus, agreements established in a series of trade negotiations known as the General Agreement on Tariffs and Trade (GATT) provided the basic rules of world trade from 1948 as a de facto organization.

During the eighth round of GATT negotiations (1986–1994, referred to as the Uruguay Round), the WTO was created as a full institution to succeed GATT and include the agreements under its operations. The WTO officially came into existence on January 1, 1995, and is headquartered in Geneva, Switzerland. Although the WTO is not a specialized agency, like the IMF and World Bank, it signed a cooperation agreement with the UN in November 1995, which guides their interactions as a related organization and includes participation on the Chief Executives Board for Coordination alongside the specialized agencies, programmes, and funds. Institutions in the UN System, such as the Food and Agriculture Organization, also have observer status in the WTO.

RESPONSIBILITIES

The WTO's aim is to promote international trade, reduce barriers to trade, and foster global economic growth and development. The organization's mandate includes promoting open borders and markets, securing most-favored-nation principles, and encouraging nondiscriminatory practices. The organization also seeks to promote transparency in international trade as well as foster domestic and international policies to enhance each member state's development goals.

STRUCTURE

The WTO's primary decision-making is conducted by its 164 member states (with Afghanistan the latest to join in 2016) through the Ministerial Conference. In this regard, unlike the World Bank and IMF, decision-making authority is not allocated to the organization. Member states retain authority and meet every two years. Most decisions are made by consensus. Much of the work of the WTO falls to the General Council, which is also composed of member state delegations. The General Council meets in Geneva several times each year and can serve as both the Trade Policy Review Body and the Dispute Settlement Body. There are three substantive Councils (Trade in Goods, Trade in Services, and Trade-Related Aspects of Intellectual Property Rights) under the General Council, each of which has additional subcommittees focused on particular areas. Additional committees under the General Committee address areas including the environment and regional trade agreements, and the General Committee also gets reports from the "plurilateral" agreement bodies (which are not signed by all WTO members) of trade in civil aircraft and government procurement. The Appellate Body reviews appeals in disputes between member states, and the body's decisions, after being approved by the Dispute Settlement Body, must be followed.

To join the WTO, states must submit a memorandum concerning all relevant trade aspects to the organization and then conduct parallel bilateral agreements with each WTO member. The WTO can then approve the terms of accession with a two-thirds vote in favor. Increasingly, regional organizations are becoming effective negotiating blocs within the WTO, and the European Union (along with its member states) holds independent membership. The WTO Secretariat is led by a Director-General, along with four Deputy Director-Generals, and operates with an annual budget of almost 200 million Swiss francs (as of 2018) provided by the member states along with other minor sources of income like publication sales.

ACTIVITIES

The WTO's main activities include negotiating the reduction of obstacles to trade (such as import tariffs) and establishing protocols governing the conduct of international trade (including antidumping, subsidies, and product standards). The organization also monitors whether states are following rules regarding trade in goods, services, and intellectual property rights. The WTO provides a forum for states to negotiate terms of trade as well as a legal framework to address disputes and monitor compliance with agreements. The agreements established are legal contracts that grant members trade rights, promote transparency, and provide for a stable global trading system. One of the WTO's primary activities is dispute settlement. Members are encouraged to resolve conflicts bilaterally, however, if that is not feasible, they can submit a dispute to a panel of experts established by the Dispute Settlement Body. As of early 2020, just under six hundred disputes have been submitted to the WTO. Recently, WTO's activities expanded to include the promotion of sustainable development and the related Sustainable Development Goals. For developing states, the WTO assists with technical and legal support in preparing for global negotiations. In addition, the organization engages in research, sponsors conferences, and provides economic analysis, trade reports, and forecasts. The WTO also works with related parts of the UN System, such as signing a memorandum of understanding in 2003 to partner with the UN Conference on Trade and Development.

CHALLENGES AND REFORM

The WTO faces ongoing challenges. Agriculture remains a contentious policy issue, and subsidies to farmers is a perpetually problematic barrier to level trading. In addition, critics find that WTO processes marginalize developing states and contribute to a global trading system that advantages wealthy countries. Another challenge area for the WTO is the growth in alternative venues, particularly at the regional level. In addition, the scope of negotiations in the Doha Round, launched in 2001, is moving well beyond tariffs to address sustainable trading practices, intellectual property rights, and issues of public health. In December 2019, the WTO's dispute settlement process was significantly undermined when the Trump administration's policy of blocking appointments to the Appellate Body meant that this body had to cease operations. Despite these challenges, the WTO has succeeded in expanding its membership rate, with the members now encompassing 98 percent of global trade. Membership in the WTO enhances capacity and access to economic research and data on trade. In addition, the WTO has crafted agreements that are subject to international monitoring and continues to provide an important dispute resolution forum.

See also: Economic and Social Council; Economic Development; Food and Agriculture Organization; International Monetary Fund; International Telecommunication Union; United Nations Conference on Trade and Development; United Nations Industrial Development Organization; World Bank Group; World Intellectual Property Organization; World Tourism Organization.

FURTHER READING

Flentø, Daniel, and Stefano Ponte. 2017. "Least-developed Countries in a World of Global Value Chains: Are WTO Trade Negotiations Helping?" *World Development* 94 (June): 366–74.

Hoda, Anwarul. 2018. *Tariff Negotiations and Renegotiations Under the GATT and the WTO: Procedures and Practices.* Second edition. Cambridge: Cambridge University Press.

Hoekman, Bernard M., and Petros C. Mavroidis. 2016. *The World Trade Organization: Law, Economics, and Politics.* Second edition. London: Routledge.

Margulis, Matias E. 2018. "Negotiating for the Margins: How the UN Shapes the Rules of the WTO." *Review of International Political Economy* 25 (3): 362–91.

United Nations Headquarters in New York City. Many Secretariat departments and offices are housed in New York, along with meeting halls for other principal organs and a number of funds and programmes. There are also three official offices in Geneva, Switzerland, Vienna, Austria, and Nairobi, Kenya, along with other parts of the United Nations System located throughout the world. (Makoto Honda/Dreamstime.com)

The Charter of the United Nations was drafted at the San Francisco Conference on International Organization and then signed on June 26, 1945. The Charter is a binding international treaty that serves as the equivalent of the constitution of the organization. (World History Archive/Alamy Stock Photo)

General Assembly Hall at United Nations Headquarters in New York City. This meeting space can accommodate representatives from all 193 member states as well as observers. (Demerzel21/Dreamstime.com)

A hearing on the frontier dispute between Cambodia and Thailand at the International Court of Justice (ICJ) in The Hague, Netherlands, in 2013. The ICJ, often referred to as the World Court, is the principal judicial organ of the United Nations. (Digikhmer/Dreamstime.com)

Training exercises by United Nations Peacekeepers at the Five Hills Training Area in Mongolia. Peacekeeping operations are a valuable tool for United Nations' efforts to maintain international peace and security and must be approved by the Security Council. (U.S. Army National Guard)

The United Nations Development Programme (UNDP) assists with the reconstruction and revival of economic activity in Ecuador after a 2016 earthquake. Promoting economic and social cooperation is a founding purpose of the United Nations. UNDP oversees thousands of development projects in approximately 170 countries. (UNDP Ecuador)

World Food Day celebration in Dhaka, Bangladesh, on October 16, 2016, commemorating the founding of the Food and Agriculture Organization (FAO) on that date in 1945. Headquartered in Rome, the FAO is one of the specialized agencies that signed an agreement to be part of the United Nations System. (Mamunur Rashid/Alamy Stock Photos)

The Dilmun Burial Mounds in Bahrain were built between 2200 and 1750 BCE. The United Nations Educational, Scientific and Cultural Organization, a United Nations specialized agency, designated these as a World Heritage site in 2019, recognizing their cultural significance. (John Elk III/Alamy Stock Photo)

Following the December 26, 2004, tsunami, the World Health Organization (WHO) worked to provide essential supplies to the people on the island of Sumatra in Indonesia. WHO is headquartered in Geneva, Switzerland, and serves as a United Nations specialized agency working to promote health and well-being across the globe. (U.S. Navy)

Children studying a science textbook provided by the United Nations Children's Fund (UNICEF) in Norton, Zimbabwe, in 2018. UNICEF, one of the programmes and funds in the United Nations System, works to promote humanitarian work with children throughout the world. (Cecil Dzwowa/Dreamstime.com)

United Nations High Commissioner for Refugees (UNHCR) staff registering refugees displaced by the war in Syria (2011–) on the island of Kos, Greece, in 2015. UNHCR assists millions of people who are forced to leave their homes. (Dimaberkut/Dreamstime.com)

A Human Rights Council meeting at its headquarters in Geneva, Switzerland, on September 15, 2017, discussing the integration of gendered perspectives. The Human Rights Council began operations in 2006, replacing the Commission on Human Rights. The body works to protect human rights, one of the three core purposes of the United Nations. (Siavosh Hosseini/Alamy Stock Photo)

International Atomic Energy Agency (IAEA) Headquarters building at the United Nations Centre in Vienna, Austria. In 1959, the IAEA signed an agreement to work with the United Nations as a related organization. The organization promotes global cooperation to safeguard nuclear capabilities for peaceful uses. (Ralf Punkenhofer/Dreamstime.com)

Dag Hammarskjöld, the second United Nations Secretary-General, was from Sweden and served from 1953–1961. He played a central role in the creation of the United Nations' peacekeeping approach and died in a plane crash during a peace mission in the Congo. (Corel)

Kofi Annan, the seventh United Nations Secretary-General, was from Ghana and served from 1997–2006. He was the first office holder to rise through the ranks of the United Nations Secretariat and is known for his reform agenda. (U.S. Mission to the United Nations)

António Guterres, the ninth and current United Nations Secretary-General, is from Portugal and took office in January 2017. Prior to assuming this office, he was the Prime Minister of Portugal (1995–2002) and served as the head of the United Nations High Commissioner for Refugees (2005–2015). (U.K. Foreign and Commonwealth Office)

Louise Fréchette, the first Deputy Secretary-General of the United Nations, is from Canada. The position was created in late 1997 as part of Secretary-General Kofi Annan's reform recommendations. Fréchette took office in 1998 and served until 2006. (PA Images/Alamy Stock Photo)

Samantha Power served as the United States Ambassador to the United Nations and led the United States' Permanent Mission in New York City from 2013–2017. Power was appointed by President Barack Obama and is remembered for her advocacy of human rights and the release of women political prisoners. (U.S. Department of State)

Li Bingbing, Chinese actress and United Nations Environment Programme (UNEP) Goodwill Ambassador, observes elephant behavior at Samburu National Reserve in Kenya in May 2013. UNEP is headquartered in Nairobi and encourages countries to limit pollution and protect natural resources. (Xinhua/Alamy Stock Photo)

PART IV

Individual Actors in the United Nations System

INTRODUCTION

As established in Parts II and III, analysis of the United Nations (UN) System requires a detailed exploration of a wide range of institutions and entities. Yet, in order to fully understand how these institutions operate and make decisions, it is important to examine the individual actors who lead the UN's work. Most notably, the Secretary-General serves as the UN's executive head, guiding UN affairs and acting as the public face of the UN to the world. This section opens by providing an overview of the Office of Secretary-General and then profiles all nine of the individuals, from Trygve Lie to António Guterres, to hold the office thus far. In 1997, a new position, Deputy Secretary-General, was established in the UN Secretariat (with the first Deputy Secretary-General, Louise Fréchette, taking office in 1998). The Secretary-General's efforts to address conflicts and global issues are supported by a number of Special Representatives. The Secretary-General is not the only executive head in the UN System. Different institutions have their own leaders. In particular, the executive heads of specialized agencies, such as the Director-General of the World Health Organization, can play an important role due to their organization's distinct autonomous status within the UN System (see Part III for more details on the specialized agencies). Unlike the Secretary-General and other executive heads who hold office for multiple years, the heads of other principal organs in the UN serve for a much shorter time frame. The President of the General Assembly is elected to guide the Assembly for a one-year session, while the Presidents of the Security Council rotate on a monthly basis. Since the UN is an organization made up of sovereign member states, the activities of state ambassadors and delegates must also be examined. To further illustrate the role played by such individuals, the Ambassador position of one of the great powers at the UN, the United States, is detailed. Finally, moving beyond UN staff and member state representatives, other individuals perform a wide array of service in promoting the work and mission of the UN under titles such as Goodwill Ambassador and Messenger of Peace.

SECRETARIES-GENERAL

Office of Secretary-General

The Secretary-General is the executive head of the UN Secretariat. Officeholders serve a five-year term with no term limit, although none have held office for more than two terms. The details of the office are set out in Chapter XV: The Secretariat of the UN Charter. Article 97 establishes the Secretary-General as the "chief administrative officer" of the UN. Administrative control is reinforced in Article 101, which lists appointing staff as one of the office's duties. Article 98 instructs the Secretary-General to carry out functions assigned by the principal organs and to prepare an annual report for the General Assembly, as well as allowing the officeholder to attend meetings of the principal organs. Article 99 provides the most independent legal power specified in the Charter, stating, "The Secretary-General may bring to the attention of the Security Council any matter in which his opinion may threaten the maintenance of international peace and security." However, this article is very rarely directly invoked by officeholders.

SELECTING THE SECRETARY-GENERAL

As specified in Article 97 of the Charter, "The Secretary-General shall be appointed by the General Assembly upon the recommendation of the Security Council." In practice, the Security Council has dominated this process. Since the permanent five (P-5) members of the Security Council can use their veto to reject a candidate, there are often great power struggles over who should be selected, and it is highly unlikely that an individual from one of these countries will ever serve as Secretary-General. Thus, the Secretaries-General selected are often compromise candidates viewed as acceptable to all of the P-5. The General Assembly has traditionally simply approved whatever candidate emerged from Security Council deliberations. However, for the 2016 selection of António Guterres, the General Assembly was more engaged in the process. This included holding public question-and-answer sessions with the candidates. Despite this more open process and a significant public campaign arguing that this was finally the time for a female Secretary-General to be selected, controversially all Secretaries-General to this point have been men. The Secretary-Generalship rotates across geographic regions. After two West European (Norway and Sweden) Secretaries-General to start, the office shifted to an Asian national (Burma) before returning back to Western Europe (Austria), then on to South America (Peru), Africa (Egypt and then Ghana), Asia (Republic of Korea), and now back to Western Europe (Portugal). However, the East European region has thus far not had a Secretary-General.

United Nations Secretaries-General	
Trygve Lie (Norway)	1946–1953
Dag Hammarskjöld (Sweden)	1953–1961
U Thant (Burma)	1961–1971
Kurt Waldheim (Austria)	1972–1981
Javier Pérez de Cuéllar (Peru)	1982–1991
Boutros Boutros-Ghali (Egypt)	1992–1996
Kofi Annan (Ghana)	1997–2006
Ban Ki-moon (Republic of Korea)	2007–2016
António Guterres (Portugal)	2017–

EVOLUTION AND DEBATE OVER THE ROLE OF THE SECRETARY-GENERAL

The Secretary-General's contributions have evolved beyond the relatively limited formal job description provided in the Charter. Officeholders can employ the listed powers in a more extensive manner than originally imagined, and additional activities expanded the office's mandate. The Secretary-General shapes the organization through overseeing the budget and staffing the Secretariat. Their strategic position, gained by serving formally as a representative in meetings and informally through a range of contacts with member state representatives and other actors engaged in UN decision-making, provides Secretaries-General with political leverage. Secretaries-General are closely involved in efforts to maintain international peace and security. Article 99 responsibilities are widely interpreted to allow a Secretary-General to monitor and take independent action to address breaches of the peace. They provide third-party peaceful settlement, such as serving as a mediator to a conflict, personally or through appointing Special Representatives or working with "groups of friends." The mandates of peacekeeping missions can be shaped by Secretaries-General, and they play a central role in overseeing the implementation of peacekeeping operations.

Officeholders can also play an important agenda-setting role through their use of public pronouncements, including their use of the annual report, speeches, public statements, publicity, and extensive travel. When using their "bully pulpit" (speaking out from a high-profile position) in this manner, the Secretary-General can draw upon the moral authority of their office to press for global problems to be addressed. Reflecting this authority, the Secretary-General is referred to by some as the "secular Pope." Secretaries-General are also viewed as having the potential to serve as "norm entrepreneurs," framing issues and approaches for addressing those issues in a particular way for the global community.

At the same time, there is ongoing debate over the proper role of a Secretary-General. The question is whether an officeholder should serve as a "Secretary" or a "General." Those in favor of the "Secretary" emphasis view the office as subservient to member state interests. Thus, the officeholder should serve as a bureaucratic manager carrying out the instructions of the members and respecting constraints on their activities. Alternatively, those calling for a "General" point to the need for a visionary leader who can provide vital independent action and challenge constraints placed upon the office. Other analysts stress the need for a strategic Secretary-General who recognizes the limits of the office but still carefully works to have an influential role within those constraints.

See also: António Guterres; Ban Ki-moon; Boutros Boutros-Ghali; Charter of the United Nations; Dag Hammarskjöld; General Assembly; Javier Pérez de Cuéllar; Kofi Annan; Kurt Waldheim; Peaceful Settlement; Peacekeeping; Preparatory Commission for the Comprehensive Nuclear-Test-Ban Treaty Organization; Secretariat; Role of Great Powers; Secretariat; Security Council; Special Representatives of the United Nations Secretary-General; Trygve Lie; U Thant; United Nations Budget and Financing; Voting and Negotiating Blocs; Women and Gender.

FURTHER READING

Gordenker, Leon. 2010. *The UN Secretary-General and Secretariat*. Second edition. New York: Routledge.

Kille, Kent J. 2006. *From Manager to Visionary: The Secretary-General of the United Nations*. New York: Palgrave Macmillan.

Mouat, Lucia. 2014. *The United Nations' Top Job: A Close Look at the Work of Eight Secretaries-General*. North Charleston, SC: CreateSpace.

Trygve Lie

The first UN Secretary-General, Trygve Lie, started his political career at the national level in Norway, after years of engagement with labor and trade union issues, when he was elected to Parliament in 1935. He held a number of ministerial roles, including Foreign Minister, during the difficult political times leading up to and during World War II, when Norway was invaded by Nazi Germany in 1940. Lie was in charge of the delegation from Norway to the 1945 San Francisco Conference that established the UN Charter. He also led the Norwegian delegation to the first session of the General Assembly held in January 1946.

Lie was originally a candidate to be President of the General Assembly but lost out to Paul-Henri Spaak. He was then put forth as a candidate to be Secretary-General. Lie was not the top pick of any of the major powers in the Security Council but was deemed acceptable when the United States and Soviet Union deadlocked over their preferred alternatives. Lie took office in February 1946. He lacked Soviet support for a second term, but nonetheless, in November 1950, Lie's time in office was extended by three years (dating from February 1951). However, faced with great difficulties from both the Soviets and Americans, Lie resigned in November 1952. He remained in office until his successor, Dag Hammarskjöld, took over the office in April 1953.

ROLE AS SECRETARY-GENERAL

As the first permanent Secretary-General (Lie replaced Gladwyn Jebb, who was Executive Secretary of the UN Preparatory Commission and then Acting Secretary-General before Lie took office), Lie was tasked with establishing the administration and permanent headquarters for the UN. The Secretariat structure had to be organized and staffed. Lie worked out of offices in various locations in New York for most of his time as Secretary-General. He played a key role in establishing the current UN Headquarters location and buildings, although he was only able to work there for a few months before leaving office.

Lie faced an array of threats to international peace and security. His first challenge came immediately in 1946, when the Soviet Union resisted withdrawing its troops in a timely manner from Iran following the end of World War II. Lie intervened in Security Council discussions to provide his view. Soon afterward (1947–1949) he had to cope with the clash over Palestine when the British asked for UN assistance in determining the future of the Palestine mandate. He also sought to mediate between the United States and Soviet Union, as in the case of the Berlin Blockade of 1948–1949, although the two countries were not receptive to his offer. Lie is particularly well known for his ten-point, twenty-year program to achieve peace through the UN. Although Lie used speeches and traveled widely in 1950 on a "peace tour" to promote his ideas, he was unable to build consensus for action. Instead, in the first instance of what some consider to be a UN collective security action, Lie and the UN were drawn into the Korean War (1950–1953), with Lie siding with UN action to be taken against the North Koreans.

ADVANCES AND CHALLENGES WHILE IN OFFICE

Key precedents and capabilities for the Secretary-Generalship were established under Lie, as his activities charted the path for future officeholders. Examples include establishing the right of the Secretary-General to address the Security Council, the ability to appoint Special Representatives, and engagement in suggesting solutions to global conflicts. Lie's ideas and advice were not always heeded by the member states, but his efforts provided an important basis for the Secretaries-General who followed.

At the same time, based on his experience, Lie famously described being Secretary-General as the "most impossible job in the world." In particular, Lie struggled in the face of the divisive Cold War. Following Lie's support for UN intervention in Korea, the angered Soviet Union refused to work with his office. The U.S. clash with communism carried over into UN Headquarters. In the heart of the McCarthy era efforts by the United States to root out suspected communists, the Federal Bureau of Investigation insisted on being given access to UN Headquarters in New York to interview U.S. citizens working there. Allowing this to occur under his watch severely damaged Secretariat morale and support for Lie. After leaving the UN, Lie returned to Norway, where he had limited further engagement with international affairs, although he did serve in the Norwegian

> **Trygve Lie's Twenty-Year Peace Program Points (1950)**
>
> 1. Inauguration of periodic meetings of the Security Council, attended by foreign ministers or heads or other members of governments, as provided by the United Nations Charter and the rules of procedure; together with further development and use of other United Nations machinery for negotiation, mediation and conciliation of international disputes.
> 2. A new attempt to make progress toward establishing an international control system for atomic energy that will be effective in preventing its use for war and promoting its use for peaceful purposes.
> 3. A new approach to the problem of bringing the armaments race under control, not only in the field of atomic weapons, but in other weapons of mass destruction and in conventional armaments.
> 4. A renewal of serious efforts to reach agreement on the armed forces to be made available under the Charter to the Security Council for enforcement of its decisions.
> 5. Acceptance and application of the principle that it is wise and right to proceed as rapidly as possible toward universality of membership.
> 6. A sound and active program of technical assistance for economic development and encouragement of broad scale capital investment, using all appropriate private, governmental and intergovernmental resources.
> 7. More vigorous use by all Member Governments of the Specialized Agencies of the United Nations to promote, in the words of the Charter, "higher standards of living, full employment and conditions of economic and social progress."
> 8. Vigorous and continued development of the work of the United Nations for wider observance and respect for human rights and fundamental freedoms throughout the world.
> 9. Use of the United Nations to promote, by peaceful means instead of by force, the advancement of dependent, colonial or semi-colonial peoples, towards a place of equality in the world.
> 10. Active and systematic use of all the powers of the Charter and all the machinery of the United Nations to speed up the development of international law towards an eventual enforceable world law for a universal world society.
>
> Source: *The United Nations, 1945–53: The Development of a World Organization.* Harry S. Truman Library and Museum.

government again between 1963 and 1965 as Minister of Industry and then Minister of Trade, before passing away in 1968.

See also: Collective Security; Dag Hammarskjöld; Office of Secretary-General; President of General Assembly; Role of Great Powers; Secretariat; Special Representatives of the United Nations Secretary-General; United Nations Headquarters; United Nations Historical Background.

FURTHER READING

Barros, James. 1989. *Trygve Lie and the Cold War: The UN Secretary-General Pursues Peace, 1946–1953.* DeKalb: Northern Illinois University Press.

Lie, Trygve. 1954. *In the Cause of Peace: Seven Years with the United Nations.* New York: Macmillan.

Ravndal, Ellen Jenny. 2017. "'A Force for Peace': Expanding the Role of the UN Secretary-General Under Trygve Lie, 1946–1953." *Global Governance* 23 (3): 443–59.

Dag Hammarskjöld

Dag Hammarskjöld served as the second UN Secretary-General from April 1953 to September 1961. Hammarskjöld came to the UN with significant public service experience. From 1930 to 1934, he served as secretary of the Royal Commission on Unemployment before moving to the National Bank of Sweden for a year. In 1936, he was selected to be Permanent Undersecretary of the Swedish Ministry of Finance and went on to provide important advising regarding Sweden's financial policies. He served overlapping posts when he also held the position of Chairman of the National Bank of Sweden's Board between 1941 and 1948. Hammarskjöld was very engaged in the international realm, including helping to negotiate a Swedish-United States trade agreement and serving as the Swedish representative to the Organization for European Economic Cooperation and the Marshall Plan. He held several high-level positions connected to the Foreign Ministry and represented Sweden in the UN General Assembly from 1951 to 1953.

Hammarskjöld's nomination to be Secretary-General came at a tense time during the Cold War as hostilities escalated between the United States and Soviet Union. His predecessor, Trygve Lie, had resigned in late 1952. Hammarskjöld was a compromise candidate from nonaligned Sweden, as both the United States and the Soviet Union believed he would serve as a quiet civil servant without favoritism to either side. Hammarskjöld did not seek the office and was surprised by the nomination. He was initially hesitant to accept but determined this was an important task he could not decline. Following his 1957 reappointment, he served until 1961 when he was killed in a plane crash in Northern Rhodesia (now Zambia) during a peace mission in the Congo.

ROLE AS SECRETARY-GENERAL

Upon taking office, Hammarskjöld immediately faced a diplomatic showdown between the United States and Communist China. Two years prior, China captured several American airmen during the Korean War and accused them of spying. The United States viewed the Chinese as violating the Korean Armistice Agreement and brought the situation to the General Assembly. The General Assembly called on the Secretary-General to safeguard the release of the airmen. In response, Hammarskjöld met with the Chinese leadership in Peking, and the airmen were ultimately released. His use of quiet diplomacy is now known as the "Peking Formula" and became Hammarskjöld's trademark approach to peaceful settlement. Another notable test came in 1956 when Egypt's President Nasser nationalized the Suez Canal, which provoked a French and British attack. Working with Canadian representative Lester Pearson, Hammarskjöld sought to create a UN force to monitor the cease-fire. The result was the first armed UN peacekeeping operation, the UN Emergency Force created in November 1956, which set essential precedents for future peacekeeping missions. Hammarskjöld was also engaged in establishing the 1958 UN Observer Group in Lebanon.

In 1960, the Congo gained independence from Belgium, but a complex conflict continued and the Congolese Prime Minster and President requested UN involvement. Hammarskjöld directly invoked Article 99 of the UN Charter for the first time in history, bringing the situation to the attention of the Security Council. He also pressed for the creation of a robust peacekeeping mission, the UN Operation in the Congo, and was personally involved in seeking peace in the Congo right up to his untimely death. During the Congolese crisis, Hammarskjöld met his greatest personal opposition and faced threats to the Secretary-Generalship itself. The Soviet leader Nikita Khrushchev decided that Hammarskjöld's actions in the Congo were against Soviet interests and accused Hammarskjöld of imperialist sympathies and favoritism. The Soviets proposed changing the Secretary-Generalship into a troika (triple) executive, but Hammarskjöld effectively opposed this move. Hammarskjöld's clear disapproval of the Soviet proposal reflected his emphasis on the importance of the UN and the need for an independent Secretariat. One of his most notable public statements reinforcing this theme is his widely cited 1961 speech at Oxford. Hammarskjöld also impacted internal UN administration, particularly during his first term, through dictating the structure of the Secretariat, hiring practices, handling of reports, and budgetary matters. Other notable UN developments under Hammarskjöld's stewardship include his organization of the first two conferences on the Peaceful Uses of Atomic Energy in Geneva in 1955 and 1958.

ADVANCES AND CHALLENGES WHILE IN OFFICE

Hammarskjöld faced multiple challenges while in office with great power strife, attacks on the neutrality of the UN, and efforts to alter the office of Secretary-General. Yet, he is widely viewed as one of the most influential individuals to hold this position, and his leadership is credited with bolstering the new organization's credibility and fostering respect for international law. Hammarskjöld is regarded as a highly professional and even brilliant diplomat with a deep commitment to international organization. Many note that he was a man of personal charisma and deep moral conviction. John F. Kennedy, U.S. President at the time of his death, praised Hammarskjöld as "the greatest statesman of our century." In 1961, Hammarskjöld was posthumously awarded a Nobel Peace Prize.

See also: Office of Secretary-General; Peaceful Settlement; Peacekeeping; Secretariat; Trygve Lie; U Thant; United Nations Budget and Financing.

FURTHER READING

Fröhlich, Manuel. 2007. *Political Ethics and the United Nations: Dag Hammarskjöld as Secretary-General*. London: Routledge.

Lyon, Alynna J. 2007. "Moral Motives and Policy Actions: The Case of Dag Hammarskjöld at the United Nations." *Public Integrity* 9 (1): 79–95.

Urquhart, Brian. 1972. *Hammarskjöld*. New York: Alfred A. Knopf.

U Thant

U Thant, the third UN Secretary-General, was the first officeholder from outside of Western Europe. He was from Burma (now Myanmar) and, following Burmese independence from British colonial control and Japanese occupation during World War II, held a range of high-ranking positions in the government. Thant first engaged with the UN in Burma's delegation in 1952. He also represented Burma in international meetings of the Non-Aligned Movement and assisted with the planning of the 1955 Asian-African Conference. He took over as the Permanent Representative for Burma to the UN in 1957, chairing several committees, and served as a Vice-President of the General Assembly for the 1959–1960 session.

Thant began his time in office as Acting Secretary-General in November 1961, as he took over the Secretary-Generalship when Dag Hammarskjöld died in a plane crash that September. A year later he was formally appointed as the third Secretary-General, with his five-year term back dated to when he first started as Acting Secretary-General. Thant initially resisted serving a second term as Secretary-General, but after gaining stronger Security Council support for his role in relation to UN peacekeeping operations, he agreed to continue in office for another five years. However, when this five-year period was drawing close to completion, he was clear that he was unwilling to serve a third term and was also suffering from health issues that would make it difficult for him to continue.

ROLE AS SECRETARY-GENERAL

Thant's predecessor, Hammarskjöld, died while pursuing peace in the Congo. A flare-up in violence in that country in December 1961 immediately challenged Thant. He asserted the powers of his office to successfully encourage a peacekeeping response. He was also involved in the creation of a number of new peacekeeping operations, including in West New Guinea (1962), Yemen (1963), and Cyprus (1964). Controversially, in 1967 he presided over the removal of the first UN peacekeeping operation, the UN Emergency Force, between Israel and Egypt, which then saw the resumption of war between these two countries. Thant was also drawn into the United States-Soviet Union Cold War clash. First, during the Cuban Missile Crisis (1962), Thant sought to defuse the tensions, sending letters to both sides encouraging a peaceful resolution and then personally traveling to Cuba. Second, and less well received by the United States, he tried to promote negotiations to bring the Vietnam War to a close. Finally, Thant also worked to get the Security Council to take action to address the 1971 India-Pakistan war, which ultimately led to the creation of Bangladesh. With the Soviets supporting India but the United States backing Pakistan, the Security Council was largely deadlocked, and his efforts were unsuccessful.

As the first Secretary-General from the developing world, Thant supported expanding and adding additional economic and social programs at the UN. While Thant was not closely engaged in Secretariat administrative issues, the addition of these programs also led to increasing the level of staffing support in these areas. The budgetary implications of undertaking these initiatives were criticized by some countries, including a call by both the Americans and Soviets for a budget freeze at the UN. The financial pressures on the organization were intensified due to the fact that France and the Soviet Union refused to pay their share to support peacekeeping operations.

ADVANCES AND CHALLENGES WHILE IN OFFICE

The UN's financial crisis made managing UN affairs difficult for Thant. Despite financial limitations, he is applauded for using creative means to create and fund new peacekeeping missions. His tenure also included a focus on income and racial inequality (including apartheid in South Africa). He promoted economic development and advancing the remaining areas under colonialism to self-governance. These moves gained Thant support among many of the newer members of the UN, most of which had emerged from colonial control like Thant's native Burma. While his agenda was sidelined in places due to Cold War politics, compared to the complete breakdown of relations between great powers and the previous two Secretaries-General (Trygve Lie and Hammarskjöld) Thant was able to maintain some form of relationship with both the United States and the Soviet Union. At the same time, the inability for the most part to broker peaceful relations between the Cold War adversaries was a great frustration for Thant. After leaving office at the end of 1971 in poor health, Thant was a fellow at the Adlai Institute of International Affairs before passing away in 1974.

See also: Dag Hammarskjöld; Economic Development; Membership; Office of Secretary-General; Peacekeeping; Role of Great Powers; Secretariat; Security Council; Self-Determination; Trygve Lie; United Nations Budget and Financing; United Nations Population Fund.

FURTHER READING

Dorn, A. Walter, and Robert Pauk. 2012. "The Closest Brush: How a UN Secretary-General Averted Doomsday." *Bulletin of the Atomic Scientists* 68 (6): 79–84.

Firestone, Bernard J. 2001. *The United Nations under U Thant, 1961–1971*. Lanham, MD: Scarecrow Press.

Thant, U. 1978. *View from the UN*. Garden City, NY: Doubleday.

Kurt Waldheim

Before serving as the fourth UN Secretary-General, Kurt Waldheim had a diverse diplomatic career representing Austria in international affairs. This involved direct connections to the UN, including guiding Austria's first delegation to the UN when the country joined the organization in 1955 and later returning to the UN as the Austrian Permanent Representative (1964–1968 and 1970–1971) leading up to his time as Secretary-General. In addition, shortly before being selected as Secretary-General, he was an unsuccessful candidate to become the President of Austria in the 1971 election.

After his failed Presidency bid, Waldheim switched his attention to becoming Secretary-General. He lobbied for the position in the first instance of an individual campaigning for the office. The Chinese initially vetoed his candidacy, as they were insisting on an officeholder from a developing country, but he ultimately won the Security Council recommendation in December 1971 and took up his first term of office in January 1972. He was reappointed to a second five-year term and then sought an unprecedented third term. However, this time the Chinese vetoed his candidacy multiple times, and the Secretary-Generalship eventually shifted to Javier Pérez de Cuéllar instead.

ROLE AS SECRETARY-GENERAL

There were three peacekeeping operations, all in the Middle East, established during Waldheim's tenure: the Second UN Emergency Force (1973–1979) between Egypt and Israel, the UN Disengagement Observer Force (1974–ongoing) in the Golan Heights area between Israel and Syria, and the UN Interim Force in Lebanon (1978–ongoing) as a buffer force between Israel and Lebanon. Waldheim was not closely involved in the formulation of these missions, which were mainly pushed for by the United States, and did not press for peacekeeping to be extended to other regions during his time in office. Waldheim was more active in peaceful settlement initiatives. However, he was cautious and most often only took such action when encouraged by major powers or the conflicting parties. Waldheim placed a particular emphasis on mediating the conflict between Greece and Turkey over Cyprus, although this effort made little headway.

In 1979, Waldheim called for the Security Council to take action on the American hostages being held in Iran. This was one of the few instances of a Secretary-General directly invoking the office's Article 99 powers to bring a conflict to the attention of the Security Council. However, it appears that this use of Article 99, and the follow-up trip to Iran that he undertook, was the result of behind-the-scenes pressure from the United States. Waldheim provided little leadership of administrative affairs in the Secretariat. He mainly used his powers in this area to gain favor with countries by appointing their nationals to posts. His public pronouncements were cautious and deferred to the wishes of the member states, and he did not seek to develop new ideas or norms to guide UN or global affairs.

ADVANCES AND CHALLENGES WHILE IN OFFICE

Waldheim was a bureaucratic manager who primarily acted to carry out policy instead of seeking to drive or initiate UN activities. He downplayed the possible power of the office, although he did insist on proper protocol and respect for the office when traveling or at meetings, and focused instead on the limitations of the Secretary-Generalship. His handling of the office in this manner meant that there were not significant innovations or advances for the office of Secretary-General during his tenure. Thus, for some analysts Waldheim is disparaged as an ineffective Secretary-General, but others applaud Waldheim for his discretion and for seeking to serve the needs of the member states.

Waldheim's time as Secretary-General is also controversial since, after he left office, allegations arose regarding his activities during World War II. Accusations emerged that he hid the length of his military service and that he had possible connections to war crimes and Nazi sympathies. Some analysts suggest that Waldheim's tenure as Secretary-General was tainted because the great powers were aware of his war record and used this as leverage against him. Yet, most examinations of his time in office conclude that his behavior was not driven by concerns over possible revelations of his war record, but rather a general reflection of his personal style. After leaving the office of Secretary-General at the end of 1981, Waldheim returned to Austria. Several years later, he again ran for President. His campaign was a success, and he served in office from 1986 to 1992. The revelations of his wartime past that emerged due to his campaigning for the Presidency, often referred to as the "Waldheim Affair," precluded his running for a second term in office and ended his political career. He died in Austria in 2007.

See also: Javier Pérez de Cuéllar; Office of Secretary-General; Peaceful Settlement; Peacekeeping; Role of Great Powers; Secretariat; Security Council.

FURTHER READING

Finger, Seymour M., and Arnold A. Saltzman. 1990. *Bending with the Winds: Kurt Waldheim and the United Nations*. New York: Praeger.

Kille, Kent J. 2018. "Kurt Waldheim, 1972–1981." In *The UN Secretary-General and the Security Council: A Dynamic Relationship*, edited by Manuel Fröhlich and Abiodun Williams, 94–115. Oxford: Oxford University Press.

Waldheim, Kurt. 1986. *In the Eye of the Storm: A Memoir*. Bethesda, MD: Adler & Adler.

Javier Pérez de Cuéllar

Javier Pérez de Cuéllar, the fifth UN Secretary-General, had an illustrious career in the diplomatic service representing his home country of Peru. Along with holding a number of posts in the Ministry of Foreign Affairs and serving as Ambassador to countries such as the Soviet Union and Switzerland, his diplomatic career also took him to the UN. He first traveled to the UN as part of the delegation from Peru for the inaugural General Assembly session in 1946. He returned for a regular role representing Peru at the UN starting with the 25th General Assembly session in 1970, taking over as Permanent Representative from 1971 to 1975. His duties included representing Peru in the Security Council from 1973 to 1974, where he held the month-long Presidency of the Security Council in 1974. From 1975 to 1977, Pérez de Cuéllar served within the UN as the Special Representative of Secretary-General Kurt Waldheim to Cyprus. He returned to the UN as Under-Secretary-General for Special Political Affairs in 1979.

Pérez de Cuéllar was assisting Waldheim again in 1981, this time as personal envoy to Afghanistan, when Waldheim failed in his bid to secure a third term as Secretary-General. With the Security Council deadlocked and the Chinese insisting on a Secretary-General from a developing country, Pérez de Cuéllar emerged from a group of possible candidates as acceptable to the major powers on the Security Council. The General Assembly agreed with Pérez de Cuéllar's selection in mid-December 1981, and he took office at the start of 1982. Although initially hesitant to serve a second term, and recovering from heart surgery, the Security Council encouraged him to continue in office. He was reappointed in October 1986 and served the full second five-year term to the end of 1991.

ROLE AS SECRETARY-GENERAL

Pérez de Cuéllar attempted to personally engage to promote the peaceful settlement of disputes. His first challenge was the 1982 British-Argentinian clash over the Falklands Islands (also known as the Malvinas Islands), where his involvement could not keep the two countries from going to war. Across his first term in office, Pérez de Cuéllar faced similar frustrations as his mediation attempts often made little progress. Promoting disarmament was a key priority for Pérez de Cuéllar, yet his efforts had limited impact, and most central negotiations ended up taking place bilaterally between the United States and the Soviet Union. In a major speech on "The Role of the Secretary-General" at Oxford in May 1986, Pérez de Cuéllar stressed the useful role that an independent and impartial Secretary-General could play.

No new peacekeeping missions were created during Pérez de Cuéllar's first term and the beginning of his second term. However, in 1988 both the UN Good Offices Mission in Afghanistan and Pakistan and the UN Iran-Iraq Military Observer Group were initiated. The first UN Angola Verification Mission started operations in early 1989, followed by missions in Namibia and Central America. In 1991, additional operations were deployed in Angola, Cambodia, El Salvador, Western Sahara, and between Iraq and Kuwait. In 1988, UN peacekeeping forces were awarded the Nobel Peace Prize, which Pérez de Cuéllar accepted on behalf of the organization. With the UN more engaged in addressing areas of conflict, Pérez de Cuéllar became closely involved in peaceful settlement across these situations.

ADVANCES AND CHALLENGES WHILE IN OFFICE

When Pérez de Cuéllar began as Secretary-General, he faced a very challenging time for the UN. He entered office the same month as U.S. President Ronald Reagan, who ratcheted up Cold War tensions with the Soviet Union. In addition, the UN faced a great reduction in financial support from the Reagan administration, which further impeded the organization's ability to act. Pérez de Cuéllar pragmatically recognized the limits to what his office could do in the face of these difficulties. However, as United States-Soviet relations thawed in the late 1980s and the Cold War came to a close, this opened up greater opportunities for the UN and the Secretary-General. Pérez de Cuéllar's diplomatic skill and cultivation of relationships with the member states kept the UN functioning and ensured that he was well placed to take advantage of the change in circumstances. Following his time as Secretary-General, Pérez de Cuéllar undertook a failed campaign for President of Peru in 1995 and held office for a brief time as President of the Council of Ministers (2000–2001). He served as Peru's Ambassador to France before retiring in 2004. He passed away in March 2020 at the age of one hundred.

See also: Boutros Boutros-Ghali; General Assembly; Kurt Waldheim; Office of Secretary-General; Peaceful Settlement; Peacekeeping; President of Security Council; Special Representatives of the United Nations Secretary-General; United Nations Budget and Financing.

FURTHER READING

Lankevich, George J. 2001. *The United Nations under Javier Pérez de Cuéllar, 1982–1991*. Lanham, MD: Scarecrow Press.

Pérez de Cuéllar, Javier. 1997. *Pilgrimage for Peace: A Secretary General's Memoir*. New York: St. Martin's Press.

Rieffer-Flanagan, Barbara Ann, and David P. Forsythe. 2007. "Religion, Ethics, and Reality: A Study of Javier Perez de Cuellar." In *The UN Secretary-General and Moral Authority: Ethics and Religion in International Leadership*, edited by Kent J. Kille, 229–64. Washington, DC: Georgetown University Press.

Boutros Boutros-Ghali

The sixth UN Secretary-General, Boutros Boutros-Ghali, came from a politically connected, Coptic Christian family in Egypt. Boutros-Ghali served as a professor of international law and international relations and had a distinguished career representing the Egyptian government. He reached the level of Deputy Prime Minister for Foreign Affairs, but his minority religious background kept him from achieving the position of Foreign Minister (customarily held by a Muslim). His diplomatic engagements representing Egypt included participation in the General Assembly in 1979, 1982, and 1990. His academic career linked him to the UN, as he authored a book on the UN (in Arabic) and served on a committee in the International Labour Organization (ILO) and the International Law Commission of the UN. He was also an unsuccessful candidate for the executive head positions at the ILO and the UN Educational, Scientific and Cultural Organization.

Boutros-Ghali was the first African (and to date the only Arab) Secretary-General. Based on the principle of geographical rotation for selecting the Secretary-General, as Latin American Javier Pérez de Cuéllar's time in office drew to a close in 1991 the UN's focus turned to Africa for his replacement. Boutros-Ghali was supported by France for the position, in part due to his strong French language skills. While the United States and United Kingdom instead pushed for Canadian Brian Mulroney, they ultimately abstained instead of vetoing Boutros-Ghali's candidacy in the November 1991 Security Council vote. The General Assembly approved the selection, and Boutros-Ghali took office at the start of 1992. While Boutros-Ghali actively sought a second term, his clashes with the Clinton administration led the United States to veto his candidacy in a 14–1 Security Council vote. Thus, Boutros-Ghali left office at the end of 1996 and is the only UN Secretary-General to not hold a second term. Since Africa's "turn" holding the Secretary-Generalship was not over, the search for his replacement stayed within Africa, ultimately leading to the selection of Kofi Annan from Ghana.

ROLE AS SECRETARY-GENERAL

Boutros-Ghali is especially well known for writing three major reports as Secretary-General: *An Agenda for Peace* (1992), *An Agenda for Development* (1994), and *An Agenda for Democratization* (1996). *An Agenda for Peace*, written in response to a request from the Security Council, reviews the UN's abilities for preventive diplomacy, peaceful settlement, and peacekeeping. Boutros-Ghali also used the report to introduce the UN to postconflict peacebuilding and pointed to the potential for UN cooperation with regional organizations. *An Agenda for Development* and *An Agenda for Democratization* were both in response to General Assembly requests. In *An Agenda for Development*, he emphasized development as a central human right that underpins achieving peace and security. *An Agenda for Democratization* was released by Boutros-Ghali just before he left office.

Taking office shortly after the end of the Cold War, Boutros-Ghali dealt with an array of new peace and security challenges. Highlights include promoting peace in Cambodia (1991), Mozambique (1992), El Salvador (1992), and Guatemala (1996). However, major setbacks occurred as well, including a failed mediation over Cyprus (1992), a disastrous UN-authorized U.S. incursion into Somalia (1992), and the inability to address mass violence in Rwanda (1994) or protect civilians in the "safe haven" of Srebrenica during the violent breakup of Yugoslavia (1995). For UN administration, Boutros-Ghali emphasized modernizing the structure of and limiting the number of positions in the Secretariat. In addition, he stressed the need for limiting, streamlining, and providing better oversight of budget expenditures to protect the organization from the threat of bankruptcy.

ADVANCES AND CHALLENGES WHILE IN OFFICE

Boutros-Ghali is noted for seeking to provide strong leadership. This approach brought about advances for the UN and the office of Secretary-General. His efforts to reshape understanding about the best approaches to peace and development led observers to label him as a "norm entrepreneur." At the same time, this brought him into conflict with the United States, which was seeking to assert itself as a new unipolar power in the world after decades of struggle with the Soviet Union. The United States was also upset with the failed mission in Somalia and sought to pin the blame on the UN. In addition, Boutros-Ghali's effort to gain a second term coincided with U.S. President William Clinton's reelection campaign in 1996, so he got caught up in domestic U.S. political wrangling.

Following his time at the UN, Boutros-Ghali remained active in international affairs. He shifted from leading the UN to become the first Secretary-General of the Organisation Internationale de la Francophonie in 1997, serving in this role through 2002. More broadly, reflecting his priorities as UN Secretary-General, he was active in a variety of capacities to continue to promote peace, development, and democracy across the globe. He passed away in 2016 and was honored with a national funeral in Egypt.

See also: Executive Heads of Specialized Agencies; International Labour Organization; Javier Pérez de Cuéllar; Kofi Annan; Office of Secretary-General; Peacebuilding; Peaceful Settlement; Peacekeeping; Regionalism; Secretariat; United Nations Budget and Financing; United Nations Educational, Scientific and Cultural Organization.

FURTHER READING

Boutros-Ghali, Boutros. 1999. *Unvanquished: A U.S.-U.N. Saga.* New York: Random House.

Burgess, Stephen F. 2001. *The United Nations under Boutros Boutros-Ghali, 1992–1997.* Lanham, MD: Scarecrow Press.

Rushton, Simon. 2008. "The UN Secretary-General and Norm Entrepreneurship: Boutros Boutros-Ghali and Democracy Promotion." *Global Governance* 14 (1): 95–110.

Kofi Annan

Kofi Annan, the seventh Secretary-General, was the first officeholder to rise through the UN ranks. Except for a brief period working in his home country as Managing Director of the Ghana Tourist Development Board, his career before becoming Secretary-General was based in the UN System. Annan started as a budget officer in the World Health Organization in 1962. He held multiple posts after that, including at the Economic Commission for Africa, the UN High Commissioner for Refugees, the UN Emergency Force, and Secretariat positions at UN Headquarters in New York and Geneva. By 1987, Annan achieved the rank of Assistant Secretary-General, and in 1993, he was named Under-Secretary-General for Peacekeeping Operations. In 1995–1996, he served for five months as Special Representative to the Former Yugoslavia under Boutros Boutros-Ghali, his predecessor as Secretary-General, before returning to his Under-Secretary-General position.

When Boutros-Ghali's candidacy for a second term was vetoed in the Security Council by the United States, Annan was supported as a replacement, which would keep the Secretary-Generalship held by an African national. He was unanimously approved by the Security Council and then given full General Assembly support in December 1996, taking office at the beginning of January 1997. Although it meant that an African held the office for three straight terms instead of rotating to a new region after two terms as usual, Annan was encouraged to continue in office. Annan was approved for a second five-year term (to start January 2002) in June 2001, well before his first term was set to expire at the end of that year.

ROLE AS SECRETARY-GENERAL

Annan focused on reforming the organization. He enacted initial reforms in March 1997 and followed this up in July 1997 with a far-reaching report *Renewing the United Nations: A Programme for Reform.* Annan organized a Millennium Summit and Assembly in 2000, influencing the agenda by releasing *We the Peoples: The Role of the United Nations in the 21st Century* in advance. In his second term, he submitted a 2002 report *Strengthening the United Nations: An Agenda for Further Change* and in 2005 released *In Larger Freedom: Towards Development, Security and Human Rights for All.* Annan also targeted particular areas of UN engagement, such as peacekeeping when he created a panel of advisers who issued the 2000 *Report of the Panel on United Nations Peace Operations* (i.e., the "Brahimi Report").

Annan was attentively engaged in budgetary affairs. He sought greater connections and support from the private sector. This included announcing the UN Global Compact in 1999, which provides principles to guide business activities and draws on the private sector to support UN work. Annan was also very active in a wide range of peaceful settlement efforts. Major instances include negotiating the 1998 Memorandum of Understanding with Iraq and developing the so-called Annan Plan (2002–2004) for peace in Cyprus. In addition, he was closely involved in guiding existing peacekeeping missions and the creation of new operations, with sixteen peacekeeping forces in the field at the end of his tenure in December 2006.

ADVANCES AND CHALLENGES WHILE IN OFFICE

Annan's intensive reform agenda reshaped the UN. For instance, the position of Deputy Secretary-General, the Human Rights Council, and the Peacebuilding Commission were all created during his tenure, and the Millennium Development Goals were launched in 2000. He closely communicated with and bolstered the morale of the Secretariat. He cultivated relations with the member states to build consensus and encourage implementation of his ideas. Annan also promoted the UN to the global community, helping to raise the public profile of the organization. He shaped UN peaceful settlement efforts and peacekeeping operations. The UN and Annan were jointly awarded the Nobel Peace Prize in 2001. The international security environment became more challenging following the terrorist attacks on September 11, 2001, in the United States. Annan was drawn back into Iraq, pulling out UN staff after a suicide bombing on UN Headquarters in Baghdad and questioning the international legality of U.S. intervention. Annan also faced backlash over the UN's handling of the Oil-for-Food Program in Iraq. The combination of these events damaged Annan's relationship with the United States and made the latter part of his second term challenging.

After leaving office, Annan set up a nonprofit organization, the Kofi Annan Foundation, which encourages stronger global governance. He remained personally involved in a number of international initiatives, such as heading the foundation of the World Organization Against Torture and the Panel of Eminent African Personalities addressing electoral violence in Kenya. He also worked with The Elders (serving as Chair from 2013 to 2018), a group of global leaders founded in 2007 to promote peace and human rights. In 2012, he served as UN special envoy addressing the civil war in Syria. In 2016, he led a commission investigating the

> *Oil-for-Food Programme*
>
> The Oil-for-Food Programme was created by the Security Council in 1995 through Resolution 986. The program allowed Iraq, which had been under UN economic sanctions imposed in 1990 following the invasion of Kuwait, to sell a set amount of oil in exchange for "essential civilian needs," such as food and medicine, under UN supervision. The program was dissolved in 2003 after efforts to enhance the program were unsuccessful and the subsequent Iraq War changed the conditions of the UN presence in Iraq. The program was controversial because the country's leader, Saddam Hussein, abused the conditions of the program and illegally smuggled oil for profit. A U.S. Central Intelligence Agency investigation found that Hussein secured around $1.7 billion in kickbacks and surcharges and an additional $10.9 billion through smuggling oil. A later investigation found almost half of the forty-five hundred companies that contracted with the program were paying illegal surcharges. A UN Independent Inquiry Committee, led by former U.S. Federal Reserve Chairman Paul Volcker, found the administration and management of the program to be "ineffective, wasteful, and unsatisfactory." Within the United States, there were also accusations that Secretary-General Kofi Annan failed to carry out proper inquiries, particularly those involving his son, Kojo. Investigations were also launched by the Iraqi Governing Council and the U.S. Government Accountability Office. The general conclusion was that there was no misconduct by Annan. As a result of the scandal, Annan created a new UN Ethics Office and "whistleblower" policies to provide an avenue for future reporting of corruption.

violence against the Rohingya in Myanmar. He died in 2018 and was honored with a state funeral in Ghana.

See also: Ban Ki-moon; Boutros Boutros-Ghali; Deputy Secretary-General; Disarmament Commission; Goodwill Ambassadors and Messengers of Peace, Human Rights Council; Human Security; Nongovernmental Organizations; Office of Secretary-General; Peacebuilding Commission; Peaceful Settlement; Peacekeeping; Responsibility to Protect; Secretariat; Special Representatives of the United Nations Secretary-General; United Nations Budget and Financing; United Nations Conferences and Summits; United Nations High Commissioner for Refugees; United Nations Reform; World Health Organization.

FURTHER READING

Annan, Kofi A., with Nader Mousavizadeh. 2012. *Interventions: A Life in War and Peace.* New York: Penguin Press.

Meisler, Stanley. 2007. *Kofi Annan: A Man of Peace in a World of War.* Hoboken, NJ: John Wiley & Sons.

Traub, James. 2006. *The Best Intentions: Kofi Annan and the UN in the Era of American World Power.* New York: Farrar, Straus, and Giroux.

Ban Ki-moon

Ban Ki-moon took office as the eighth UN Secretary-General following an extended career in the Republic of Korea's Ministry of Foreign Affairs. Across almost four decades, he worked his way up from junior foreign service officer to Foreign Minister. His positions included several engagements with the UN. In 1975, he was assigned to the foreign ministry's UN division and later operated as director of the division. He served as first secretary in the Korean permanent observer mission at UN Headquarters. He also chaired the Preparatory Commission for the Comprehensive Nuclear-Test-Ban Treaty Organization in 1999. When Han Seung-soo was President of the General Assembly from 2001 to 2002, Ban served as Chef de Cabinet.

From 1992 to 2006, the Secretary-Generalship was held by individuals from the African region, so the search for the next Secretary-General focused on Asia. After announcing his candidacy in February 2006, Ban traveled widely as part of his campaign for the office, including visiting all fifteen Security Council countries. He built support and won an initial Security Council straw poll in July as well as additional polls in September and early October. On October 9, the Security Council formally voted to unanimously support Ban. The General Assembly approved Ban as Secretary-General on October 13. Ban took office on January 1, 2007, for a five-year term and was reappointed early (in June 2011) for a second term from January 2012 to December 2016.

ROLE AS SECRETARY-GENERAL

Following Kofi Annan into office, there were expectations that Ban would maintain the focus on UN reform. His first reform initiative to restructure peacekeeping led to the creation of the Department of Field Support in March 2007. However, his plan to merge the Departments of Political Affairs and Disarmament Affairs failed, and instead he settled for renaming the latter Department as the Office for Disarmament Affairs. He also highlighted strengthening the Department of Political Affairs. Later reforms included creating the Office of Administration of Justice in 2009. Ban's emphasis on women's empowerment is reflected in the creation of the UN Entity for Gender Equality and the Empowerment of Women (UN Women) in 2010.

Addressing climate change was a top priority on Ban's agenda. He stressed the threat posed by climate change and the need for action, including inviting leaders to a summit on climate change in 2007, convening the 2014 Climate Summit, and attending the 2015 UN Climate Change Conference that led to the Paris Agreement. Ban oversaw the shift from the Millennium Development Goals (2000–2015) to the Sustainable Development Goals (2015–2030). At the start of his second term, Ban summarized his agenda around five central points: sustainable development; improving preventive capabilities to address disasters, violent conflict, human rights, and economic shocks; building a safer and more secure world; supporting countries in transition; and addressing the needs of women and youth. Ban faced a wide array of pressing security issues, including the Darfur region of the Sudan, Central African Republic, Côte d'Ivoire, Democratic Republic of the Congo, Kosovo, Libya, North Korean and Iranian nuclear proliferation, Mali, Israeli-Palestinian clashes, Sri Lanka, Syria, Ukraine, and the increase in refugees and need for humanitarian assistance.

ADVANCES AND CHALLENGES WHILE IN OFFICE

Ban's focus on climate change helped to keep this issue highlighted on the global agenda. However, efforts to build agreements and create policy faced many setbacks, and the Paris Agreement is attributed more to other actors than as a sign of Ban's success. Ban is recognized for promoting gender parity in senior management positions. However, after positive steps in this direction, some critique his overall record since many more men than women were appointed in 2015 and 2016. Others are critical of his handling of administrative affairs during his transition into office, including relying on South Korean advisers and hiring a Deputy Secretary-General with whom he had no connection. Ban is often described as quiet and low-key, which carried over to his preference for quiet diplomacy. He encouraged preventive diplomacy and promoted the responsibility to protect, yet critics contend that a stronger voice was needed to bolster peacekeeping and better protect civilians from humanitarian crises. While Ban is viewed by some as being too deferential to the member states, especially the permanent members of the Security Council, he tended to take stronger public stances in his later years in office.

As Ban's time as Secretary-General came to an end, there was speculation that he would return home to run for President at the start of 2017. However, in February he publicly announced that he would not seek election. Instead, Ban helped found the nonprofit Ban Ki-moon Centre for Global Citizens in Vienna, Austria, which he cochairs with the former President of Austria, Heinz Fischer. Ban also returned to international organization leadership when he was elected as President of the Assembly and Chair of the Council at the Global Green Growth Institute, based in Seoul, starting in February 2018.

See also: Arms Control and Disarmament, Deputy Secretary-General, Environmental Protection, Human Security, Kofi Annan, Peacekeeping, Preparatory Commission for the Comprehensive Nuclear-Test-Ban Treaty Organization; Responsibility to Protect; Secretariat; Sustainable Development Goals; United Nations Conferences and Summits; United Nations Entity for Gender Equality and the Empowerment of Women; United Nations Reform.

FURTHER READING

Gowan, Richard. 2011. "Floating Down the River of History: Ban Ki-Moon and Peacekeeping, 2007–2011." *Global Governance* 17 (4): 399–416.

Jesensky, Marcel. 2019. *The United Nations Under Ban Ki-Moon*. New York: Palgrave Macmillan.

Plate, Tom. 2012. *Conversations with Ban Ki-Moon: What the United Nations Is Really Like: The View from the Top*. Singapore: Marshall Cavendish.

António Guterres

António Guterres took office as the ninth UN Secretary-General on January 1, 2017. Guterres has a long history of political engagement. He was elected to the

Portuguese parliament in 1976 and attained the position of Prime Minister from 1995 to 2002. He served two years in the Parliamentary Assembly of the Council of Europe in the early 1980s and held the rotating presidency of European Council for the first six months of 2000. From 1999 to 2005, he was also the President of Socialist International, a global body that brings together democratic socialist parties. Guterres had leadership experience in the UN System shortly before taking over as Secretary-General, serving as UN High Commissioner for Refugees from 2005 to 2015.

During the search for the ninth Secretary-General, there were calls to choose the first officeholder from Eastern Europe and pressure to select the first woman. Out of the thirteen candidates, both criteria were well represented, with nine from Eastern Europe and seven women. Four of the candidates met both benchmarks, including one of the presumed front-runners Irina Bokova, a Bulgarian who served as Director-General of the UN Educational, Scientific and Cultural Organization between 2009 and 2017. The selection process underwent significant changes to become more open and transparent. Building out of General Assembly Resolution 69/321 (September 2015), in December 2015 the Presidents of General Security and Security Council jointly released a letter calling for countries to nominate candidates by submitting their qualifications and vision statement to be publicly posted. Between April and June 2016 (and one session in early October for a late entrant), the candidates engaged in public informal dialogues, where they presented their ideas and answered questions from member state delegates and civil society. Six straw polls were taken by the Security Council from July to October, with Guterres emerging from the start as the favored candidate. He was unanimously selected by the Security Council on October 6 and approved by the General Assembly on October 13.

ROLE AS SECRETARY-GENERAL

In his vision for the UN, Guterres consistently stresses the common values that bind everyone together: peace, justice, respect, human rights, tolerance, and solidarity. Promoting gender equality and empowerment is a major point of emphasis for Guterres, including achieving gender parity in top Secretariat appointments, ensuring greater gender balance for Special Representatives, and stressing a zero-tolerance approach to sexual harassment. For peace and security, Guterres highlights conflict prevention, and he launched new proposals for disarmament with the 2018 report *Securing Our Common Future: An Agenda for Disarmament*. Guterres initiated the first strategy at the UN to address new technologies, as well as a High-level Panel on Digital Cooperation, and the Department of Public Information was altered to the Department of Global Communications. Guterres inherited the 2030 Agenda launched in 2015, with related Sustainable Development Goals, and has focused on repositioning UN development efforts to achieve this agenda. There are three pillars to Guterres's UN reform efforts: development, management, and peace and security. Implementation of major organizational structural changes started January 1, 2019. A special United to Reform website details the steps taken and ongoing plans. For instance, Secretariat departments were altered to create the Departments of Operational Support; Management Strategy, Policy and Compliance; Peace Operations; and Political and Peacebuilding Affairs. Along with encouraging greater coordination within the UN System, Guterres also supports partnerships with regional organizations, international financial institutions, civil society, and the private sector.

ADVANCES AND CHALLENGES WHILE IN OFFICE

The public selection process provides Guterres with a level of legitimacy to draw upon. He also came into office with extensive leadership experience at both the national and international levels. Regardless, there are critics who challenge his position due to the failure to select a woman as Secretary-General. While groups such as the International Center for Research on Women acknowledge progress on gender made under Guterres, they also argue that he should be doing more in areas such as transparency in resource allocation to gender issues and ensuring a more independent system for sexual harassment complaints. Analysts point to Guterres's balanced approach to the office, asserting his authority but in a careful manner designed not to aggravate the member states. Yet, he faces a particularly challenging international environment. U.S. President Donald Trump took office several weeks after Guterres became Secretary-General with an "America First" platform that questions UN multilateral approaches. For example, the United States pulled out of the Paris Agreement, and the Trump administration criticized the World Health Organization's handling of the coronavirus pandemic. However, Guterres has advocated for continued positive initiatives to address climate change and global efforts to mitigate the pandemic. The rise of populism across the world makes building cooperation based on the common values expressed by Guterres difficult. As of late 2019, the UN also faced a particularly daunting budget shortage. Guterres must address these challenges while continuing to reform and bolster UN engagement in global affairs.

See also: Arms Control and Disarmament; Cybersecurity; Environmental Protection; Office of Secretary-General; Peaceful Settlement; Preparatory Commission for the Comprehensive Nuclear-Test-Ban Treaty Organization; President of General Assembly; President of Security Council; Secretariat; Sustainable Development Goals; United Nations Budget and Financing; United Nations High Commissioner for Refugees; United Nations Population Fund; United Nations Educational, Scientific and Cultural Organization; United Nations Reform; Women and Gender.

FURTHER READING

Haack, Kirsten. 2018. "The UN Secretary-General, Role Expansion and Narratives of Representation in the 2016 Campaign." *The British Journal of Politics and International Relations* 20 (4): 898–912.

Ramcharan, Bertrand. 2019. "António Guterres's Strategy for Modernizing the UN." *Global Governance* 25 (1): 13–21.

Thakur, Ramesh. 2017. "Choosing the Ninth United Nations Secretary-General: Looking Back, Looking Ahead." *Global Governance* 23 (1): 1–13.

Deputy Secretary-General

The UN Deputy Secretary-General assists the Secretary-General with managing administrative affairs, building coordination across parts of the UN System, and promoting the UN's status and engagement in economic and social areas. The idea of Deputy Secretary-General was discussed at the San Francisco Conference founding the UN in 1945, including a proposal by the Soviet Union for five Deputy Secretaries-General. One would support the Secretary-General, while the other four would be assigned to the Economic and Social Council, General Assembly, Security Council, and Trusteeship Council, respectively. Concerns about the proposed selection process undermined support for this plan, and the final version of the Charter only listed the Secretary-General for UN leadership.

As part of Secretary-General Kofi Annan's focus on UN reforms, his July 1997 *Renewing the United Nations: A Programme for Reform* called for a Deputy Secretary-General. The General Assembly approved the creation of the office in late 1997 as part of Resolution 52/12B. The resolution explains "the Secretary-General will appoint the Deputy Secretary-General following consultations with Member States and in accordance with Article 101" of the Charter. Annan's choice for the first Deputy Secretary-General was Louise Fréchette, who was Canada's Permanent Representative to the UN from 1992 to 1995. Fréchette took office in March 1998.

RESPONSIBILITIES

Based on the recommendations in Annan's reform report, the General Assembly resolution specified delegated responsibilities in five areas. First, to assist with managing Secretariat operations. Second, when the Secretary-General was absent from UN Headquarters, or at other times requested by the Secretary-General, to act in the place of the Secretary-General. Third, to provide support to the Secretary-General to encourage coherence across activities and institutions in the UN System as well as "elevating the profile and leadership of the United Nations in the economic and social spheres." Fourth, the Deputy Secretary-General can serve as a representative to conferences and other functions. Fifth, the open-ended duty "to undertake such assignments as may be determined by the Secretary-General." The Deputy Secretary-General also chairs groups such as the UN Sustainable Development Group, which assists with coordinating development policy and operations, and the Advisory Board of the UN Fund for International Partnerships (within the UN Office for Partnerships), which oversees the relationship with the UN Foundation established by Ted Turner in 1998 to support UN ideals and activities.

When Fréchette left office in March 2006, Annan moved Mark Malloch-Brown into the position in April. At the time Malloch-Brown was Annan's Chef de Cabinet and also had previous experience as head of the UN Development Programme. The General Assembly resolution notes that "the term of office of the Deputy Secretary-General will not exceed that of the Secretary-General," so Malloch-Brown only served for nine months as Annan departed at the end of December. Annan's successor, Ban Ki-moon, chose Asha-Rose Migiro to be his first Deputy

United Nations Deputy Secretaries-General	
Louise Fréchette (Canada)	March 1998–March 2006
Mark Malloch Brown (United Kingdom)	April 2006–December 2006
Asha-Rose Migiro (Tanzania)	February 2007–June 2012
Jan Eliasson (Sweden)	July 2012–December 2016
Amina Mohammed (Nigeria)	January 2017–

Secretary-General. Migiro was Foreign Minister in Tanzania before taking the office. Jan Eliasson from Sweden, who had extensive UN experience including serving as President of the General Assembly and undertaking a range of mediation and humanitarian work, took over as Deputy Secretary-General in July 2012. He served under Ban until they left office together at the end of 2016. António Guterres selected Amina Mohammed as Deputy Secretary-General, and they both entered office in January 2017. Mohammed previously served in the Nigerian government, focusing in particular on sustainable development, and was Ban's Special Adviser for establishing the 2030 Agenda for Sustainable Development.

ADVANCES AND CHALLENGES

The Secretary-General's involvement in managing peacekeeping, peaceful settlement, and promoting global issues has been bolstered since 1946 by appointing a wide range of Special Representatives as well as Messengers of Peace to highlight and promote the UN's work. The addition of the Deputy Secretary-General provides a central level of administrative support and reduces the workload of the Secretary-General. Unlike the (thus far) all-male Secretary-Generalship, the Deputy Secretary-General office is a high-level UN leadership position that has been filled by women. Annan selected a woman as the first holder of the office, and two of the four subsequent Deputy Secretaries-General are also women. The capabilities of the Deputy Secretary-General are challenged due to holding a lower profile compared to the Secretary-General. Critics also question how Deputy Secretaries-General have handled the office and whether the most qualified individuals are always selected. For example, Fréchette was critiqued for her management oversight, which led to her resignation. Migiro had limited management skills, and her brief UN experience beforehand was serving on the Committee on the Elimination of Discrimination against Women in 2000. After decades of the Secretary-General serving alone, the Deputy Secretary-General position continues to evolve as an important dimension of UN System leadership.

See also: António Guterres; Ban Ki-moon; Charter of the United Nations; Economic and Social Council; General Assembly; Goodwill Ambassadors and Messengers of Peace;

Kofi Annan; Office of Secretary-General; President of General Assembly; Secretariat; Security Council; Special Representatives of the United Nations Secretary-General; Sustainable Development; Sustainable Development Goals; Trusteeship Council; United Nations Conferences and Summits; United Nations Development Programme; United Nations Historical Background; United Nations Reform; Women and Gender.

FURTHER READING

Fréchette, Louise. 2003. "A New Development Agenda: Outlining the Challenges to Development in the 21st Century: A Conversation with Louise Fréchette." *Harvard International Review* 25 (1): 40–41.

Jere, reGina Jane. 2017. "Interview Amina J. Mohammed: 'You Cannot Put a Band-Aid on the World's Problems.'" *New African* 576: 20–23.

Malloch-Brown, Mark. 2011. *The Unfinished Global Revolution: The Pursuit of a New International Politics*. New York: Penguin Press.

Special Representatives of the United Nations Secretary-General (SRSGs)

Demands on the UN Secretary-General's time for addressing global issues are extensive. To assist with handling their duties, Secretaries-General appoint individuals to represent their office in peacefully resolving conflicts, running peacekeeping operations, and promoting thematic areas. The exact titles vary, including "personal representative," "envoy," and "special adviser," but these individuals are commonly known as Special Representatives of the UN Secretary-General (SRSGs). Outside of a broad interpretation of Article 101 of the Charter specifying "the staff shall be appointed by the Secretary-General under regulations established by the General Assembly," there is no specific basis for SRSGs in the Charter. Instead, the SRSGs essentially operate as an extension of the Secretary-General's powers and capabilities. From the early days of the UN, it quickly became clear that the Secretary-General could not personally be directly involved in all of the organization's missions. The first representative of the Secretary-General was established in 1946 to coordinate the transfer of League of Nations assets to the UN. That same year a personal representative was placed on the Special Committee on Palestine. The following year the first UN peacekeeping observation mission in India and Pakistan was assigned a personal representative. SRSGs ensure that the Secretary-General has someone to represent their interests, to act as their eyes and ears to report back from the field, and to provide helpful expertise.

UN ENGAGEMENT

A central role for SRSGs is serving as the head of a peacekeeping mission. These SRSGs have authority over operations and work to ensure that the mission's mandate is carried out. Since peacekeeping operations are established by the Security Council, SRSGs must report to and build a relationship with the Council.

Other SRSGs are assigned to mediate or seek other paths to peacefully resolve conflicts. These SRSGs are often not based in the conflict areas, like the heads of peacekeeping missions, but come and go depending on the peaceful settlement activities underway. Finally, there are a number of SRSGs assigned to address a particular thematic issue area. They are expected to draw attention to the issue, encourage action to be taken, and assist with developing policy options. Offices of the Special Representative of the Secretary-General established in the Secretariat include those for Children and Armed Conflict, Sexual Violence in Conflict, and Violence Against Children. SRSGs have been assigned to issues as diverse as HIV/AIDS, climate change, migration, and global education.

The backgrounds of SRSGs vary widely. Some come from other positions within the UN System, whether working within the Secretariat or serving as a member state delegate. Others come from outside the UN System, including from other international organizations, nongovernmental organizations, or the diplomatic service of a country. While some SRSGs only serve once, others hold multiple posts across time. Notable examples include Lakhdar Brahimi, who served as SRSG across Haiti, South Africa, Afghanistan, Iraq, and Syria, and Sergio Vierra de Mello, who died in a bomb explosion at his last posting in Iraq. Martii Ahtisaari was recognized for his work, including guiding Kosovo negotiations and transition away from Serbia, with the Nobel Peace Prize in 2008. Several individuals who went on to become Secretary-General also previously served as SRSGs. Javier Pérez de Cuéllar was Special Representative to Cyprus and then the Secretary-General's personal representative to Afghanistan. Kofi Annan was Special Representative to the Former Yugoslavia before taking office as Secretary-General, and after leaving office he returned to UN service to assist as a special envoy mediating in Syria.

ADVANCES AND CHALLENGES

SRSGs play a central role in addressing conflicts across the world. Although SRSGs existed from the first year of UN operations, there was a significant increase in the number of appointments and areas of engagement starting in the early 1990s following the end of the Cold War. SRSGs can employ their authority to provide independent leadership to influence policy, advocate for preferred approaches, and guide administrative affairs. One of the challenges for SRSGs is the historical gender imbalance, as a limited number of women were traditionally appointed to serve in this capacity. This began to shift under the Secretary-Generalship of Ban Ki-moon and has been an area of emphasis for António Guterres. The Secretary-General often faces political pressure over whom to appoint as countries lobby for their nationals to be given a SRSG position or claim that individuals who do not match a country's interests are unsuitable. SRSGs need a clear and focused mandate from the Security Council, but a tendency to apply a generic peacekeeping model to situations, and to expand the mission mandate over time, undermines their ability to address the complexities they find in the field. SRSGs also often claim that they do not have the necessary resources to carry out their mission. With so many conflicts and issues requiring global attention, SRSGs will remain a vital part of UN engagement.

See also: António Guterres; Ban Ki-moon; Javier Pérez de Cuéllar; Kofi Annan; Member State Ambassadors and Delegates; Office of Secretary-General; Peacebuilding; Peaceful Settlement; Peacekeeping; Secretariat; Security Council; Trygve Lie.

FURTHER READING

Fröhlich, Manuel. 2013. "The Special Representatives of the United Nations Secretary-General." In *Routledge Handbook of International Organization*, edited by Bob Reinalda, 231–43. London: Routledge.

Karlsrud, John. 2013. "Special Representatives of the Secretary-General as Norm Arbitrators? Understanding Bottom-up Authority in UN Peacekeeping." *Global Governance* 19 (4): 525–44.

Peck, Connie. 2015. "Special Representatives of the Secretary-General." In *The UN Security Council in the Twenty-First Century*, edited by Sebastian von Einsiedel, 457–74. Boulder, CO: Lynne Rienner.

President of General Assembly

The President of the General Assembly presides over the 193-member Assembly. The basis of the office is found in Article 21 of the UN Charter, which states, "The General Assembly . . . shall elect its President for each session." Yet, the President and the powers for this position are not explicitly mentioned elsewhere in the Charter. The Rules of Procedure of the General Assembly provide greater details. For the election, each member state is entitled to one vote, and the President is selected by a simple majority. However, since the Presidency rotates across the five geographic regions, such a vote is only necessary if the regional group does not come to a clear agreement on their candidate. The President serves a one-year term and is elected in advance of the start of a new General Assembly session. They are not allowed to be reelected. Presidents are elected as an individual and not as a representative of a member state. There are also twenty-one Vice-Presidents elected. Five of the Vice-Presidents are always from the permanent members of the Security Council (P-5), with the rest based on geographic representation, but this precludes the P-5 from holding the Presidency since the office-holder cannot be from the same country as the Vice-Presidents.

RESPONSIBILITIES

The President manages the proceedings of the General Assembly. As stated in the Rules of Procedure, the President "remains under the authority of the General Assembly" and does not vote. The President is called upon to enforce the rules of procedure. Such responsibilities include opening debate, setting the agenda, establishing speaker times, ruling on points of order, and suspending or adjourning meetings. The Assembly's General Committee, which includes the Vice-Presidents and the Chairs of the six Main Committees, is chaired by the President. Informally, the President works to seek solutions to member state disagreements and to promote consensus support for proposals. Ad hoc working groups may also be established by the President, as well as informal thematic debates separate from the regular General Assembly sessions. The President represents the General Assembly in the world and at meetings across the UN System.

The Office of the President is supported by a temporary staff consisting of around twenty-five to thirty-five individuals. This includes several staff members, supported by the UN's regular budget on one-year contracts, who are chosen by the President. Diplomatic staff members, who remain paid by their home governments, are provided on a voluntary basis by member states. Staff members from UN agencies are also provided to support the office, and the President has their own spokesperson. Financial support for the office is relatively limited. The regular UN budget allocation of around $300,000 does not meet full expenditure needs. In 2010, a Trust Fund was set up to support the President's office as well. Additional funds may also be raised from generous member states, which can fluctuate depending on how much the home country of the President provides support, although such funding should now be routed through the Trust Fund.

ADVANCES AND CHALLENGES

In recent years, many member states have become more reliant on the President to mediate disputes and serve as a consensus builder to help overcome differences. Mogens Lykketoft, President of the 70th session of the General Assembly (2015–2016), led the Assembly to be more engaged in the selection process of the Secretary-General (which culminated in the election of António Guterres). This included presiding over informal dialogues where those seeking the Secretary-Generalship, who had submitted information about their candidacies in advance, answered questions posed by member states and civil society.

The President is a neutral party while in office. Yet, as they are a member of a national delegation, their objectivity can be difficult to maintain. For example, questions have been raised about some Presidents seeking to influence the agenda in a biased manner. The President lacks the influence that the heads of other agencies in the UN System hold. The limited budget also affects the work of the office. There are calls for the President of the General Assembly to coordinate to a greater degree with the President of the Security Council. Although the UN promotes gender equality, the Presidency of the General Assembly has been dominated by men (with only four women holding the position as of the 2019–2020 session). Reform suggestions include making the selection process more competitive instead of having individuals put forth by a regional bloc, establishing a permanent staff for the office who would serve across Presidents, bolstering the budget, and having the President serve for more than one year in office.

See also: António Guterres; Ban Ki-moon; Charter of the United Nations; Deputy Secretary-General; Executive Heads of Specialized Agencies; General Assembly;

High-level Political Forum on Sustainable Development; Office of Secretary-General; President of Security Council; Research and Training Institutes; Role of Great Powers; Security Council; Trygve Lie; U Thant; Voting and Negotiating Blocs.

FURTHER READING

Al-Nasser, Nassir Abdulaziz. 2014. *A Year at the Helm of the United Nations General Assembly: A Vision for Our Century.* New York: New York University Press.

Christensen, Tomas Anker. 2018. "President or Paper Tiger? The Role of the President of the General Assembly of the United Nations." Berlin: Friedrich-Ebert-Stiftung. Available at https://www.fesny.org/article/president-or-paper-tiger-the-role-of-the-president-of-the-general-assembly-of-the-united-nations/.

Khan, Muhammad Zafrulla. 1964. "The President of the General Assembly of the United Nations." *International Organization* 18 (2): 231–40.

President of Security Council

The President of the Security Council serves as the presiding officer of the Council. Article 30 of the UN Charter gives the Security Council the authority to establish its own rules of procedure, including the method for choosing a President. The Provisional Rules of Procedure (S/96) established in 1946 created these guidelines, with Chapter IV (Rules 18, 19, and 20) along with other rules, covering the Presidency. The Presidency rotates on an English alphabetical basis, for a one-month term, among all members of the Security Council. With fifteen members and twelve months in the year, this rotation carries over between months to ensure that all non-permanent members of the Security Council serve as President at least once in their two-year term. However, some member states serve two terms as President during a two-year cycle depending on where they fall in the rotation.

RESPONSIBILITIES

Several powers and responsibilities are conferred to the President. The President is required to hold a meeting at least every fourteen days but must call a meeting when requested by any member of the Security Council or if a dispute is brought to the Council by other means. Once a meeting is scheduled, the President sets the agenda, oversees the meeting, and generally provides the order for the prioritization of motions and for recognizing members to speak. According to Rule 30, member states may challenge a procedural matter via a point of order, and the President must respond with a ruling before any other matters, substantive or procedural, are addressed. However, the President's ruling may be then be challenged and overruled by the Security Council. The President is also required, unless the Security Council "decides otherwise" (Rule 59), to refer all requests for UN membership received from the Secretary-General to a special committee of the Council.

The President also guides informal sessions of the Security Council. In addition, Rule 19 of the Provisional Rules of Procedure states that "under the authority of the Security Council" the President "shall represent it in its capacity as an organ of the United Nations." As the Security Council's representative, the President encourages implementation of Security Council resolutions, guides interactions with other parts of the UN System, and provides statements and press briefings. The President may also act on behalf of the Security Council for diplomatic initiatives or communication.

DUAL ROLE OF THE PRESIDENT AND INFORMAL POWERS

Presidents hold an unusual position as they are expected to maintain two separate roles. They act as the representative of their member state but also serve as the representative of the Security Council, including delivering statements on behalf of the Council. In many instances, this dual role can create a conflict of interest as a Security Council President pushes their country's priorities. However, the experience of serving as President also helps to build understanding of Security Council processes and connects the members through shared experience. Rule 20 of the Provisional Rules of Procedure states that any President who is "directly connected" to an issue shall inform the Security Council and step down and be replaced by the next member in line. However, the language provides many loopholes for Presidents deciding whether to abdicate or not. In a historic first, during the Presidential terms of France in March and Germany in April 2019, the two European Union states shared their Presidency. Although the roles were still technically occupied by one state at a time, the two states decided to operate as a "dual presidency."

There is debate over whether the President should play a passive or an active role. Views on this are influenced by which country the President represents, the global and historical context, and the issues on the agenda during their term. The President is expected to engage in a diplomatic fashion distinct from their role as a member state when acting as President, although they continue to vote based on their country's interests. Serving as President creates an advantage for any state holding the position as their diplomatic power is expanded and there is greater opportunity to resolve conflicts in line with their state's priorities. They can do this informally by facilitating private discussions between members or formally through speeches or public engagement. Recently, the position has evolved from a largely procedural one to a more substantive role as Presidents are, with Security Council members' consent, increasingly highlighting themes in the monthly agenda.

See also: António Guterres; Charter of the United Nations; Javier Pérez de Cuéllar; Membership; Role of Great Powers; Security Council.

FURTHER READING

Jaipal, Rikhi. 1978. "A Personal View of Consensus Making in the UN Security Council." *International Security* 2 (4): 195–200.

Pogany, Istvan. 1982. "The Role of the President of the U.N. Security Council." *The International and Comparative Law Quarterly* 31 (2): 231–45.
Sievers, Loraine, and Sam Daws. 2014. "The People." In *The Procedure of the UN Security Council*. Fourth edition, 110–25. Oxford: Oxford University Press.

Executive Heads of Specialized Agencies

Leadership at the UN is usually associated with the UN Secretary-General. Yet, many of the different bodies within the UN System have their own executive head leadership. For example, the UN Environment Programme is led by an Executive Director nominated by the UN Secretary-General and then approved by the UN General Assembly. However, the specialized agencies hold a distinctive place in the UN System. These are autonomous institutions that have signed formal agreements to coordinate as part of the UN System but maintain legal independence and operate according to their own structure and rules. A key implication of this level of autonomy is that the specialized agencies elect their own executive heads and these individuals can undertake a more independent leadership role in the international arena. In fact, since some of the specialized agencies predate the founding of the UN in 1945, including the International Telecommunications Union and Universal Postal Union from the nineteenth century and the International Labour Organization established in 1919, their executive heads have operated and shaped global affairs before the UN even existed.

RESPONSIBILITIES

The exact powers and capabilities of an executive head depends on the particular specialized agency. The different roles are reflected in the varied titles used. The majority (seven of the fifteen) hold the title Director-General, but there are also five organizations headed by a Secretary-General, two Presidents, and one Managing Director. The shift in title at the UN Industrial Development Organization (UNIDO) emphasizes this point. Before having its status upgraded to specialized agency in 1985, UNIDO was led by an Executive Director chosen by the UN Secretary-General. Now that the institution is a specialized agency, UNIDO's executive head is titled Director-General and selected by the organization. Similarly, in the early days of the International Meteorological Organization, operations were overseen by a Chief of the Secretariat, but a Secretary-General is in charge of the modern World Meteorological Organization.

The executive heads interact with each other, and other parts of the UN System, when their interorganizational work or related events bring them into contact. A formal central coordinating mechanism is the Chief Executives Board for Coordination (CEB). This body, in 2001 renamed from the previous Administrative Committee on Coordination that was set up in 1946, is chaired by the UN Secretary-General and meets twice a year. Along with the heads of the specialized agencies, the CEB brings together the leaders of thirty-one UN bodies total to consult, share knowledge, and develop recommendations to support coordinating administrative management and policies across the UN System.

Specialized Agency Executive Head Position Titles

Specialized Agency	Title
Food and Agriculture Organization	Director-General
International Civil Aviation Organization	Secretary-General
International Fund for Agricultural Development	President
International Labour Organization	Director-General
International Maritime Organization	Secretary-General
International Monetary Fund	Managing Director
International Telecommunications Union	Secretary-General
UN Educational, Scientific and Cultural Organization	Director-General
UN Industrial Development Organization	Director-General
UN World Tourism Organization	Secretary-General
Universal Postal Union	Director-General
World Bank	President
World Health Organization	Director-General
World Intellectual Property Organization	Director-General
World Meteorological Organization	Secretary-General

ADVANCES AND CHALLENGES

Executive heads of specialized agencies play an important leadership role within and outside of the UN System. The first individuals to hold office in an organization, such as the World Health Organization's (WHO) initial Director-General Brock Chisholm (1948–1953), face different leadership expectations and challenges from those following in the position who are supposed to maintain the organization or those who are called on to reform the institution. The size of the staff and resources available to an executive head differ greatly across the specialized agencies. Although there are significant female executive heads, such as Gro Harlem Brundtland (1998–2003) at WHO and Christine Lagarde (2011–2019) at the International Monetary Fund (IMF), gender inequality is a major issue for specialized agencies as far more men than women have served in office. The quality of leadership varies widely across time and organizations. Controversial specialized agency leaders include Amadou M'Bow (1974–1987) at the UN Educational, Scientific and Cultural Organization and Edouard Saouma (1976–1993) at the Food and Agriculture Organization. As these two examples also illustrate, some executive heads hold office for an extended period, while others have a much shorter time in office to shape the organization.

The country of origin can also impact the leadership provided by an executive head. A major shift occurred from the International Telegraph Union, which was always led by a Swiss national, to the updated International Telecommunications Union with leaders from eleven different countries since 1948. Leadership selection at the World Bank (always from the United States) and IMF (always a European) is critiqued, especially by developing countries that feel they are excluded. Finally, despite the existence of the CEB, specialized agency executive heads wielding independent leadership authority greatly complicate coordination with the UN System. Even the leadership title, with five specialized agency Secretaries-General, can confuse and undermine the leadership provided by the UN Secretary-General. In addition, since country membership of specialized agencies can diverge from the overarching UN organization, their executive heads must answer to different constituencies and work to meet their distinct interests.

See also: Food and Agriculture Organization; International Labour Organization; International Monetary Fund; International Telecommunication Union; Membership; Office of Secretary-General; United Nations Educational, Scientific and Cultural Organization; United Nations Environment Programme; United Nations Industrial Development Organization; Universal Postal Union; World Bank Group; World Meteorological Organization.

FURTHER READING

Farley, John. 2008. *Brock Chisholm, the World Health Organization, and the Cold War.* Vancouver: UBC Press.

Reinalda, Bob, Kent J. Kille, and Jaci Eisenberg, eds. 2020. *IO BIO: Biographical Dictionary of Secretaries-General of International Organizations.* Available at www.ru.nl/fm/iobio.

Schechter, Michael G. 2012. "Confronting the Challenges of Political Leadership in International Organizations." In *Comparative Political Leadership*, edited by Ludger Helms, 249–71. New York: Palgrave Macmillan.

Member State Ambassadors and Delegates

Member states maintain offices at the UN, which are referred to as a Permanent Mission. These centers of operation serve as a country's diplomatic embassy at the UN. The head of the mission is the Permanent Representative, often referred to as the UN Ambassador. UN Ambassadors may be political appointees or career diplomats. The personnel accredited to represent a member state at UN meetings, known as delegates, make up the state's delegation. The successful operation of a Permanent Mission relies on coordination with delegates to prepare for meetings and events. Their presence at the UN provides for formal and informal diplomatic interactions. Permanent Missions serve as both a forum for meetings and an administrative headquarters for member states. The Permanent Mission also publicizes the member state's policy positions and provides information on their activities, staff, and events.

UN ENGAGEMENT

Permanent Representatives and delegates can have significant agenda-setting capacity in UN bodies. Their role and impact vary across different parts of the UN System. For example, in the 193-member General Assembly delegates usually work together in voting and negotiating blocs. These are often based on geographical region, but also common interests on a particular global issue. In the fifteen-member Security Council, the representatives of the permanent members (P-5) hold a particularly important place in guiding Council affairs compared to the representatives from the ten non-permanent members. Outside of representation at formal meetings, the collection of Permanent Missions engage with one another so regularly that they have formed a microcommunity of actors known as the UN Village where a wide range of informal interactions occur.

Member states depend on the ability of their Ambassadors and delegates to negotiate and advocate for their interests at the UN. The ability for a country's representative to achieve their goals is greatly dependent on their resources and capabilities. The staff and resource support provided by the Permanent Mission is vital to backing the efforts of the delegation and is often dependent on the overall level of member state power. Influential capabilities include financial leverage, a country's historical level of engagement and reputation at the UN, and level of expertise on the issue being discussed. Along with the P-5 powers, other countries that tend to provide strong backing to their delegations at the UN include: Australia, Canada, Germany, Japan, and Nordic countries such as Sweden. In addition, powerful countries in a particular region can exert their influence at the UN, such as Brazil, India, and Nigeria.

The success of each delegation is not solely a reflection of their country's influential position. Skilled representatives can also overcome being outside of the majority by implementing minority-based strategies or brokering between different factions during negotiations. The personal skills, experiences, and personalities can also have a major impact on the role played by Ambassadors and delegates. For instance, individuals' knowledge, motivation, and negotiating skill shape the personal strategies employed when interacting with other representatives. Experienced delegates also use detailed knowledge of UN rules and procedures to their advantage.

ADVANCES AND CHALLENGES

Much of the work done by UN Ambassadors and delegates occurs during formal meetings. However, informal settings and opportunities for engagement are also a vital part of reaching agreements. These include caucusing during pauses to formal meetings, discussions in the corridors, and social gatherings over meals and at receptions. In this manner, the member state representatives build networks and further diplomatic engagement. Thus, the UN provides a vital arena for diplomatic interaction and assists in building cooperation and consensus over addressing global problems. However, the relative size of each Permanent Mission and the ability to fully staff their offices vary substantially. While P-5 countries, and those with extensive financial capacity, have a full staff and a position on every policy issue, smaller Missions are not so fortunate. Missions that suffer from lack of funding or inadequate staff are at a disadvantage when drafting policy positions and resolutions. Even geographical location can impact the operations of Ambassadors and delegates. When seeking feedback or instructions from the home government, many represent countries that exist in a time zone that is not compatible with UN Headquarters in New York (Eastern Standard Time). UN Ambassadors and delegates are central to the decision-making process at the organization, but the differences in support and capabilities of these actors are an important consideration when examining UN activities.

See also: General Assembly; Role of Great Powers; Security Council; United Nations Headquarters; United States Ambassadors to the United Nations; Voting and Negotiating Blocs.

FURTHER READING

Gaudiosi, Rebecca E. Webber, Jimena Leiva-Roesch, and Ye-Min Wu. 2019. *Negotiating at the United Nations: A Practitioner's Guide*. London: Routledge.

Rosenthal, Gert. 2017. *Inside the United Nations: Multilateral Diplomacy Up Close*. London: Routledge.

Smith, Courtney B. 2006. "Member States and Delegates." In *Politics and Process at the United Nations: The Global Dance*, 19–51. Boulder, CO: Lynne Rienner.

United States Ambassadors to the United Nations

As the United States is one of the most influential countries, the U.S. Permanent Representative, also known as the UN Ambassador, is a highly visible figure and often plays a crucial role in the engagement with global issues at the UN. A Presidential Executive Order in April 1947 established the U.S. Mission to the UN. The Chief of Mission is the Representative of the United States to the UN, with the rank of Ambassador Extraordinary and Plenipotentiary. The U.S. President nominates the Ambassador, with the position confirmed by the Senate. The professional background of those holding the position varies over time, ranging from political appointees with little diplomatic experience to subject matter experts.

UN ENGAGEMENT

The U.S. Ambassador to the UN serves several roles. They represent the U.S. delegation in meetings at the UN. In addition, they serve as head of one of the largest missions, with approximately 117 mission staff members listed at the UN as of February 2019 (compared to 88 for China and 87 for Russia). This position also acts as a liaison between the U.S. President and the UN. Finally, since countries representing the entire world come to UN Headquarters in New York, the U.S. Ambassador often meets with other diplomats outside of formal UN meetings. As the United States holds a permanent seat on the Security Council and is

United States Ambassadors to the United Nations (1946–2019)

1946	Edward Reilly Stettinius Jr.
1947–1953	Warren Robinson Austin
1953–1960	Henry Cabot Lodge Jr.
1960–1961	James Jeremiah Wadsworth
1961–1965	Adlai Ewing Stevenson II
1965–1968	Arthur Joseph Goldberg
1968	George Wildman Ball
1968–1969	James Russell Wiggins
1969–1971	Charles Woodruff Yost
1971–1973	George Herbert Walker Bush
1973–1975	John Alfred Scali
1975–1976	Daniel Patrick Moynihan
1976–1977	William Warren Scranton
1977–1979	Andrew Jackson Young
1979–1981	Donald F. McHenry
1981–1985	Jeane Jordan Kirkpatrick
1985–1989	Vernon A. Walters
1989–1992	Thomas Reeve Pickering
1992–1993	Edward Joseph Perkins
1993–1997	Madeleine Korbel Albright
1997–1998	William Blaine (Bill) Richardson
1999–2001	Richard Charles Albert Holbrooke
2001–2004	John Dimitri Negroponte
2004–2005	John Claggett Danforth
2005–2006	John R. Bolton
2007–2009	Zalmay Khalilzad
2009–2013	Susan Rice
2013–2017	Samantha Power
2017–2018	Nikki R. Haley
2019–	Kelly Knight Craft

the largest financial contributor to the UN, this elevates the potential for an Ambassador's influence. At the same time, great power political clashes, an extensive UN bureaucracy, and lack of political will often undermine their capacity to have a significant impact.

Because U.S. Ambassadors are appointed by the President, changes in the administration shift the United States' approach to the UN overall and the expected role of the position. Some Presidents elevate the UN Ambassador to a cabinet level position (i.e., William Clinton and Barack Obama), and the position holder can also sit on the National Security Council and work between Washington, DC, and New York. Depending on the administration, the level of autonomy granted to U.S. Ambassadors at the UN to pursue their preferences also shifts across time. Some Ambassadors act more as an extension of existing U.S. foreign policy, serving as a bridge between the requests of Washington and the UN. All U.S. Ambassadors to the UN are tasked with furthering U.S. foreign policy objectives and as such will work more closely with some UN entities than others. For example, while the U.S. consistently attends Security Council meetings, at certain points in time the United States has withdrawn from other UN agencies, such as the Human Rights Council and UN Educational, Scientific and Cultural Organization. The influence of U.S. representatives to the UN looks very different in the General Assembly than at the Security Council. In the General Assembly, the United States is one of 193 member states with equal voting power with all other members. In the Security Council, the United States can use its veto power to block any resolution.

NOTABLE U.S. AMBASSADORS TO THE UN

Noteworthy U.S. Ambassadors to the UN include former President George H.W. Bush (1971–1973), Daniel Patrick Moynihan (1975–1976), and Richard Holbrooke (1999–2001). Several women have served in this position, including Jeane Kirkpatrick (1981–1985), appointed by Ronald Reagan, and Madeleine Albright (1993–1997), who served under Clinton. John Bolton's (2005–2006) tenure at the UN as an interim appointee of the George W. Bush administration is remembered as a particularly confrontational time between the United States and the UN. Susan Rice (2009–2013), Obama's first UN Ambassador, was instrumental in gaining support for sanctions on Iran and North Korea and military action in Libya in 2011, yet also received criticism after the 2012 attacks on the U.S. embassy in that country. Samantha Power (2013–2017), the second representative for Obama, is known for her work on human rights and the release of women political prisoners. Nikki Haley (2017–2018), Donald Trump's first UN Ambassador, played an active role despite assuming the position with limited foreign policy experience. In September 2019, Kelly Knight Craft began representing the Trump Administration. U.S. Ambassadors to the UN set the tone for United States' engagement in the organization and can provide essential leadership and momentum for global initiatives. At the same time, they can also set a defensive posture and undermine global cooperation.

See also: General Assembly; Human Rights Council; Member State Ambassadors and Delegates; Role of Great Powers; Security Council; United Nations Educational, Scientific and Cultural Organization.

FURTHER READING

Albright, Madeleine K. 2003. "United Nations." *Foreign Policy* 138 (October): 16–24.

Luck, Edward. 1999. *Mixed Messages: American Politics and International Organization 1919–1999.* Washington, DC: Brookings Institution Press.

Lyon, Alynna J. 2016. *US Politics and the United Nations: A Tale of Dysfunctional Dynamics.* Boulder, CO: Lynne Rienner.

Goodwill Ambassadors and Messengers of Peace

Goodwill Ambassadors and Messengers of Peace are distinguished individuals, often celebrities, who work with the UN to raise awareness about global issues. Popular figures like boxer Muhammad Ali, anthropologist Jane Goodall, musician Stevie Wonder, and activist Malala Yousafzai have all lent their status to bring attention to the UN and the issues the organization supports. Starting with the Goodwill Ambassadors in 1954 and extending to the Messengers of Peace in 1997, the UN partners with eminent personalities to promote a diverse array of issues. Individuals with a range of backgrounds in the public eye, including artists, authors, musicians, movie stars, and sports figures, bring media attention to global problems and raise funds for UN initiatives. Their fame is used to promote UN causes on the world stage through public appearances, media events, and humanitarian work. Examples include actors Anne Hathaway's campaign against child marriage for the UN Entity for Gender Equality and the Empowerment of Women (UN Women) and Leonardo DiCaprio's work to raise awareness about climate change.

UN ENGAGEMENT

Messengers of Peace are appointed by the Secretary-General, whereas Goodwill Ambassadors are selected by the executive heads of particular specialized agencies and many of the programmes and funds in the UN System (although the Secretary-General must be informed before their designation is recognized). Individuals are chosen for two-year terms, which can be renewed. While some entities have mature programs, such as the UN Children's Fund and the UN High Commissioner for Refugees, others, like the World Food Programme, have relatively young programs. Along with DiCaprio, Goodall, Wonder, and Yousafzai, in 2019 there were nine additional recognized Messengers of Peace: Princess Haya Bint Al Hussein, Daniel Barenboim, Paulo Coelho, Michael Douglas, Lang Lang, Yo-Yo Ma, Midori, Edward Norton, and Charlize Theron. The larger set of Goodwill Ambassadors greatly expands the number of individuals promoting the UN. In 2016, the UN reported over four hundred active Goodwill Ambassadors and

> **Examples of United Nations Goodwill Ambassadors**
>
> Food and Agriculture Organization—Gong Li (China), Actress
>
> Joint UN Programme on HIV/AIDS—Toumani Diabaté (Mali), Musician
>
> UN Children's Fund—Lionel Messi (Argentina), Football Player
>
> UN Development Programme—Antonio Banderas (Spain), Actor
>
> UN Educational, Scientific and Cultural Organization—Alicia Alonso (Cuba), Ballerina and Choreographer
>
> UN Entity for Gender Equality and the Empowerment of Women—Nicole Kidman (Australia), Actress
>
> UN Environment Programme—Jack Johnson (United States), Musician
>
> UN High Commissioner for Refugees—Adel Imam (Egypt), Actor
>
> UN Industrial Development Organization—Marc Van Montagu (Belgium), Scientist
>
> UN Office on Drugs and Crime—Mira Sorvino (United States), Actress
>
> UN Population Fund—Queen Mother Ashi Sangay Choden Wangchuck (Bhutan)
>
> World Food Programme—Michael Kors (United States), Fashion Designer
>
> World Health Organization—Yohei Sasakawa (Japan), Chairman of The Nippon Foundation

Messengers of Peace holding fifteen different titles within three categories (international, regional, and national).

For example, Amal Clooney, a noted human rights lawyer, was Goodwill Ambassador for the UN Office on Drugs and Crime for the Dignity of Survivors of Human Trafficking and has advocated for the prevention of rape as a weapon of war. Amal Clooney's husband, actor George Clooney, served as a Messenger of Peace with an emphasis on promoting peacekeeping and reducing violence in the Darfur region in Sudan. Actress Angelina Jolie has worked extensively with the UN High Commissioner for Refugees, serving as a Goodwill Ambassador (2001–2012) and then being appointed as a Special Envoy in April 2012. Champions for Sport are a particular form of Goodwill Ambassador designated by the UN Educational, Scientific and Cultural Organization to engage sports personalities in promoting the organization's message. Examples include track and field sprinter Veronica Campbell-Brown, ice hockey player Vyacheslav Fetisov, tennis player Justine Henin, and Formula One race car driver Michael Schumacher.

ADVANCES AND CHALLENGES

High levels of media coverage elevate the communication capacity of Goodwill Ambassadors and Messengers of Peace. They also have unique influence as global personalities not confined by country borders. They can attract a global audience to raise awareness and generate public, and at times even financial, support for UN programs. In some circumstances, they have shaped the discourse through agenda setting around particular UN issues. Their popularity can connect their fans and followers with global issues that may otherwise go unrecognized or unsupported and can highlight the UN's work in these areas.

However, there are concerns that famous personalities engaging in global diplomacy can oversimplify complex issues and only have a minor, episodic impact. Critics suggest that celebrity-based activism may also be motivated by selfish desires for publicity that can drain legitimacy away from crucial causes. Moreover, adding more intermediaries to an already complex system of UN agencies can strain both resources and staff. Other critics emphasize the need for policy experts to set the agenda instead of celebrities. Goodwill Ambassadors and Messengers of Peace can be a great asset to the UN when correctly involved. In 2003, the UN adopted the "Guidelines for the Designation of Goodwill Ambassadors and Messengers of Peace" to promote best practices in the designation and engagement of these individuals.

See also: Executive Heads of Specialized Agencies; Office of Secretary-General; United Nations Children's Fund; United Nations Educational, Scientific and Cultural Organization; United Nations Entity for Gender Equality and the Empowerment of Women; United Nations High Commissioner for Refugees; United Nations Population Fund; World Food Programme.

FURTHER READING

Alleyne, Mark D. 2005. "The United Nations' Celebrity Diplomacy." *SAIS Review* 25 (1): 175–85.

Lim, Young Joon. 2014. "Promoting the Image of the United Nations." *Journalism History* 40 (3): 187–96.

Wheeler, Mark. 2011. "Celebrity Diplomacy: United Nations' Goodwill Ambassadors and Messengers of Peace." *Celebrity Studies* 2 (1): 6–18.

PART V

United Nations Concepts and Issues

INTRODUCTION

As an organization with 193 member states from every corner of the globe, the United Nations (UN) is responsible for and engages with an immense array of issues that transcend borders and affect people around the world. As set out in the Charter, the UN's original mandate focused on maintaining international peace and security, promoting international economic and social cooperation, and ensuring respect for human rights. UN security efforts include arms control and disarmament, collective security, and peaceful settlement. Economic and social cooperation encompasses issues as varied as economic development, health, and refugees and migration. Human rights, covering areas as diverse as women's rights and self-determination, are promoted across a number of UN institutions as well as working with nongovernmental organizations. The UN's handling of these issue areas evolves across time. For instance, the rise of terrorism and cybersecurity threats engages the UN in the security realm in new and unexpected ways. New issue areas not considered by UN founders, in particular environmental protection and the global commons, and increasing emphasis on existing issues, such as women and gender and indigenous peoples, also altered the UN's agenda.

As part of the organization's effort to address global problems, the UN has explored, in regular UN meetings as well as a series of conferences and summits, different ways to think about these issues and how to better the lives of people across the globe. Economic development has been combined with environmental protection to emphasize the new approach of sustainable development, and currently the linked Sustainable Development Goals (2015–2030) guide much of the work across the UN System. Traditional approaches to security have been extended through the creation of peacekeeping and peacebuilding operations. The very notion of what it means to maintain international peace and security has shifted with the introduction of new norms like human security and the responsibility to protect civilians against mass violence. Across time, the UN's membership, headquarters (from New York to Geneva, Vienna, and Nairobi), and level of regional engagement expanded, and the organization is also involved in a diverse set of reform efforts. Work at the UN across all issue areas requires careful budgeting and financial support, as well as close consideration of the views and involvement of the great powers and a variety of voting and negotiating blocs.

The Part V entries begin by explaining the emergence of the concept or issue and how this concern became part of the UN's agenda. This is followed by details of UN engagement, including related institutions, documents, and international events. Finally, the advances the UN has promoted as well as the challenges it faces in each issue area are also explored.

Arms Control and Disarmament

The possession and proliferation of weapons is a major issue in the realm of international security. Arms control is designed to regulate weapons, disarmament pursues the reduction or elimination of weapons, while nonproliferation seeks to limit the spread or increase of weapons. The international community first collectively engaged in disarmament negotiations with the 1899 Hague Peace Conference, but this effort failed to prevent World War I. The League of Nations' Covenant pointed to controlling arms, and a World Disarmament Conference was held in Geneva in 1932, but Europe was again plunged into destructive violence with World War II. Despite these failures, the UN seized on the need for disarmament and arms limitations as part of its mission to maintain international peace and security. While the UN Charter does not explicitly mention arms control or disarmament to frame the organization's purposes and principles, the body of the document connects this to the work of the Security Council (Article 26) and "the regulation of armaments, and possible disarmament" for addressing threats to peace (Article 47). Additionally, the General Assembly's "general principles" for maintaining international peace and security include "governing disarmament and the regulation of armaments" (Article 11). The need to address armaments was reinforced shortly after the signing of the Charter in June 1945, when the United States dropped atomic weapons on Japan in August. In fact, the first General Assembly resolution ever passed focused on this development and called for the control and peaceful use of atomic capabilities and the avoidance of weapons of mass destruction (WMDs).

UN ENGAGEMENT

In recognition of the need to safely and securely develop nuclear technology, the International Atomic Energy Agency (IAEA) began operations in 1957. The IAEA connects to the UN System as a related organization, as do the Organization for the Prohibition of Chemical Weapons and the Preparatory Commission for the Comprehensive Nuclear-Test-Ban Treaty Organization. The UN developed its own disarmament governance as well. The Disarmament Commission serves as a forum for discussing and making recommendations, the UN Institute for

Disarmament Research gathers data and provides analysis, and the Secretariat provides support through the Office for Disarmament Affairs. The Conference on Disarmament meets separately from the UN, although the body does provide a report to the General Assembly. The General Assembly further considers disarmament issues through the First Committee (Disarmament and International Security) and organized three special sessions on disarmament (1978, 1982, and 1988), although plans to hold a fourth session have stalled. The UN helped to put in place numerous international agreements. Limits on WMDs are an area of great emphasis, with a series of distinct treaties addressing nuclear, biological, and chemical weapons. Most recently, the UN adopted the Treaty on the Prohibition of Nuclear Weapons in 2017 (which will enter into force when fifty countries have ratified the agreement, as of early 2020 there were thirty-six ratifications). However, an array of conventional weapons are also addressed, including ammunition, small arms, light weapons, landmines, cluster bombs, and the trade of arms. The UN is also involved in disarmament as part of the peacebuilding process, helping to guide the disarming, demobilization, and reintegration of combatants into society.

ADVANCES AND CHALLENGES

The UN provides a useful forum for discussing and establishing new norms and agreements governing arms control and disarmament. However, many key negotiations and pacts take place outside of the official confines of the UN, with the major powers guiding and dominating the process in areas of concern to them ever since U.S. and Soviet actions at the onset of the Cold War. Progress is also limited due to the ongoing debate over whether arms undermine efforts to build peace or are necessary for enforcing global security. While advances are in place regarding rules for the use, limitations on, and removal of certain weapons, UN capabilities for implementation are generally limited. Along with existing arms issues, the UN faces challenges in coping with new areas, such as outer space arms control, as well as weapon developments brought about by technological innovation. A long road remains before weapons are removed as a central dimension of international relations, yet with maintaining international peace and security as a central purpose the UN will continue to promote arms control and disarmament efforts.

See also: António Guterres; Ban Ki-moon; Cybersecurity; Disarmament Commission; General Assembly; International Atomic Energy Agency; Organization for the Prohibition of Chemical Weapons; Preparatory Commission for the Comprehensive Nuclear-Test-Ban Treaty Organization; Research and Training Institutes; Secretariat; United Nations Purposes.

FURTHER READING

Blavoukos, Spyros, and Dimitris Bourantonis. 2014. "Calling the Bluff of the Western Powers in the United Nations Disarmament Negotiations, 1954–55." *Cold War History* 14 (3): 359–76.

Krause, Keith. 2018. "Arms Control and Disarmament." In *The Oxford Handbook on the United Nations*. Second edition, edited by Thomas G. Weiss and Sam Daws, 383–95. Oxford: Oxford University Press.

Weiss, Thomas G., and Ramesh Thakur. 2010. "Arms Control and Disarmament." In *Global Governance and the UN: An Unfinished Journey*, 90–127. Bloomington: Indiana University Press.

Collective Security

Countries often cooperate with one another to increase security and minimize the chance of war. One example of this is the collective security approach, which is designed to keep peaceful relations within a group of countries. Under a collective security arrangement, it is agreed that no country will use violence against another participating country. If a member of the collective agreement does use military action against another member, then the group pledges to respond to the aggression and restore the peace. The hope is that the threat of such an overwhelming collective response will deter potential attackers for using violence. Collective security differs from an alliance, which is a group of countries that form an agreement to jointly defend themselves against an attack from outside the group.

An alliance-based balance of power system was employed for centuries in the European security system. Following World War I, the 1919 Treaty of Versailles set out collective security as an alternative approach to be implemented through the League of Nations. Although the League struggled and Europe resumed fighting in World War II, the UN's approach to international security was built upon the collective security model. The principles set out in Article 2 of the UN Charter include, "All Members shall refrain in their international relations from the threat or use of force against the territorial integrity or political independence of any state." The Security Council's enforcement powers in Chapter VII of the Charter ("Action with Respect to the Threats to the Peace, Breaches of the Peace, and Acts of Aggression") provide strong support for this approach.

UN ENGAGEMENT

Despite the emphasis on creating a robust UN collective security system, this method rarely works as intended. Responding to invasions of Korea and Kuwait are the two instances that come closest to the UN engaging in collective security. In June 1950, North Korea invaded South Korea. The Security Council called on all members to counter the attack based on its authority under Chapter VII. While fifteen other countries (along with South Korea) operated in a coalition under the UN flag, the operation was dominated by U.S. forces and decision-making and is often viewed as collective self-defense instead of a true collective security exercise. In addition, as the Security Council deadlocked on further action in Korea, this necessitated expanding General Assembly authority to act through the passing of the "Uniting for Peace" Resolution in November 1950. In 1990, when Iraq occupied a portion of neighboring Kuwait the Security Council passed resolutions authorizing collective action to restore Kuwait's sovereignty, but again the United

States and its allies directed the military planning and operations. In addition, the progress in using a collective response was undermined in 2003 when the United States failed to secure Security Council support for further action against Iraq but proceeded with the military operation anyway.

ADVANCES AND CHALLENGES

Collective security requires consensus and commitment from the member states to carry out the organization's procedures. This has not been the case at the UN. Security Council action can be paralyzed by one of the five permanent members wielding their veto vote, which was particularly problematic during the Cold War clash between the United States and the Soviet Union. When the Security Council is ready to act, the UN lacks key resources set out in Chapter VII. Neither the armed forces that were supposed to be available on call (Article 43) nor the Military Staff Committee to assist with planning (Articles 46 and 47) were established. When the United States is not willing to commit military forces and planning this limits UN enforcement capabilities. Collective security is designed to counter war between countries, which does not address much of the violence that occurs in the world today. This includes the rise in civil conflict within countries and transnational terrorist violence carried out by nonstate actors. UN advances in maintaining peace and security have occurred in other areas, such as the creation of peacekeeping missions. Broader understanding of what it means to be secure, such as the promotion of human security, also moves the UN further away from a focus on collective security. However, in case of a future military incursion by one member state into another, a UN collective security response remains a possibility.

See also: Charter of the United Nations; Human Security; Peacekeeping; Role of Great Powers; Security Council; Terrorism; Trygve Lie; United Nations Principles.

FURTHER READING

Anderson, Kenneth. 2009. "United Nations Collective Security and the United States Security Guarantee in an Age of Rising Multipolarity: The Security Council as Talking Shop of the Nations." *Chicago Journal of International Law* 10 (1): 55–90.

McCoubrey, Hilaire, and Justin Morris. 2000. "The Concept of Collective Security." In *Regional Peacekeeping in the Post-Cold War Era*, 1–23. The Hague: Kluwer Law International.

Nasu, Hitoshi. 2011. "The Expanded Conception of Security and International Law: Challenges to the UN Collective Security System." *Amsterdam Law Forum* 3 (3): 15–33.

Cybersecurity

Information and communication technologies (ICTs) are an essential part of life in the twenty-first century. The growing dependency on technology includes managing medical records, operating banking services, maintaining government databases, and running municipal power grids. This creates increased vulnerabilities, making data and computer processing the target of cyberattacks by both state and nonstate actors. Significant attacks include in Estonia (2007), Georgia (2008), the use of Stuxnet against Iran (revealed in 2010), Ukraine (2017), and the global WannaCry ransomware (2017). In his 2018 *Agenda for Disarmament*, Secretary-General António Guterres declared, "Malicious acts in cyberspace are contributing to diminishing trust among States." These emerging and complex threats push the UN to respond and create comprehensive guidelines regulating cyber behavior.

UN ENGAGEMENT

The UN began addressing information security in 1998 when Russia introduced General Assembly Resolution 53/70, which identified cyber vulnerabilities as a national security threat. The World Summit on the Information Society (WSIS), organized by the International Telecommunications Union (ITU), was held in 2003 and 2005. This led to the creation in 2006 of the Internet Governance Forum, which provides a multistakeholder meeting for policy dialogue hosted by a different country each year. In advance of the WSIS, in 2012 General Assembly Resolution 57/239 called for the "creation of a global culture of cybersecurity." Extending from this, a UN Group of Governmental Experts on Developments in the Field of Information and Telecommunications in the Context of International Security (GGE) was established starting in 2004 and convened five times. The second, third, and fourth GGEs produced consensus reports outlining guidelines for cyber conduct. However, since that time, the members of the GGE have largely disagreed, particularly due to conflicting opinions of major powers. Thus, recent attempts to establish cybersecurity regulations have produced a two-track process.

This parallel approach (designed to span 2019–2021) was launched when the General Assembly passed Resolutions 73/27 and 73/266 addressing information, telecommunications, and cyberspace in relation to international security. An Open-Ended Working Group (OEWG) was created alongside a newly constituted GGE (on Advancing Responsible State Behavior in Cyberspace in the Context of International Security). The OEWG's first substantive session met in September 2019 and serves as an open forum for any UN member state that wants to participate as well as have consultative meetings with interested stakeholders, including businesses, nongovernmental organizations, and researchers. Divisions over the proper approach to cyber affairs have largely prevented progress in the Security Council, although when Resolution 2341 regarding terrorist attacks on critical infrastructure was passed in 2017 many delegates pointed to the connection with cyberattacks. Other parts of the UN System shape the organization's work on cybersecurity. The ITU sets International Telecommunication Regulations and created the Global Cybersecurity Index, as part of the body's Global Cybersecurity Agenda, to measure the state of international cybersecurity and raise awareness. The UN Institute for Disarmament Research holds an annual Cyber Stability Conference, which discusses the state of global cybersecurity policy as well as ways to combat ICT threats.

ADVANCES AND CHALLENGES

While cybersecurity remains a contentious issue, progress has been made and several treaties on crime address global standards for internet use. The 2001 Convention on Cybercrime, established by the Council of Europe, was the first international agreement to define what constituted a crime in cyberspace and created a network of countries to investigate and prevent attacks. The 2000 Convention against Transnational Organized Crime provides relevant dimensions (even though the internet is not explicitly referenced), and the 2001 Optional Protocol to the Convention on the Rights of a Child notes the role of the internet for distributing child pornography. Yet, the ability to set standards for conduct in cyberspace is slowed by great power politics and pushback against regulations on state actions. For example, the Shanghai Cooperation Organization (SCO), a coalition between China, Russia, Kazakhstan, Kyrgyzstan, Tajikistan, and Uzbekistan (India and Pakistan joined in 2017), presented an International Code of Conduct for Information Security in 2011 (and again in 2015) calling for the establishment of cyber sovereignty, which declares that governing the internet is solely a country's right and responsibility within its own borders. This approach is criticized by Western democracies as threatening human rights, undermining freedom of information, blocking the role of civil society and the private sector, and enabling authoritarian government control of communications. This is countered by the SCO, which accuses countries like the United States of espionage in cyberspace and violations of sovereignty. Another challenge is that both state and nonstate actors are engaged in cyberattacks and, therefore, require two distinct sets of regulations. As cyberattacks are transnational and transcend several issue areas, including national security, economic development, and human rights, the UN is in a unique position to host ongoing and inclusive dialogue and help advance global policies that will create secure and peaceful uses of cyberspace.

See also: António Guterres; Arms Control and Disarmament; Human Rights; International Telecommunication Union, Research and Training Institutes; Terrorism.

FURTHER READING

Finnemore, Martha, and Duncan B. Hollis. 2016. "Constructing Norms for Global Cybersecurity." *American Journal of International Law* 110 (3): 425–79.

Henriksen, Anders. 2019. "The End of the Road for the UN GGE Process: The Future Regulation of Cyberspace." *Journal of Cybersecurity* 5 (1). https://doi.org/10.1093/cybsec/tyy009.

Van Puyvelde, Damien, and Aaron F. Brantly. 2019. C*ybersecurity: Politics, Governance, and Conflict in Cyberspace*. Cambridge: Polity.

Economic Development

Economic development presents a significant challenge as billions of people around the world live in extreme poverty and must cope with malnutrition, disease, and a lack of basic necessities. There remain significant economic disparities between countries, and many developing countries are plagued by high levels of debt, stagnation, and unemployment. The UN Charter stresses addressing such problems, listing one of the UN's purposes as promoting international economic and social cooperation, and Article 55 pledges to foster "economic and social progress and development."

UN ENGAGEMENT

The UN's commitment to economic development was clear from the start as the General Assembly's Economic and Financial Committee (the Second Committee) was tasked with addressing financing, economic policy, and poverty. The Economic and Social Council, a new organ not included in the UN's predecessor the League of Nations, was mandated to raise standards of living and promote financial progress. This work is supported by five Regional Commissions that facilitate information sharing and cooperation to meet regional needs. The General Assembly also created the Expanded Programme of Technical Assistance in 1949 to coordinate UN agencies and assist countries with development plans, training programs, and grants. In 1958, the General Assembly formed the UN Special Fund to encourage financing, technical assistance, and large projects. In 1965, the programs were consolidated to create the UN Development Programme. The 1960s were proclaimed the UN Development Decade, followed by three additional development decades.

A wide range of other UN entities engage in development work, including the International Labour Organization, the UN Industrial Development Organization, the World Food Programme, and the UN Conference on Trade and Development. UN funds support development efforts by raising needed contributions and engaging in other activities, including the UN Capital Development Fund, the UN Population Fund, the International Fund for Agricultural Development, and the UN Development Fund for Women (merged into the UN Entity for Gender Equality and the Empowerment of Women). Several conferences, such as those on Environment and Development (1992) and Population and Development (1994), also expanded the UN's scope of work. In 2000, the UN spearheaded the Millennium Development Goals (MDGs) initiative that redefined the UN's objectives, including poverty and hunger eradication, environmental sustainability, enhancing health care, and gender equality. When the MDGs expired in 2015, they were replaced by the Sustainable Development Goals (2015–2030), which further tied economic inequality with development and preservation of natural resources alongside social progress.

ADVANCES AND CHALLENGES

Economic development has different possible meanings. For some it is the process of transforming low-income economies into industrial economies, while for others it means advancing broader human security. The different interpretations and unequal progress led the UN to spearhead changes in understanding the causes of underdevelopment and potential solutions, as well as shifting focus from building a country's economy to poverty reduction. The geographical regions emphasized by the UN also changed from postwar reconstruction in Europe and Asia to decolonialization in Africa in the 1960s. In the 1990s, the UN spearheaded the creation of benchmarks with targets and measurable indicators. The demands for economic development also changed as the global population grew from around 2 billion in 1945 to an estimated 7.8 billion in early 2020, in a world also facing increased environmental pressures.

While the UN is the center of much global development activity, the organization's impact on fostering economic progress is less clear. One frequent criticism is that the development focus is Western-centered and does not account for local priorities. International loans and industrialization seldom alleviate cycles of debt and poverty and can harm the environment. Much of the work on development takes place within the Western-dominated International Monetary Fund and World Bank Group. In addition, many point to progress being undermined by a lack of coordination within the UN System. Regardless, important contributions are found in the Human Development Index (a measure of income, education, and life expectancy), and there is evidence of global poverty reduction (particularly in Asian states), decreasing child mortality rates, and increasing global life expectancy. Overall, the UN provides an important venue to define the problems and goals of economic development. The UN has pioneered many ideas about development, set priorities, developed measures, and emphasized that economic development should be an investment into the well-being of future generations.

See also: Charter of the United Nations; Economic and Social Council; General Assembly; Human Security; International Fund for Agricultural Development; International Labour Organization; International Monetary Fund; International Seabed Authority; Regional Commissions; Sustainable Development; Sustainable Development Goals; United Nations Conference on Trade and Development; United Nations Conferences and Summits; United Nations Development Programme; United Nations Entity for Gender Equality and the Empowerment of Women; United Nations Industrial Development Organization; United Nations Population Fund; United Nations Purposes; World Bank Group; World Food Programme; World Trade Organization.

FURTHER READING

Baumann, Max-Otto. 2018. "Forever North–South? The Political Challenges of Reforming the UN Development System." *Third World Quarterly* 39 (4): 626–41.

Marshall, Katherine. 2018. "Global Development Governance." In *International Organization and Global Governance.* Second edition, edited by Thomas G. Weiss and Rorden Wilkinson, 616–29. New York: Routledge.

Stokke, Olav. 2009. *The UN and Development: From Aid to Cooperation.* Bloomington: Indiana University Press.

Environmental Protection

The industrial era changed the relationship between humans and the planet as hunting and gathering shifted to agribusiness and large-scale resource extraction. These alterations led to an increase in population and a range of environmental challenges. Issues like ozone depletion, loss of biodiversity, and planetary climate change transcend national borders and highlight the need for global cooperation. While the environment was not on the UN's agenda when the organization was founded in 1945, preserving natural resources like forests and clean water has become a pressing issue. Today, the UN takes the lead on many environmental issues. The organization creates forums for discussion to set priorities and create goals, as well as monitoring and preventing pollution.

UN ENGAGEMENT

A range of UN organizations, conferences, and agreements address environmental protection. Early on, the Food and Agricultural Organization and UN Educational, Scientific and Cultural Organization (UNESCO) were called on to safeguard certain natural resources like biodiversity. By the late 1960s, growing concerns about rising pollution led to calls for global action. In 1968, UNESCO hosted a conference on biosphere protection and the General Assembly passed Resolution 2398, noting "that the relationship between man and his environment is undergoing profound changes in the wake of modern scientific and technological developments," and called for international conferences and policies. From this point forward, UN-sponsored conferences became a central approach for promoting environmental protection. The 1972 UN Conference on the Human Environment in Stockholm, Sweden, included over a hundred countries and a parallel forum with several hundred nongovernmental organizations. The meeting released the Stockholm Declaration and an action plan with 109 recommendations for environmental action. In addition, the conference led to the creation of the UN Environment Programme, an institution that monitors global environmental conditions and promotes environmental coordination and policies.

In 1979, the World Meteorological Organization hosted the first World Climate Conference and concluded that human activity would alter the planet's climate. In 1987, the World Commission on Environment and Development issued a key report titled *Our Common Future* (known as the Brundtland Report). The 1992 UN Conference on Environment and Development in Rio de Janeiro is also notable, with the creation of Agenda 21, a nonbinding sustainable development plan. This conference, referred to as the Earth Summit, resulted in the creation of the Commission on Sustainable Development to monitor and follow up on conference outcomes (this body was replaced by the High-level Political Forum on Sustainable Development [HLPF] in 2013) and the UN Framework Convention on Climate Change to limit greenhouse gas emissions. Other significant UN contributions include a series of meetings known as the Conference of the Parties (COP). COP-1 was held in 1995 in Germany and the twenty-fifth meeting in 2019 in Spain. Two of the most significant meetings include Kyoto in 1992, which resulted in the Kyoto Protocol, and COP-21 (2015), which generated the Paris Agreement. The Paris Agreement includes an ambitious target to prevent global temperature rise from exceeding 2 degrees Celsius through countries taking individual climate actions (referred to as nationally determined contributions). The Paris Agreement was signed by 175 countries on April 22, 2016, the first day it

> **Selected United Nations Environmental Protection Conferences and Meetings**
>
> 1972—UN Conference on the Human Environment ("Stockholm Conference") held in Stockholm, Sweden
>
> 1979—World Climate Conference held in Geneva, Switzerland
>
> 1985–1990 Intergovernmental conferences focusing on climate change (Villach 1985, Toronto 1988, Ottawa 1989, Tata 1989, The Hague 1989, Noordwijk 1989, Cairo 1989, and Bergen 1990)
>
> 1990—Second World Climate Conference held in Geneva, Switzerland
>
> 1992—UN Conference on Environment and Development ("Rio Summit" or "Earth Summit") held in Rio de Janeiro, Brazil
>
> 1995—First Session of the Conference of the Parties to the UN Framework Convention on Climate Change (COP 1) held in Berlin, Germany
>
> 1997—UN General Assembly Special Session for Review and Appraisal of the Implementation of Agenda 21 held in New York City, United States ("Earth Summit +5")
>
> 1997—COP 3 held in Kyoto, Japan
>
> 2002—World Summit on Sustainable Development ("Rio+10") held in Johannesburg, South Africa
>
> 2005—COP 11 and the first meeting of the Parties to the Kyoto Protocol (CMP 1) held in Montreal, Canada
>
> 2009—COP 15 and CMP 5 held in Copenhagen, Denmark ("Copenhagen Summit")
>
> 2012—UN Conference on Sustainable Development ("Rio+20") held in Rio de Janeiro, Brazil
>
> 2015—UN Sustainable Development Summit held in New York City, United States
>
> 2015—COP 21 and CMP 11 held in Paris, France
>
> 2016—COP 22, CMP 12, and the first meeting of the Parties to the Paris Agreement (CMA 1) held in Marrakesh, Morocco
>
> 2019—UN Climate Action Summit held at UN Headquarters in New York City
>
> 2019—COP 25, CMP 15, and CMA 2 held in Madrid, Spain

opened for signatures (as of December 2019, there are 195 signatories, 187 of which have ratified the agreement in some manner).

ADVANCES AND CHALLENGES

The UN is a leading actor in raising awareness of the need for environmental protection, compiling scientific information, creating international law, and crafting goals to guide country efforts. An example of success is found in the 1987 Montreal Protocol on Substances that Deplete the Ozone Layer, which addressed damage to the ozone layer. Other advances include UN Environment Programme's (UNEP) creation of environmental assessment reports, regulations of drinking

Selected United Nations Environmental Protection Agreements and Plans

1971—Ramsar Convention on Wetlands of International Importance especially as Waterfowl Habitat (entered into force 1975)

1972—Declaration of the UN Conference on the Human Environment ("Stockholm Declaration") and Action Plan for the Human Environment

1972—Convention Concerning the Protection of the World Cultural and Natural Heritage (entered into force 1975)

1972—Convention on the Prevention of Marine Pollution by the Dumping of Wastes and Other Matter (entered into force 1975)

1973—International Convention for the Prevention of Pollution from Ships (MARPOL, entered into force 1983)

1973—Convention on the International Trade in Endangered Species of Wild Fauna and Flora (CITES, entered into force 1975)

1979—Convention on Long-Range Transboundary Air Pollution (entered into force 1983)

1985—Vienna Convention for the Protection of the Ozone Layer (entered into force 1988)

1987—Montreal Protocol on Substances that Deplete the Ozone Layer (entered into force 1989)

1987—*Our Common Future*, Report of the World Commission on Environment and Development ("Brundtland Report")

1989—Basel Convention on the Control of Transboundary Movements of Hazardous Wastes and Their Disposal (entered into force 1992)

1992—Rio Declaration on Environment and Development

1992—Agenda 21 from the UN Conference on Environment and Development

1992—Forest Principles from the UN Conference on Environment and Development

1992—Convention on Biological Diversity (entered into force 1993)

1992—UN Framework Convention on Climate Change (UNFCCC, entered into force 1994)

1994—UN Convention to Combat Desertification in Those Countries Experiencing Serious Drought and/or Desertification, Particularly in Africa (entered into force 1996)

1997—Kyoto Protocol to the UNFCCC (entered into force 2005)

1997—Convention on the Law of the Non-navigational Uses of International Watercourses (entered into force 2014)

2001—Stockholm Convention on Persistent Organic Pollutants (entered into force 2004)

2002—Johannesburg Declaration on Sustainable Development and Plan of Implementation

2004—International Convention for the Control and Management of Ships' Ballast Water and Sediments (entered into force 2017)

2006—International Tropical Timber Agreement (entered into force 2011)

2009—Copenhagen Accord from the 15th session of the Conference of the Parties to the UNFCCC

2012—"The Future We Want" from the UN Conference on Sustainable Development

> 2013—Minamata Convention on Mercury (entered into force 2017)
>
> 2015—"Transforming Our World: The 2030 Agenda for Sustainable Development" from the UN Sustainable Development Summit
>
> 2015—Paris Agreement from the 21st Conference of the Parties to the UNFCCC

water, prevention of oil spills, and hazardous waste, and international pesticide standards. Recently, the scope of environmental protection concerns has expanded. For instance, in 2009 the Office of the UN High Commissioner for Human Rights connected climate change with human rights. The Security Council has also begun to link climate change with threats to international peace and security. The great majority of the seventeen Sustainable Development Goals contain an element on environment protection.

One challenge the UN faces concerns compliance with international agreements, which is often undermined by a lack of political will and clear leadership. For example, the United States, once a leader in environmental policy, announced its withdrawal from the Paris Agreement in 2017. Critics add that organizational support, particularly UNEP, is persistently underfunded. Efforts toward conservation bring out tensions between developed and developing areas, and protests from countries that seek to prioritize economic development. Yet, this clash of priorities has shifted to create the innovative idea of sustainable development and the related goals. Overall, the UN serves as a global leader encouraging balance between the demands of development and preservation of natural resource for future generations.

See also: Ban Ki-moon; Food and Agriculture Organization; Global Commons; High-level Political Forum on Sustainable Development; Human Rights; International Civil Aviation Organization; International Maritime Organization; International Seabed Authority; Nongovernmental Organizations; Security Council; Sustainable Development; Sustainable Development Goals; United Nations Conferences and Summits; United Nations Educational, Scientific and Cultural Organization; United Nations Environment Programme; United Nations Human Settlements Programme; World Meteorological Organization.

FURTHER READING

Conca, Ken. 2015. *An Unfinished Foundation: The United Nations and Global Environmental Governance.* Oxford: Oxford University Press.

Elliott, Lorraine. 2004. *The Global Politics of the Environment.* Second edition. New York: New York University Press.

Scott, Shirley V., and Charlotte Ku, eds. 2018. *Climate Change and the UN Security Council.* Cheltenham, UK: Edward Elgar.

Global Commons

The global commons refer to areas with natural resources that are not under the control of a single country or set of countries. The four traditional global commons zones are Antarctica, the atmosphere, the high seas, and outer space. Resources in these areas should be accessible and shared as a common heritage. Governance of the global commons helps to prevent the long-standing "tragedy of the commons," where an individual's incentive to use as many resources as possible undermines the mutual sharing and long-term maintenance of resources in an area. International efforts to monitor and regulate the global commons grew as countries developed capabilities to expand travel and impact global commons areas. Since the UN's creation in 1945, the organization has been increasingly engaged in managing the global commons as technological developments provided greater access to and increased pressure on these resources.

UN ENGAGEMENT

The UN is actively involved in regulating the use of the seas. The UN Convention on the Law of the Sea and the International Seabed Authority guide the use of ocean resources, including deep seabed mining. The International Maritime Organization oversees a wide range of shipping regulations. Governance of the polar regions is more limited in scope and primarily outside of the UN System. The Antarctic Treaty System, which began with the 1959 Antarctic Treaty, provides protections and a consultative framework for addressing Antarctic resources but operates separately from the UN. Starting with twelve countries, as of early 2020 there are fifty-four countries engaged with the Antarctic discussions, twenty-nine with consultative status and twenty-five non-consultative countries that can attend meetings but not make decisions. The question of Antarctica has appeared sporadically on the General Assembly's agenda. In addition, various UN bodies engage with the Antarctic Treaty System, including the UN Environment Programme's (UNEP) monitoring of environmental conditions, preparing reports, and attending consultative meetings.

The atmosphere is an area of increasing concern due to the impact of pollution on the protective ozone layer and greenhouse gases that lead to climate change. The UN is a key organization for bringing countries together to coordinate and seek solutions to reduce these threats. For example, UNEP plays a useful role in countering ozone layer depletion and sponsoring negotiations that led to the important 1987 Montreal Protocol on Substances that Deplete the Ozone Layer. In terms of climate change, a wide range of UN organizations, conferences, and agreements focus on countering this growing threat. These include the UN Intergovernmental Panel on Climate Change and the UN Framework Convention on Climate Change. Space exploration and the possibility of resource extraction, and concerns over the possible militarization of outer space, also pushed the international community into action. The UN initially reacted to space exploration by founding the Committee on the Peaceful Uses of Outer Space in 1959. The influential work of this committee helped lead to the 1967 Treaty on Principles Governing the Activities of States in the Exploration and Use of Outer Space, Including the Moon and Other Celestial Bodies (Outer Space Treaty) and the 1979 Agreement Governing the Activities of States on the Moon and Other Celestial Bodies

(Moon Treaty). Geostationary satellite orbital slots are a valuable telecommunications resource, which fall under the mandate of the International Telecommunications Union.

ADVANCES AND CHALLENGES

The UN promotes the maintenance and protection of the global commons through international agreements and regulatory organizations. However, many countries resist treating Antarctica as a global resource and bringing this area under UN oversight. With climate change, the Arctic is becoming more accessible and raises similar questions about oversight versus individual country jurisdiction claims. The polar regions illustrate how governing the global commons presents a continual challenge as countries seek to extend their individual sovereign control over areas of strategic interest. The UN is based on respecting state sovereignty, so the desire for international community versus country control remains an ongoing tension. The differences between economically developed and less developed countries also carry over into the global commons debate. Developing countries often lack the funds and technology to access global commons resources, yet want them to be equitably maintained for future use. In addition, some argue for global commons protection to be expanded to areas such as biodiversity and rain forests. Pressures on the global commons continue to grow as technological and scientific advances make these areas more accessible and large-scale environmental damage expands. These challenges ensure that the UN will continue to work to preserve these vital resources.

See also: Environmental Protection; International Maritime Organization; International Seabed Authority; International Telecommunication Union; Trusteeship Council; United Nations Environment Programme.

FURTHER READING

Buck, Susan J. 1998. *The Global Commons: An Introduction.* Washington, DC: Island Press.
Schrijver, Nico. 2010. "Management of the Global Commons." In *Development without Destruction: The UN and Global Resource Management*, 75–113. Bloomington: Indiana University Press.
Vogler, John. 2012. "Global Commons Revisited." *Global Policy* 3 (1): 61–71.

Health

Health issues transcend borders, as people across the globe share concern over common health problems and infectious diseases, such as the Ebola virus and the coronavirus (COVID-19), ignore national boundaries. The need to coordinate to stop the spread of disease was recognized early on, and there is a long history of international efforts to regulate this area. Efforts to block cholera epidemics led to cooperation in the nineteenth century in the form of sanitary councils put into place in seaport cities on the borders of Europe. A series of international health conferences were held, starting in Paris in 1851. International health institutions were established in the early twentieth century, including the Pan American Sanitary Bureau, the International Office of Public Health, and the League of Nations' Health Organization. The UN moved quickly to establish a universal agency with a broad health mandate. The World Health Organization (WHO) began operations in 1948 and remains an important specialized agency in the UN System.

UN ENGAGEMENT

In the twenty-first century, health is a crucial part of the UN's development targets in the eight Millennium Development Goals (MDGs, 2000–2015) and the seventeen Sustainable Development Goals (SDGs, 2015–2030). MDGs 4, 5, and 6 specifically targeted health issues: reduce child mortality, improve maternal health, and combat HIV/AIDS, malaria, and other diseases. In addition, MDG 8 on global partnerships for development included providing access to affordable drugs. SDG 3 most explicitly promotes healthy lives and well-being. This goal encompasses infectious diseases (including HIV/AIDS, malaria, tuberculosis, and hepatitis B) and noncommunicable diseases (such as heart disease, cancer, and diabetes). Unsafe drinking water, lack of sanitation and hygiene, and air pollution within the home and outside are targeted as well. Reproductive, maternal, newborn, and child health are also emphasized, along with improving health systems and funding. In fact, almost all of the SDGs contain something connected to health.

WHO provides broad-ranging engagement in addressing health issues. A more recent UN body is the Joint United Nations Programme on HIV/AIDS (UNAIDS), which began operations in 1996. Since health connects to so many different issues, many institutions in the UN System have a health component as part of their disaster relief or long-term work. For example, the UN Children's Fund includes programs on child and maternal health. Along with the SDGs, the UN promotes health through other specific agreements (e.g., the WHO Framework Convention on Tobacco Control adopted in 2003, the Global Action Plan for the Prevention and Control of Noncommunicable Diseases 2013–2020, and conventions against narcotic drugs). World Health Day is recognized every April 7, the day in 1948 when WHO's Constitution was ratified.

ADVANCES AND CHALLENGES

Compared to the condition of the world population's health at the time of UN founding in 1945, the commitment to addressing global health by the international community has brought about great progress. Certain communicable diseases, such as polio and smallpox, are now extremely limited. Other important health indicators, such as infant mortality rates, are also much improved. Health is now recognized as a fundamental human right for all. The link between underdevelopment and health problems is recognized in UN goals. Dimensions of health that were ignored at the global level, such as mental health, have drawn increased attention at the UN. At the same time, the world is faced with new dangerous communicable disease threats, including H1N1 flu, coronavirus (COVID-19), and the Ebola virus. The rapid spread of such diseases is difficult to control given globalized transportation. Diseases are also building resistance to drugs and antibiotics. Health emergencies have led to the "securitization" of global health by some. Others are concerned that a security emphasis on health undermines collaborative efforts to address the long-term health problems of vulnerable populations by creating an "us" versus "them" feeling and stressing crisis situations. There are an increasing number of health organizations in the international arena. Reform suggestions include more centralization and coordination of resources committed to global health. Other recommendations include the creation of a UN Panel on Global Health to bring together all public and private health actors. Global health will continue to be a critical issue that also impacts international commerce. The UN System's ability to provide a venue for tracking pandemics, coordinating mitigation efforts, and providing assistance is vital for making the world a healthy place to live.

See also: Human Rights; Joint United Nations Programme on HIV/AIDS; Sustainable Development Goals; United Nations Children's Fund; World Health Organization.

FURTHER READING

Birn, Anne-Emanuelle. 2009. "The Stages of International (Global) Health: Histories of Success or Successes of History?" *Global Public Health* 4 (1): 50–68.
Mackey, Tim K., and Bryan A. Liang. 2013. "A United Nations Global Health Panel for Global Health Governance." *Social Science & Medicine* 76 (January): 12–15.
Packard, Randall M. 2016. *A History of Global Health: Interventions into the Lives of Other Peoples.* Baltimore, MD: Johns Hopkins University Press.

Human Rights

Human rights are the basic protections and freedoms to which all people are entitled regardless of nationality, gender, ethnic origin, religion, language, or other status. The idea of citizen rights first emerged at the domestic level, such as in the French Declaration of the Rights of Man and the United States' Bill of Rights. Although some progress was made in the Geneva Conventions for protecting civilians, prisoners of war, and medical personal during wartime and under the League of Nations and International Labour Organization founded following World War I, the UN provided a revolutionary step forward in the expression of human rights at the international level. After World War II, many saw a connection between violations of human rights and threats to international peace and security. The UN Charter is a vital document placing human rights fully onto the global agenda. Human rights are referenced seven times, including the Preamble statement declaring that one purpose of the UN is "to reaffirm faith in fundamental human rights, in the dignity and worth of the human person, in the equal rights of men and women."

UN ENGAGEMENT

Human rights are a core pillar of the UN System. For seventy-five years, the UN has been at the forefront in establishing the rights everyone is entitled to as well as creating instruments to monitor violations and assisting governments in establishing and codifying rights. Observers identify three generations of human rights. First-generation rights are political and civil rights and include life, liberty, freedom of religion, speech, and peaceful assembly. Second-generation rights focus on socioeconomic rights such as the right to housing, work, and education. The third generation of human rights refers to the collective rights of particular groups or communities, and a healthy environment.

The Charter never defined human rights, but, in 1948, the General Assembly approved the Universal Declaration of Human Rights (UDHR) that listed the common standards for all people (see Part VI). Although the UDHR is not legally binding, the document is translated into over five hundred languages and has shaped the constitutions of many countries. Along with a number of additional nonbinding declarations, years of negotiations between countries with different political structures, legal systems, and cultural traditions produced a range of binding international human rights treaties. These include the International Covenant on Civil and Political Rights (entered into force in 1976), which prohibits negative acts such as torture, slavery, and arbitrary arrest and ensures protections for rights such as freedom of religion and expression. The International Covenant on Economic, Social, and Cultural Rights (entered into force in 1976) includes rights to safe and healthy working conditions, to form unions, to education, and access to adequate housing, food, and clothing. These two treaties in combination with the UDHR are often referred to as the International Bill of Human Rights. Separate treaties, for instance, the Convention on the Elimination of All Forms of Discrimination against Women (entered into force in 1981), protect specific disadvantaged groups.

The UN also sponsors international conferences on human rights, including the World Conference on Human Rights held in 1993 that led to the Vienna Declaration and Programme of Action and the creation of the Office of High Commissioner for Human Rights. Other notable UN agents that promote and monitor human rights include the Human Rights Council, the General Assembly's Third Committee, and treaty-based committees. In addition, many other UN entities promote human rights, such as the UN Entity for Gender Equality and the Empowerment of Women, the UN Educational, Scientific and Cultural Organization, and the International Labour Organization.

ADVANCES AND CHALLENGES

Since 1948, human rights have expanded to include the rights of children, women, migrant workers, and provisions against racial discrimination. Human rights are increasingly mentioned in Security Council and General Assembly resolutions. Key human rights elements are in the Sustainable Development Goals and are included in issues such as health, housing, and gender equality. At the

> ### Human Rights Conventions
>
> 1948—Convention on the Prevention and Punishment of the Crime of Genocide (entered into force 1951)
>
> 1951—Convention Relating to the Status of Refugees (entered into force 1954) (protocol extending time frame and geographical coverage of Convention entered into force 1967)
>
> 1952—Convention on the International Right of Correction (entered into force 1962)
>
> 1954—Convention Relating to the Status of Stateless Persons (entered into force 1960)
>
> 1961—Convention on the Reduction of Statelessness (entered into force 1975)
>
> 1962—Convention on Consent to Marriage, Minimum Age for Marriage and Registration of Marriages (entered into force 1964)
>
> 1965—International Convention on the Elimination of All Forms of Racial Discrimination (entered into force 1969)
>
> 1966—International Covenant on Civil and Political Rights (entered into force 1976)
>
> 1966—International Covenant on Economic, Social and Cultural Rights (entered into force 1976)
>
> 1968—Convention on the Non-Applicability of Statutory Limitations of War Crimes and Crimes against Humanity (entered into force 1970)
>
> 1973—International Convention on the Suppression and Punishment of the Crime of Apartheid (entered into force 1976)
>
> 1979—Convention on the Elimination of All Forms of Discrimination against Women (entered into force 1981)
>
> 1984—Convention against Torture and Other Cruel, Inhuman, or Degrading Treatment or Punishment (entered into force 1987)
>
> 1985—International Convention Against Apartheid in Sports (entered into force 1988)
>
> 1989—Convention on the Rights of the Child (entered into force 1990)
>
> 1989—Indigenous and Tribal Peoples Convention (International Labour Organization Convention 169, entered into force 1991)
>
> 1990—International Convention on the Protection of the Rights of All Migrant Workers and Members of Their Families (entered into force 2003)
>
> 2006—Convention on the Rights of Persons with Disabilities (entered into force 2008)
>
> 2006—International Convention for the Protection of All Persons from Enforced Disappearances (entered into force 2010)

same time, Charter Article 2(7) protects member state sovereignty and prohibits the UN from imposing standards and protections. The recently established norm of the responsibility to protect challenges this and asserts that, in cases of mass atrocities, a country may relinquish sovereignty and the international community holds a responsibility to protect civilians. However, mass violence continues in cases like Myanmar (2016–2017), Syria (2011–), and Yemen (2015–). Ongoing violations, such as the exploitation of children and marginalization of women,

> **Human Rights Declarations**
>
> 1948—Universal Declaration of Human Rights
>
> 1959—Declaration of the Rights of the Child (based on the 1924 League of Nations' Geneva Declaration of the Rights of the Child)
>
> 1968—Proclamation of Tehran, The International Conference on Human Rights
>
> 1971—Declaration on the Rights of Mentally Retarded Persons
>
> 1974—Declaration on the Protection of Women and Children in Emergency and Armed Conflict
>
> 1975—Declaration on the Rights of Disabled Persons
>
> 1978—Declaration on Race and Racial Prejudice
>
> 1981—Declaration on the Elimination of All Forms of Intolerance and of Discrimination Based on Religion or Belief
>
> 1984—Declaration on the Right of Peoples to Peace
>
> 1986—Declaration on the Right to Development
>
> 1993—Vienna Declaration and Programme of Action, World Conference on Human Rights
>
> 1993—Declaration on the Elimination of Violence Against Women
>
> 1998—Declaration on the Right and Responsibility of Individuals, Groups and Organs of Society to Promote and Protect Universally Recognized Human Rights and Fundamental Freedoms
>
> 2001—Universal Declaration on Cultural Diversity
>
> 2001—Durban Declaration and Programme of Action, World Conference Against Racism
>
> 2007—UN Declaration on the Rights of Indigenous People
>
> 2011—Declaration on Human Rights Education and Training
>
> 2018—Declaration on the Rights of Peasants and Other People Working in Rural Areas

LGBTQ persons, and refugees, also reflect failures. The UN's ability to address violations lies with its member states. They can block UN action, or simply fail to act, as they closely guard sovereign control over their territory. Despite these difficulties, the UN promotes an ambitious agenda to preserve human dignity and apply these standards to every person on the planet.

See also: Charter of the United Nations; Economic and Social Council; Environmental Protection; General Assembly; Health; Human Rights Council; Human Security; Indigenous Peoples; International Criminal Court; International Labour Organization; Peacebuilding; Refugees and Migration; Responsibility to Protect; Self-Determination; Sustainable Development Goals; Terrorism; United Nations Children's Fund; United Nations Conferences and Summits; United Nations Educational, Scientific and Cultural Organization; United Nations Entity for Gender Equality and the Empowerment of Women; United Nations Purposes; Women and Gender.

FURTHER READING

Donnelly, Jack, and Daniel Whelan. 2017. *International Human Rights*. Fifth edition. London: Routledge.

Forsythe, David P. 2017. *Human Rights in International Relations*. Fourth edition. Cambridge: Cambridge University Press.

Mills, Kurt, and David J. Karp, eds. 2015. *Human Rights Protection in Global Politics: Responsibilities of States and Non-State Actors*. London: Palgrave Macmillan.

Human Security

A central purpose of the UN is the maintenance of international peace and security. At the founding of the UN in 1945, the focus was on peaceful relations between countries. However, the UN's understanding of and engagement with "security" has evolved over time. Human security focuses on the security needs of everyday people. This concept not only broadens the scope of what actors should be made secure but also explains what it means to be secure. Populations should be guarded against the threat of violent conflict but also provided with human rights safeguards, essential social and economic development needs, and environmental protection.

The key first step for placing human security on the UN's agenda was the UN Development Programme's 1994 Human Development Report. Under Secretary-General Kofi Annan, starting at the 2000 UN Millennium Summit and reinforced in his 2005 report *In Larger Freedom: Towards Development, Security and Human Rights for All*, he encouraged developing the UN's conceptualization and implementation of human security. This included the establishment of the independent Commission on Human Security, which produced the guiding 2003 report *Human Security Now*.

UN ENGAGEMENT

Human security has reshaped the way that the UN engages with security issues. The organization continues to discuss approaches to human security and to issue reports and resolutions supporting the need to maintain a human security lens when looking at building peace. This includes General Assembly thematic debates on human security in 2008, 2011, and 2014. A high-level gathering with country representatives, civil society members, and UN officials was convened in 2013 following the passing of General Assembly Resolution 66/290 in 2012. This resolution emphasized the value of human security and endorsed a common understanding of the term, including "the right of people to live in freedom and dignity, free from poverty and despair." Secretary-General Ban Ki-moon issued three reports on human security and established the position of Special Adviser on Human Security.

The work initiated by the Commission on Human Security is carried forward today by an independent Advisory Board on Human Security. The Advisory Board's role includes providing advice to the UN's Human Security Unit, which promotes incorporating a human security approach throughout the UN System and manages the UN Trust Fund for Human Security. This trust fund supports projects that incorporate a human security approach and finances efforts across all regions of the globe. For example, empowering rural communities in postconflict Liberia across multiple sectors, including managing peaceful negotiations, improving farming and technical capabilities, and improving local economic capacity, and reducing violence in El Salvador by addressing the interconnected threats posed by organized crime, violent attacks, gender inequality, and a lack of secure social services. As human security links peace and security, development, and human rights, the Inter-Agency Working Group on Human Security draws together representatives engaged in these areas from across the UN System. The working group made important contributions to the 2015 *Framework for Cooperation for the System-wide Application of Human Security*. This framework urges more effective collaboration between the different parts of the UN System, sets out principles to guide the application of human security—including the need to be people centered, comprehensive, and provide protection and empowerment—and encourages a stronger implementation of human security.

ADVANCES AND CHALLENGES

The concept of human security is a major shift in the understanding of security and the idea is now infused across the UN System. However, the very breadth of a human security approach is a central concern to critics. By labeling an issue as a security threat, this can bring greater attention, priority, and resources. Yet, if everything is a security issue, then how can the global community prioritize its responses? There are also concerns raised that labeling areas as security-related can encourage military solutions instead of social or economic assistance. Human security is also overshadowed at times by other security emphases. For example, the stress on counterterrorism following the September 11, 2001 attacks in the United States drew more attention to more traditional security approaches. In addition, the responsibility to protect concept emerged at the UN around the same time as human security and is often given greater attention by analysts. At the same time, the Sustainable Development Goals established in 2015 to set the UN's 2030 Agenda are based on a human security approach, so human security continues to be relevant to UN thinking moving forward.

See also: Ban Ki-moon; Environmental Protection; Human Rights; Kofi Annan; Responsibility to Protect; Sustainable Development Goals; Terrorism; United Nations Conferences and Summits; United Nations Development Programme; United Nations Purposes.

FURTHER READING

MacFarlane, S. Neil, and Yuen Foong Khong. 2006. *Human Security and the UN: A Critical History*. Bloomington: Indiana University Press.

Ogata, Sadako, and Johan Cels. 2003. "Human Security: Protecting and Empowering the People." *Global Governance* 9 (3): 273–82.

Page, Edward, and Michael Redclift, eds. 2002. *Human Security and the Environment: International Comparisons*. Cheltenham, UK: Edward Elgar.

Indigenous Peoples

Although the Preamble to the UN Charter opens with "We the peoples of the United Nations," indigenous peoples faced a long and difficult path for participation in the UN. The label of indigenous peoples captures the shared existence of representing and preserving the distinct ancestral culture, language, and identity of those who were historically displaced from their traditional place in a territory through the invasive occupation by outsiders. Indigenous peoples often continue to stand separate from the other parts of society where they live, which can lead to them being disadvantaged, marginalized, and oppressed. There are an estimated 370 million indigenous peoples in the world across over ninety countries, with examples including the Aborigines in Australia, the Inuit in the Arctic, and different native peoples within the Americas.

There are a wide variety of indigenous peoples, but they come together as a global movement to address common grievances over mistreatment and lack of recognition within their resident states. There were early efforts to press for indigenous rights at the League of Nations, but greater progress was made as the issue moved on to the UN agenda. In the early decades of the UN, indigenous peoples struggled to be treated as a distinct group with specific protections. Increased pressure in the 1970s culminated in the establishment of the Working Group on Indigenous Populations (WGIP) in the Sub-Commission on the Promotion and Protection of Human Rights in 1982.

UN ENGAGEMENT

The WGIP, and other human rights mechanisms, was altered with the establishment of the Human Rights Council in 2006. Within the Human Rights Council, there is now instead the Expert Mechanism on the Rights of Indigenous Peoples, along with a Special Rapporteur on the Rights of Indigenous Peoples. The separate Office of the UN High Commissioner for Human Rights also provides support for indigenous rights. In addition, a Permanent Forum on Indigenous Issues began operations under the Economic and Social Council in 2002. A number of institutions in the UN System have policies in support of indigenous peoples, ranging from addressing their development needs in the UN Development Programme, International Fund for Agricultural Development, and World Bank to supporting cultural and linguistic diversity at the UN Educational, Scientific and Cultural Organization.

There is no definitive definition of indigenous peoples within the UN, but most often cited is the important Study of the Problem of Discrimination Against Indigenous Populations submitted in the early 1980s by the Special Rapporteur of the Sub-Commission on Prevention of Discrimination and Protection of Minorities José Martínez Cobo. The only legally binding treaty on indigenous rights is the International Labour Organization's 1989 Indigenous and Tribal Peoples Convention (Convention 169, entered into force in 1991), which updated and replaced Convention 107 from 1957. While not legally binding, the essential, comprehensive document is the UN Declaration on the Rights of Indigenous Peoples (UNDRIP), which was approved by the General Assembly in 2007 after over two decades of work. Commitment to the Declaration's goals was reinforced at the 2014 World Conference on Indigenous Peoples. The UN also promoted respect for indigenous peoples through the 1993 International Year of the World's Indigenous People and two International Decades of the World's Indigenous People (1995–2004 and 2005–2014).

ADVANCES AND CHALLENGES

Since appearing on the UN agenda as a distinct group, indigenous peoples have made notable advances institutionally, including the establishment of the new Permanent Forum, and conceptually, particularly with the long-sought UNDRIP that has generated much attention and analysis. While the nonbinding UNDRIP is often viewed as taking on the status of customary international law protections, the need to improve implementation is stressed along with calls for creating a legally binding indigenous rights treaty. Others argue that indigenous peoples' issues should not be addressed under traditional UN rights approaches, instead emphasizing that indigenous people are connected to decolonization and self-determination land claims. This is tied to calls for stronger indigenous recognition and representation at UN venues beyond being treated as nongovernmental actors. Indigenous peoples have developed supportive working partnerships with various UN bodies, although reviews point to the need for reform in areas such as improving interagency collaboration on indigenous issues, bolstering indigenous consultation access, advancing country-level programming and funding, and ensuring that indigenous peoples are treated distinctly from other marginalized groups. Overall, indigenous peoples have created an important space within the UN beyond that of other vulnerable groups.

See also: Human Rights Council; International Fund for Agricultural Development; International Labour Organization; Permanent Forum on Indigenous Issues; Self-Determination; United Nations Conferences and Summits; United Nations Development Programme; United Nations Educational, Scientific and Cultural Organization; World Bank Group.

FURTHER READING

Dahl, Jens. 2012. *The Indigenous Space and Marginalized Peoples in the United Nations.* New York: Palgrave Macmillan.

Hohmann, Jessie, and Marc Weller, eds. 2018. *The UN Declaration on the Rights of Indigenous Peoples: A Commentary.* Oxford: Oxford University Press.

Morgan, Rhiannon. 2011. *Transforming Law and Institution: Indigenous Peoples, the United Nations and Human Rights.* Burlington, VT: Ashgate.

Membership

The UN is a universal organization with 193 member states. This is a great increase over the fifty-one founding members in 1945. As specified in Article 4 of the UN Charter, to join the organization a country should be a "peace-loving state" willing to "accept the obligations contained in" the Charter. The General Assembly is responsible for admitting new members, but this is contingent on a recommendation from the Security Council. A country wishing to join the UN first submits their application to the Secretary-General. The Security Council reviews the application, and the vote to approve membership is subject to veto by any of the permanent five members. Final approval by the General Assembly requires a two-thirds majority vote.

UN ENGAGEMENT

Membership in the UN was controversial from the start. At the San Francisco Conference founding the UN, there was disagreement over whether or not to allow in Argentina, which had supported Nazi Germany. A deal was made to accept Argentina along with Belorussia and Ukraine, republics of the Soviet Union, which some countries did not view as independent. Cold War disputes over accepting new members continued across the first decade of the UN's existence. Communist countries connected to the Soviet Union were blocked by the United States, while the Soviets vetoed countries friendly to the United States. Only nine countries gained membership by 1950. In 1948, the first advisory opinion of the International Court of Justice was issued, with the court ruling that each application must be evaluated on the merits in the Charter and could not include other political conditions. The logjam was broken by a package deal in 1955 with sixteen countries, balanced between the United States and the Soviet blocs, admitted.

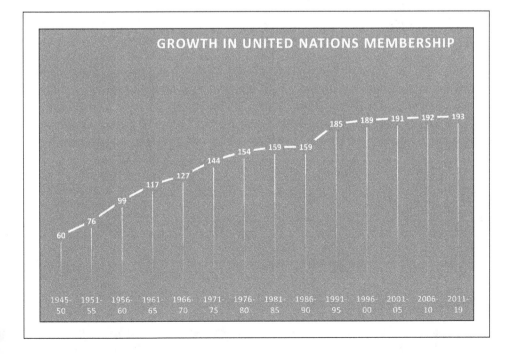

World War II Axis power Japan was admitted in 1956 but divided East and West Germany waited until 1973 (and took on membership as unified Germany in 1990). A significant period of enlargement occurred with decolonization in Africa during the 1960s, bringing membership up from 76 in 1955 to 122 by 1966. Membership continued to grow slowly until many newly independent countries were admitted following the breakup of the Soviet Union and Yugoslavia in the early 1990s. Switzerland is an unusual case, refusing membership due to its longstanding policy of neutrality until joining in 2002 as the 190th member. The most recent member added is South Sudan in 2011.

ADVANCES AND CHALLENGES

The UN has achieved near-universal membership. Going from 51 to 193 members altered UN operations. The rise in developing country membership shifted the agenda of the General Assembly and led to the creation of new programmes, such as the UN Development Programme. The Economic and Social Council expanded from eighteen to fifty-four members, but the Security Council only added three additional non-permanent seats to grow from twelve to fifteen members. Member state representation is at times controversial. A major example is the clash between the People's Republic of China and Taiwan. The Nationalist government based in Taiwan kept UN representation following the Communist revolution in 1949, but this shifted to the People's Republic in 1971. Since both claim to be the legitimate government of all China, the two could not be admitted separately like South and North Korea in 1991.

Unlike its predecessor, the League of Nations, the UN does not have a process for withdrawing. In 1965, Indonesia indicated that it was withdrawing in protest over Malaysia's election to the Security Council. This was not recognized by the UN, and Indonesia resumed cooperation with full membership rights in 1966. Member states can be suspended or expelled by the UN (Charter, Articles 5 and 6), but this has never happened despite efforts against South Africa during its policy of racial segregation and apartheid. Others still seek UN membership. A high-profile example is the Palestinian effort, which made some progress as the Palestinians are now one of two (along with the Holy See) recognized as a "non-member state" permanent observer at the UN. The Palestinians also obtained full membership status in several UN bodies, including the UN Educational, Scientific and Cultural Organization in 2011. This reflects the challenge of how the membership rosters of autonomous UN specialized agencies vary by agency and are different from other parts of the UN System.

See also: Charter of the United Nations; Economic and Social Council; General Assembly; International Court of Justice; Security Council; Self-Determination; United Nations Development Programme; United Nations Educational, Scientific and Cultural Organization; United Nations Historical Background.

FURTHER READING

Grant, Thomas D. 2009. *Admission to the United Nations: Charter Article 4 and the Rise of Universal Organization.* Leiden, Netherlands: Martinus Nijhoff Publishers.

Kolb, Robert. 2010. "Membership in the United Nations." In *An Introduction to the Law of the United Nations*, 106–14. Portland, OR: Hart Publishing.

Schwelb, Egon. 1967. "Withdrawal from the United Nations: The Indonesian Intermezzo." *The American Journal of International Law* 61 (3): 661–72.

Nongovernmental Organizations (NGOs)

The UN is an international governmental organization made up of member states. However, there are a wide range of nonstate actors from global civil society that influence and work with the UN, including academic and expert communities, foundations, think tanks, independent commissions, social movements, and transnational networks. Many refer to these groups as the "Third UN," alongside the member states (First UN) and Secretariat staff (Second UN). Nongovernmental organizations (NGOs), a formally organized group of citizens acting on behalf of shared ideals, are a particularly significant type of civil society actor at the UN. NGOs participated at the 1945 San Francisco Conference when the UN was created. This is reflected in the opening phrase of the UN Charter, "We the peoples of the United Nations," and Article 71: "The Economic and Social Council may make suitable arrangements for consultation with non-governmental organizations which are concerned with matters within its competence." The Economic and Social Council (ECOSOC) established consultative status for NGOs, with the number holding this status increasing over time from forty-one in 1948 to over five thousand.

UN ENGAGEMENT

NGO applications for consultative status are handled by ECOSOC's Committee on Non-Governmental Organizations. Consultative arrangements were reviewed and updated in ECOSOC Resolutions 288B (1950), 1296 (1968), and 1996/31 (1996). NGOs must submit reports every four years to demonstrate compliance with these rules, and their status can be suspended or removed. Based on how the groups contribute to ECOSOC, there are three different categories of consultative status: General, Special, and Roster. There is a great variety in numbers across the categories, with 140 recognized as General, almost 1,000 categorized as Roster, and over 4,000 labeled Special as of early 2020. The Department of Public Information, now the Department of Global Communications (DGC), also has a long-standing relationship with NGOs. The DGC has a separate accreditation process, based on NGO ability to publicize and advocate for UN activities, although around half of these NGOs also hold ECOSOC consultative status. There is a Civil Society Resource Centre through the DGC, as well as briefings and an annual UN Civil Society Conference. In 1975, the Non-Governmental Liaison Service was created to assist NGOs with understanding the UN System and is now a part of the DGC. Further support is provided by the NGO Branch of the Secretariat's Department of Economic and Social Affairs. The independent Conference of NGOs in Consultative Relationship with the UN (CoNGO) assists with NGO engagement at the UN.

NGOs have informal access to the General Assembly and Security Council, as well as relations with most specialized agencies and other entities in the UN System. Secretary-General Kofi Annan encouraged greater connections with NGOs and other forms of global civil society, including establishing a High-Level Panel of Eminent Persons on UN Civil Society Relations and a UN Global Compact to build linkages with the private sector. Based on their expertise, NGOs play an educational role and are relied on for their information and specialized knowledge. NGOs also undertake an advocacy role, seeking to set the agenda, influence decision-making, and guide the development of international standards. NGOs are very active at UN conferences, including holding parallel meetings, and use these opportunities to coordinate approaches and build networks. The implementation of and compliance with international treaties is monitored by NGOs. Finally, NGOs have a significant operational role, partnering with the UN to provide assistance in the field.

ADVANCES AND CHALLENGES

NGOs use their formal consultative status, as well as informal interactions that build out of their access to the UN, to serve as influential actors at the UN. Their role has grown over time, adding many more consultative NGOs, broadening dialogue at the UN beyond member state perspectives, pressing for action to be taken, and building stronger operational connections. The UN and NGOs developed a mutually reinforcing relationship. The UN benefits from NGO information and operational support, while NGOs use UN access and resources to press for progress on issues. At the same time, NGOs challenge the UN by monitoring the organization's activities and pressuring for reforms. Some in the NGO community are concerned that they are sacrificing independence and autonomy by working with the UN. In return, some question the legitimacy of NGOs by pointing to their lack of representation, accountability, and transparency. The UN and NGOs are bound together but continue to work on improving coordination and complementing each other's relative strengths and limitations to best address global issues.

See also: Charter of the United Nations; Economic and Social Council; Environmental Protection; General Assembly; High-level Political Forum on Sustainable Development; Human Rights Council; Indigenous Peoples; International Maritime Organization; International Organization for Migration; Joint United Nations Programme on HIV/AIDS; Kofi Annan; Peacebuilding Commission; Secretariat; United Nations Children's Fund; United Nations Conference on Trade and Development; United Nations Conferences and Summits; United Nations Educational, Scientific and Cultural Organization; United Nations Environment Programme; United Nations High Commissioner for Refugees; United Nations Human Settlements Programme; United Nations Population Fund; Universal Postal Union; World Health Organization; World Intellectual Property Organization; World Meteorological Organization; World Tourism Organization.

FURTHER READING

Martens, Kerstin. 2005. *NGOs and the United Nations: Institutionalization, Professionalization and Adaptation.* New York: Palgrave Macmillan.

Ruhlman, Molly A. 2015. *Who Participates in Global Governance: States, Bureaucracies, and NGOs in the United Nations*. London: Routledge.

Weiss, Thomas G., Tatiana Carayannis, and Richard Jolly. 2009. "The 'Third' United Nations." *Global Governance* 15 (1): 123–42.

Peacebuilding

The Preamble to the UN Charter prioritizes the promotion of international peace and security. However, this commitment was traditionally to address issues between countries, not within them. Violent conflicts in the 1990s raised the need for an organized approach after countries like Cambodia, El Salvador, and Sierra Leone needed international support to rebuild. These early efforts revealed the challenges of supporting countries in their efforts to create an environment that would prevent the reoccurrence of violence. Secretary-General Boutros Boutros-Ghali focused the UN on "post-conflict peace-building" as part of his 1992 report *An Agenda for Peace*. The UN has since adopted a more comprehensive view of peacebuilding that links the concepts of peace, security, economic development, sustainability, and human rights.

UN ENGAGEMENT

In 2005, the Peacebuilding Commission (PBC) was created to bring a more coordinated and comprehensive approach to supporting a country's peacebuilding efforts. The organization provides a forum for multiple stakeholders. The UN also acknowledged the need for resources and the important role financing plays in the success of postconflict transition, creating the Peacebuilding Fund, which is supported by voluntary contributions, in 2006. The final part of the UN peacebuilding architecture is the Peacebuilding Support Office. The peacebuilding approach seeks to move beyond reaction to crises to lay the foundation for preventative mechanisms that will block future sources of violence.

The UN has conducted peacebuilding operations across the world, including Afghanistan, Bosnia and Herzegovina, Burundi, Cambodia, El Salvador, Guatemala, Iraq, Kosovo, Liberia, Mozambique, Sierra Leone, and Timor-Leste. Most UN peacebuilding operations are overseen by the Security Council (although the General Assembly played an important role in Guatemala). Often a representative of the Secretary-General is appointed to create a leadership hub for the entire operation. The PBC provides guidance and helps to secure resources but does not have enforcement capacity or a significant presence on the ground. However, the PBC can recommend coordination of agencies in assisting with issues such as refugee return, monitoring cease-fires, demilitarization of combatants, setting up and observing elections, and supporting the protection of human rights. In addition, most postconflict countries require extensive economic development assistance as their economies are not able to provide the needed essentials. Peacebuilding actions may also include stabilization, building political infrastructure, and truth and reconciliation efforts.

ADVANCES AND CHALLENGES

The idea of peacebuilding is controversial, with different critiques ranging from those who see the approach as a tool for neocolonialism to those who argue that the UN should focus more on conflict prevention. In the years following the September 11, 2001 attacks on the United States, the idea of peacebuilding became more focused on security as many Western states began to see postconflict states as potential breeding grounds for terrorism. In this light, peacebuilding became associated with enhanced military operations, counterinsurgency, and counterterrorism. This is particularly true in the cases of Afghanistan and Iraq. Other sources of contention include issues with the creation of a set of peacebuilding principles and measures of success. There are those who define success in a narrow context and focus in on basic security and stability, whereas others believe that peacebuilding should lay the foundations for a more just, equitable, and sustainable society. One essential principle is "first do no harm," in which stakeholders refrain from pursing their own strategic interests and exploiting a weakened society. Other lessons include the need for timely action, priorities based on each country's goals, long-term commitments, and the need for sufficient resources.

Understanding the need to assist with rebuilding shattered societies is an important advancement. The UN has gained significant understanding of peacebuilding as a complex undertaking and requiring a sustained commitment. One perpetual challenge remains a lack of an integrated approach, where many actors on the ground can result in multiple operations engaged with different agendas. There is also the challenge of transitioning away from a foreign military providing security to the domestic government taking on this responsibility. Furthermore, some push for an integrated approach, especially since violence is viewed as a threat to the UN's human rights agenda, efforts to promote economic development, and the implementation of the Sustainable Development Goals. A lack of political will is also a challenge. Countries with the most capacity to assist, particularly the United States and Western European states, are less interested in intervening as the experiences of Iraq and Afghanistan did not produce the desired results. There is also debate over whether there should be more focus on preventive peacebuilding versus postconflict peacebuilding. In partnership with the World Bank, in 2018 the UN published *Pathways for Peace: Inclusive Approaches to Preventing Violent Conflict*. This study estimates that preventive peacebuilding could save up to $70 billion annually.

See also: Arms Control and Disarmament; Boutros Boutros-Ghali; Economic Development; Human Rights; Peacebuilding Commission; Security Council; Special Representatives of the United Nations Secretary-General; Sustainable Development Goals; Terrorism; World Bank Group.

FURTHER READING

Cavalcante, Fernando. 2019. *Peacebuilding in the United Nations: Coming into Life*. New York: Palgrave Macmillan.

De Soto, Alvaro, and Graciana Del Castillo. 2016. "Obstacles to Peacebuilding Revisited." *Global Governance* 22 (2): 209–27.

Ozerdem, Alpaslan, and SungYong Lee. 2015. *International Peacebuilding: An Introduction.* New York: Routledge.

Peaceful Settlement

Peaceful settlement is built into the UN Charter as an important dimension of maintaining international peace and security. The principles guiding the UN include Article 2(3): "All Members shall settle their international disputes by peaceful means in such a manner that international peace and security, and justice, are not endangered." How the UN addresses peaceful settlement is detailed in Chapter VI: Pacific Settlement of Disputes (Articles 33–38). This includes listing out the peaceful settlement approaches and emphasizing the role of the Security Council. Negotiations are direct discussions between the official representatives of the conflicting parties. However, a neutral third party often works with the disputants. With good offices, a third party acts as an intermediary to promote communication and build trust. In mediation, the third party discusses the substance of the conflict and provides suggestions for resolution. Fact-finding, or inquiry, independently establishes fundamental information underlying the dispute. Conciliation both investigates the facts and recommends solutions. With arbitration, a panel provides a legally binding decision on the dispute. Adjudication, or judicial settlement, uses preexisting courts to impart a legally binding ruling. Article 52, under Regional Arrangements, also encourages peaceful settlement to be handled at the regional level.

UN ENGAGEMENT

The Security Council investigates and provides recommendations on a range of conflicts, although very rarely does the Council suggest the use of arbitration or the International Court of Justice (ICJ). However, countries do go directly to the ICJ to get a formal ruling in cases such as border disputes, interpretation of treaties, and principles of international law. The most frequent Security Council recommendation is for the disputants to work out their differences through negotiations. The Security Council's fact-finding missions at times feed into judicial engagement. For example, the findings of fact-finding commissions brought about the creation of the International Criminal Tribunals for the former Yugoslavia and for Rwanda. With the permanent International Criminal Court now in place, fact-finding can lead to referrals by the Security Council, as in the case of the Darfur region of Sudan. Such commissions of inquiry are now often established by the Human Rights Council.

Compared to the Security Council, the General Assembly plays a secondary role in peaceful settlement efforts. However, the General Assembly can act when the Security Council is deadlocked, as supported by the Assembly's 1950 "Uniting for Peace" Resolution. The General Assembly provides guidance for peaceful settlement. In particular, the 1982 Manila Declaration on Peaceful Settlement of International Disputes (Resolution 37/10) presents an overview of the principles as well as the roles to be played by different parts of the UN System. Other resolutions address particular areas, such as 46/59 (1991) on fact-finding, 50/50 (1995) on conciliation, 53/101 (1998) on negotiation, and 70/304 (2016) on mediation. Further guidance is stipulated in the Office for Legal Affairs' *Handbook on the Peaceful Settlement of Disputes between States* (1992). The Secretary-General plays a key role using good offices and mediation, both when mandated and under the office's independent initiative. Along with personal involvement, officeholders designate Special Representatives. The Secretary-General is also supported by a "group of friends" or "contact group" made up of countries providing assistance for specific cases, or more generally as in the Group of Friends of Mediation. A Mediation Support Unit was created in 2006 and is connected to the online support tool UN Peacemaker. This was supplemented in 2017 with the High-Level Advisory Board on Mediation, which emerged from the Secretary-General's report *United Nations Activities in Support of Mediation*.

ADVANCES AND CHALLENGES

Peaceful settlement has been a core part of the UN's mission from the start, and the organization continues to evolve and adapt. UN efforts are challenged in long-standing intractable conflicts, like Cyprus, where peaceful settlement efforts have lasted for decades without a clear result. With the central role of the Security Council, UN effectiveness relies on great power support and when their interests clash this undermines UN engagement. The UN also faces competition from other actors, including countries operating on their own, regional organizations, and nongovernmental organizations. One approach taken by the UN to address this is building partnerships, particularly with regional organizations. Observers point out that the UN should provide greater gender equity in peace processes and the inclusion of gendered perspectives, which resulted in the 2017 report *Guidance on Gender and Inclusive Mediation Strategies*.

See also: General Assembly; Human Rights Council; International Court of Justice; International Criminal Court; Office of Secretary-General; Regionalism; Security Council; Special Representatives of the United Nations Secretary-General; United Nations Principles.

FURTHER READING

Frulli, Micaela. 2012. "Fact-Finding or Paving the Road to Criminal Justice? Some Reflections on United Nations Commissions of Inquiry." *Journal of International Criminal Justice* 10 (5): 1323–38.

Iji, Tetsuro. 2017. "The UN as an International Mediator: From the Post–Cold War Era to the Twenty-First Century." *Global Governance* 23 (1): 83–100.

Merrills, John G. 2017. *International Dispute Settlement*. Sixth edition. Cambridge: Cambridge University Press.

Peacekeeping

Although the Charter never mentions peacekeeping, this approach to promote the UN's mandate to maintain peace and security has become a centerpiece of the organization's activities. Peacekeeping is often informally referred to as "Chapter VI ½" operations, situated between the peaceful settlement of disputes authorized in Chapter VI of the Charter and enforcement operations called for in Chapter VII. Traditionally, peacekeeping refers to the use of international personnel to maintain peaceful relations after a conflict has diminished. Three original principles guide traditional peacekeeping: consent of the parties involved in the conflict, peacekeeper impartiality, and avoiding the use of force except in situations of self-defense or defending the mission's mandate. After the Cold War ended, there was a great increase in the number of peacekeeping operations deployed across the 1990s. Since the September 11, 2001 terrorist attacks in the United States, the Security Council has created fewer missions, but these often have more robust mandates for peacekeepers to pursue combatants. Another development in peacekeeping includes the UN's collaboration and co-deployments with regional organizations, particularly the African Union.

UN ENGAGEMENT

The first peacekeeping mission originated in 1948 when the Security Council authorized UN military observers to monitor a peace agreement between Israel and its Arab neighbors in the UN Truce Supervision Organization (UNTSO). The first full peacekeeping mission, the UN Emergency Force during the 1956 Suez Canal crisis, employed an impartial UN force to promote stability. The operation was the innovation of the second Secretary-General Dag Hammarskjöld and the Canadian Foreign Minister Lester Pearson. The UN has since facilitated over

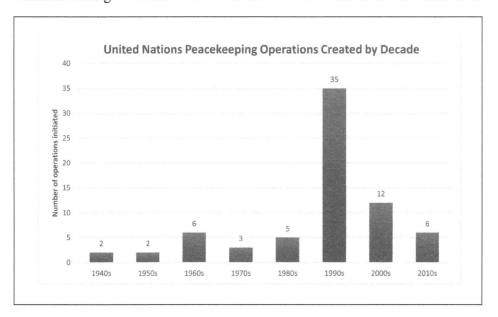

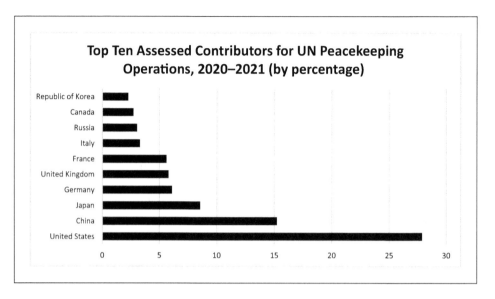

70 peacekeeping operations, with 13 ongoing operations as of early 2020 and 3,925 peacekeepers killed in action reported by the UN as of March 2020. Peacekeeping was originally focused on supporting cease-fires and stabilizing postconflict situations. Peacekeeping operations have greatly expanded in scope. For instance, the 1999 operation in Kosovo included training local law enforcement, holding elections, and state-building tasks like providing an interim government. Peacekeeping also often includes humanitarian assistance and the protection of civilian populations and refugees, such as the missions in the Democratic Republic of the Congo (most recent mission launched in 2010) and Mali (starting in 2013).

Because the UN does not have a standing military force, peacekeeping personnel are contributed by the member states. Countries supplying military personnel and equipment are reimbursed by the UN, but civilian personnel, including police, receive payment from the operation's peacekeeping budget. Funding for peacekeeping is also the responsibility of UN member states. The General Assembly utilizes a scale of assessments to determine the required contribution from each country to the peacekeeping budget. For 2019–2020, the budget for UN peacekeeping operations was $6.5 billion. This number is relatively small in comparison to overall world military expenditures (a reported $1,822 billion in 2018). These funds finance eleven of the thirteen peacekeeping missions. UNTSO and the UN Military Observer Group in India and Pakistan (established 1949), the two oldest peacekeeping operations, receive funding from the UN regular budget. Many countries provide additional resources, such as transportation and supplies.

ADVANCES AND CHALLENGES

As the nature of global conflict has changed, peacekeeping operations often face conflicts that spillover into several countries but have authorization only to operate in one county. In addition, UN faced criticism of several 1990s operations, particularly Somalia (1992–1993 and 1993–1995), Rwanda (1993–1994), and Bosnia (1995–2002). In response, the UN commissioned the *Report of the Panel on United Nations Peace Operations* (2000), also known as the Brahimi Report, which highlighted the need for resources and the problems with operations trying to secure countries that were not yet "postconflict." With further mandate expansions incorporating state building and the protection of civilians, Secretary-General Ban Ki-moon organized a High-Level Independent Panel on Peace Operations, which noted in its report (2015) "a widening gap between what is being asked of UN peace operations today and what they are able to deliver." Critics also point out that more robust tactics like authorization to pursue combatants compromises the impartiality of UN operations and can undermine the protection of civilians and rule of law. The UN often remains reactive rather than proactive, and resources are persistently stretched too thin. In addition, there are cases where peacekeepers themselves have perpetuated violence on the very populations they were sent to protect. At the same time, many analysts note that UN peacekeeping operations are sent to the most difficult places and are effective at reducing the chance of violence reoccurring (such as Mozambique 1992–1994 and Sierra Leone 1998–1999 and 1999–2005) and have helped avoid war (such as monitoring the divided Cyprus since 1964).

See also: Ban Ki-moon; Charter of the United Nations; Collective Security; Dag Hammarskjöld; Office of Secretary-General; Peacebuilding; Peaceful Settlement; Refugees and Migration; Regionalism; Role of Great Powers; Security Council; Terrorism; United Nations Budget and Financing.

FURTHER READING

Fortna, Virginia Page. 2008. *Does Peacekeeping Work? Shaping Belligerents' Choices After Civil War.* Princeton, NJ: Princeton University Press.

Guéhenno, Jean-Marie. 2015. *The Fog of Peace: A Memoir of International Peacekeeping in the 21st Century.* Washington, DC: Brookings Institution Press.

Howard, Lise Morjé. 2019. *Power in Peacekeeping.* Cambridge: Cambridge University Press.

Refugees and Migration

The movement of people from their homes is a major challenge facing the global community. There are a variety of classifications for such individuals. This includes migrants (individuals who shifted from their usual place residence), those leaving their original country out of fear (refugees), and those forced out of their home but still living within their country of origin (internally displaced persons). Many people are displaced in times of conflict, but the international community originally focused on this as a temporary and limited geographical problem. This approach started with the League of Nations' High Commissioner for Refugees in 1921 and work with European refugees. Given the disruptions caused by World War II, European refugees were immediately part of the UN agenda. This process started before the end of the war and the founding of the UN, with the allied countries establishing the United Nations Relief and Rehabilitation Administration in 1943. Under the UN organization, another interim body, the International Refugee Organization, was created to provide assistance in 1947. To handle ongoing refugee pressures, the UN High Commissioner for Refugees (UNHCR) began operations in 1951.

UN ENGAGEMENT

Despite the UN's hope that refugees would be a temporary issue following the great wars in Europe, the issue persisted and UNHCR's work was extended beyond the body's planned limited time frame and the organization is now engaged in helping refugees across the globe. Another institution, the UN Relief and Works Agency for Palestinian Refugees in the Near East (UNRWA), was established on a temporary basis after the 1948 Arab-Israeli war. Yet, UNRWA's mandate is continuously renewed and remains closely involved in working with Palestinian refugees. The International Organization for Migration, with organizational precursors dating back to provisional bodies focused solely on Europe starting in 1951, expanded its mission, membership, and resources over time and formally connected to the UN System as a related organization in 2016. Other UN institutions also provide services to displaced persons. For example, the World Food Programme addresses nutritional needs in times of humanitarian crisis. Given the scope of the problem and range of agencies involved, the UN founded the Global Migration Group in 2006, which was replaced with the UN Network on Migration in 2018, to improve coordination and consultation.

The UN also established several important international agreements. The 1951 Convention Relating to the Status of Refugees, supplemented by a 1967 Protocol, defines refugee status and the protections and assistance with which refugees should be provided. World Refugee Day is celebrated every June 20 in honor of the signing of the Convention. A central area of migration concern is the rights of migrant workers, which is addressed by the International Convention on the Protection of the Rights of All Migrant Workers and Members of Their Families (adopted by the General Assembly in 1990 and entered into force in 2003) and monitored by the Committee on Migrant Workers. A recent push to strengthen UN engagement culminated in the 2016 New York Declaration for Refugees and Migrants. Building out of this, in December 2018 the UN adopted the first agreement to cover all dimensions of migration, the Global Compact for Safe, Orderly and Regular Migration, and a separate Global Compact on Refugees. The High-level Dialogue on International Migration and Development was changed into the International Migration Review Forum to assess progress on the first Global Compact starting in 2022 (see A/RES/73/241 in Part VI). There is also a Migration Multi-Partner Trust Fund. Finally, the UN holds conferences to address particular areas, including the International Conferences for Assistance to Refugees in Africa (1981 and 1984), and certain issues, such as first issuing the Guiding Principles on Internal Displacement in 1998 and recognizing these Principles at the 2005 World Summit.

ADVANCES AND CHALLENGES

From the early days of treating refugees and migration as an impermanent, European issue, the UN has made much progress in establishing lasting institutions and international agreements. However, the ongoing and evolving global movement of people, including new challenges such as climate change, creates major pressures on the UN. While the 1951 Refugee Convention was innovative for its time, the creators of this document could not have envisaged the scope of modern refugee and migration crises. The UN struggles with addressing the needs of emergency and longer-term displaced populations in a world of rising populism, which hardens borders to accepting people from other countries. The UN recently took steps with the new Global Compacts, although both are nonbinding and resisted by some countries, including the United States, and will continue to evolve with the needs of the world's displaced people.

See also: Human Rights; International Organization for Migration; Peacekeeping; United Nations High Commissioner for Refugees; United Nations Conferences and Summits; United Nations Relief and Works Agency for Palestine Refugees in the Near East; World Food Programme.

FURTHER READING

Betts, Alexander, and Gil Loescher, eds. 2011. *Refugees in International Relations*. Oxford: Oxford University Press.

Fiddian-Qasmiyeh, Elena, Gil Loescher, Katy Long, and Nando Sigona, eds. 2014. *The Oxford Handbook of Refugee and Forced Migration Studies*. Oxford: Oxford University Press.

Geiger, Martin, and Antoine Pécoud, eds. 2010. *The Politics of International Migration Management*. New York: Palgrave Macmillan.

Regionalism

The UN is an organization with universal membership, open to all eligible countries, designed to bring together countries on a global scale to address international issues. Whether or not to include regional arrangements as part of the UN was debated at the founding of the institution. As World War II ended, some countries, including the United States, saw a centralized universal organization as the best path to future peace. Other countries, such as the United Kingdom under Prime Minister Winston Churchill, argued that several regional organizations would be more effective. In meetings held before gathering to draft the UN Charter, the decision was made to devise a universal organization, but one that would include reference to regional arrangements for promoting peace and security. At the 1945 San Francisco Conference founding the UN, the need for regionalism to be emphasized in the Charter was advocated by smaller countries, particularly Latin American countries that had a regional approach dating back to the first International Conference of American States in 1889.

Chapter VIII, "Regional Arrangements," of the Charter details the role of regional organizations relative to the UN when addressing peace and security. Article 52 establishes that "regional arrangements or agencies" are allowed, as long as they are consistent with UN purposes and principles, and peaceful settlement of disputes should be attempted prior to referral to the Security Council. Article 53 specifies that the Security Council may use regional bodies to address local disputes, but regional enforcement efforts should not be employed without Security Council authorization. Article 54 requires the Security Council to be "kept fully informed" about regional activities. In addition, Article 51 in Chapter VI states, "Nothing in the present Charter shall impair the inherent right of individual or collective self-defense," which has been used to justify the creation of regional alliances like the North Atlantic Treaty Organization (NATO). Overall, the Charter accommodates regional organizations, although Security Council's precedence over regional efforts is stressed.

UN ENGAGEMENT

The UN created Regional Commissions under the Economic and Social Council. These bodies adapt economic goals and projects to regional contexts. The first two were established in Europe and Asia in 1947 and grew to cover five regions by 1973. In the realm of peace and security, the UN increasingly works with regional organizations based outside of the UN System. Secretary-General Boutros Boutros-Ghali emphasized greater cooperation with regional organization in his 1992 *Agenda for Peace* report. The General Assembly reinforced this perspective in the 1994 "Declaration on the Enhancement of Cooperation between the United Nations and Regional Arrangements or Agencies in the Maintenance of International Peace and Security." Developments in the field brought the UN and regional organization security operations into close collaboration, such as NATO's strong military role in Kosovo and Libya. The African Union is an important partner in African peacekeeping missions, highlighted by the joint mission in the Darfur region of Sudan. Other notable regional organizations include the Association of Southeast Asian Nations, Economic Community of West African States, League of Arab States, Organization of American States, and Organization on Security and Co-operation in Europe. Regional organizations also operate within the UN to promote their interests during negotiations and decision-making, with the European Union's level of coordinated engagement particularly notable.

ADVANCES AND CHALLENGES

UN involvement with regional organizations evolved over time. Following the Cold War, where the U.S.–Soviet clash impeded efforts to engage with regional organizations, the UN now frequently cooperates with regional institutions. Whether this shift is a good idea is often debated. Advantages of UN-regional coordination include the ability to leverage regional organizations' proximity to local conflicts, which allows them to react more quickly and tailor operations to regional needs. In addition, the UN can bolster regional efforts by providing resources and a neutral viewpoint on the best approach and practices. Coordination can improve operational effectiveness and efficiency. Yet, critics are concerned that powerful countries in a region will gain too much influence over operations and shape these to match their interests. Proponents of universal organizations also question whether including regional actors undermines cooperation, building consensus, and addressing issues at the global level. UN operations are now often closely intertwined with regional efforts, so the relative strengths of the different organizations can be used to best address shared problems and issues.

See also: Boutros Boutros-Ghali; Charter of the United Nations; Membership; Peaceful Settlement; Peacekeeping; Regional Commissions; Security Council; United Nations Historical Background; Voting and Negotiating Blocs.

FURTHER READING

Hettne, Björn, and Fredrik Söderbaum. 2006. "The UN and Regional Organizations in Global Security: Competing or Complementary Logics?" *Global Governance* 12 (3): 227–32.

Wallensteen, Peter, and Anders Bjurner, eds. 2015. *Regional Organizations and Peacemaking: Challengers to the UN?* New York: Routledge.

Walter, Christian. 2012. "Introduction to Chapter VIII." In *The Charter of the United Nations: A Commentary.* Third edition, edited by Bruno Simma, et al., 1429–44. Oxford: Oxford University Press.

Responsibility to Protect (R2P)

Beginning in 1948 with the Convention on the Prevention and Punishment of the Crime of Genocide (which entered into force in 1951), the UN made a commitment to protect people from genocide and mass killings. At the same time, countries with sovereign control are supposed to be free from interference in their domestic affairs unless there is an expressed invitation. Sovereignty is a central UN principle, with Article 2(7) of the Charter stating, "Nothing contained in the present Charter shall authorize the United Nations to intervene in matters which are essentially within the domestic jurisdiction of any state." These two values create a tension, and the UN has struggled with how to respond to mass atrocities. Ultimately, the UN adopted the responsibility to protect (R2P) norm, which calls on the international community to protect people against mass atrocities, including genocide, crimes against humanity, and ethnic cleansing. Under R2P, the idea of sovereignty shifts to emphasize the need for a country to take care of its civilian population. Countries have a responsibility to protect their citizens, but if they fail then the international community has a responsibility to intervene.

UN ENGAGEMENT

The early 1990s saw the legal precedent established for UN intervention to protect civilians. In 1991, the Security Council passed Resolution 688 after the

Convention on the Prevention and Punishment of the Crime of Genocide (1948, Articles I–VI)

Article I

The Contracting Parties confirm that genocide, whether committed in time of peace or in time of war, is a crime under international law which they undertake to prevent and to punish.

Article II

In the present Convention, genocide means any of the following acts committed with intent to destroy, in whole or in part, a national, ethnical, racial or religious group, as such:

(a) Killing members of the group;

(b) Causing serious bodily or mental harm to members of the group;

(c) Deliberately inflicting on the group conditions of life calculated to bring about its physical destruction in whole or in part;

(d) Imposing measures intended to prevent births within the group;

(e) Forcibly transferring children of the group to another group.

Article III

The following acts shall be punishable:

(a) Genocide;

(b) Conspiracy to commit genocide;

(c) Direct and public incitement to commit genocide;

(d) Attempt to commit genocide;

(e) Complicity in genocide.

Article IV

Persons committing genocide or any of the other acts enumerated in Article III shall be punished, whether they are constitutionally responsible rulers, public officials or private individuals.

Article V

The Contracting Parties undertake to enact, in accordance with their respective Constitutions, the necessary legislation to give effect to the provisions of the present Convention, and, in particular, to provide effective penalties for persons guilty of genocide or any of the other acts enumerated in Article III.

Article VI

Persons charged with genocide or any of the other acts enumerated in Article III shall be tried by a competent tribunal of the State in the territory of which the act was committed, or by such international penal tribunal as may have jurisdiction with respect to those Contracting Parties which shall have accepted its jurisdiction.

Source: United Nations. "Convention on the Prevention and Punishment of the Crime of Genocide." https://www.un.org/en/genocideprevention/documents/atrocity-crimes/Doc.1_Convention%20on%20the%20Prevention%20and%20Punishment%20of%20the%20Crime%20of%20Genocide.pdf.

Persian Gulf War to assist the Kurds in Northern Iraq. The operation did not request authorization from the Iraqi government and, in doing so, altered the terms under which the UN can intervene. The 1994 genocide in Rwanda and ethnic cleansing a year later in Bosnia resulted in increased calls for UN action to protect such populations. In a 1998 lecture, Secretary-General Kofi Annan identified "two sovereignties" and proclaimed that the Charter "was issued in the name of 'the peoples,' not the governments of the United Nations. . . . The Charter protects the sovereignty of peoples. . . . Sovereignty implies responsibility, not just power." This builds on Article 55 that commits the UN to promote "universal respect for, and observance of, human rights and fundamental freedoms" and Article 56 that pledges all members "to take joint and separate action" to achieve Article 55.

In December 2001, the report of the International Commission on Intervention and State Sovereignty found that state sovereignty carries an obligation to protect domestic populations from terrible human rights violations. If a country does not live up to its responsibility to protect its citizens, that country may potentially give up its sovereign freedom from intervention (and outlining criteria justifying such intervention). In 2005, the UN World Summit Outcome Document supported and clarified the application of R2P, stating that if a government fails to protect its population from mass atrocities then the international community has a responsibility to prevent, act, and help rebuild through either providing necessary support to the government or through a direct intervention. In April 2006, the Security Council indicated support of R2P for the first time, and, in September 2009, the General Assembly reaffirmed the commitment to R2P in Resolution 63/308. Ever since Ban Ki-moon's January 2009 report *Implementing the Responsibility to Protect*, the Secretary-General submits an annual report on the status of R2P (which is discussed at the General Assembly) and the Secretary-General also appoints a Special Adviser on the Responsibility to Protect (supported by the UN Office on Genocide Prevention and the Responsibility to Protect). In practice, interventions under R2P are authorized by the Security Council and carried out multilaterally.

ADVANCES AND CHALLENGES

The R2P norm was acted upon in Kenya (2007–2008) after a contentious election and widespread violence that resulted in over one thousand deaths and approximately five hundred thousand people displaced from their homes. Another R2P intervention came in 2011 when the Libyan government, led by Muammar Gaddafi, carried out mass violence against civilians. In response, the Security Council passed Resolution 1973 authorizing the use of force to protect human rights through a North Atlantic Treaty Organization (NATO) intervention. However, with this progress there is also regression, as both China and Russia claim that the NATO operation overstepped its mandate when the government was overthrown. In addition, the terrorist attacks of September 2001 shifted the focus on mass atrocities to counterterrorism. R2P as a norm is not binding or enforceable and is vulnerable to political will. Since the Libyan intervention, the UN record on

R2P is problematic as the Security Council has not effectively intervened in several cases of mass atrocities, including Syria (2011–), Yemen (2015–), and Myanmar (2016–2017). At the same time, R2P continues to grow and gather support as an idea. As of December 2019, R2P is mentioned in over eighty Security Council resolutions or Presidential statements and the Human Rights Council has expressed support through it use of resolutions, special sessions, and investigations. R2P represents a significant UN innovation with growing progress, but also political backlash to overcome.

See also: Ban Ki-moon; Charter of the United Nations; Human Rights; Human Rights Council; Human Security; Kofi Annan; Security Council; Terrorism; United Nations Principles.

FURTHER READING

Bellamy, Alex J., and Edward C. Luck. 2018. *The Responsibility to Protect: From Promise to Practice.* Cambridge: Polity.

Thakur, Ramesh. 2019. *Reviewing the Responsibility to Protect: Origins, Implementation and Controversies.* London: Routledge.

Weiss, Thomas G. 2016. *Humanitarian Intervention.* Third edition. Cambridge: Polity Press.

Role of Great Powers

The UN was forged from great power consensus as the victors of World War II, specifically the United States, the United Kingdom, the Soviet Union (now Russia), France, and China, shaped the UN System. In particular, reflecting U.S. President Franklin D. Roosevelt's model of powerful countries serving as global "policemen" to protect international peace and security, the five great powers guaranteed themselves a privileged position at the UN with permanent seats on the Security Council that includes veto power over Council votes. Thus, these countries are often referred to as the permanent five (P-5).

UN ENGAGEMENT

UN actions and the ability to respond to breaches of the peace are determined by great power politics. During the Cold War, power struggles between the United States and the Soviet Union led to gridlock in the Security Council. The two countries frequently vetoed resolutions regarding areas such as Germany, Korea, and Vietnam. Although there were moments of cooperation, like the Suez Canal crisis in 1956, the UN became a venue for both ideological battles and divisions over allies. The General Assembly's 1950 "Uniting for Peace" Resolution attempted to bypass stalemates in Security Council, but division also seeped into the Assembly. For example, the Group of 77 (G-77), a group of Global South countries that formed a coalition to increase leverage, emerged and the General Assembly passed several resolutions regarding Israel and Zionism.

With the end of the Cold War, tensions between Russia and the United States waned temporarily only to reemerge in 1999 over the humanitarian intervention in Kosovo. Divisive relations are again prevalent as the Russians and the Chinese have vetoed resolutions addressing situations such as Syria (2011–) and the Arab spring (2010–2011). While the so-called P-3 (the United States, the United Kingdom, and France) are often in agreement, there are exceptions such as the lead up to the Iraq War (2003). France and the United Kingdom also differ with the United States over support for the International Criminal Court, the Comprehensive Nuclear-Test-Ban Treaty, and global efforts to mitigate climate change.

ADVANCES AND CHALLENGES

Great powers are often engaged at the UN to impede action being taken by the organization, particularly against themselves or their allies. For instance, Russia blocked all condemnations of its incursion into Crimea (2014). Thus, a persistent issue for the UN is whether the organization can moderate great power impulses and create a more rule-bound global system. Yet, the great powers are major financial contributors and the work of the UN could not continue without them. Together, the P-5 contributed 45 percent of the UN's regular operating budget for 2020. When the other five top contributors (Japan, Germany, Italy, Brazil, and Canada) are included, this rises to 69 percent. The United States presents a mixed record of support despite its privileged position. While the United States is the most significant source of funding for the UN (based on the "capacity to pay" assessment formula), it is also unreliable and has withheld funds and unilaterally cut funding to many UN bodies.

Security Council membership can elevate the influence of the P-5. For instance, Russia kept its permanent seat and veto power despite the country's declining

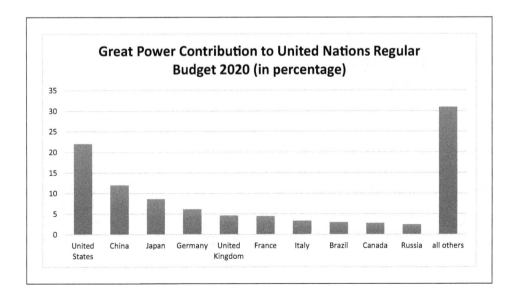

economic position during the 1990s. Historically, China's role has been hesitant, yet it is growing significantly due to increasing economic power and capacity to pay a larger share of the UN's assessed regular budget (rising from 1 percent in 2000 to just under 8 percent in 2017 and then up to 12 percent for 2020). France and the United Kingdom are often tentative when it comes to bold moves in the Security Council. Yet, both jealously protect their position from other rising powers, like India and Brazil, that claim their growing power should grant them a permanent seat on the Security Council. Despite Roosevelt's plan for great powers serving as policemen, powerful countries are typically not interested in intervening where they do not have strategic interest, such as the failure of the UN to address the Rwandan genocide in 1994. Yet, the great power tug of war is not the only dynamic within the UN. The creation of the Sustainable Development Goals and bodies like the UN Development Programme demonstrate that the UN can also serve as an advocate for weaker powers and marginalized people.

See also: Collective Security; General Assembly; International Criminal Court; Office of Secretary-General; Peacekeeping; Preparatory Commission for the Comprehensive Nuclear-Test-Ban Treaty Organization; Security Council; Sustainable Development Goals; United Nations Budget and Financing; United Nations Development Programme; United Nations Historical Background; United Nations Reform; United States Ambassadors to the United Nations.

FURTHER READING

Cronin, Bruce. 2002. "The Two Faces of the United Nations: The Tension between Intergovernmentalism and Transnationalism." *Global Governance* 8 (1): 53–71.

Engelbrekt, Kjell. 2016. *High-Table Diplomacy: The Reshaping of International Security Institutions*. Washington, DC: Georgetown University Press.

Krisch, Nico. 2008. "The Security Council and the Great Powers." In *The United Nations Security Council and War*, edited by Dominik Zaum, Vaughan Lowe, Adam Roberts, and Jennifer Welsh, 133–53. Oxford: Oxford University Press.

Self-Determination

The exact definition and application of self-determination is debated in the international arena, but in general the term refers to the ability of a people to govern themselves. Self-determination at times brings political units together, for example, the reunification of Germany, but often leads to a drive for freedom from political control through decolonization, ethnonationalism fragmentation, and sovereign claims of indigenous peoples. U.S. President Woodrow Wilson advocated for the principle of self-determination to build a peaceful order following World War I. Although the League of Nations did not fully embrace this approach, a mandate system for colonial territories lost during the war was established. The UN built upon this to establish the Trusteeship Council to guide what were now referred to as trust territories. However, the UN also went much further in the Charter founding the organization, notably specifying in Article 1(2) that one of the purposes was "to develop friendly relations among nations based on respect for the principle of equal rights and self-determination of peoples" and reiterating this language in Article 55 of Charter Chapter IX on International Economic and Social Cooperation.

UN ENGAGEMENT

While the Charter emphasized "self-determination of peoples," what such self-determination would look like or to what peoples this would apply was not specified. The UN did establish the International Trusteeship System, guided by the Trusteeship Council, in Chapter XII of the Charter. In addition, the Chapter XI Declaration Regarding Non-Self-Governing Territories helped to set the basis for the broader decolonization that would occur under the UN. Starting with fifty-one member states, UN membership expanded in the 1960s with the addition of newly decolonized countries. An important step in this process was the 1960 General Assembly Resolution 1514 (XV), the Declaration on the Granting of Independence to Colonial Countries and Peoples, which was followed by the establishment of a Special Committee on Decolonization. In celebration of the twenty-fifth anniversary of the UN's founding, the General Assembly reinforced self-determination in the Declaration on Principles of International Law Concerning Friendly Relations and Co-operation among States.

Self-determination is a key human right at the UN, with the same phrase "All peoples have the right of self-determination" listed in Article 1 of both the International Covenant on Civil and Political Rights and the International Covenant on Economic, Social, and Cultural Rights and reinforced in the Vienna Declaration and Programme of Action adopted at the 1993 World Conference on Human Rights. Indigenous peoples press for their right to self-determination through the UN, which includes the establishment of a Permanent Forum on Indigenous Issues. A number of civil conflicts within states based on the principle of self-determination are faced by the UN. Some were resolved through the creation of new states with UN involvement, such as Timor-Leste and South Sudan. Others continue to draw UN attention, such as mediation of Western Sahara's efforts to break away from Morocco, which was ruled as reflecting the principle of self-determination in an advisory opinion by the ICJ in 1975. Political entities continue to press for self-determination and UN recognition, including the Palestinians whom the organization engages with via the UN Relief Works Agency for Palestinian Refugees in the Near East.

ADVANCES AND CHALLENGES

Since 1945, the UN has placed self-determination squarely on the global agenda and the work advancing self-determination is viewed as one of the organization's success stories. However, challenges remain for the UN going forward, including ongoing disagreements over what exactly self-determination means and how to address competing claims for self-determination, which are expressed both peacefully and through the use of violence. The UN faces a long-standing tension between the principles of self-determination versus respect for state sovereignty and prohibitions against intervening in a state's domestic jurisdiction that are enshrined in the Charter. Calls for reform include suggestions for adapting the inactive Trusteeship Council to new areas of self-determination. In 2000, an international conference held in Geneva on the right to self-determination and the UN led to proposals such as establishing an Office of High Commissioner for Self-Determination and a Self-Determination Commission, but these have not been carried out by the UN.

See also: Human Rights; Indigenous Peoples; International Court of Justice; Membership; Permanent Forum on Indigenous Issues; Trusteeship Council; United Nations Principles; United Nations Purposes; United Nations Relief and Works Agency for Palestine Refugees in the Near East.

FURTHER READING

Quane, Helen. 1998. "The United Nations and the Evolving Right to Self-Determination." *The International and Comparative Law Quarterly* 47 (3): 537–72.

Sureda, A. Rigo. 1973. *The Evolution of the Right of Self-Determination: A Study of United Nations Practice.* Leiden, Netherlands: A. W. Sijthoff.

White, Peter B., David E. Cunningham, and Kyle Beardsley. 2018. "Where, When, and How Does the UN Work to Prevent Civil War in Self-Determination Disputes?" *Journal of Peace Research* 55 (3): 380–94.

Sustainable Development

The UN Charter, established in 1945, committed the organization to promoting economic development. Yet, the demands for development, as well as ideas about what development means, shifted over the decades. Early on the UN assisted individual countries with establishing their needs and priorities. There is now consensus that these efforts need to be comprehensive and coordinated at a global rather than a country level. Historically, development projects included efforts to promote industrialization and large-scale investment. Today, there is awareness that industrialization efforts may harm the environment and the ability of a country's natural systems to support future generations. Thus, the concept of development evolved from a country-based focus on the reduction of poverty to an integrative effort that supports environmentally sustainable approaches. As expressed in the widely cited 1987 report of the World Commission on Environment and Development *Our Common Future* (known as the Brundtland Report), sustainable development is "development that meets the needs of the present without compromising the ability of future generations to meet their own needs."

UN ENGAGEMENT

Although the concept of sustainable development emerged as part of environmental movements in the 1950s, the UN first considered notions of "ecodevelopment" at the 1972 Conference on the Human Environment held in Stockholm,

Sweden. Ecodevelopment, which is a conceptual precursor to sustainable development, was championed by the UN Environment Programme across the 1970s. By the 1980s, developing countries were wrestling with how to advance economically without destroying the environment in the process, as was the historical path followed previously by most developed countries. The World Commission on Environment and Development, chaired by Gro Harlem Brundtland, was established in 1983 and their 1987 report placed the idea of sustainable development as making development progress alongside needed environmental protections firmly on the international agenda. The 1992 UN Conference on Environment and Development held in Rio de Janeiro, Brazil, brought high-level representatives together from across the globe to work on sustainable development proposals. The conference produced the Rio Declaration on Environment and Development, which set out the principles to be followed, and a plan of action referred to as Agenda 21. The conference also produced a Statement of Forest Principles and conventions on biological diversity and climate change.

Progress on sustainable development was reviewed at a special session of the General Assembly in 1997 and at the 2002 World Summit on Sustainable Development held in Johannesburg, South Africa. The UN returned to Rio in 2012 to hold the Conference on Sustainable Development. One of the eight Millennium Development Goals (MDGs) established in 2000 was "to ensure environmental sustainability." In advance of the MDGs expiring in 2015, new Sustainable Development Goals (SDGs) were crafted based around three pillars of sustainable development (economic growth, environmental protection, and social progress). The list of seventeen specific goals was approved in 2015 with the passing of the UN's 2030 Agenda for Sustainable Development. The UN established a Commission on Sustainable Development in 1992, which has since been replaced by the High-level Political Forum on Sustainable Development. Sustainable development is a central focus for many other UN bodies. For instance, the World Health Organization is broadly engaged in promoting the health dimensions of sustainable development and the SDGs.

ADVANCES AND CHALLENGES

Sustainable development represents a major shift in development thinking at the UN. The organization played a central role in developing this new norm and priority of development. UN activities are focused on promoting and putting sustainable development into practice, including stressing the driving role of the SDGs. However, the concept of sustainable development has its critics. The idea that economic development, environmental protection, and social progress can all be integrated and balanced in the pursuit of a sustainable future is questioned. From a development perspective, concerns are raised that incorporating environmental and social safeguards will undermine overcoming poverty. From the environmental side, the argument is that connecting this to other issues is distracting from an essential focus on addressing the environment in the face of pending crises such as climate change. The funding levels required to carry out sustainable development on a global scale are high, and this has limited full implementation thus far. The UN is fully committed to the sustainable development approach and any understanding of the organization's engagement with global issues should be viewed through this lens.

See also: Economic Development; Environmental Protection; High-level Political Forum on Sustainable Development; Sustainable Development Goals; United Nations Conferences and Summits; United Nations Environment Programme; United Nations Purposes; World Health Organization; World Trade Organization.

FURTHER READING

Ashford, Nicholas A., and Ralph P. Hall. 2011. "The Emergence of Sustainable Development." In *Technology, Globalization, and Sustainable Development: Transforming the Industrial State*, 122–41. New Haven, CT: Yale University Press.

Browne, Stephen. 2017. *Sustainable Development Goals and UN Goal-Setting.* New York: Routledge.

Sachs, Jeffrey. 2015. *The Age of Sustainable Development.* New York: Columbia University Press.

Sustainable Development Goals (SDGs)

Over the past several decades, the UN has been at the center of efforts to create, promote, and monitor global development and environmental goals. In 1992, the UN Conference on Environment and Development held in Rio de Janeiro, Brazil (referred to as the Earth Summit) crafted two conventions on the environment and proposed Agenda 21 as a blueprint to promote sustainability that included targets and action plans. At the turn of the new millennium, the UN led an ambitious plan to coordinate efforts to address poverty with a clear set of goals. When that initiative was set to expire in 2015, the UN spearheaded a new effort that combined efforts promoting development with sustainability, again creating tangible benchmarks to guide both UN agencies and countries toward a more equitable, healthy, and viable future.

UN ENGAGEMENT

The Millennium Summit, held in September 2000, highlighted development for both people and economies. Member state representatives adopted the Millennium Declaration to guide the UN's work up to 2015. The summit produced the Millennium Development Goals (MDGs), which established eight targets, including a plan to end extreme poverty and hunger and stop the spread of HIV/AIDS, malaria, and other diseases. The MDGs are notable as they redefined poverty as "multidimensional depravation," and many countries used the goals and their related benchmarks to create development policies. The MDGs also provided data and reinvigorated development aid. The goals were notable as an agreement between countries that included performance indicators and implementation strategies as well as integrating the work of UN agencies, including the International Monetary Fund and World Bank.

> **United Nations Millennium Development Goals**
>
> 1. Eradicate extreme poverty and hunger
> 2. Achieve universal primary education
> 3. Promote gender equality and empower women
> 4. Reduce child mortality
> 5. Improve maternal health
> 6. Combat HIV/AIDS, malaria, and other diseases
> 7. Ensure environmental sustainability
> 8. Develop a global partnership for development

In 2010, the Secretary-General appointed a High-level Panel on Global Sustainability to create a new set of priorities. Their January 2012 report, *Resilient People, Resilient Planet: A Future Worth Choosing*, contained fifty-six recommmendations. In June 2012, the UN Conference on Sustainable Development, known as Rio+20, followed up the Earth Summit and the 2002 World Summit on Sustainable Development held in South Africa. The outcome document, *The Future We Want*, called for the creation of the UN High-level Political Forum on Sustainable Development (HLPF) that was approved in General Assembly Resolution 67/290. The HLPF was placed under the joint jurisdiction of the Economic and Social Council (ECOSOC) and the General Assembly, replacing ECOSOC's Commission on Sustainable Development. After extensive negotiations, in September 2015 a high-level plenary General Assembly meeting adopted a document titled "Transforming our World: The 2030 Agenda for Sustainable Development." This includes seventeen Sustainable Development Goals (SDGs). The list of 17 goals and 169 targets provide a global set of priorities for the entire UN System. Of the SDGs, six focus on basic human needs (ending poverty, ensuring food security, health care, education, gender equality, and access to water and sanitation). Many prioritize environmental protection (clean energy, sustainable cities, responsible consumption and production, halting climate change, and ocean as well as land conservation). The HLPF reviews the implementation of the SDGs.

ADVANCES AND CHALLENGES

The MDGs' initiative is generally viewed as one of the most successful international antipoverty efforts. During their time period, there was a significant decline in extreme poverty, a decrease in infant mortality rates, and an increase in the number of children completing primary school. Many applaud the higher level of inclusiveness in the SDGs, both in the process of creating the goals and in the range of targets. Yet, critics find the SDGs too ambitious as they cover a broad spectrum of issues and are intended to be universally applied to all countries (even those outside of the developing world). Others point out that the SDGs are non-binding and vague. The number of goals is also critiqued, as this could dilute their

> ### United Nations Sustainable Development Goals
>
> 1. End poverty in all its forms everywhere
> 2. End hunger, achieve food security and improved nutrition and promote sustainable agriculture
> 3. Ensure healthy lives and promote well-being for all at all ages
> 4. Ensure inclusive and equitable quality education and promote lifelong learning opportunities for all
> 5. Achieve gender equality and empower all women and girls
> 6. Ensure availability and sustainable management of water and sanitation for all
> 7. Ensure access to affordable, reliable, sustainable and modern energy for all
> 8. Promote sustained, inclusive and sustainable economic growth, full and productive employment and decent work for all
> 9. Build resilient infrastructure, promote inclusive and sustainable industrialization and foster innovation
> 10. Reduce inequality within and among countries
> 11. Make cities and human settlements inclusive, safe, resilient and sustainable
> 12. Ensure sustainable consumption and production patterns
> 13. Take urgent action to combat climate change and its impacts
> 14. Conserve and sustainably use the oceans, seas and marine resources for sustainable development
> 15. Protect, restore and promote sustainable use of terrestrial ecosystems, sustainably manage forests, combat desertification and halt and reverse land degradation and halt biodiversity loss
> 16. Promote peaceful and inclusive societies for sustainable development, provide access to justice for all and build effective, accountable and inclusive institutions at all levels
> 17. Strengthen the means of implementation and revitalize the Global Partnership for Sustainable Development
>
> Source: United Nations General Assembly, Resolution A/Res/70/1. https://www.un.org/en/development/desa/population/migration/generalassembly/docs/globalcompact/A_RES_70_1_E.pdf.

effect and make it difficult to rally support from both donors and countries. Despite the critiques, both the MDGs and the SDGs represent a remarkable consensus on priorities for the UN agenda. The SDGs are consistently referenced by a wide range of UN agencies. They also provide a commitment to the most marginalized populations on the planet and a vision of hope that highlights the connections between development and stewardship for future generations.

See also: Economic Development; Environmental Protection; Food and Agriculture Organization; General Assembly; Health; High-level Political Forum on Sustainable Development; Human Rights; Human Security; International Fund for Agricultural Development; International Labour Organization; International Monetary Fund; Regional Commissions; United Nations Conferences and Summits; United Nations Educational,

Scientific and Cultural Organization; Sustainable Development; World Bank Group; World Health Organization; World Tourism Organization.

FURTHER READING

Dodds, Felix, David Donoghue, and Jimena Leiva Roesch. 2017. *Negotiating the Sustainable Development Goals: A Transformational Agenda for an Insecure World.* London: Routledge.

Gupta, Joyeeta, and Courtney Vegelin. 2016. "Sustainable Development Goals and Inclusive Development." *International Environmental Agreements: Politics, Law and Economics* 16 (3): 433–48.

Kamau, Macharia, Pamela Chasek, and David O'Connor. 2018. *Transforming Multilateral Diplomacy: The Inside Story of the Sustainable Development Goals.* London: Routledge.

Terrorism

The UN was established to handle conflict between countries. However, with the rise of violent nonstate actors and transnational terrorism, the UN incrementally added dimensions of terrorism to its agenda. The first treaty was established in 1963 with the Convention on Offences and Certain Other Acts Committed on Board Aircraft. Additional conventions cover areas such as hostage-taking and prohibitions on the use of certain materials. The General Assembly's Sixth Committee (Legal) agenda includes combating terrorism and supports drafting legal instruments. The General Assembly regularly passes resolutions denouncing terrorism, including the 1994 Declaration on Measures to Eliminate International Terrorism. Two years later, the General Assembly added an Ad Hoc Committee to develop the conventions related to terrorist bombings and acts of nuclear terrorism and then continue with "further developing a comprehensive legal framework of conventions dealing with international terrorism." While the General Assembly has tackled terrorism for decades, the Security Council rarely addressed the topic before the end of the Cold War but became more engaged in the 1990s. This included passing resolutions imposing sanctions on supporters of terrorism, such as Resolution 1267 in 1999 on the Taliban in Afghanistan and earlier resolutions against Libya (1992) and Somalia (1996). By 1999, with the passage of Resolution 1269, the Security Council also began addressing terrorism more broadly as a part of the Council's agenda on maintaining international peace and security. The September 11, 2001 terrorist attacks on the United States prompted the Security Council to take even greater action. Today, UN engagement with terrorism is wide-ranging.

UN ENGAGEMENT SINCE 9/11

On September 12, 2001, the Security Council passed Resolution 1368 allowing for self-defense as a response to terrorism. On September 28, the Security Council approved Resolution 1373 aimed at preventing and suppressing terrorist activity

> **International Counter-Terrorism Conventions**
>
> 1963—Convention on Offences and Certain Other Acts Committed on Board Aircraft (with 2014 Protocol)
>
> 1970—Convention for the Suppression of Unlawful Seizure of Aircraft (with 2010 Protocol Supplementary)
>
> 1971—Convention for the Suppression of Unlawful Acts Against the Safety of Civil Aviation (with 1988 Protocol for the Suppression of Unlawful Acts of Violence at Airports Serving International Civil Aviation)
>
> 1973—Convention on the Prevention and Punishment of Crimes Against Internationally Protected Persons
>
> 1979—International Convention Against the Taking of Hostages
>
> 1980—Convention on the Physical Protection of Nuclear Material (with 2005 Amendments)
>
> 1988—Convention for the Suppression of Unlawful Acts Against the Safety of Maritime Navigation (with 2005 Protocol)
>
> 1988—Protocol for the Suppression of Unlawful Acts Against the Safety of Fixed Platforms Located in the Continental Shelf (with 2005 Protocol)
>
> 1991—Convention on the Marking of Plastic Explosives for the Purposes of Detection
>
> 1997—International Convention for the Suppression of Terrorist Bombings
>
> 1999—International Convention for the Suppression of the Financing of Terrorism
>
> 2005—International Convention for the Suppression of Acts of Nuclear Terrorism
>
> 2010—Convention on the Suppression of Unlawful Acts Relating to International Civil Aviation

and establishing the Counter-Terrorism Committee (CTC). Additional support for the CTC was provided in 2004 with the creation of the Counter-Terrorism Committee Executive Directorate (CTED). Since then, the Security Council has continued to bolster the mandate of the CTC and CTED and pass resolutions addressing various dimensions related to terrorism. In addition, the Security Council has authorized peacekeeping missions in situations with counterterrorist operations, for example, the UN Multidimensional Stabilization Mission in Mali established in 2013.

Coming out of the 2005 World Summit, Secretary-General Kofi Annan created the Counter-Terrorism Implementation Task Force (CTITF) to coordinate across the UN System and carry out the Global Counter-Terrorism Strategy (passed by the General Assembly in 2006). The UN Counter-Terrorism Centre (UNCCT) was established in 2011 to assist countries with implementing the directives in the Global Strategy. In 2017, as part of reforms promoted by Secretary-General António Guterres, the CTITF and the UNCCT joined the newly established UN Office of Counter-Terrorism. The office provides strategic leadership for General Assembly mandates, coordinates the members of the Global Counter-Terrorism

Coordination Compact (which replaced the CTITF in 2018), increases state capacity on counterterrorism efforts, and promotes counterterrorism awareness. Other UN entities actively work to combat terrorism, including the UN Office on Drugs and Crime at its Terrorism Prevention Branch, the Analytical Support and Sanctions Monitoring Team, and a support system for victims of terrorism.

ADVANCES AND CHALLENGES

UN entities and programs provide a range of counterterrorism operations and services. Security Council resolutions create legal obligations for member states and establish a communications network, as well as punitive measures to both punish and deter terrorist organizations. While there is progress, agreeing on a common definition of terrorism is persistently controversial. As early as 1972 and the attack that killed Israeli athletes at the Munich Olympic Games, countries in the General Assembly failed to agree on a common definition of terrorism. While countries are moving closer to consensus, efforts to approve a Comprehensive International Convention on Terrorism are still ongoing. Within the UN framework, countries have established several basic elements of terrorism: a criminal act (including, murder, taking hostages, property damage, and the threat of violence) intended to spread fear and coerce government authorities. Critics point out that UN legal parameters to criminalize and punish terrorism open the door for countries to violate human rights. For example, the Office of the UN High Commissioner for Human Rights issued a warning that the war on terror may be used to erode civil liberties and due process. In addition, as the Security Council increasingly calls on peacekeepers to confront extremist organizations, this challenges the UN's commitment to neutrality and has resulted in significant peacekeeping casualties. Finally, many of the provisions rely on country compliance, but this remains inconsistent due to both political concerns and technical obstacles. Overall, the UN's global counterterrorism system provides strategic leadership, promotes international coordination, and creates practical preventive measures.

See also: Cybersecurity, General Assembly, Human Rights, International Civil Aviation Organization, International Maritime Organization, Kofi Annan, Peacebuilding, Peacekeeping, Security Council, World Tourism Organization.

FURTHER READING

Boulden, Jane, and Thomas G. Weiss, eds. 2004. *Terrorism and the UN: Before and after September 11.* Bloomington: Indiana University Press.

Joyner, Christopher C. 2004. "The United Nations and Terrorism: Rethinking Legal Tensions between National Security, Human Rights, and Civil Liberties." *International Studies Perspectives* 5 (3): 240–57.

Messmer, William B., and Carlos L. Yordán. 2011. "A Partnership to Counter International Terrorism: The UN Security Council and the UN Member States." *Studies in Conflict & Terrorism* 34 (11): 843–61.

United Nations Budget and Financing

For most organizations, setting the budget and providing financing are technical issues. As the UN relies primarily on member states for the organization's financing, the budget process is impacted by political disputes. The Secretary-General is responsible for preparing the budget. Article 17 of the UN Charter states that the General Assembly shall "consider and approve the budget," with the Fifth Committee (Administrative and Budgetary) serving this key role. The General Assembly also elects a sixteen-person expert Advisory Committee on Administrative and Budgetary Questions, which reports through the Fifth Committee along with a Committee for Programme and Coordination, a Committee on Contributions, and Board of Auditors. The budget approval process is lengthy, with estimates required to be submitted in advance. The first UN budget in 1946 was around $20 million. By comparison, the regular UN budget approved for 2020 is just over $3 billion.

UN ENGAGEMENT

The UN's budget is composed of the regular budget, the peacekeeping budget, and extrabudgetary expenditures supported by voluntary contributions. The regular budget is financed through mandatory contributions, known as assessments, based on each country's "capacity to pay." The formula to calculate assessed contributions is established by each member state's share of gross national income and may be adjusted if a country has a high debt ratio or low per capita income. Additionally, there is a minimum share of 0.001 percent for all countries, a maximum rate of 0.01 percent for least developed countries, and a ceiling of 22 percent of the budget for the largest contributor (the United States). The regular budget covers all administrative costs and necessary capital improvements. The peacekeeping budget operates separately. Peacekeeping assessments are based on each state's political and economic status, with the Security Council's five permanent members obligated to contribute a greater portion of the peacekeeping budget. The 2019–2020 peacekeeping budget was $6.5 billion.

Countries may also offer additional voluntary contributions to specific funds or projects. Some UN programmes and funds, for instance, the UN Children's Fund and the UN Development Programme, are financed completely through voluntary contributions from the UN member states as well as other governmental and private sources. A number of specialized agencies, such as the World Health Organization, are increasingly reliant on voluntary contributions as well. In general, voluntary contributions have greatly increased since the UN's creation and have significantly grown in the new millennium to levels beyond all other areas of the UN budget, with one study reporting a jump from $7.5 billion in 2003 to $30 billion by 2015. The ability to earmark funds enhances the appeal of funding for countries, yet this prevents UN entities from having direct control over the disbursement of the funds. Wealthy donors, such as the Bill and Melinda Gates Foundation (focused on health and reducing poverty) and Ted Turner (established the UN Foundation), can also provide support for particular areas.

ADVANCES AND CHALLENGES

Issues with assessed contributions include lack of reliable data, varying definitions of national income, and reluctance of member states to accept the scale for payments. Countries also deliberately withhold funding to manipulate both policies and reform efforts at the UN in response to allegations, such as inefficiencies and mismanagement. While the United States is the UN's largest contributor, it often withholds funds or unilaterally cuts funds for specific entities. At times, the U.S. Congress has capped UN peacekeeping assessment at 25 percent. However, the UN peacekeeping assessment formula exceeds this cap. For instance, the United States is called upon to pay 27.89 percent of peacekeeping costs for 2019–2020. In another example, the United States stopped providing voluntary funding to the UN Relief and Works Agency for Palestine Refugees in the Near East in 2018. When funds are withheld from the regular budget, this places the member states in arrears and compromises the UN's ability to effectively budget. Cutbacks to or full removal of voluntary funding greatly impacts the services that can be provided. The financial deficit at which the UN operates is thus tied to a lack of political will to provide appropriate funds. This pattern creates chronic challenges and undermines the capacity of UN agencies to implement programs and the organization's overall solvency.

The UN has made efforts to be more efficient. For instance, the approved budget for the 2018–2019 session was reduced 5 percent budget from the previous two-year period. However, the actual budget increased by $130 million in comparison to 2016–2017 after a mid-point adjustment in late 2018. To avoid such alterations, starting with the 2020 budget the General Assembly approved shifting to an annual operating budget (the approach previously used until 1973) instead of a two-year cycle. In addition, the UN has spearheaded initiatives to supplement member dues with private sector donations, although this is not without its own challenges as there are concerns that those donating might try to use contributions to leverage favorable policies. Financing the UN is an essential part of member states' commitment to shared responsibility and supporting UN work across the globe.

See also: Charter of the United Nations; General Assembly; Office of Secretary-General; Peacekeeping; Security Council; United Nations Children's Fund; United Nations Development Programme; United Nations Relief and Works Agency for Palestine Refugees in the Near East; World Health Organization.

FURTHER READING

Graham, Erin R. 2017. "The Institutional Design of Funding Rules at International Organizations: Explaining the Transformation in Financing the United Nations." *European Journal of International Relations* 23 (2): 365–90.

Hüfner, Klaus. 2019. *Financing the United Nations: An Introduction.* Berlin: Frank & Timme.

Laurenti, Jeffrey. 2018. "Financing." In *The Oxford Handbook on the United Nations.* Second edition, edited by Thomas G. Weiss and Sam Daws, 250–79. Oxford: Oxford University Press.

United Nations Conferences and Summits

The UN System includes a variety of entities and venues for diplomacy. Along with work in regular UN bodies, the organization also hosts issue-specific conferences and summits. These short-term events respond to emerging issues as well as emphasize ongoing concerns. Summits are high-profile meetings that bring together political leaders, or other high-level representatives, of countries. Conferences are broader meetings, which at times can also include world leaders, but have a wider range of country representatives and other actors. Although the UN Charter does not specify the use of such meetings, Article 1(4) stating that the UN is "to be a centre for harmonizing the actions of nations" justifies these events. Both conferences and summits help to shape the global "to-do" list, create international agreements, form policies, and encourage institutional changes.

UN ENGAGEMENT

Many conferences and summits are organized in response to resolutions from either the General Assembly or Economic and Social Council. Often a Preparatory Committee is established for planning and coordination. Thus, many times the summit or conference is the final meeting at the end of an extended process. Conferences often provide opportunities for participants not normally included in UN discussions, including representatives from civil society. These events can include separate NGO forums where diverse organizations meet to find common goals and strategies and in some cases shape international policy. A notable example is the 1996 Ottawa Conference and the resulting treaty to ban landmines. Country representatives also benefit from access to scientists, researchers, and people on the ground dealing with a particular issue.

The first UN-sponsored conference, the International Conference on Trade and Employment (1947–1948), was held in Havana, Cuba. Conferences are often key turning points that engage the UN with new issues, such as the 1972 Conference on the Human Environment held in Stockholm, Sweden. As this event illustrates, conferences regularly establish outcome documents to guide the handling of global issues, in this situation the Stockholm Declaration, and can also lead to the establishment of new institutions, in this case the UN Environment Programme. There are also often a series of conferences that build upon one another, as happened with the 1995 Beijing Women's Conference, which was the fourth World Conference on Women (following 1975 in Mexico City, 1980 in Copenhagen, and 1985 in Nairobi). Recent conferences have addressed areas as diverse as climate change, financing for development, human rights, human settlements, indigenous peoples, population, sustainable development, and water. A major example of a UN summit is the Millennium Summit, a three-day meeting of leaders held in September 2000, which led to these leaders approving the UN Millennium Declaration to help guide to organization as it entered the new century. A follow-up World Summit was held five years later to evaluate progress.

ADVANCES AND CHALLENGES

Conferences and summits can impact global priorities and publicize the need for action as well as promote the creation of new or altered UN entities. Summits bring together the highest levels of member state governance to emphasize the importance of an issue, and decisions made at these meetings carry greater weight than regular UN meetings or resolutions. Conferences provide the opportunity for a wider range of participants and actors to share ideas and gain new perspectives. Dialogue between participants and information shared often shapes future UN resolutions and international treaties. Additionally, conference participants bring ideas, priorities, and commitments back to their home countries.

While conferences often include NGOs, some argue that these events are largely elite driven, with powerful states setting the agenda, and claim that minority interests are not adequately represented. Other critics view these events as too much of a public show without enough substance. High-level meetings often focus on building compromise instead of establishing efficient solutions. Summits between major powers, such as in the area of disarmament, have also often been held outside of UN auspices. In addition, questions are raised on whether the money spent on holding conferences is justified, when the funds could instead be applied directly to addressing the global issue. Overall, conferences and summits illustrate the adaptability of the UN to provide attention to emerging areas and to provide a forum for the international community to address global issues.

See also: Arms Control and Disarmament; Ban Ki-moon; Economic and Social Council; Economic Development; Environmental Protection; General Assembly; Human Rights; Human Rights Council; Human Security; Indigenous Peoples; International Fund for Agricultural Development; International Seabed Authority; International Telecommunication Union; Kofi Annan; Nongovernmental Organizations; Refugees and Migration; Sustainable Development; Sustainable Development Goals; United Nations Conference on Trade and Development; United Nations Environment Programme; United Nations Historical Background; United Nations Human Settlements Programme; United Nations Population Fund; Women and Gender.

FURTHER READING

Friedman, Elisabeth Jay, Kathryn Hochstetler, and Ann Marie Clark. 2005. *Sovereignty, Democracy, and Global Civil Society: State-Society Relations at UN World Conferences.* Albany: State University of New York Press.

Pianta, Michael. 2005. *UN World Summits and Civil Society: The State of the Art.* Geneva: United Nations Research Institute for Social Development.

Schechter, Michael. 2005. *United Nations Global Conferences.* London: Routledge.

United Nations Headquarters

With the development of permanent international organizations came the need for a headquarters to house the staff and hold regular meetings. Early hubs for international organization headquarters include Geneva, Switzerland, home to a wide range of international governmental and nongovernmental organizations, and The Hague, Netherlands, the center for international law and courts. The League of Nations, the universal organization founded after World War I, was based in Geneva. This included the construction of the Palais des Nations to house the organization, which is still used by the UN today. However, instead of staying in Geneva, the UN sought a new headquarters location. Thus, after the UN was created in 1945, the organization lacked a permanent place to meet. The UN Headquarters complex in New York familiar today to people around the world was not in place before the early 1950s.

The very first UN meetings were held in early 1946 in London in the United Kingdom. Various locations in the United States were considered after the U.S. Congress invited the UN to place its headquarters there, but New York City won the day. Financier John D. Rockefeller Jr. provided $8.5 million to the UN to buy land in Manhattan alongside the East River (an area referred to as Turtle Bay). While construction was underway, the Secretariat was temporarily located at Hunter College in the Bronx and then Lake Success in Long Island. UN Headquarters stretches along First Avenue between 42nd and 48th Streets, encompassing four main, linked buildings: the thirty-nine-story Secretariat building, the General Assembly Building with a large General Assembly Hall, the Conference Building (with chambers for the Economic and Social Council, Security Council, and Trusteeship Council), and the Dag Hammarskjöld Library (named in memory of the Secretary-General after he died in a plane crash in 1961). The Headquarters Agreement between the UN and the United States establishes the eighteen-acre territory as under the international legal jurisdiction of the UN. The UN operates independent security and fire forces as well as a post office on site.

UN ENGAGEMENT

A wide range of Secretariat Departments and Offices are housed in New York, along with the meeting halls of the other principal organs (except for the International Court of Justice based in The Hague) and a number of UN funds and programmes, such as the UN Development Programme. The UN also maintains three official offices in Geneva (since 1946), Vienna, Austria (opened in 1980), and Nairobi, Kenya (established in 1996). The Nairobi office encompasses environmental efforts, including the UN Environmental Programme, and is an important step in placing UN offices in less developed countries. A great variety of UN conferences have also been held across the globe, such as the 1994 International Conference on Population and Development held in Cairo, Egypt. The UN maintains five Regional Commissions, headquartered in Bangkok, Thailand; Beirut, Lebanon; Addis Ababa, Ethiopia; Geneva; and Santiago, Chile. UN Information Centres span the globe, with around sixty spread across different regions. UN specialized agencies are headquartered around the world in additional cities, including concentrations in Washington, DC (economic institutions) and Rome, Italy (food organizations). With the move of the German government back to Berlin following the reunification of Germany, Bonn repurposed itself as a UN city, hosting entities such as the Secretariat of the UN Framework Convention on Climate Change.

ADVANCES AND CHALLENGES

Original construction of UN Headquarters in New York was supported by a $65 million interest-free loan from the United States (which was paid off in 1982), along with a $6.6 million donation from the Ford Foundation for the library. However, as the UN buildings aged, they were in dire need of a complete overhaul. After years of delay, the General Assembly approved a $1.88 billion plan for full renovations, and the project got underway in 2008. Most renovations were completed by September 2014 in time for the opening of the 69th session of the General Assembly, with the final cost running to $2.31 billion. The UN maintained operations during the reconstruction in surrounding office space and in a temporary building built on the North Lawn. Although the UN has operations and offices around the world, UN Headquarters in New York remains a symbol of the organization and draws over one million tourists each year.

See also: Dag Hammarskjöld; Economic and Social Council; General Assembly; International Court of Justice; Nongovernmental Organizations; Regional Commissions; Secretariat; Security Council; Trusteeship Council; United Nations Conferences and Summits; United Nations Environment Programme.

FURTHER READING

Hanlon, Pamela. 2017. *A Worldly Affair: New York, the United Nations, and the Story Behind Their Unlikely Bond.* New York: Empire State Editions.
Mires, Charlene. 2013. *Capital of the World: The Race to Host the United Nations.* New York: New York University Press.
Monfried, Andrea, ed. 2015. *The United Nations at 70: Restoration and Renewal: The Seventieth Anniversary of the United Nations and the Restoration of the New York Headquarters.* New York: Rizzoli International Publications.

United Nations Reform

Calls for UN reform began the moment the organization was created, and adjustments at the UN are always ongoing. Two factors push this dynamic. First, the original design established at the San Francisco Conference in 1945 represented many compromises. Second, the UN must adapt to an ever-changing global political environment. Reforms are generally divided into three categories: reform of UN bodies, bureaucratic reform to address issues of efficiency and implementation, and inclusivity. Inclusivity addresses both the actors that engage the UN, such as nongovernmental organizations, and issues at the organization, such as gender equality. There has also been a push to innovate and respond to emerging threats, including terrorism, cybersecurity, and climate change.

UN ENGAGEMENT

While the drafters of the UN Charter acknowledged the need for review and reform, the process of altering the Charter is challenging. Article 108 of the Charter requires amendments to be ratified by two-thirds of the member states and all five permanent members in the Security Council. To date, this has happened only five times: three Articles impacted by Security Council enlargement (Article 23 on membership in the Council, Article 27 on voting in the Council, and Article 109 in regard to Council votes needed for calling a General Conference to review the Charter) and expansion of the Economic and Social Council (ECOSOC) twice altering Article 61 on ECOSOC membership. The growth in overall UN membership, particularly through the addition of countries following decolonization, pushed significant changes at the UN. ECOSOC grew from eighteen to twenty-seven (1965) and again to the current fifty-four (1973). Other modifications at that time included the creation of new entities at the UN, such as the UN Conference on Trade and Development (1964) and the UN Development Programme (1965). With more members, calls for Security Council reform gained momentum as well and, in 1965, the Council expanded from eleven to fifteen and outlined the geographic distribution of the ten nonpermanent members. Despite these changes, Security Council reform is an ongoing topic and there are many proposals focused on further expanding membership as well as altering the use of the veto.

Encouragement for reforms gained prominence with the end of the Cold War deadlock at the UN. However, during the 1990s, the UN faced growing pains due to the increased number of peacekeeping missions and a severe budget crisis as the United States, the UN's largest financial contributor, demanded change. Secretaries-General from that point forward have offered many blueprints for reform to address criticism as well as to provide innovative programs. Kofi Annan is particularly noted for his extensive "quiet revolution" for implementing reforms. Some of the most impactful UN reforms include efforts toward gender parity, simplification of bureaucracy, and increased accountability of peacekeeping operations. Annan created an ethics office, a zero-tolerance policy for sexual exploitation, and whistleblower protections to improve accountability. António Guterres highlighted gender parity when he took office in 2017. He has also emphasized reform for development, management, and peace and security, including major structural reforms implemented at the beginning of 2019.

ADVANCES AND CHALLENGES

Over seventy-five years, the UN has seen the addition of new bodies, ranging from the UN Environment Programme (1972) to the Peacebuilding Commission (2005), and alteration of existing bodies, as in the case of the Human Rights Council (2006). The organization has promoted new methods of conflict resolution, including peacekeeping and the responsibility to protect, and established important new initiatives, such as the Sustainable Development Goals. In addition, there are significant modifications to international legal capacities with the first war crimes court, the International Criminal Tribunal for the Former Yugoslavia

(1993), and the creation of the International Criminal Court (2002). Yet, there is work to be done as some organs, like the Trusteeship Council, have lost their relevance but have not been dissolved or altered to serve a new purpose. Many support the creation of a rapid reaction force, while others support more enhanced collaboration with regional institutions like the African Union. While some reforms enhance capacity, reforms can at times scramble resources and deplete existing programs in favor of constantly changing priorities. In some cases, observers claim that recent reform efforts focusing on security priorities, largely in response to U.S. demands to address terrorism, are to the detriment of human rights protections. Despite extensive modifications, elements of the UN remain a 1940s artifact with redundancies, underfunding, and lack of accountability. At the same time, the UN has endured, and although grand reform efforts have largely faltered, incremental adjustments ensure that the organization is a dynamic and continually relevant actor in global affairs.

See also: António Guterres; Ban Ki-moon; Charter of the United Nations; Cybersecurity; Economic and Social Council; Environmental Protection; High-level Political Forum on Sustainable Development; Human Rights; International Criminal Court; Joint United Nations Programme on HIV/AIDS; Kofi Annan; Membership; Nongovernmental Organizations; Peacebuilding Commission; Peacekeeping; Regionalism; Secretariat; Security Council; Sustainable Development Goals; Terrorism; Trusteeship Council; United Nations Conference on Trade and Development; United Nations Development Programme; United Nations Environment Programme; United Nations Historical Background; Women and Gender.

FURTHER READING

Luck, Edward C. 2005. "How Not to Reform the United Nations." *Global Governance* 11 (4): 407–14.

Müller, Joachim, ed. 2016. *Reforming the United Nations: A Chronology.* Leiden, Netherlands: Brill Nijhoff.

Weiss, Thomas G. 2016. *What's Wrong with the United Nations and How to Fix It.* Third edition. Malden, MA: Polity Press.

Voting and Negotiating Blocs

Political bodies of all forms have groups, also known as blocs, which express views from a common position. In the UN, member states often base their voting and negotiating stances on geographic proximity, regional organization, and issues of shared interest. These groups shape the UN agenda and are essential for understanding how decisions are made at the UN.

UN ENGAGEMENT

Voting in elections at the UN are traditionally based on regional categories. This process started informally in 1946 by using electoral slates designed to provide for geographical representation. In 1963, the General Assembly formally approved regionally based elections that led to the five current electoral groups: African (currently fifty-four countries), Asia-Pacific (fifty-five), Eastern European (twenty-three), Latin American and Caribbean (known as GRULAC, thirty-three), and Western European and Others (WEOG; twenty-nine). Three countries hold interesting positions in relation to these groups. Turkey participates in both Asia-Pacific and WEOG, but only WEOG for elections. Israel struggled to find a group home but has since joined WEOG, along with the rest of the "others" Australia, Canada, and New Zealand. The United States does not belong to any of the regional groups but observes at WEOG meetings and is treated as a WEOG member for elections.

The UN Charter presents a clear basis for regional representation in the Security Council. Article 23(1) states that "due regard" should be paid "to equitable geographical distribution" when the General Assembly votes to elect the nonpermanent members of the Security Council. The ten nonpermanent members are divided by one to Eastern Europe, two to WEOG, two to GRULAC, three to Africa, and two to Asia-Pacific (with one member being an Arab country from either of the latter two groups). General Assembly elections for other parts of the UN are similarly geographically based, such as the Economic and Social Council. Other agencies within the UN System have their own election criteria to ensure representation. For example, the UN Educational, Scientific and Cultural Organization also employs regional electoral groups for selecting the Executive Board.

Other forms of groups are also important for negotiations and voting in UN bodies and international conferences. Regional organizations are active in the UN. The European Union is particularly noted for its efforts to coordinate members, including being recognized as an observer with enhanced status by the General Assembly in 2011. Subregional groups, such as the cohesive five Nordic countries, are also present. Broader groups with shared interests have shaped the UN agenda, especially large groups of less developed countries such as the Group of 77 (G-77, now up to 134 countries) and the Non-Aligned Movement. Groups of countries with a specific interest also work together in the UN. For example, the Alliance of Small Island States lobbies for action against climate changes. Many working groups form on a temporary basis to address a particular situation. This includes "Friends of the Secretary-General" and contact groups, which help to guide conflicts to a peaceful resolution.

ADVANCES AND CHALLENGES

The extensive use of blocs in the UN advances the political process in certain ways. Small countries are able to work with others who share their interests to get their voices heard and impact voting outcomes. Groups provide access to a wider array of information and channels of communication between members. Establishing a group position on issues can smooth the negotiating process instead of sorting through all 193 individual member state positions as the UN tackles a crowded agenda. However, the compromises reached in such a process can lead to decisions based on the "lowest common denominator." This leads to weakened policies and limits the impact of UN decisions for addressing global problems. The political process at the UN can be slowed, or even derailed, once groups lock into set positions. Individual states' voices can also get lost. While a large set of less powerful countries can come together to dominate votes in the UN (as in the case of the G-77), they often lack the capability to ensure that these decisions are carried out. The role of blocs is complex but greatly impact processes within the UN System.

See also: Economic and Social Council; General Assembly; Membership; Regionalism; Security Council; United Nations Educational, Scientific and Cultural Organization.

FURTHER READING

Blavoukos, Spyros, Dimitris Bourantonis, Ioannis Galariotis, and Maria Gianniou. 2016. "The European Union's Visibility and Coherence at the United Nations General Assembly." *Global Affairs* 2 (1): 35–45.

Laatikainen, Katie Verlin. 2017. "Conceptualizing Groups in UN Multilateralism: The Diplomatic Practice of Group Politics." *The Hague Journal of Diplomacy* 12 (2–3): 113–37.

Smith, Courtney B. 2006. "Groups and Blocs." In *Politics and Process at the United Nations: The Global Dance*, 53–78. Boulder, CO: Lynne Rienner.

Women and Gender

Although women make up half of the world's population, they have a small presence in governing within countries and at the global level. Many women lack essential human rights and access to health care, education, and the workplace. The UN Population Fund (UNFPA) estimates that one in every three women will be the victims of physical or sexual abuse. The marginalization of women slows human progress, undermines economic development, and disrupts peace processes. The UN is an important venue for those advocating for gender equality, including the promotion of political rights, access to education, employment, reproductive rights, establishing standards and legal protections, and raising awareness. Concerns about gendered phrasing ensured that the Preamble of the UN Charter called for promoting "equal rights of men and women" instead of "equal rights of men."

UN ENGAGEMENT

In 1946, the Economic and Social Council created the Commission on the Status of Women (CSW) to promote "women's rights in political, economic, social, and educational fields." The CSW contributed to the writing of the Universal Declaration of Human Rights (see Part VI) and lobbied against using the term "men" to refer to all humanity. In 2010, the General Assembly created a new body, UN Entity for Gender Equality and the Empowerment of Women (UN Women), which brought together existing structures to better coordinate gender equity and empowerment efforts. Toward creating legal protections, in 1967 the General Assembly unanimously passed the Declaration on the Elimination of Discrimination against Women. Another notable development was the 1979 Convention on the Elimination of All Forms of Discrimination against Women (CEDAW). This treaty is often identified as the "women's bill of rights," supporting gender equality and "fundamental freedoms in the political, economic, social, cultural, civil or any other field." While 189 countries ratified CEDAW (which entered into force in 1981), many expressed reservations about specific items. Notably, the United States is a signatory but has not ratified the treaty.

The UN also sponsored a series of international conferences in Mexico City, Mexico (1975); Copenhagen, Denmark (1980); Nairobi, Kenya (1985); and Beijing, China (1995). The 1995 conference established a Platform of Action calling on the UN and its member states to address issues of education, employment, health, and women as victims of violence and armed conflict and established follow-up evaluations (held every five years). The year 2020 marked the twenty-fifth anniversary and latest follow-up session (limited to one day and suspended due to COVID-19). These reviews provide a valuable opportunity for building awareness, consensus, and support for global advocacy. The Security Council also addressed the issue of gender in the groundbreaking Resolution 1325 in October 2000 (see Part VI), which called for increased inclusion of women in the prevention, management, and resolution of violent conflict. In addition, the Millennium Development Goal 3 and Sustainable Development Goal 5 seek to establish gender equality and empower all women. Other notable UN contributions include the UN Decade for Women (1975–1985) and an International Women's Day (March 8). Furthermore, both the General Assembly and Economic and Social Council adopted resolutions calling for "gender mainstreaming," which places gender perspectives and equality central to UN policies and programs.

ADVANCES AND CHALLENGES

Gender is an issue that cuts across key areas, including development, sustainability, peacebuilding, and human rights. Yet, progress within the UN has met with backlash, and there are concerns that further meetings and conferences may be used by some countries to seek to erode the advancements achieved. Reproductive rights are controversial, and several actors at the UN are pushing back to advocate for reduced rights and access (e.g., the Holy See, conservative Islamic countries, and, at times, the United States). Despite a commitment to "50-50" gender parity for UN staff by 2028 and the 2017 System-wide Strategy on Gender Parity, the UN still has far to go given the current level of gender disparity, although progress has already been made in top Secretariat appointments under Secretary-General António Guterres, who made this a strategic priority. Yet, evidence indicates a UN "glass ceiling," as women are woefully underrepresented in leadership positions and a woman has yet to serve as Secretary-General. Some fault the UN's bureaucracy and culture as obstacles to change. The demands for protections are also expanding to include persons with diverse gender identities and members of the LGBTQ community. Despite the challenges, the UN is increasing awareness that women are essential stakeholders in the peacebuilding process and an important part of promoting human rights and development.

See also: António Guterres; Economic Development; Functional Commissions; Health; Human Rights; Peacebuilding; Security Council; Sustainable Development Goals; United Nations Children's Fund; United Nations Conferences and Summits; United Nations Entity for Gender Equality and the Empowerment of Women; United Nations Population Fund; United Nations Reform.

FURTHER READING

Bunch, Charlotte. 2018. "Women's Rights and Gender Integration." In *The Oxford Handbook on the United Nations*. Second edition, edited by Thomas G. Weiss and Sam Daws, 601–18. Oxford: Oxford University Press.

Labonte, Melissa, and Gaynel Curry. 2016. "Women, Peace, and Security: Are We There Yet?" *Global Governance* 22 (3): 311–19.

Pietilä, Hilkka, and Jeanne Vickers. 1990. *Making Women Matter: The Role of the United Nations*. London: Zed Books.

PART VI

Documents

CHARTER OF THE UNITED NATIONS

Preamble

We the peoples of the United Nations

determined

to save succeeding generations from the scourge of war, which twice in our lifetime has brought untold sorrow to mankind, and

to reaffirm faith in fundamental human rights, in the dignity and worth of the human person, in the equal rights of men and women and of nations large and small, and

to establish conditions under which justice and respect for the obligations arising from treaties and other sources of international law can be maintained, and

to promote social progress and better standards of life in larger freedom,

and for these ends

to practice tolerance and live together in peace with one another as good neighbours, and

to unite our strength to maintain international peace and security, and

to ensure, by the acceptance of principles and the institution of methods, that armed force shall not be used, save in the common interest, and

to employ international machinery for the promotion of the economic and social advancement of all peoples,

have resolved to combine our efforts to accomplish these aims

Accordingly, our respective Governments, through representatives assembled in the city of San Francisco, who have exhibited their full powers found to be in good and due form, have agreed to the present Charter of the United Nations and do hereby establish an international organization to be known as the United Nations.

Chapter 1: Purposes and Principles

Article 1

The Purposes of the United Nations are:

1. To maintain international peace and security, and to that end: to take effective collective measures for the prevention and removal of threats to the peace, and for the suppression of acts of aggression or other breaches of the peace, and to bring about by peaceful means, and in conformity with the principles of justice and international law, adjustment or settlement of international disputes or situations which might lead to a breach of the peace;

2. To develop friendly relations among nations based on respect for the principle of equal rights and self-determination of peoples, and to take other appropriate measures to strengthen universal peace;
3. To achieve international co-operation in solving international problems of an economic, social, cultural, or humanitarian character, and in promoting and encouraging respect for human rights and for fundamental freedoms for all without distinction as to race, sex, language, or religion; and
4. To be a centre for harmonizing the actions of nations in the attainment of these common ends.

Article 2

The Organization and its Members, in pursuit of the Purposes stated in Article 1, shall act in accordance with the following Principles:

1. The Organization is based on the principle of the sovereign equality of all its Members.
2. All Members, in order to ensure to all of them the rights and benefits resulting from membership, shall fulfill in good faith the obligations assumed by them in accordance with the present Charter.
3. All Members shall settle their international disputes by peaceful means in such a manner that international peace and security, and justice, are not endangered.
4. All Members shall refrain in their international relations from the threat or use of force against the territorial integrity or political independence of any state, or in any other manner inconsistent with the Purposes of the United Nations.
5. All Members shall give the United Nations every assistance in any action it takes in accordance with the present Charter, and shall refrain from giving assistance to any state against which the United Nations is taking preventive or enforcement action.
6. The Organization shall ensure that states which are not Members of the United Nations act in accordance with these Principles so far as may be necessary for the maintenance of international peace and security.
7. Nothing contained in the present Charter shall authorize the United Nations to intervene in matters which are essentially within the domestic jurisdiction of any state or shall require the Members to submit such matters to settlement under the present Charter; but this principle shall not prejudice the application of enforcement measures under Chapter VII.

Chapter II: Membership

Article 3

The original Members of the United Nations shall be the states which, having participated in the United Nations Conference on International Organization at San Francisco, or having previously signed the Declaration by United Nations of 1 January 1942, sign the present Charter and ratify it in accordance with Article 110.

Article 4

1. Membership in the United Nations is open to all other peace-loving states which accept the obligations contained in the present Charter and, in the judgment of the Organization, are able and willing to carry out these obligations.
2. The admission of any such state to membership in the United Nations will be effected by a decision of the General Assembly upon the recommendation of the Security Council.

Article 5

A Member of the United Nations against which preventive or enforcement action has been taken by the Security Council may be suspended from the exercise of the rights and privileges of membership by the General Assembly upon the recommendation of the Security Council. The exercise of these rights and privileges may be restored by the Security Council.

Article 6

A Member of the United Nations which has persistently violated the Principles contained in the present Charter may be expelled from the Organization by the General Assembly upon the recommendation of the Security Council.

Chapter III: Organs

Article 7

1. There are established as principal organs of the United Nations: a General Assembly, a Security Council, an Economic and Social Council, a Trusteeship Council, an International Court of Justice and a Secretariat.
2. Such subsidiary organs as may be found necessary may be established in accordance with the present Charter.

Article 8

The United Nations shall place no restrictions on the eligibility of men and women to participate in any capacity and under conditions of equality in its principal and subsidiary organs.

Chapter IV: The General Assembly

Composition

Article 9

1. The General Assembly shall consist of all the Members of the United Nations.
2. Each Member shall have not more than five representatives in the General Assembly.

Functions and Powers

Article 10

The General Assembly may discuss any questions or any matters within the scope of the present Charter or relating to the powers and functions of any organs provided for in the present Charter, and, except as provided in Article 12, may make recommendations to the Members of the United Nations or to the Security Council or to both on any such questions or matters.

Article 11

1. The General Assembly may consider the general principles of cooperation in the maintenance of international peace and security, including the principles governing disarmament and the regulation of armaments, and may make recommendations with regard to such principles to the Members or to the Security Council or to both.
2. The General Assembly may discuss any questions relating to the maintenance of international peace and security brought before it by any Member of the United Nations, or by the Security Council, or by a state which is not a Member of the United Nations in accordance with Article 35, paragraph 2, and, except as provided in Article 12, may make recommendations with regard to any such questions to the state or states concerned or to the Security Council or to both. Any such question on which action is necessary shall be referred to the Security Council by the General Assembly either before or after discussion.
3. The General Assembly may call the attention of the Security Council to situations which are likely to endanger international peace and security.
4. The powers of the General Assembly set forth in this Article shall not limit the general scope of Article 10.

Article 12

1. While the Security Council is exercising in respect of any dispute or situation the functions assigned to it in the present Charter, the General Assembly shall not make any recommendation with regard to that dispute or situation unless the Security Council so requests.
2. The Secretary-General, with the consent of the Security Council, shall notify the General Assembly at each session of any matters relative to the maintenance of international peace and security which are being dealt with by the Security Council and shall similarly notify the General Assembly, or the Members of the United Nations if the General Assembly is not in session, immediately the Security Council ceases to deal with such matters.

Article 13

1. The General Assembly shall initiate studies and make recommendations for the purpose of:
    a. promoting international co-operation in the political field and encouraging the progressive development of international law and its codification;
    b. promoting international co-operation in the economic, social, cultural, educational, and health fields, and assisting in the realization

of human rights and fundamental freedoms for all without distinction as to race, sex, language, or religion.
c. The further responsibilities, functions and powers of the General Assembly with respect to matters mentioned in paragraph 1 (b) above are set forth in Chapters IX and X.

Article 14

Subject to the provisions of Article 12, the General Assembly may recommend measures for the peaceful adjustment of any situation, regardless of origin, which it deems likely to impair the general welfare or friendly relations among nations, including situations resulting from a violation of the provisions of the present Charter setting forth the Purposes and Principles of the United Nations.

Article 15

1. The General Assembly shall receive and consider annual and special reports from the Security Council; these reports shall include an account of the measures that the Security Council has decided upon or taken to maintain international peace and security.
2. The General Assembly shall receive and consider reports from the other organs of the United Nations.

Article 16

The General Assembly shall perform such functions with respect to the international trusteeship system as are assigned to it under Chapters XII and XIII, including the approval of the trusteeship agreements for areas not designated as strategic.

Article 17

1. The General Assembly shall consider and approve the budget of the Organization.
2. The expenses of the Organization shall be borne by the Members as apportioned by the General Assembly.
3. The General Assembly shall consider and approve any financial and budgetary arrangements with specialized agencies referred to in Article 57 and shall examine the administrative budgets of such specialized agencies with a view to making recommendations to the agencies concerned.

Voting

Article 18

1. Each member of the General Assembly shall have one vote.
2. Decisions of the General Assembly on important questions shall be made by a two-thirds majority of the members present and voting. These questions shall include: recommendations with respect to the maintenance of international peace and security, the election of the non-permanent members of the Security Council, the election of the members of the Economic and Social Council, the election of members of the

Trusteeship Council in accordance with paragraph 1 (c) of Article 86, the admission of new Members to the United Nations, the suspension of the rights and privileges of membership, the expulsion of Members, questions relating to the operation of the trusteeship system, and budgetary questions.

3. Decisions on other questions, including the determination of additional categories of questions to be decided by a two-thirds majority, shall be made by a majority of the members present and voting.

Article 19

A Member of the United Nations which is in arrears in the payment of its financial contributions to the Organization shall have no vote in the General Assembly if the amount of its arrears equals or exceeds the amount of the contributions due from it for the preceding two full years. The General Assembly may, nevertheless, permit such a Member to vote if it is satisfied that the failure to pay is due to conditions beyond the control of the Member.

Procedure

Article 20

The General Assembly shall meet in regular annual sessions and in such special sessions as occasion may require. Special sessions shall be convoked by the Secretary-General at the request of the Security Council or of a majority of the Members of the United Nations.

Article 21

The General Assembly shall adopt its own rules of procedure. It shall elect its President for each session.

Article 22

The General Assembly may establish such subsidiary organs as it deems necessary for the performance of its functions.

Chapter V: The Security Council

Composition

Article 23

1. The Security Council shall consist of fifteen Members of the United Nations. The Republic of China, France, the Union of Soviet Socialist Republics, the United Kingdom of Great Britain and Northern Ireland, and the United States of America shall be permanent members of the Security Council. The General Assembly shall elect ten other Members of the United Nations to be non-permanent members of the Security Council, due regard being specially paid, in the first instance to the contribution of Members of the United Nations to the maintenance of international peace and security and to the other purposes of the Organization, and also to equitable geographical distribution.

2. The non-permanent members of the Security Council shall be elected for a term of two years. In the first election of the non-permanent members after the increase of the membership of the Security Council from eleven to fifteen, two of the four additional members shall be chosen for a term of one year. A retiring member shall not be eligible for immediate re-election.
3. Each member of the Security Council shall have one representative.

Functions and Powers

Article 24

1. In order to ensure prompt and effective action by the United Nations, its Members confer on the Security Council primary responsibility for the maintenance of international peace and security, and agree that in carrying out its duties under this responsibility the Security Council acts on their behalf.
2. In discharging these duties the Security Council shall act in accordance with the Purposes and Principles of the United Nations. The specific powers granted to the Security Council for the discharge of these duties are laid down in Chapters VI, VII, VIII, and XII.
3. The Security Council shall submit annual and, when necessary, special reports to the General Assembly for its consideration.

Article 25

The Members of the United Nations agree to accept and carry out the decisions of the Security Council in accordance with the present Charter.

Article 26

In order to promote the establishment and maintenance of international peace and security with the least diversion for armaments of the world's human and economic resources, the Security Council shall be responsible for formulating, with the assistance of the Military Staff Committee referred to in Article 47, plans to be submitted to the Members of the United Nations for the establishment of a system for the regulation of armaments.

Voting

Article 27

1. Each member of the Security Council shall have one vote.
2. Decisions of the Security Council on procedural matters shall be made by an affirmative vote of nine members.
3. Decisions of the Security Council on all other matters shall be made by an affirmative vote of nine members including the concurring votes of the permanent members; provided that, in decisions under Chapter VI, and under paragraph 3 of Article 52, a party to a dispute shall abstain from voting.

Procedure
Article 28

1. The Security Council shall be so organized as to be able to function continuously. Each member of the Security Council shall for this purpose be represented at all times at the seat of the Organization.
2. The Security Council shall hold periodic meetings at which each of its members may, if it so desires, be represented by a member of the government or by some other specially designated representative.
3. The Security Council may hold meetings at such places other than the seat of the Organization as in its judgment will best facilitate its work.

Article 29
The Security Council may establish such subsidiary organs as it deems necessary for the performance of its functions.

Article 30
The Security Council shall adopt its own rules of procedure, including the method of selecting its President.

Article 31
Any Member of the United Nations which is not a member of the Security Council may participate, without vote, in the discussion of any question brought before the Security Council whenever the latter considers that the interests of that Member are specially affected.

Article 32
Any Member of the United Nations which is not a member of the Security Council or any state which is not a Member of the United Nations, if it is a party to a dispute under consideration by the Security Council, shall be invited to participate, without vote, in the discussion relating to the dispute. The Security Council shall lay down such conditions as it deems just for the participation of a state which is not a Member of the United Nations.

Chapter VI: Pacific Settlement of Disputes

Article 33

1. The parties to any dispute, the continuance of which is likely to endanger the maintenance of international peace and security, shall, first of all, seek a solution by negotiation, enquiry, mediation, conciliation, arbitration, judicial settlement, resort to regional agencies or arrangements, or other peaceful means of their own choice.
2. The Security Council shall, when it deems necessary, call upon the parties to settle their dispute by such means.

Article 34
The Security Council may investigate any dispute, or any situation which might lead to international friction or give rise to a dispute, in order to determine whether the continuance of the dispute or situation is likely to endanger the maintenance of international peace and security.

Article 35

1. Any Member of the United Nations may bring any dispute, or any situation of the nature referred to in Article 34, to the attention of the Security Council or of the General Assembly.
2. A state which is not a Member of the United Nations may bring to the attention of the Security Council or of the General Assembly any dispute to which it is a party if it accepts in advance, for the purposes of the dispute, the obligations of pacific settlement provided in the present Charter.
3. The proceedings of the General Assembly in respect of matters brought to its attention under this Article will be subject to the provisions of Articles 11 and 12.

Article 36

1. The Security Council may, at any stage of a dispute of the nature referred to in Article 33 or of a situation of like nature, recommend appropriate procedures or methods of adjustment.
2. The Security Council should take into consideration any procedures for the settlement of the dispute which have already been adopted by the parties.
3. In making recommendations under this Article the Security Council should also take into consideration that legal disputes should as a general rule be referred by the parties to the International Court of Justice in accordance with the provisions of the Statute of the Court.

Article 37

1. Should the parties to a dispute of the nature referred to in Article 33 fail to settle it by the means indicated in that Article, they shall refer it to the Security Council.
2. If the Security Council deems that the continuance of the dispute is in fact likely to endanger the maintenance of international peace and security, it shall decide whether to take action under Article 36 or to recommend such terms of settlement as it may consider appropriate.

Article 38

Without prejudice to the provisions of Articles 33 to 37, the Security Council may, if all the parties to any dispute so request, make recommendations to the parties with a view to a pacific settlement of the dispute.

Chapter VII: Action with Respect to Threats to the Peace, Breaches of the Peace, and Acts of Aggression

Article 39

The Security Council shall determine the existence of any threat to the peace, breach of the peace, or act of aggression and shall make recommendations, or decide what measures shall be taken in accordance with Articles 41 and 42, to maintain or restore international peace and security.

Article 40
In order to prevent an aggravation of the situation, the Security Council may, before making the recommendations or deciding upon the measures provided for in Article 39, call upon the parties concerned to comply with such provisional measures as it deems necessary or desirable. Such provisional measures shall be without prejudice to the rights, claims, or position of the parties concerned. The Security Council shall duly take account of failure to comply with such provisional measures.

Article 41
The Security Council may decide what measures not involving the use of armed force are to be employed to give effect to its decisions, and it may call upon the Members of the United Nations to apply such measures. These may include complete or partial interruption of economic relations and of rail, sea, air, postal, telegraphic, radio, and other means of communication, and the severance of diplomatic relations.

Article 42
Should the Security Council consider that measures provided for in Article 41 would be inadequate or have proved to be inadequate, it may take such action by air, sea, or land forces as may be necessary to maintain or restore international peace and security. Such action may include demonstrations, blockade, and other operations by air, sea, or land forces of Members of the United Nations.

Article 43

1. All Members of the United Nations, in order to contribute to the maintenance of international peace and security, undertake to make available to the Security Council, on its call and in accordance with a special agreement or agreements, armed forces, assistance, and facilities, including rights of passage, necessary for the purpose of maintaining international peace and security.
2. Such agreement or agreements shall govern the numbers and types of forces, their degree of readiness and general location, and the nature of the facilities and assistance to be provided.
3. The agreement or agreements shall be negotiated as soon as possible on the initiative of the Security Council. They shall be concluded between the Security Council and Members or between the Security Council and groups of Members and shall be subject to ratification by the signatory states in accordance with their respective constitutional processes.

Article 44
When the Security Council has decided to use force it shall, before calling upon a Member not represented on it to provide armed forces in fulfilment of the obligations assumed under Article 43, invite that Member, if the Member so desires, to participate in the decisions of the Security Council concerning the employment of contingents of that Member's armed forces.

Article 45
In order to enable the United Nations to take urgent military measures, Members shall hold immediately available national air-force contingents for combined international enforcement action. The strength and degree of readiness of these contingents and plans for their combined action shall be determined within the limits laid down in the special agreement or agreements referred to in Article 43, by the Security Council with the assistance of the Military Staff Committee.

Article 46
Plans for the application of armed force shall be made by the Security Council with the assistance of the Military Staff Committee.

Article 47

1. There shall be established a Military Staff Committee to advise and assist the Security Council on all questions relating to the Security Council's military requirements for the maintenance of international peace and security, the employment and command of forces placed at its disposal, the regulation of armaments, and possible disarmament.
2. The Military Staff Committee shall consist of the Chiefs of Staff of the permanent members of the Security Council or their representatives. Any Member of the United Nations not permanently represented on the Committee shall be invited by the Committee to be associated with it when the efficient discharge of the Committee's responsibilities requires the participation of that Member in its work.
3. The Military Staff Committee shall be responsible under the Security Council for the strategic direction of any armed forces placed at the disposal of the Security Council. Questions relating to the command of such forces shall be worked out subsequently.
4. The Military Staff Committee, with the authorization of the Security Council and after consultation with appropriate regional agencies, may establish regional sub-committees.

Article 48

1. The action required to carry out the decisions of the Security Council for the maintenance of international peace and security shall be taken by all the Members of the United Nations or by some of them, as the Security Council may determine.
2. Such decisions shall be carried out by the Members of the United Nations directly and through their action in the appropriate international agencies of which they are members.

Article 49
The Members of the United Nations shall join in affording mutual assistance in carrying out the measures decided upon by the Security Council.

Article 50

If preventive or enforcement measures against any state are taken by the Security Council, any other state, whether a Member of the United Nations or not, which finds itself confronted with special economic problems arising from the carrying out of those measures shall have the right to consult the Security Council with regard to a solution of those problems.

Article 51

Nothing in the present Charter shall impair the inherent right of individual or collective self-defence if an armed attack occurs against a Member of the United Nations, until the Security Council has taken measures necessary to maintain international peace and security. Measures taken by Members in the exercise of this right of self-defence shall be immediately reported to the Security Council and shall not in any way affect the authority and responsibility of the Security Council under the present Charter to take at any time such action as it deems necessary in order to maintain or restore international peace and security.

Chapter VIII: Regional Arrangements

Article 52

1. Nothing in the present Charter precludes the existence of regional arrangements or agencies for dealing with such matters relating to the maintenance of international peace and security as are appropriate for regional action provided that such arrangements or agencies and their activities are consistent with the Purposes and Principles of the United Nations.
2. The Members of the United Nations entering into such arrangements or constituting such agencies shall make every effort to achieve pacific settlement of local disputes through such regional arrangements or by such regional agencies before referring them to the Security Council.
3. The Security Council shall encourage the development of pacific settlement of local disputes through such regional arrangements or by such regional agencies either on the initiative of the states concerned or by reference from the Security Council.
4. This Article in no way impairs the application of Articles 34 and 35.

Article 53

1. The Security Council shall, where appropriate, utilize such regional arrangements or agencies for enforcement action under its authority. But no enforcement action shall be taken under regional arrangements or by regional agencies without the authorization of the Security Council, with the exception of measures against any enemy state, as defined in paragraph 2 of this Article, provided for pursuant to Article 107 or in regional arrangements directed against renewal of aggressive policy on the part of any such state, until such time as the Organization may, on request of the Governments concerned, be charged with the responsibility for preventing further aggression by such a state.

2. The term enemy state as used in paragraph 1 of this Article applies to any state which during the Second World War has been an enemy of any signatory of the present Charter.

Article 54
The Security Council shall at all times be kept fully informed of activities undertaken or in contemplation under regional arrangements or by regional agencies for the maintenance of international peace and security.

Chapter IX: International Economic and Social Co-operation

Article 55
With a view to the creation of conditions of stability and well-being which are necessary for peaceful and friendly relations among nations based on respect for the principle of equal rights and self-determination of peoples, the United Nations shall promote:

a. higher standards of living, full employment, and conditions of economic and social progress and development;
b. solutions of international economic, social, health, and related problems; and international cultural and educational cooperation; and
c. universal respect for, and observance of, human rights and fundamental freedoms for all without distinction as to race, sex, language, or religion.

Article 56
All Members pledge themselves to take joint and separate action in co-operation with the Organization for the achievement of the purposes set forth in Article 55.

Article 57

1. The various specialized agencies, established by intergovernmental agreement and having wide international responsibilities, as defined in their basic instruments, in economic, social, cultural, educational, health, and related fields, shall be brought into relationship with the United Nations in accordance with the provisions of Article 63.
2. Such agencies thus brought into relationship with the United Nations are hereinafter referred to as specialized agencies.

Article 58
The Organization shall make recommendations for the co-ordination of the policies and activities of the specialized agencies.

Article 59
The Organization shall, where appropriate, initiate negotiations among the states concerned for the creation of any new specialized agencies required for the accomplishment of the purposes set forth in Article 55.

Article 60
Responsibility for the discharge of the functions of the Organization set forth in this Chapter shall be vested in the General Assembly and, under the authority of

the General Assembly, in the Economic and Social Council, which shall have for this purpose the powers set forth in Chapter X.

Chapter X: The Economic and Social Council

Composition

Article 61

1. The Economic and Social Council shall consist of fifty-four Members of the United Nations elected by the General Assembly.
2. Subject to the provisions of paragraph 3, eighteen members of the Economic and Social Council shall be elected each year for a term of three years. A retiring member shall be eligible for immediate re-election.
3. At the first election after the increase in the membership of the Economic and Social Council from twenty-seven to fifty-four members, in addition to the members elected in place of the nine members whose term of office expires at the end of that year, twenty-seven additional members shall be elected. Of these twenty-seven additional members, the term of office of nine members so elected shall expire at the end of one year, and of nine other members at the end of two years, in accordance with arrangements made by the General Assembly.
4. Each member of the Economic and Social Council shall have one representative.

Functions and Powers

Article 62

1. The Economic and Social Council may make or initiate studies and reports with respect to international economic, social, cultural, educational, health, and related matters and may make recommendations with respect to any such matters to the General Assembly to the Members of the United Nations, and to the specialized agencies concerned.
2. It may make recommendations for the purpose of promoting respect for, and observance of, human rights and fundamental freedoms for all.
3. It may prepare draft conventions for submission to the General Assembly, with respect to matters falling within its competence.
4. It may call, in accordance with the rules prescribed by the United Nations, international conferences on matters falling within its competence.

Article 63

1. The Economic and Social Council may enter into agreements with any of the agencies referred to in Article 57, defining the terms on which the agency concerned shall be brought into relationship with the United Nations. Such agreements shall be subject to approval by the General Assembly.
2. It may co-ordinate the activities of the specialized agencies through consultation with and recommendations to such agencies and through

recommendations to the General Assembly and to the Members of the United Nations.

Article 64

1. The Economic and Social Council may take appropriate steps to obtain regular reports from the specialized agencies. It may make arrangements with the Members of the United Nations and with the specialized agencies to obtain reports on the steps taken to give effect to its own recommendations and to recommendations on matters falling within its competence made by the General Assembly.
2. It may communicate its observations on these reports to the General Assembly.

Article 65

The Economic and Social Council may furnish information to the Security Council and shall assist the Security Council upon its request.

Article 66

1. The Economic and Social Council shall perform such functions as fall within its competence in connection with the carrying out of the recommendations of the General Assembly.
2. It may, with the approval of the General Assembly, perform services at the request of Members of the United Nations and at the request of specialized agencies.
3. It shall perform such other functions as are specified elsewhere in the present Charter or as may be assigned to it by the General Assembly.

Voting

Article 67

1. Each member of the Economic and Social Council shall have one vote.
2. Decisions of the Economic and Social Council shall be made by a majority of the members present and voting.

Procedure

Article 68

The Economic and Social Council shall set up commissions in economic and social fields and for the promotion of human rights, and such other commissions as may be required for the performance of its functions.

Article 69

The Economic and Social Council shall invite any Member of the United Nations to participate, without vote, in its deliberations on any matter of particular concern to that Member.

Article 70

The Economic and Social Council may make arrangements for representatives of the specialized agencies to participate, without vote, in its deliberations and in those of the commissions established by it, and for its representatives to participate in the deliberations of the specialized agencies.

Article 71

The Economic and Social Council may make suitable arrangements for consultation with non-governmental organizations which are concerned with matters within its competence. Such arrangements may be made with international organizations and, where appropriate, with national organizations after consultation with the Member of the United Nations concerned.

Article 72

1. The Economic and Social Council shall adopt its own rules of procedure, including the method of selecting its President.
2. The Economic and Social Council shall meet as required in accordance with its rules, which shall include provision for the convening of meetings on the request of a majority of its members.

Chapter XI: Declaration regarding Non-Self-Governing Territories

Article 73

Members of the United Nations which have or assume responsibilities for the administration of territories whose peoples have not yet attained a full measure of self-government recognize the principle that the interests of the inhabitants of these territories are paramount, and accept as a sacred trust the obligation to promote to the utmost, within the system of international peace and security established by the present Charter, the well-being of the inhabitants of these territories, and, to this end:

a. to ensure, with due respect for the culture of the peoples concerned, their political, economic, social, and educational advancement, their just treatment, and their protection against abuses;
b. to develop self-government, to take due account of the political aspirations of the peoples, and to assist them in the progressive development of their free political institutions, according to the particular circumstances of each territory and its peoples and their varying stages of advancement;
c. to further international peace and security;
d. to promote constructive measures of development, to encourage research, and to co-operate with one another and, when and where appropriate, with specialized international bodies with a view to the practical achievement of the social, economic, and scientific purposes set forth in this Article; and
e. to transmit regularly to the Secretary-General for information purposes, subject to such limitation as security and constitutional considerations may require, statistical and other information of a technical nature relating to economic, social, and educational conditions in the territories for which they are respectively responsible other than those territories to which Chapters XII and XIII apply.

Article 74
Members of the United Nations also agree that their policy in respect of the territories to which this Chapter applies, no less than in respect of their metropolitan areas, must be based on the general principle of good-neighbourliness, due account being taken of the interests and well-being of the rest of the world, in social, economic, and commercial matters.

Chapter XII: International Trusteeship System

Article 75
The United Nations shall establish under its authority an international trusteeship system for the administration and supervision of such territories as may be placed thereunder by subsequent individual agreements. These territories are hereinafter referred to as trust territories.

Article 76
The basic objectives of the trusteeship system, in accordance with the Purposes of the United Nations laid down in Article 1 of the present Charter, shall be:

   a. to further international peace and security;
   b. to promote the political, economic, social, and educational advancement of the inhabitants of the trust territories, and their progressive development towards self-government or independence as may be appropriate to the particular circumstances of each territory and its peoples and the freely expressed wishes of the peoples concerned, and as may be provided by the terms of each trusteeship agreement;
   c. to encourage respect for human rights and for fundamental freedoms for all without distinction as to race, sex, language, or religion, and to encourage recognition of the interdependence of the peoples of the world; and
   d. to ensure equal treatment in social, economic, and commercial matters for all Members of the United Nations and their nationals, and also equal treatment for the latter in the administration of justice, without prejudice to the attainment of the foregoing objectives and subject to the provisions of Article 80.

Article 77

1. The trusteeship system shall apply to such territories in the following categories as may be placed thereunder by means of trusteeship agreements:
    a. territories now held under mandate;
    b. territories which may be detached from enemy states as a result of the Second World War; and
    c. territories voluntarily placed under the system by states responsible for their administration.
2. It will be a matter for subsequent agreement as to which territories in the foregoing categories will be brought under the trusteeship system and upon what terms.

Article 78

The trusteeship system shall not apply to territories which have become Members of the United Nations, relationship among which shall be based on respect for the principle of sovereign equality.

Article 79

The terms of trusteeship for each territory to be placed under the trusteeship system, including any alteration or amendment, shall be agreed upon by the states directly concerned, including the mandatory power in the case of territories held under mandate by a Member of the United Nations, and shall be approved as provided for in Articles 83 and 85.

Article 80

1. Except as may be agreed upon in individual trusteeship agreements, made under Articles 77, 79, and 81, placing each territory under the trusteeship system, and until such agreements have been concluded, nothing in this Chapter shall be construed in or of itself to alter in any manner the rights whatsoever of any states or any peoples or the terms of existing international instruments to which Members of the United Nations may respectively be parties.
2. Paragraph 1 of this Article shall not be interpreted as giving grounds for delay or postponement of the negotiation and conclusion of agreements for placing mandated and other territories under the trusteeship system as provided for in Article 77.

Article 81

The trusteeship agreement shall in each case include the terms under which the trust territory will be administered and designate the authority which will exercise the administration of the trust territory. Such authority, hereinafter called the administering authority, may be one or more states or the Organization itself.

Article 82

There may be designated, in any trusteeship agreement, a strategic area or areas which may include part or all of the trust territory to which the agreement applies, without prejudice to any special agreement or agreements made under Article 43.

Article 83

1. All functions of the United Nations relating to strategic areas, including the approval of the terms of the trusteeship agreements and of their alteration or amendment shall be exercised by the Security Council.
2. The basic objectives set forth in Article 76 shall be applicable to the people of each strategic area.
3. The Security Council shall, subject to the provisions of the trusteeship agreements and without prejudice to security considerations, avail itself of the assistance of the Trusteeship Council to perform those functions of the United Nations under the trusteeship system relating to political, economic, social, and educational matters in the strategic areas.

Article 84

It shall be the duty of the administering authority to ensure that the trust territory shall play its part in the maintenance of international peace and security. To this end the administering authority may make use of volunteer forces, facilities, and assistance from the trust territory in carrying out the obligations towards the Security Council undertaken in this regard by the administering authority, as well as for local defence and the maintenance of law and order within the trust territory.

Article 85

1. The functions of the United Nations with regard to trusteeship agreements for all areas not designated as strategic, including the approval of the terms of the trusteeship agreements and of their alteration or amendment, shall be exercised by the General Assembly.
2. The Trusteeship Council, operating under the authority of the General Assembly shall assist the General Assembly in carrying out these functions.

Chapter XIII: The Trusteeship Council

Composition

Article 86

1. The Trusteeship Council shall consist of the following Members of the United Nations:
    a. those Members administering trust territories;
    b. such of those Members mentioned by name in Article 23 as are not administering trust territories; and
    c. as many other Members elected for three-year terms by the General Assembly as may be necessary to ensure that the total number of members of the Trusteeship Council is equally divided between those Members of the United Nations which administer trust territories and those which do not.
2. Each member of the Trusteeship Council shall designate one specially qualified person to represent it therein.

Functions and Powers

Article 87

The General Assembly and, under its authority, the Trusteeship Council, in carrying out their functions, may:

a. consider reports submitted by the administering authority;
b. accept petitions and examine them in consultation with the administering authority;
c. provide for periodic visits to the respective trust territories at times agreed upon with the administering authority; and
d. take these and other actions in conformity with the terms of the trusteeship agreements.

Article 88

The Trusteeship Council shall formulate a questionnaire on the political, economic, social, and educational advancement of the inhabitants of each trust territory, and the administering authority for each trust territory within the competence of the General Assembly shall make an annual report to the General Assembly upon the basis of such questionnaire.

Voting

Article 89

1. Each member of the Trusteeship Council shall have one vote.
2. Decisions of the Trusteeship Council shall be made by a majority of the members present and voting.

Procedure

Article 90

1. The Trusteeship Council shall adopt its own rules of procedure, including the method of selecting its President.
2. The Trusteeship Council shall meet as required in accordance with its rules, which shall include provision for the convening of meetings on the request of a majority of its members.

Article 91

The Trusteeship Council shall, when appropriate, avail itself of the assistance of the Economic and Social Council and of the specialized agencies in regard to matters with which they are respectively concerned.

Chapter XIV: The International Court of Justice

Article 92

The International Court of Justice shall be the principal judicial organ of the United Nations. It shall function in accordance with the annexed Statute, which is based upon the Statute of the Permanent Court of International Justice and forms an integral part of the present Charter.

Article 93

1. All Members of the United Nations are ipso facto parties to the Statute of the International Court of Justice.
2. A state which is not a Member of the United Nations may become a party to the Statute of the International Court of Justice on conditions to be determined in each case by the General Assembly upon the recommendation of the Security Council.

Article 94

1. Each Member of the United Nations undertakes to comply with the decision of the International Court of Justice in any case to which it is a party.

2. If any party to a case fails to perform the obligations incumbent upon it under a judgment rendered by the Court, the other party may have recourse to the Security Council, which may, if it deems necessary, make recommendations or decide upon measures to be taken to give effect to the judgment.

Article 95
Nothing in the present Charter shall prevent Members of the United Nations from entrusting the solution of their differences to other tribunals by virtue of agreements already in existence or which may be concluded in the future.

Article 96

a. The General Assembly or the Security Council may request the International Court of Justice to give an advisory opinion on any legal question.
b. Other organs of the United Nations and specialized agencies, which may at any time be so authorized by the General Assembly, may also request advisory opinions of the Court on legal questions arising within the scope of their activities.

Chapter XV: The Secretariat

Article 97
The Secretariat shall comprise a Secretary-General and such staff as the Organization may require. The Secretary-General shall be appointed by the General Assembly upon the recommendation of the Security Council. He shall be the chief administrative officer of the Organization.

Article 98
The Secretary-General shall act in that capacity in all meetings of the General Assembly, of the Security Council, of the Economic and Social Council, and of the Trusteeship Council, and shall perform such other functions as are entrusted to him by these organs. The Secretary-General shall make an annual report to the General Assembly on the work of the Organization.

Article 99
The Secretary-General may bring to the attention of the Security Council any matter which in his opinion may threaten the maintenance of international peace and security.

Article 100

1. In the performance of their duties the Secretary-General and the staff shall not seek or receive instructions from any government or from any other authority external to the Organization. They shall refrain from any action which might reflect on their position as international officials responsible only to the Organization.
2. Each Member of the United Nations undertakes to respect the exclusively international character of the responsibilities of the Secretary-General

and the staff and not to seek to influence them in the discharge of their responsibilities.

Article 101

1. The staff shall be appointed by the Secretary-General under regulations established by the General Assembly.
2. Appropriate staffs shall be permanently assigned to the Economic and Social Council, the Trusteeship Council, and, as required, to other organs of the United Nations. These staffs shall form a part of the Secretariat.
3. The paramount consideration in the employment of the staff and in the determination of the conditions of service shall be the necessity of securing the highest standards of efficiency, competence, and integrity. Due regard shall be paid to the importance of recruiting the staff on as wide a geographical basis as possible.

Chapter XVI: Miscellaneous Provisions

Article 102

1. Every treaty and every international agreement entered into by any Member of the United Nations after the present Charter comes into force shall as soon as possible be registered with the Secretariat and published by it.
2. No party to any such treaty or international agreement which has not been registered in accordance with the provisions of paragraph 1 of this Article may invoke that treaty or agreement before any organ of the United Nations.

Article 103

In the event of a conflict between the obligations of the Members of the United Nations under the present Charter and their obligations under any other international agreement, their obligations under the present Charter shall prevail.

Article 104

The Organization shall enjoy in the territory of each of its Members such legal capacity as may be necessary for the exercise of its functions and the fulfilment of its purposes.

Article 105

1. The Organization shall enjoy in the territory of each of its Members such privileges and immunities as are necessary for the fulfilment of its purposes.
2. Representatives of the Members of the United Nations and officials of the Organization shall similarly enjoy such privileges and immunities as are necessary for the independent exercise of their functions in connection with the Organization.
3. The General Assembly may make recommendations with a view to determining the details of the application of paragraphs 1 and 2 of this

Article or may propose conventions to the Members of the United Nations for this purpose.

Chapter XVII: Transitional Security Arrangements

Article 106
Pending the coming into force of such special agreements referred to in Article 43 as in the opinion of the Security Council enable it to begin the exercise of its responsibilities under Article 42, the parties to the Four-Nation Declaration, signed at Moscow, 30 October 1943, and France, shall, in accordance with the provisions of paragraph 5 of that Declaration, consult with one another and as occasion requires with other Members of the United Nations with a view to such joint action on behalf of the Organization as may be necessary for the purpose of maintaining international peace and security.

Article 107
Nothing in the present Charter shall invalidate or preclude action, in relation to any state which during the Second World War has been an enemy of any signatory to the present Charter, taken or authorized as a result of that war by the Governments having responsibility for such action.

Chapter XVIII: Amendments

Article 108
Amendments to the present Charter shall come into force for all Members of the United Nations when they have been adopted by a vote of two thirds of the members of the General Assembly and ratified in accordance with their respective constitutional processes by two thirds of the Members of the United Nations, including all the permanent members of the Security Council.

Article 109

1. A General Conference of the Members of the United Nations for the purpose of reviewing the present Charter may be held at a date and place to be fixed by a two-thirds vote of the members of the General Assembly and by a vote of any nine members of the Security Council. Each Member of the United Nations shall have one vote in the conference.
2. Any alteration of the present Charter recommended by a two-thirds vote of the conference shall take effect when ratified in accordance with their respective constitutional processes by two thirds of the Members of the United Nations including all the permanent members of the Security Council.
3. If such a conference has not been held before the tenth annual session of the General Assembly following the coming into force of the present Charter, the proposal to call such a conference shall be placed on the agenda of that session of the General Assembly, and the conference shall be held if so decided by a majority vote of the members of the General Assembly and by a vote of any seven members of the Security Council.

Chapter XIX: Ratification and Signature

Article 110

1. The present Charter shall be ratified by the signatory states in accordance with their respective constitutional processes.
2. The ratifications shall be deposited with the Government of the United States of America, which shall notify all the signatory states of each deposit as well as the Secretary-General of the Organization when he has been appointed.
3. The present Charter shall come into force upon the deposit of ratifications by the Republic of China, France, the Union of Soviet Socialist Republics, the United Kingdom of Great Britain and Northern Ireland, and the United States of America, and by a majority of the other signatory states. A protocol of the ratifications deposited shall thereupon be drawn up by the Government of the United States of America which shall communicate copies thereof to all the signatory states.
4. The states signatory to the present Charter which ratify it after it has come into force will become original Members of the United Nations on the date of the deposit of their respective ratifications.

Article 111

The present Charter, of which the Chinese, French, Russian, English, and Spanish texts are equally authentic, shall remain deposited in the archives of the Government of the United States of America. Duly certified copies thereof shall be transmitted by that Government to the Governments of the other signatory states.

IN FAITH WHEREOF the representatives of the Governments of the United Nations have signed the present Charter.

DONE at the city of San Francisco the twenty-sixth day of June, one thousand nine hundred and forty-five.

Source: United Nations, *Charter of the United Nations*, 1945, available at: https://www.un.org/en/charter-united-nations/

UNIVERSAL DECLARATION OF HUMAN RIGHTS

Preamble

Whereas recognition of the inherent dignity and of the equal and inalienable rights of all members of the human family is the foundation of freedom, justice and peace in the world,

Whereas disregard and contempt for human rights have resulted in barbarous acts which have outraged the conscience of mankind, and the advent of a world in which human beings shall enjoy freedom of speech and belief and freedom from fear and want has been proclaimed as the highest aspiration of the common people,

Whereas it is essential, if man is not to be compelled to have recourse, as a last resort, to rebellion against tyranny and oppression, that human rights should be protected by the rule of law,

Whereas it is essential to promote the development of friendly relations between nations,

Whereas the peoples of the United Nations have in the Charter reaffirmed their faith in fundamental human rights, in the dignity and worth of the human person and in the equal rights of men and women and have determined to promote social progress and better standards of life in larger freedom,

Whereas Member States have pledged themselves to achieve, in co-operation with the United Nations, the promotion of universal respect for and observance of human rights and fundamental freedoms,

Whereas a common understanding of these rights and freedoms is of the greatest importance for the full realization of this pledge,

Now, therefore,

The General Assembly

Proclaims this Universal Declaration of Human Rights as a common standard of achievement for all peoples and all nations, to the end that every individual and every organ of society, keeping this Declaration constantly in mind, shall strive by teaching and education to promote respect for these rights and freedoms and by progressive measures, national and international, to secure their universal and effective recognition and observance, both among the peoples of Member States themselves and among the peoples of territories under their jurisdiction.

Article 1

All human beings are born free and equal in dignity and rights. They are endowed with reason and conscience and should act towards one another in a spirit of brotherhood.

Article 2

Everyone is entitled to all the rights and freedoms set forth in this Declaration, without distinction of any kind, such as race, colour, sex, language, religion, political or other opinion, national or social origin, property, birth or other status.

Furthermore, no distinction shall be made on the basis of the political, jurisdictional or international status of the country or territory to which a person belongs, whether it be independent, trust, non-self-governing or under any other limitation of sovereignty.

Article 3

Everyone has the right to life, liberty and security of person.

Article 4

No one shall be held in slavery or servitude; slavery and the slave trade shall be prohibited in all their forms.

Article 5

No one shall be subjected to torture or to cruel, inhuman or degrading treatment or punishment.

Article 6

Everyone has the right to recognition everywhere as a person before the law.

Article 7

All are equal before the law and are entitled without any discrimination to equal protection of the law. All are entitled to equal protection against any discrimination in violation of this Declaration and against any incitement to such discrimination.

Article 8

Everyone has the right to an effective remedy by the competent national tribunals for acts violating the fundamental rights granted him by the constitution or by law.

Article 9

No one shall be subjected to arbitrary arrest, detention or exile.

Article 10

Everyone is entitled in full equality to a fair and public hearing by an independent and impartial tribunal, in the determination of his rights and obligations and of any criminal charge against him.

Article 11

1. Everyone charged with a penal offence has the right to be presumed innocent until proved guilty according to law in a public trial at which he has had all the guarantees necessary for his defence.
2. No one shall be held guilty of any penal offence on account of any act or omission which did not constitute a penal offence, under national or international law, at the time when it was committed. Nor shall a heavier penalty be imposed than the one that was applicable at the time the penal offence was committed.

Article 12

No one shall be subjected to arbitrary interference with his privacy, family, home or correspondence, nor to attacks upon his honour and reputation. Everyone has the right to the protection of the law against such interference or attacks.

Article 13

1. Everyone has the right to freedom of movement and residence within the borders of each State.
2. Everyone has the right to leave any country, including his own, and to return to his country.

Article 14

1. Everyone has the right to seek and to enjoy in other countries asylum from persecution.
2. This right may not be invoked in the case of prosecutions genuinely arising from non-political crimes or from acts contrary to the purposes and principles of the United Nations.

Article 15

1. Everyone has the right to a nationality.
2. No one shall be arbitrarily deprived of his nationality nor denied the right to change his nationality.

Article 16

1. Men and women of full age, without any limitation due to race, nationality or religion, have the right to marry and to found a family. They are entitled to equal rights as to marriage, during marriage and at its dissolution.
2. Marriage shall be entered into only with the free and full consent of the intending spouses.
3. The family is the natural and fundamental group unit of society and is entitled to protection by society and the State.

Article 17

1. Everyone has the right to own property alone as well as in association with others.
2. No one shall be arbitrarily deprived of his property.

Article 18

Everyone has the right to freedom of thought, conscience and religion; this right includes freedom to change his religion or belief, and freedom, either alone or in community with others and in public or private, to manifest his religion or belief in teaching, practice, worship and observance.

Article 19

Everyone has the right to freedom of opinion and expression; this right includes freedom to hold opinions without interference and to seek, receive and impart information and ideas through any media and regardless of frontiers.

Article 20

1. Everyone has the right to freedom of peaceful assembly and association.
2. No one may be compelled to belong to an association.

Article 21

1. Everyone has the right to take part in the government of his country, directly or through freely chosen representatives.
2. Everyone has the right of equal access to public service in his country.
3. The will of the people shall be the basis of the authority of government; this will shall be expressed in periodic and genuine elections which shall be by universal and equal suffrage and shall be held by secret vote or by equivalent free voting procedures.

Article 22

Everyone, as a member of society, has the right to social security and is entitled to realization, through national effort and international co-operation and in accordance with the organization and resources of each State, of the economic, social and cultural rights indispensable for his dignity and the free development of his personality.

Article 23

1. Everyone has the right to work, to free choice of employment, to just and favourable conditions of work and to protection against unemployment.
2. Everyone, without any discrimination, has the right to equal pay for equal work.
3. Everyone who works has the right to just and favourable remuneration ensuring for himself and his family an existence worthy of human dignity, and supplemented, if necessary, by other means of social protection.
4. Everyone has the right to form and to join trade unions for the protection of his interests.

Article 24

Everyone has the right to rest and leisure, including reasonable limitation of working hours and periodic holidays with pay.

Article 25

1. Everyone has the right to a standard of living adequate for the health and well-being of himself and of his family, including food, clothing, housing and medical care and necessary social services, and the right to security in the event of unemployment, sickness, disability, widowhood, old age or other lack of livelihood in circumstances beyond his control.
2. Motherhood and childhood are entitled to special care and assistance. All children, whether born in or out of wedlock, shall enjoy the same social protection.

Article 26

1. Everyone has the right to education. Education shall be free, at least in the elementary and fundamental stages. Elementary education shall be compulsory. Technical and professional education shall be made generally available and higher education shall be equally accessible to all on the basis of merit.
2. Education shall be directed to the full development of the human personality and to the strengthening of respect for human rights and fundamental freedoms. It shall promote understanding, tolerance and friendship among all nations, racial or religious groups, and shall further the activities of the United Nations for the maintenance of peace.
3. Parents have a prior right to choose the kind of education that shall be given to their children.

Article 27

1. Everyone has the right freely to participate in the cultural life of the community, to enjoy the arts and to share in scientific advancement and its benefits.
2. Everyone has the right to the protection of the moral and material interests resulting from any scientific, literary or artistic production of which he is the author.

Article 28

Everyone is entitled to a social and international order in which the rights and freedoms set forth in this Declaration can be fully realized.

Article 29

1. Everyone has duties to the community in which alone the free and full development of his personality is possible.
2. In the exercise of his rights and freedoms, everyone shall be subject only to such limitations as are determined by law solely for the purpose of securing due recognition and respect for the rights and freedoms of others and of meeting the just requirements of morality, public order and the general welfare in a democratic society.
3. These rights and freedoms may in no case be exercised contrary to the purposes and principles of the United Nations.

Article 30

Nothing in this Declaration may be interpreted as implying for any State, group or person any right to engage in any activity or to perform any act aimed at the destruction of any of the rights and freedoms set forth herein.

Source: UN General Assembly. *Universal Declaration of Human Rights.* UN General Assembly Resolution 217A (III), A/810 at 71, 1948.

United Nations General Assembly   A/RES/73/241

Seventy-third session
Agenda item 22 (b)

**Resolution adopted by the General Assembly
on 20 December 2018**

[*on the report of the Second Committee (A/73/540/Add.2)*]

73/241. International migration and development

The General Assembly,

Recalling its resolutions 58/208 of 23 December 2003, 59/241 of 22 December 2004, 60/227 of 23 December 2005, 61/208 of 20 December 2006, 63/225 of 19 December 2008, 65/170 of 20 December 2010, 67/219 of 21 December 2012, 69/229 of 19 December 2014 and 71/237 of 21 December 2016 on international migration and development, its resolution 68/4 of 3 October 2013, by which it adopted the Declaration of the High-level Dialogue on International Migration and Development, its resolution 60/206 of 22 December 2005 on the facilitation and reduction of the cost of transfer of migrant remittances, its resolutions 62/156 of 18 December 2007, 64/166 of 18 December 2009, 66/172 of 19 December 2011, 68/179 of 18 December 2013, 69/167 of 18 December 2014 and 70/147 of 17 December 2015 on the protection of migrants and its resolution 62/270 of 20 June 2008 on the Global Forum on Migration and Development, and recalling also chapter X of the Programme of Action of the International Conference on Population and Development[1] and Commission on Population and Development resolutions 2006/2 of 10 May 2006,[2] 2008/1 of 11 April 2008,[3] 2013/1 of 26 April 2013[4] and 2014/1 of 11 April 2014,[5]

Reaffirming its resolution 70/1 of 25 September 2015, entitled "Transforming our world: the 2030 Agenda for Sustainable Development", in which it adopted a comprehensive, far-reaching and people-centred set of universal and transformative Sustainable Development Goals and targets, its commitment to working tirelessly for the full implementation of the Agenda by 2030, its recognition that eradicating poverty in all its forms and dimensions, including extreme poverty, is the greatest global challenge and an indispensable requirement for sustainable development, its commitment to achieving sustainable development in its three dimensions—economic, social and environmental—in a balanced and integrated manner, and to building upon the achievements of the Millennium Development Goals and seeking to address their unfinished business,

---

1 *Report of the International Conference on Population and Development, Cairo, 5–13 September 1994* (United Nations publication, Sales No. E.95.XIII.18), chap. I, resolution 1, annex.
2 See *Official Records of the Economic and Social Council, 2006, Supplement No. 5* (E/2006/25), chap. I, sect. B.
3 Ibid., 2008, *Supplement No. 5* (E/2008/25), chap. I, sect. B.
4 Ibid., 2013, *Supplement No. 5* (E/2013/25), chap. I, sect. B.
5 Ibid., 2014, *Supplement No. 5* (E/2014/25), chap. I, sect. B.

Reaffirming also its resolution 69/313 of 27 July 2015 on the Addis Ababa Action Agenda of the Third International Conference on Financing for Development, which is an integral part of the 2030 Agenda for Sustainable Development, supports and complements it, helps to contextualize its means of implementation targets with concrete policies and actions, and reaffirms the strong political commitment to address the challenge of financing and creating an enabling environment at all levels for sustainable development in the spirit of global partnership and solidarity,

Reaffirming further the New York Declaration for Refugees and Migrants, adopted at the high-level plenary meeting of the General Assembly on addressing large movements of refugees and migrants, held at United Nations Headquarters on 19 September 2016,[6]

Reaffirming the New Urban Agenda, which was adopted at the United Nations Conference on Housing and Sustainable Urban Development (Habitat III), held in Quito from 17 to 20 October 2016,[7] and recognizing the linkages between migration and sustainable urbanization and sustainable urban development,

Reaffirming also the Paris Agreement,[8] and encouraging all its parties to fully implement the Agreement, and parties to the United Nations Framework Convention on Climate Change[9] that have not yet done so to deposit their instruments of ratification, acceptance, approval or accession, where appropriate, as soon as possible,

Recalling the Sendai Declaration and the Sendai Framework for Disaster Risk Reduction 2015–2030, adopted at the Third United Nations World Conference on Disaster Risk Reduction,[10] and those provisions that are applicable to migrants,

Recalling also the second High-level Dialogue on International Migration and Development, held in New York on 3 and 4 October 2013, which addressed constructively the issue of international migration and development and explored the opportunities and the challenges that international migration presents, including the protection of the human rights of migrants and the contribution of migrants to development,

Recalling further the Declaration of the High-level Dialogue on International Migration and Development adopted on 3 October 2013 on the occasion of the High-level Dialogue,

Reaffirming the Universal Declaration of Human Rights,[11] recalling the International Covenant on Civil and Political Rights,[12] the International Covenant on Economic, Social and Cultural Rights,[12] the International Convention on the Elimination of All Forms of Racial Discrimination,[13] the Convention on the

---

6 Resolution 71/1.
7 Resolution 71/256, annex.
8 Adopted under the UNFCCC in FCCC/CP/2015/10/Add.1, decision 1/CP.21.
9 United Nations, *Treaty Series*, vol. 1771, No. 30822.
10 Resolution 69/283, annexes I and II.
11 Resolution 217 A (III).
12 See resolution 2200 A (XXI), annex.

Elimination of All Forms of Discrimination against Women,[14] the Convention on the Rights of the Child[15] and the Convention on the Rights of Persons with Disabilities,[16] and recalling also the Declaration on the Right to Development,[17]

Encouraging States that have not done so to consider ratifying or acceding to the International Convention on the Protection of the Rights of All Migrant Workers and Members of Their Families[18] and to consider acceding to relevant conventions of the International Labour Organization, as appropriate,

Recalling the importance of the decent work agenda of the International Labour Organization, including for migrant workers, the eight fundamental Conventions of that Organization and the Global Jobs Pact adopted by the International Labour Conference at its ninety-eighth session as a general framework within which each country can formulate policy packages specific to its situation and national priorities in order to promote a job-intensive recovery and sustainable development,

Recognizing the valuable contribution of the Global Forum on Migration and Development to addressing the multidimensional nature of international migration and promoting balanced and comprehensive approaches and dialogue on migration and development, and acknowledging that it has proved to be a valuable forum for holding frank and open discussions, including through multi-stakeholder dialogues, and that it has helped to build trust among participating stakeholders through the exchange of experiences and good practices and by virtue of its voluntary, intergovernmental, non-binding and informal character and the engagement of civil society actors as well as the private sector,

Acknowledging the important and complex interrelationship between international migration and development and the need to deal with the challenges and opportunities that migration presents to countries of origin, transit and destination, recognizing that migration brings benefits and challenges to the global community, and confirming the importance of including the matter in relevant debates and discussions held at the global, regional and national levels, as appropriate, including at the level of the United Nations and other international organizations, in relation to development,

1. *Takes note* of the report of the Secretary-General;[19]
2. *Recognizes* the need to strengthen synergies between international migration and development at all levels, including the global, regional, national and local levels, as appropriate;
3. *Recommits* to ensuring full respect for the human rights and fundamental freedoms of all migrants, regardless of their migration status, and

---

13 United Nations, *Treaty Series*, vol. 660, No. 9464.
14 Ibid., vol. 1249, No. 20378.
15 Ibid., vol. 1577, No. 27531.
16 Ibid., vol. 2515, No. 44910.
17 Resolution 41/128, annex.
18 United Nations, *Treaty Series*, vol. 2220, No. 39481.
19 A/73/286.

supporting countries of origin, transit and destination in the spirit of international cooperation, taking into account national circumstances;

4. *Notes* the convening of the Intergovernmental Conference to Adopt the Global Compact for Safe, Orderly and Regular Migration in Marrakech, Morocco, on 10 and 11 December 2018;

5. *Also notes* that the Global Compact for Safe, Orderly and Regular Migration[20] is the first intergovernmentally negotiated outcome, prepared under the auspices of the United Nations, to cover international migration in all its dimensions;

6. *Recognizes* that the High-level Dialogues on International Migration and Development have served as forums to advance discussions on the multidimensional aspects of international migration and development in order to identify appropriate ways and means to maximize its development benefits and minimize its negative impacts;

7. *Notes* that, with the adoption of the Global Compact, the High-level Dialogue on International Migration and Development shall be repurposed into the International Migration Review Forum, which will serve as the primary intergovernmental global platform for Member States to discuss and share progress on the implementation of all aspects of the Global Compact, including as it relates to the 2030 Agenda for Sustainable Development,[21] and with the participation of all relevant stakeholders, and that the Forum is to be held every four years, beginning in 2022;

8. *Decides* to convene, in the first half of 2019, a one-day high-level debate on international migration and development, under the auspices of the President of the General Assembly, in lieu of the 2019 High-level Dialogue, to inform the high-level political forum on sustainable development, which will review the Goals and targets relevant to migration of the 2030 Agenda for Sustainable Development, taking into consideration the outcomes of other processes related to international migration and development;

9. *Welcomes* the decision of the Secretary-General to establish a United Nations network on migration;

10. *Requests* the Secretary-General to submit to the General Assembly, at its seventy-fifth session, a report on the implementation of the present resolution;

11. *Decides* to include in the provisional agenda of its seventy-fifth session, under the item entitled "Globalization and interdependence", the sub-item entitled "International migration and development".

62nd plenary meeting
20 December 2018

Source: United Nations General Assembly, Resolution 73/241 (2018).

---

20 Resolution 73/195, annex.
21 Resolution 70/1.

United Nations Security Council   **S/RES/1325 (2000)**

Resolution 1325 (2000)

Adopted by the Security Council at its 4213th meeting, on 31 October 2000

The Security Council,

Recalling its resolutions 1261 (1999) of 25 August 1999, 1265 (1999) of 17 September 1999, 1296 (2000) of 19 April 2000 and 1314 (2000) of 11 August 2000, as well as relevant statements of its President, and *recalling also* the statement of its President to the press on the occasion of the United Nations Day for Women's Rights and International Peace (International Women's Day) of 8 March 2000 (SC/6816),

Recalling also the commitments of the Beijing Declaration and Platform for Action (A/52/231) as well as those contained in the outcome document of the twenty-third Special Session of the United Nations General Assembly entitled "Women 2000: Gender Equality, Development and Peace for the Twenty-First Century" (A/S-23/10/Rev.1), in particular those concerning women and armed conflict,

Bearing in mind the purposes and principles of the Charter of the United Nations and the primary responsibility of the Security Council under the Charter for the maintenance of international peace and security,

Expressing concern that civilians, particularly women and children, account for the vast majority of those adversely affected by armed conflict, including as refugees and internally displaced persons, and increasingly are targeted by combatants and armed elements, and *recognizing* the consequent impact this has on durable peace and reconciliation,

Reaffirming the important role of women in the prevention and resolution of conflicts and in peace-building, and *stressing* the importance of their equal participation and full involvement in all efforts for the maintenance and promotion of peace and security, and the need to increase their role in decision-making with regard to conflict prevention and resolution,

Reaffirming also the need to implement fully international humanitarian and human rights law that protects the rights of women and girls during and after conflicts,

Emphasizing the need for all parties to ensure that mine clearance and mine awareness programmes take into account the special needs of women and girls,

Recognizing the urgent need to mainstream a gender perspective into peacekeeping operations, and in this regard *noting* the Windhoek Declaration and the Namibia Plan of Action on Mainstreaming a Gender Perspective in Multidimensional Peace Support Operations (S/2000/693),

Recognizing also the importance of the recommendation contained in the statement of its President to the press of 8 March 2000 for specialized training for all peacekeeping personnel on the protection, special needs and human rights of women and children in conflict situations,

Recognizing that an understanding of the impact of armed conflict on women and girls, effective institutional arrangements to guarantee their protection and full participation in the peace process can significantly contribute to the maintenance and promotion of international peace and security,

Noting the need to consolidate data on the impact of armed conflict on women and girls,

1. *Urges* Member States to ensure increased representation of women at all decision-making levels in national, regional and international institutions and mechanisms for the prevention, management, and resolution of conflict;
2. *Encourages* the Secretary-General to implement his strategic plan of action (A/49/587) calling for an increase in the participation of women at decision-making levels in conflict resolution and peace processes;
3. *Urges* the Secretary-General to appoint more women as special representatives and envoys to pursue good offices on his behalf, and in this regard *calls on* Member States to provide candidates to the Secretary-General, for inclusion in a regularly updated centralized roster;
4. *Further urges* the Secretary-General to seek to expand the role and contribution of women in United Nations field-based operations, and especially among military observers, civilian police, human rights and humanitarian personnel;
5. *Expresses* its willingness to incorporate a gender perspective into peacekeeping operations, and *urges* the Secretary-General to ensure that, where appropriate, field operations include a gender component;
6. *Requests* the Secretary-General to provide to Member States training guidelines and materials on the protection, rights and the particular needs of women, as well as on the importance of involving women in all peacekeeping and peace-building measures, *invites* Member States to incorporate these elements as well as HIV/AIDS awareness training into their national training programmes for military and civilian police personnel in preparation for deployment, and *further requests* the Secretary-General to ensure that civilian personnel of peacekeeping operations receive similar training;
7. *Urges* Member States to increase their voluntary financial, technical and logistical support for gender-sensitive training efforts, including those undertaken by relevant funds and programmes, inter alia, the United Nations Fund for Women and United Nations Children's Fund, and by the Office of the United Nations High Commissioner for Refugees and other relevant bodies;

8. *Calls on* all actors involved, when negotiating and implementing peace agreements, to adopt a gender perspective, including, inter alia:
    a. The special needs of women and girls during repatriation and resettlement and for rehabilitation, reintegration and post-conflict reconstruction;
    b. Measures that support local women's peace initiatives and indigenous processes for conflict resolution, and that involve women in all of the implementation mechanisms of the peace agreements;
    c. Measures that ensure the protection of and respect for human rights of women and girls, particularly as they relate to the constitution, the electoral system, the police and the judiciary;
9. *Calls upon* all parties to armed conflict to respect fully international law applicable to the rights and protection of women and girls, especially as civilians, in particular the obligations applicable to them under the Geneva Conventions of 1949 and the Additional Protocols thereto of 1977, the Refugee Convention of 1951 and the Protocol thereto of 1967, the Convention on the Elimination of All Forms of Discrimination against Women of 1979 and the Optional Protocol thereto of 1999 and the United Nations Convention on the Rights of the Child of 1989 and the two Optional Protocols thereto of 25 May 2000, and to bear in mind the relevant provisions of the Rome Statute of the International Criminal Court;
10. *Calls on* all parties to armed conflict to take special measures to protect women and girls from gender-based violence, particularly rape and other forms of sexual abuse, and all other forms of violence in situations of armed conflict;
11. *Emphasizes* the responsibility of all States to put an end to impunity and to prosecute those responsible for genocide, crimes against humanity, and war crimes including those relating to sexual and other violence against women and girls, and in this regard *stresses* the need to exclude these crimes, where feasible from amnesty provisions;
12. *Calls upon* all parties to armed conflict to respect the civilian and humanitarian character of refugee camps and settlements, and to take into account the particular needs of women and girls, including in their design, and recalls its resolutions 1208 (1998) of 19 November 1998 and 1296 (2000) of 19 April 2000;
13. *Encourages* all those involved in the planning for disarmament, demobilization and reintegration to consider the different needs of female and male ex-combatants and to take into account the needs of their dependants;
14. *Reaffirms* its readiness, whenever measures are adopted under Article 41 of the Charter of the United Nations, to give consideration to their potential impact on the civilian population, bearing in mind the special needs of women and girls, in order to consider appropriate humanitarian exemptions;

15. *Expresses* its willingness to ensure that Security Council missions take into account gender considerations and the rights of women, including through consultation with local and international women's groups;
16. *Invites* the Secretary-General to carry out a study on the impact of armed conflict on women and girls, the role of women in peace-building and the gender dimensions of peace processes and conflict resolution, and *further invites* him to submit a report to the Security Council on the results of this study and to make this available to all Member States of the United Nations;
17. *Requests* the Secretary-General, where appropriate, to include in his reporting to the Security Council progress on gender mainstreaming throughout peacekeeping missions and all other aspects relating to women and girls;
18. *Decides* to remain actively seized of the matter.

Source: United Nations Security Council, Resolution 1325 (2000).

Appendix: United Nations International Days (as of 2020)

January 4—World Braille Day

January 24—International Day of Education

January 27—International Day of Commemoration in Memory of the Victims of the Holocaust

February 6—International Day of Zero Tolerance to Female Genital Mutilation

February 10—World Pulses Day

February 11—International Day of Women and Girls in Science

February 13—World Radio Day

February 20—World Day of Social Justice

February 21—International Mother Language Day

March 1—Zero Discrimination Day

March 3—World Wildlife Day

March 8—International Women's Day

March 20—International Day of Happiness

March 20—French Language Day

March 21—International Day for the Elimination of Racial Discrimination

March 21—World Poetry Day

March 21—International Day of Nowruz

March 21—World Down Syndrome Day

March 21—International Day of Forests

March 22—World Water Day

March 23—World Meteorological Day

March 24—World Tuberculosis Day

March 24—International Day for the Right to the Truth Concerning Gross Human Rights Violations and for the Dignity of Victims

March 25—International Day of Remembrance of the Victims of Slavery and the Transatlantic Slave Trade

March 25—International Day of Solidarity with Detained and Missing Staff Members

April 2—World Autism Awareness Day

April 4—International Day for Mine Awareness and Assistance in Mine Action

April 5—International Day of Conscience

April 6—International Day of Sport for Development and Peace

April 7—International Day of Reflection on the 1994 Genocide against the Tutsi in Rwanda

April 7—World Health Day

April 12—International Day of Human Space Flight

April 14—World Chagas Disease Day

April 20—Chinese Language Day

April 21—World Creativity and Innovation Day

April 22—International Mother Earth Day

April 23—World Book and Copyright Day

April 23—English Language Day

April 23—Spanish Language Day

April (Fourth Thursday)—International Girls in ICT Day

April 24—International Day of Multilateralism and Diplomacy for Peace

April 25—International Delegate's Day

April 25—World Malaria Day

April 26—International Chernobyl Disaster Remembrance Day

April 26—World Intellectual Property Day

April 28—World Day for Safety and Health at Work

April 30—International Jazz Day

May 2—World Tuna Day

May 3—World Press Freedom Day

May—"Vesak," the Day of the Full Moon

May 8–9—Time of Remembrance and Reconciliation for Those Who Lost Lives during the Second World War

May (Second Saturday)—World Migratory Bird Day

May 15—International Day of Families

May 16—International Day of Living Together in Peace

May 16—International Day of Light

May 17—World Telecommunication and Information Society Day

May 20—World Bee Day

May 21—International Tea Day

May 21—World Day for Cultural Diversity for Dialogue and Development

May 22—International Day for Biological Diversity
May 23—International Day to End Obstetric Fistula
May 29—International Day of UN Peacekeepers
May 31—World No Tobacco Day
June 1—Global Day of Parents
June 3—World Bicycle Day
June 4—International Day of Innocent Children Victims of Aggression
June 5—World Environment Day
June 5—International Day for the Fight against Illegal, Unreported and Unregulated Fishing
June 6—Russian Language Day
June 7—World Food Safety Day
June 8—World Oceans Day
June 12—World Day Against Child Labour
June 13—International Albinism Awareness Day
June 14—World Blood Donor Day
June 15—World Elder Abuse Awareness Day
June 16—International Day of Family Remittances
June 17—World Day to Combat Desertification and Drought
June 18—Sustainable Gastronomy Day
June 19—International Day for the Elimination of Sexual Violence in Conflict
June 20—World Refugee Day
June 21—International Day of Yoga
June 21—International Day of the Celebration of the Solstice
June 23—United Nations Public Service Day
June 23—International Widows' Day
June 25—Day of the Seafarer
June 26—International Day against Drug Abuse and Illicit Trafficking
June 26—United Nations International Day in Support of Victims of Torture
June 27—Micro-, Small and Medium-sized Enterprises Day
June 29—International Day of the Tropics
June 30—International Asteroid Day
June 30—International Day of Parliamentarism
July (First Saturday)—International Day of Cooperatives
July 11—World Population Day
July 15—World Youth Skills Day
July 18—Nelson Mandela International Day
July 20—World Chess Day

July 28—World Hepatitis Day
July 30—International Day of Friendship
July 30—World Day against Trafficking in Persons
August 9—International Day of the World's Indigenous Peoples
August 12—International Youth Day
August 19—World Humanitarian Day
August 21—International Day of Remembrance and Tribute to the Victims of Terrorism
August 22—International Day Commemorating the Victims of Acts of Violence Based on Religion or Belief
August 23—International Day of Remembrance of the Slave Trade and Its Abolition
August 29—International Day against Nuclear Tests
August 30—International Day of the Victims of Enforced Disappearances
September 5—International Day of Charity
September 7—International Day of Clean Air for Blue Skies
September 8—International Literacy Day
September 12—United Nations Day for South-South Cooperation
September 15—International Day of Democracy
September 16—International Day for the Preservation of the Ozone
September 17—World Patient Safety Day
September 18—International Equal Pay Day
September 21—International Day of Peace
September 23—International Day of Sign Languages
September 26—International Day for the Total Elimination of Nuclear Weapons
September (Last Thursday)—World Maritime Day
September 27—World Tourism Day
September 28—International Day for Universal Access to Information
September 29—International Day of Awareness of Food Loss and Waste
September 30—International Translation Day
October 1—International Day of Older Persons
October 2—International Day of Non-Violence
October 5—World Teachers' Day
October (First Monday)—World Habitat Day
October 9—World Post Day
October 10—World Mental Health Day
October 11—International Day of the Girl Child
October (Second Saturday)—World Migratory Bird Day

October 13—International Day for Disaster Risk Reduction
October 15—International Day of Rural Women
October 16—World Food Day
October 17—International Day for the Eradication of Poverty
October 20 (Every Five Years, Beginning in 2010)—World Statistics Day
October 24—United Nations Day
October 24—World Development Information Day
October 27—World Day for Audiovisual Heritage
October 31—World Cities Day
November 2—International Day to End Impunity for Crimes against Journalists
November 5—World Tsunami Awareness Day
November 6—International Day for Preventing the Exploitation of the Environment in War and Armed Conflict
November 10—World Science Day for Peace and Development
November 14—World Diabetes Day
November 16—International Day for Tolerance
November (Third Sunday)—World Day of Remembrance for Road Traffic Victims
November 19—World Toilet Day
November 20—Africa Industrialization Day
November 20—World Children's Day
November 21—World Television Day
November (Third Thursday)—World Philosophy Day
November 25—International Day for the Elimination of Violence against Women
November 29—International Day of Solidarity with the Palestinian People
November 30—Day of Remembrance for all Victims of Chemical Warfare
December 1—World AIDS Day
December 2—International Day for the Abolition of Slavery
December 3—International Day of Persons with Disabilities
December 4—International Day of Banks
December 5—International Volunteer Day for Economic and Social Development
December 5—World Soil Day
December 7—International Civil Aviation Day
December 9—International Day of Commemoration and Dignity of the Victims of the Crime of Genocide and the Prevention of this Crime
December 9—International Anti-Corruption Day
December 10—Human Rights Day
December 11—International Mountain Day

December 12—International Day of Neutrality
December 12—International Universal Health Coverage Day
December 18—International Migrants Day
December 18—Arabic Language Day
December 20—International Human Solidarity Day

Bibliography

Adebajo, Adekeye, ed. 2009. *From Global Apartheid to Global Village: Africa and the United Nations*. Scottsville, South Africa: University of KwaZulu-Natal Press.

Alexander, Dan, and Bryan Rooney. 2019. "Vote-Buying by the United States in the United Nations." *International Studies Quarterly* 63 (1): 168–76.

Alger, Chadwick F., ed. 1998. *The Future of the United Nations System: Potential for the Twenty-First Century*. Tokyo: United Nations University Press.

Baehr, Peter R., and Leon Gordenker. 2005. *The United Nations: Reality and Ideal*. Fourth edition. New York: Palgrave Macmillan.

Binder, Martin. 2015. "Paths to Intervention: What Explains the UN's Selective Response to Humanitarian Crises?" *Journal of Peace Research* 52 (6): 712–26.

Bloom, Louise, and Romily Faulkner. 2016. "Innovation Spaces: Lessons from the United Nations." *Third World Quarterly* 37 (8): 1371–87.

Bode, Ingvild. 2015. *Individual Agency and Policy Change at the United Nations: The People of the United Nations*. New York: Routledge.

Boulden, Jane, Ramesh Thakur, and Thomas G. Weiss, eds. 2009. *The United Nations and Nuclear Orders*. Tokyo: United Nations University Press.

Butler, Michael J. 2012. "Ten Years After: (Re) Assessing Neo-Trusteeship and UN State-Building in Timor-Leste." *International Studies Perspectives* 13 (1): 85–104.

Carant, Jane Briant. 2017. "Unheard Voices: A Critical Discourse Analysis of the Millennium Development Goals' Evolution into the Sustainable Development Goals." *Third World Quarterly* 38 (1): 16–41.

Charron, Andrea. 2011. *UN Sanctions and Conflict: Responding to Peace and Security Threats*. New York: Routledge.

Chesterman, Simon, Ian Johnstone, David Malone, and Thomas M. Franck. 2016. *Law and Practice of the United Nations: Documents and Commentary*. Second edition. Oxford: Oxford University Press.

Clements, Kevin P., and Nadia Mizner, eds. 2008. *The Center Holds: UN Reform for 21st Century Challenges*. New Brunswick, NJ: Transaction Publishers.

Cogan, Jacob Katz, Ian Hurd, and Ian Johnstone, eds. 2016. *The Oxford Handbook of International Organizations*. Oxford: Oxford University Press.

Coning, Cedric de, Chiyuki Aoi, and John Karlsrud, eds. 2017. *UN Peacekeeping Doctrine in a New Era: Adapting to Stabilisation, Protection and New Threats*. London: Routledge.

Davies, Michael, and Richard Woodward. 2014. *International Organizations: A Companion*. Cheltenham, UK: Edward Elgar.

Dörfler, Thomas 2019. *Security Council Sanctions Governance: The Power and Limits of Rules* London: Routledge.

Dorn, A. Walter. 2011. *Keeping Watch: Monitoring, Technology and Innovation in UN Peace Operations*. Tokyo: United Nations University Press.

Doyle, Michael W., and Nicholas Sambanis. 2006. *Making War and Building Peace: United Nations Peace Operations*. Princeton, NJ: Princeton University Press.

Duque, Juan C., Michael Jetter, and Santiago Sosa. 2015. "UN Interventions: The Role of Geography." *The Review of International Organizations* 10 (1): 67–95.

Durch, William J., ed. 1993. *The Evolution of UN Peacekeeping: Case Studies and Comparative Analysis*. New York: St. Martin's Press.

Egger, Clara. 2016. "Partners for Peace, Peaceful Partners? On the Relations between UN, Regional and Non-State Peacebuilders in Somalia." *Peacebuilding* 4 (1): 11–27.

Fasulo, Linda M. 2015. *An Insider's Guide to the UN*. Third edition. New Haven, CT: Yale University Press.

Finkelstein, Lawrence S., ed. 1988. *Politics in the United Nations System*. Durham, NC: Duke University Press.

Fomerand, Jacques. 2018. *Historical Dictionary of the United Nations*. Second edition. Lanham, MD: Rowman & Littlefield.

Franck, Thomas M. 1985. *Nation against Nation: What Happened to the U.N. Dream and What the U.S. Can Do about It*. New York: Oxford University Press.

Fraser, Trudy. 2014. *Maintaining Peace and Security?: The United Nations in a Changing World*. New York: Palgrave Macmillan.

Fukuda-Parr, Sakiko, ed. 2015. *The MDGs, Capabilities and Human Rights: The Power of Numbers to Shape Agendas*. London: Routledge.

Gaĭduk, Ilya V. 2012. *Divided Together: The United States and the Soviet Union in the United Nations, 1945–1965*. Stanford, CA: Stanford University Press.

Gareis, Sven B. 2012. *The United Nations: An Introduction*. Second edition. New York: Palgrave Macmillan.

Guehenno, Jean-Marie. 2002. "The United Nations Post-Brahimi." *Journal of International Affairs* 55 (2): 489–500.

Gutner, Tamar L. 2017. *International Organizations in World Politics*. London: SAGE.

Haack, Kirsten. 2014. "Breaking Barriers? Women's Representation and Leadership at the United Nations." *Global Governance* 20 (1): 37–54.

Hampson, Fen Osler, and David Malone, eds. 2002. *From Reaction to Conflict Prevention: Opportunities for the UN System*. Boulder, CO: Lynne Rienner Publishers.

Hanhimäki, Jussi M. 2015. *The United Nations: A Very Short Introduction.* Second edition. Oxford: Oxford University Press.

Hill, Melissa, ed. 2017. *Worldmark Encyclopedia of the Nations.* Fourteenth edition. Vol. 1: United Nations. Farmington Hills, MI: Gale, Cengage Learning.

Howard, Lise Morjé. 2008. *UN Peacekeeping in Civil Wars.* Cambridge: Cambridge University Press.

Hultman, Lisa, Jacob Kathman, and Megan Shannon. 2013. "United Nations Peacekeeping and Civilian Protection in Civil War." *American Journal of Political Science* 57 (4): 875–91.

Hurd, Ian. 2017. *International Organizations: Politics, Law, Practice.* Third edition. Cambridge: Cambridge University Press.

Hwang, Wonjae, Amanda G. Sanford, and Junhan Lee. 2015. "Does Membership on the UN Security Council Influence Voting in the UN General Assembly?" *International Interactions* 41 (2): 256–78.

Jolly, Richard, Louis Emmerij, and Thomas G. Weiss. 2009. *UN Ideas That Changed the World.* Bloomington: Indiana University Press.

Joyner, Christopher C., ed. 1997. *The United Nations and International Law.* Cambridge: Cambridge University Press.

Junk, Julian, ed. 2017. *The Management of UN Peacekeeping: Coordination, Learning, and Leadership in Peace Operations.* Boulder, CO: Lynne Rienner.

Karim, Sabrina, and Kyle Beardsley. 2016. "Explaining Sexual Exploitation and Abuse in Peacekeeping Missions: The Role of Female Peacekeepers and Gender Equality in Contributing Countries." *Journal of Peace Research* 53 (1): 100–15.

Kennedy, Paul M. 2006. *The Parliament of Man: The Past, Present, and Future of the United Nations.* New York: Random House.

Kille, Kent J., ed. 2007. *The UN Secretary-General and Moral Authority: Ethics and Religion in International Leadership.* Washington, D.C.: Georgetown University Press.

Kolb, Robert. 2010. *An Introduction to the Law of the United Nations.* Portland, OR: Hart Publishing.

Kostakos, Georgios. 2018. "About Form and Function: An Overview and Typology of UN Reforms Since the 1990s." *Global Society* 32 (2): 176–97.

Krasno, Jean E., ed. 2004. *The United Nations: Confronting the Challenges of a Global Society.* Boulder, CO: Lynne Rienner.

Laatikainen, Katie Verlin, and Karen Elizabeth Smith, eds. 2006. *The European Union at the United Nations: Intersecting Multilateralisms.* New York: Palgrave Macmillan.

MacKenzie, David. 2010. *A World Beyond Borders: An Introduction to the History of International Organizations.* Toronto: University of Toronto Press.

Makdisi, Karim, and Vijay Prashad, eds. 2017. *Land of Blue Helmets: The United Nations and the Arab World.* Oakland: University of California Press.

Meisler, Stanley. 2011. *United Nations: A History.* Revised and updated edition. New York: Grove Press.

Mertus, Julie. 2009. *The United Nations and Human Rights: A Guide for a New Era*. Second edition. New York: Routledge.

Mingst, Karen A., Margaret P. Karns, and Alynna Lyon. 2017. *The United Nations in the 21st Century*. Fifth edition. Boulder, CO: Westview Press.

Moore, John Allphin, Jr., and Jerry Pubantz. 2017. *The New United Nations: International Organization in the Twenty-First Century*. Second edition. New York: Routledge.

Müller, Joachim, ed. 2010. *Reforming the United Nations: The Challenge of Working Together*. Leiden, Netherlands: Martinus Nijhoff Publishers.

Murphy, Sean D. 1996. *Humanitarian Intervention: The United Nations in an Evolving World Order*. Philadelphia: University of Pennsylvania Press.

Niemetz, Martin D. 2015. *Reforming UN Decision-Making Procedures: Promoting a Deliberative System for Global Peace and Security*. London: Routledge.

Novosseloff, Alexandra. 2018. *The UN Military Staff Committee: Recreating a Missing Capacity*. London: Routledge.

Oestreich, Joel E. 2007. *Power and Principle: Human Rights Programming in International Organizations*. Washington, D.C.: Georgetown University Press.

Olsson, Louise, and Theodora-Ismene Gizelis, eds. 2015. *Gender, Peace and Security: Implementing UNSCR 1325*. London: Routledge.

Park, Susan. 2018. *International Organisations and Global Problems: Theories and Explanations*. Cambridge: Cambridge University Press.

Passmore, Timothy J. A., Megan Shannon, and Andrew F. Hart. 2018. "Rallying the Troops: Collective Action and Self-Interest in UN Peacekeeping Contributions." *Journal of Peace Research* 55 (3): 366–79.

Pouligny, Béatrice. 2006. *Peace Operations Seen from Below: UN Missions and Local People*. Bloomfield, CT: Kumarian Press.

Price, Richard M., and Mark W. Zacher, eds. 2004. *The United Nations and Global Security*. New York: Palgrave Macmillan.

Protopsaltis, Panayotis M. 2017. "Deciphering UN Development Policies: From the Modernisation Paradigm to the Human Development Approach?" *Third World Quarterly* 38 (8): 1733–52.

Pubantz, Jerry, and John Allphin Moore Jr. 2008. *Encyclopedia of the United Nations*. Second edition. New York: Facts On File.

Puchala, Donald. 1996. "Reforming the United Nations or Going Beyond." In *U.S. Foreign Policy and the United Nations System*, edited by Charles William Maynes and Richard S. Williamson, 229–48. New York: W.W. Norton and Company.

Puchala, Donald, Katie Verlin Laatikainen, and Roger A. Coate. 2007. *United Nations Politics: International Organization in a Divided World*. Upper Saddle River, NJ: Pearson Prentice Hall.

Ramcharan, Bertrand G. 2016. *United Nations Protection of Humanity and Its Habitat: A New International Law of Security and Protection*. Leiden, Netherlands: Brill.

Reinalda, Bob. 2009. *Routledge History of International Organizations: From 1815 to the Present Day*. New York: Routledge.

Rittberger, Volker, ed. 2001. *Global Governance and the United Nations System.* Tokyo: United Nations University Press.

Roberts, Adam, and Benedict Kingsbury, eds. 1993. *United Nations, Divided World: The UN's Roles in International Relations.* Second edition. Oxford: Oxford University Press.

Rofe, J. Simon, Giles Scott-Smith, and Tom Zeiler. 2019. "The UN and the Postwar Global Order: Dumbarton Oaks in Historical Perspective after 75 Years." *Journal of Contemporary History* 54 (2): 256–64.

Saiget, Marie. 2016. "Women's Participation in African Peace Negotiations: Cooperating with the UN Agencies in Burundi and Liberia." *Peacebuilding* 4 (1): 28–40.

Salton, Herman. 2017. *Dangerous Diplomacy: Bureaucracy, Power Politics, and the Role of the UN Secretariat in Rwanda.* Oxford: Oxford University Press.

Sayward, Amy L. 2017. *The United Nations in International History.* New York: Bloomsbury Academic.

Schechter, Michael G. 2010. *Historical Dictionary of International Organizations.* Second edition. Lanham, MD: Scarecrow Press.

Schiavone, Giuseppe. 2008. *International Organizations: A Dictionary and Directory.* Seventh edition. New York: Palgrave Macmillan.

Schrijver, Nico. 2010. *Development without Destruction: The UN and Global Resource Management.* Bloomington: Indiana University Press.

Schwartzberg, Joseph E. 2013. *Transforming the United Nations System: Designs for a Workable World.* Tokyo: United Nations University Press.

Shepherd, Laura J. 2016. "Victims of Violence or Agents of Change? Representations of Women in UN Peacebuilding Discourse." *Peacebuilding* 4 (2): 121–35.

Smith, Courtney B. 2006. *Politics and Process at the United Nations: The Global Dance.* Boulder, CO: Lynne Rienner.

Spijkers, Otto. 2017. "Global Values and the Institutions of the United Nations." *Vienna Journal on International Constitutional Law* 11 (2): 211–55.

Staur, Carsten. 2013. *Shared Responsibility: The United Nations in the Age of Globalization.* Montreal: McGill-Queen's University Press.

Svenson, Nanette Archer. 2016. *The United Nations as a Knowledge System.* London: Routledge.

Taylor, Paul Graham, and A. J. R. Groom, eds. 2000. *The United Nations at the Millennium: The Principal Organs.* London: Continuum.

Thakur, Ramesh. 2017. *The United Nations, Peace and Security: From Collective Security to the Responsibility to Protect.* Second edition. Cambridge: Cambridge University Press.

Trent, John E., and Laura Schnurr. 2018. *A United Nations Renaissance: What the UN Is, and What It Could Be.* Leverkusen: Barbara Budrich.

Tryggestad, Torunn L. 2009. "Trick or Treat? The UN and Implementation of Security Council Resolution 1325 on Women, Peace, and Security." *Global Governance* 15 (4): 539–57.

United Nations Department of Public Information. 2017. *Basic Facts About the United Nations.* 42nd edition. New York: United Nations.

Vreeland, James Raymond, and Axel Dreher. 2014. *The Political Economy of the United Nations Security Council: Money and Influence.* Cambridge: Cambridge University Press.

Walling, Carrie Booth. 2013. *All Necessary Measures: The United Nations and Humanitarian Intervention.* Philadelphia: University of Pennsylvania Press.

Weiss, Thomas G. 2018. *Would the World Be Better Without the UN?* Medford, MA: Polity Press.

Weiss, Thomas G., and Sam Daws, eds. 2018. *The Oxford Handbook on the United Nations.* Second edition. Oxford: Oxford University Press.

Weiss, Thomas G., David P. Forsythe, Roger A. Coate, and Kelly-Kate Pease. 2017. *The United Nations and Changing World Politics.* Eighth edition. Boulder, CO: Westview Press.

Weiss, Thomas G., and Ramesh Thakur. 2010. *Global Governance and the UN: An Unfinished Journey.* Bloomington: Indiana University Press.

White, Nigel D. 2002. *The United Nations System: Toward International Justice.* Boulder, CO: Lynne Rienner.

Whittaker, David J. 1997. *United Nations in the Contemporary World.* New York: Routledge.

Wiseman, Geoffrey. 2015. "Diplomatic Practices at the United Nations." *Cooperation and Conflict* 50 (3): 316–33.

Yoder, Amos. 1997. *The Evolution of the United Nations System.* Third edition. Washington, D.C.: Taylor and Francis.

Zacklin, Ralph. 2010. *The United Nations Secretariat and the Use of Force in a Unipolar World: Power v. Principle.* Cambridge: Cambridge University Press.

Zanotti, Laura. 2011. *Governing Disorder: UN Peace Operations, International Security, and Democratization in the Post-Cold War Era.* University Park: Pennsylvania State University Press.

Ziring, Lawrence, Robert E. Riggs, and Jack C. Plano. 2005. *The United Nations: International Organization and World Politics.* Fourth edition. Belmont, CA: Thomson Wadsworth.

Index

Acheson, Dean, 18
Annan, Kofi, 194–196
    advances and challenges while in office, 195–196
    Annan Plan, 27, 195
    approved as Secretary-General, 194, 204
    and budgetary affairs, 195
    and Counter-Terrorism Implementation Task Force, 270
    death of, 196
    early career, 194
    and Human Rights Council, 144, 195
    and human security, 239
    and Iraq War, 25, 195
    Kofi Annan Foundation, 195
    In Larger Freedom: Towards Development, Security and Human Rights for All, 150, 195, 239
    Millennium Summit and Assembly (2000), 195, 239, 266, 275
    Nobel Peace Prize awarded to, 195
    and nongovernmental organizations, 246
    and office of Deputy Secretary-General, 201, 202
    and Oil-for-Food Programme, 196
    and Peacebuilding Commission, 150, 195
    Renewing the United Nations: A Program for Reform, 36, 138, 194–195, 201
    role as Secretary-General, 194–195
    and Secretariat reforms, 36
    and Security Council reforms, 27
    as Special Representative to the Former Yugoslavia, 194, 204
    on "two sovereignties," 259
    and UN reform, 27, 36, 138, 194–195, 201, 278
    years as Secretary-General, 181
Arab League, 7
Arab Spring, 261
Arms control and disarmament, 220–222
    advances and challenges, 221
    and Cold War politics, 221
    and General Assembly, 221
    history of, 220
    and International Atomic Energy Agency, 220–221
    and Security Council, 220
    UN engagement, 220–221
Atlantic Charter
    and Churchill, Winston, 175
    and international trade, 175
    signing of, 5

Ban Ki-moon, 196–198
    advances and challenges while in office, 198
    and climate change, 197, 198
    early career, 196–197
    and High-Level Independent Panel on Peace Operations, 253
    and human security, 239
    Implementing the Responsibility to Protect, 259
    role as Secretary-General, 197
    and Special Representatives of the UN Secretary-General, 204
    and Sustainable Development Goals, 197
    and UN reform, 197
    years as Secretary-General, 181

Boutros-Ghali, Boutros, 192–194
  advances and challenges while in office, 193–194
  An Agenda for Democratization, 193
  An Agenda for Development, 193
  An Agenda for Peace, 193, 247, 256
  death of, 194
  as "norm entrepreneur," 193
  role as Secretary-General, 193
  years as Secretary-General, 181
Bretton Woods Conference, 65, 66, 84, 175
Brown, Mark Malloch, 201–202
Bush, George H. W., 214, 215
Bush, George W., 129, 215

Charter of the United Nations, 9–11
  amendments, 10, 309
  and arms control, 220
  and collective security, 222
  and creation of UN, 7, 9
  on Deputy Secretary-General, 201
  on Economic and Social Council, 29–30, 300–302
  and economic development, 226
  on economic security, 109
  on Functional Commissions, 139
  on General Assembly, 9, 10, 16, 289–292
  and human rights, 235, 236, 237
  and indigenous peoples, 241
  on International Civil Aviation Organization, 52
  on International Court of Justice, 37, 38, 39, 306–307
  on international economic and social co-operation, 10, 299–300
  and Lie, Trygve, 182, 183, 184
  on maintenance of international peace and security, 9–10
  and nongovernmental organizations, 245
  and peacebuilding, 247
  and peaceful settlement, 249
  and peacekeeping, 251
  pocket-size print version, 9
  Preamble, 6, 9, 11, 160, 235, 241, 247, 281, 287
  on President of General Assembly, 205
  on principal organs, 9, 13, 289
  ratification of, 7, 9, 10
  on regionalism, 255–256, 298–299
  on responsibilities of General Assembly, 16
  and responsibility to protect, 257, 259
  on Secretariat, 33, 35, 307–308
  on Secretary-General, 180, 181
  on Security Council, 22–23, 25, 28, 207, 280, 292–294
  and self-determination, 262–263, 264, 302–303
  and Special Representatives of the UN Secretary-General, 203
  on specialized agencies, 47
  and sustainable development, 264
  on transnational security arrangements, 309
  on Trusteeship Council, 41, 43, 44, 305–306
  and UN budget and funding, 272
  and UN conferences and summits, 274
  on UN membership, 10, 243, 244, 288–289
  on UN principles, 11–12, 288
  on UN purposes, 11, 287–288
  and UN reform, 278
  on voting procedures, 14
  and women and gender, 281
Charter of the United Nations (document), 287–310
  on action with respect to threats to and breaches of peace and acts of aggression, 295–298
  on amendments, 309
  on declaration regarding non-self-governing territories, 302–303
  on Economic and Security Council, 300–302
  on General Assembly, 289–292
  on International Court of Justice, 306–307
  on international economic and social co-operation, 299–300
  on international trusteeship system, 303–305
  on membership, 288–289
  on miscellaneous provisions, 308–309
  on organs, 289
  on pacific settlement of disputes, 294–295
  Preamble, 287
  on purposes and principles, 287–288
  on ratification and signature, 310
  on regional arrangements, 298–299

on Secretariat, 307–308
on Security Council, 292–294
on transitional security arrangements, 309
on Trusteeship Council, 305–306
Chiang Kai-shek, 7
Churchill, Winston
and Atlantic Charter, 175
and creation of UN, 6
and death of Roosevelt, 7
and regionalism, 255
and Tehran Conference, 6
and Yalta Conference, 6
Clinton, William, 192, 193, 215
Collective security, 222–223
advances and challenges, 223
and Cold War politics, 223
and General Assembly, 222
history of, 222
and Security Council, 222–223
and Treaty of Versailles, 222
UN engagement, 222–223
Concert of Europe, 2–3, 4, 22
Congress of Vienna, 2, 3
Coronavirus (COVID-19) pandemic, 89, 200, 233, 235
Cybersecurity, 223–225
advances and challenges, 225
Convention on Cybercrime (Council of Europe), 225
and General Assembly, 224
history of, 223–224
and Security Council, 224
significant cyberattacks, 224
UN engagement, 224

Deputy Secretary-General, 201–203
advances and challenges, 202–203
and Annan, Kofi, 201
Brown, Mark Malloch, 201–202
Eliasson, Jan, 202
Fréchette, Louise, 201
list of UN Deputy Secretaries-General, 202
Migiro, Asha-Rose, 202
Mohammed, Amina, 202
responsibilities, 201–202
Disarmament Commission, 136–139
activities, 137–138
challenges and reform, 138
and Cold War politics, 136

history and creation of, 136–137, 160, 220
responsibilities, 137
structure, 137

Economic and Social Council (ECOSOC), 28–33
challenges and reforms, 31–32
and decolonialization period, 32
and High-level Political Forum on Sustainable Development, 30–32, 142–143
membership and structure, 29
and Millennium Development Goals, 31
and nongovernmental organizations, 29–30, 32
and Permanent Forum on Indigenous Issues, 44, 139, 153, 154
President and Vice-Presidents, 29
relationship with other actors, 20–30
responsibilities and operations, 30–31
size of, 29, 32
and Sustainable Development Goals, 30
Youth Forum, 31
Economic development, 225–227
advances and challenges, 226–227
and decolonialization, 227
and General Assembly, 226
history of, 225–226
and Human Development Index, 227
and Millennium Development Goals, 226
UN engagement, 226
Eliasson, Jan, 202
Environmental protection, 227–231
advances and challenges, 229–231
and climate change, 228–231
funding, 231
and General Assembly, 228
history of, 227–228
Montreal Protocol on Substances that Deplete the Ozone Layer, 78, 229, 230, 232
Our Common Future (Brundtland Report), 175, 199, 228, 230, 264
and Security Council, 231
selected UN agreements and plans, 230–231
selected UN conferences and meetings, 229
and Sustainable Development Goals, 231
UN engagement, 228–229

Executive heads of specialized agencies, 209–211
  advances and challenges, 210–211
  Brundtland, Gro Harlem, 210
  Chisholm, Brock, 210
  and controversy, 210
  and country of origin, 210
  first office-holders, 210
  and gender, 210
  Lagarde, Christine, 210
  M'Bow, Amadou, 210
  responsibilities, 209
  Saouma, Edouard, 210
  and size of staff and resources, 210
  specialized agency executive head position titles, 210

Food and Agriculture Organization (FAO), 48–52
  activities, 50–51
  budget, 50
  budget and funding, 49–50, 51
  challenges and reform, 51
  competing institutional frameworks, 51, 210
  Council, 49–50
  date joined UN, 48
  departments, 50
  Director-General, 50, 133, 210
  and environmental protection, 228
  Gong Li (Goodwill Ambassador), 217
  history and creation of, 48–49
  and International Fund for Agricultural Development, 49, 51, 55, 57, 58
  membership, 50
  Orr, John Boyd, first Director-General, 133
  responsibilities, 49
  Saouma, Edouard, Director-General, 210
  structure, 49–50
  and Sustainable Development Goals, 50
  technical committees, 50
  World Food Day, 49
  and World Food Programme, 49, 51, 133, 134, 135
  and World Health Organization, 89
Fréchette, Louise, 201
Functional Commissions, 139–141
  activities, 140
  challenges and reform, 140–141
  Commission for Social Development, 29, 139, 140, 158
  Commission on Crime Prevention and Criminal Justice, 29, 139–140, 158
  Commission on Narcotic Drugs, 139–140
  Commission on Population and Development, 127, 139, 140
  Commission on Science and Technology for Development, 139, 140, 158
  Commission on the Status of Women, 29, 113, 139, 140, 281
  responsibilities, 139
  Statistical Commission, 29, 139, 140
  structure, 139–140
  and UN Forum on Forests, 139, 140

General Assembly, 15–21
  agenda, 20
  challenges and reform, 20–21
  and Cold War, 18
  and Cold War politics, 18
  committees, 17
  decision-making process, 16–20
  electoral groups, 20
  and Millennium Development Goals, 18
  nonmember states and "observer" status, 15–16
  representation, 15–16
  resolutions, 14, 18
  responsibilities, 16
  rules of procedure and election of President, 17–18
  special sessions, 18, 19
  UN Charter on, 9, 10, 16, 289–292
  "Uniting for Peace" Resolution, 18, 23, 222, 249, 260
  universal membership, 15
  voting procedures, 14–15, 16, 18, 20
  working groups, 20
Global commons, 231–233
  advances and challenges, 233
  and Antarctica, 233
  and climate change, 232, 233
  definition of, 231
  and General Assembly, 232
  and space exploration, 232
  UN engagement, 232–233
Globalization
  and health, 235
  and International Labour Organization, 61
  and International Maritime Organization, 64–65
  and International Monetary Fund, 68

Index

and Regional Commissions, 156
and World Bank Group, 86
Goodwill Ambassadors and Messengers of Peace, 216–218
  advances and challenges, 217–218
  examples of UN Goodwill Ambassadors, 217
  history of, 216
  UN engagement, 216–217
Great Depression
  and League of Nations, 5
  and nationalistic economic policies, 65
Guterres, António, 198–200
  advances and challenges while in office, 200
  and climate change, 200
  early career, 198–199
  role as Secretary-General, 199–200
  Securing Our Common Future: An Agenda for Disarmament, 175, 199, 224
  and Special Representatives of the UN Secretary-General, 204
  and Sustainable Development Goals, 199
  and Trump, Donald, 200
  as UN High Commissioner for Refugees, 121
  and UN reform, 270, 278
  years as Secretary-General, 181

Hague Peace Conference, 3, 4, 37, 170, 220
  and Hague Conventions, 3, 4, 170, 220
  and Permanent Court of Arbitration, 3, 37
  Roosevelt, Theodore, on, 4
Hammarskjöld, Dag, 185–186
  advances and challenges while in office, 186
  and Cold War politics, 185
  and Congolese crisis, 186
  death of, 185, 187
  early career, 185
  first invocation of Article 99, 186
  "Peking Formula" of, 185
  role as Secretary-General, 185–186
  years as Secretary-General, 181
Health, 233–235
  advances and challenges, 234–235
  as fundamental right, 234
  and globalization, 235
  HIV/AIDS, 234
  infectious diseases, 233

  and Millennium Development Goals, 234
  and Sustainable Development Goals, 234
  UN engagement, 234
High-level Political Forum on Sustainable Development (HLPF), 141–144
  activities, 142–143
  challenges and reform, 143
  and Economic and Social Council, 30–31–32, 142–143
  history and creation of, 141–142
  responsibilities, 142
  structure, 142
  and Sustainable Development Goals, 141, 142–143
Hull, Cordell, 7
Human rights, 235–239
  advances and challenges, 236–238
  Conventions, 237
  Declarations, 238
  definition of, 235
  and General Assembly, 236
  and Security Council, 236
  and Sustainable Development Goals, 236
  UN engagement, 236
Human Rights Council, 144–147
  activities, 145
  and Annan, Kofi, 195
  challenges and reform, 145–147
  and Commission on Human Rights, 30, 32, 140, 144, 145, 153
  history and creation of, 144
  and indigenous peoples, 241
  and politicization, 147
  responsibilities, 144
  special sessions, 145, 146
  structure, 144–145
Human security, 239–240
  advances and challenges, 240
  Advisory Board on Human Security, 239
  and Annan, Kofi, 239
  Commission on Human Security, 239
  and General Assembly, 239
  Inter-Agency Working Group on Human Security, 240
  and Sustainable Development Goals, 240
  UN engagement, 239–240
  UN Trust Fund for Human Security, 239–240

Indigenous peoples, 241–242
    advances and challenges, 242
    and Human Rights Council, 241
    and League of Nations, 241
    Study of the Problem of Discrimination Against Indigenous Populations, 241
    UN Declaration on the Rights of Indigenous Peoples, 241–242
    UN engagement, 241–242
    Working Group on Indigenous Populations, 241
Intergovernmental Panel on Climate Change (IPCC), 96, 117
International Atomic Energy Agency (IAEA), 160–162
    activities, 161–162
    budget and funding, 161, 162
    challenges and reform, 162
    and Cold War politics, 162
    and Eisenhower, Dwight D., 160
    history and creation of, 160
    Nobel Peace Prize awarded to, 162
    responsibilities, 160
    structure, 160–161
International Civil Aviation Organization (ICAO), 52–55
    activities, 53–54
    and Air Navigation Commission, 53
    budget and funding, 53
    challenges and reform, 54–55
    and Chicago Convention, 52–55
    and Convention on International Civil Aviation, 52
    Council, 53, 54
    date joined UN, 48
    history and creation of, 52
    legal activities, 54
    membership, 53
    responsibilities, 52–53
    Secretary-General, 53, 210
    structure, 53
    and terrorist attacks, 55
International Court of Justice (ICJ), 36–40
    cases and judicial process, 38–39
    challenges and potential reform, 40
    Charter of the UN on, 37, 38, 39, 289, 295, 306–307
    and Cold War politics, 40
    first advisory opinion of, 243
    ICJ Statute, 37, 39
    jurisdiction, 39
    membership and judges, 37–38
    and *Nicaragua v. United States of America*, 38–39
    Permanent Court of Arbitration as forerunner to, 3
    as "World Court," 37
International Criminal Court (ICC), 162–165
    activities, 164
    challenges and reform, 164
    funding, 163–164
    history and creation of, 162–163
    and peaceful settlement, 249
    responsibilities, 163
    Rome Statute, 162–163, 322
    and Security Council, 24
    structure, 163–164
    and UN reform, 278–279
    withdrawals from, 164
International Criminal Tribunal for Rwanda, 22, 162, 249
International Criminal Tribunal for the former Yugoslavia, 22, 162, 249, 278
International Fund for Agricultural Development (IFAD), 55–58
    activities, 57
    budget and funding, 56
    challenges and reform, 57–58
    collaborative engagement of, 154
    date joined UN, 48
    and Food and Agriculture Organization, 49, 51, 55, 57, 58
    history and creation of, 55
    membership, 56
    President, 57, 210
    responsibilities, 56
    structure, 56–57
    and Sustainable Development Goals, 57
    voting procedures, 56–57
    and World Food Conference (1974), 55, 58
International Institute of Agriculture, 49
International Labour Organization (ILO), 58–62
    activities, 60–61
    budget and funding, 60
    central documents, 59
    challenges and reform, 61
    Constitution, 59
    and creation of UN, 47, 59
    date joined UN, 48
    Declaration Concerning the Aims and Purposes of the International Labour Organization, 59

Declaration on Fundamental Principles
 and Rights at Work, 59
Director-General, 60, 210
and globalization, 61
history and creation of, 58–59
Indigenous and Tribal Peoples
 Convention, 237, 241
International Training Center (Turin), 158
and League of Nations, 58–59, 60
membership, 60
responsibilities, 59
structure, 59–60
and Sustainable Development Goals, 61
and Treaty of Versailles, 5, 58–59
UN General Assembly A/RES/73/241
 on, 318
International Maritime Organization
 (IMO), 62–65
activities, 63–64
Assembly, 63
budget and funding, 63
challenges and reform, 64–65
date joined UN, 48
and global commons, 232
and globalization, 64–65
history and creation of, 62
Marine Environment Protection
 Committee, 63
Maritime Safety Committee, 63
membership, 63
responsibilities, 62–63
Secretary-General, 63, 210
structure, 63
and UN Convention on the Law of the
 Sea, 65
International Monetary Fund (IMF),
 65–69
activities, 68
Board of Governors, 67
and Bretton Woods Conference, 65, 66
challenges and reform, 68–69
date joined UN, 48
and global financial crisis of 2008,
 67, 68–69
and globalization, 68
history and creation of, 65–66, 84
Lagarde, Christine, Managing Director,
 210
Managing Director, 67, 210
membership, 67
responsibilities, 66–67
structure, 67

voting procedures, 15, 67
and World Bank Group, 65, 66, 67, 84, 85
International Organization for Migration
 (IOM), 165–167, 254
activities, 166
budget and funding, 166
challenges and reform, 166–167
and climate change, 166
history and creation of, 165
responsibilities, 165
structure, 165–166
and United Nations High Commissioner
 for Refugees, 166
International Seabed Authority (ISA),
 167–170
activities, 169
budget and funding, 169
challenges and reform, 169–170
and global commons, 232
history and creation of, 167
and Law of the Sea conferences and
 conventions, 167, 168
responsibilities, 167–168
structure, 168–169
and technology, 170
and UN Convention on the Law of the
 Sea, 167, 168
International Telecommunication Union
 (ITU), 69–72
activities, 70–71
budget and funding, 70, 71–72
challenges and reform, 71–72
date joined UN, 48
history and creation of, 33, 69
membership, 70
responsibilities, 69–70
Secretary-General, 210
Sectors, 70, 71
structure, 70

Jebb, Gladwyn, 183
Joint United Nations Programme on HIV/
 AIDS (UNAIDS), 147–149
activities, 148–149
challenges and reform, 149
funding, 148, 149
history and creation of, 147
Piot, Peter, first Executive Director, 149
responsibilities, 147–148
structure, 148
and Sustainable Development Goals,
 149

Kennedy, John F., 186
Khrushchev, Nikita, 186

League of Nations
  and arms control, 220
  and collective security, 222
  Covenant, 5, 220
  and creation of UN, 6, 13
  failure of, 5, 22
  and food issues, 49
  Geneva Declaration of the Rights of the Child, 238
  Health Organization, 234
  High Commissioner for Refugees, 253
  history and creation of, 4–5
  and human rights, 235
  and indigenous rights, 241
  and international labor, 5, 59
  and international meteorological efforts, 94
  and Italian invasion of Ethiopia, 5
  and Manchurian Crisis, 5
  membership, 4, 60
  organizational structure, 4–5, 33
  Permanent Court of International Justice, 3, 13, 37, 306
  permanent members, 4
  as precursor to UN, 2, 3, 4–5, 13, 40–41, 87
  purpose, 4
  Secretariat, 4–5, 33
  Secretary-General, 5
  Soviet Union expelled from, 6
  and Special Representatives of UN Secretary-General, 203
  and territorial self-governance, 40–41, 262
  and Treaty of Versailles, 4–5
  UN compared with, 5, 15, 22, 226, 244
  unanimous decision-making, 5, 15
  and universal international civil service, 33
  and Universal Postal Union, 81
  US rejection of membership in, 4
  and World Health Organization, 87
Lie, Trygve, 182–185
  advances and challenges while in office, 183–184
  and Cold War politics, 182, 183
  death of, 184
  early career, 182
  and Korean War, 183
  and Palestine, 183
  "peace tour" of, 183
  role as Secretary-General, 183
  on role of Secretary-General, 183
  Twenty-Year Peace Program Points, 184
  years as Secretary-General, 181

Member state ambassadors and delegates, 211–213
  advances and challenges, 212–213
  agenda-setting capacity, 212
  UN engagement, 212
Membership, 242–245
  advances and challenges, 244
  and Cold War politics, 243
  controversy, 243
  and General Assembly, 243
  growth in UN membership, 243, 244
  and Security Council, 243, 244
  UN engagement, 243–244
  withdrawal, 244
Migiro, Asha-Rose, 202
Millennium Development Goals
  and Annan, Kofi, 195
  and Ban Ki-moon, 197
  creation of, 266–267
  and Economic and Social Council, 31
  and economic development, 226
  and General Assembly, 18
  and health, 234
  list of eight, 267
  and sustainable development, 265
  and Sustainable Development Goals, 226, 265, 266–267
  and UN Conference on Sustainable Development, 141
  and UN Conference on Trade and Development, 106
  and UN Development Programme, 112
  and UN Educational, Scientific and Cultural Organization, 74
  and UN General Assembly A/RES/73/241 on, 317
  and UN Population Fund, 127
  and United Nations Children's Fund, 103
  and United Nations General Assembly A/RES/73/241, 317
Millennium Summit and Assembly (2000), 195, 239, 266, 275

Mohammed, Amina, 202
Montreal Protocol on Substances that Deplete the Ozone Layer, 78, 229, 230, 232
Moscow Declaration, 5, 6

Nongovernmental organizations (NGOs), 245–247
    advantages and challenges, 246
    and Annan, Kofi, 246
    definition of, 245
    and Economic and Social Council, 245
    and General Assembly, 246
    history and creation of, 245
    and Security Council, 246
    UN engagement, 245–246

Obama, Barack, 129, 215
Office of Secretary-General, 180–182
    list of UN Secretaries-General, 181
    role of the Secretary-General, 181–182
    selecting the Secretary-General, 180
    See also individual Secretaries-General
Organization for the Prohibition of Chemical Weapons (OPCW), 170–173
    activities, 172
    and Biological Weapons Convention, 170
    budget and funding, 171–172
    challenges and reform, 172
    history and creation of, 170–171
    responsibilities, 171
    structure, 171–172
    and Syria, 172
    and Tokyo sarin gas attack, 172
Our Common Future (Brundtland Report), 175, 199, 228, 230, 264

Peacebuilding, 247–249
    advances and challenges, 248
    and Boutros-Ghali, Boutros, 247
    controversy, 248
    and General Assembly, 247
    Pathways for Peace: Inclusive Approaches to Preventing Violent Conflict, 248
    Peacebuilding Commission, 247
    principles and measures of success, 248
    and Security Council, 247
    and Sustainable Development Goals, 248
    UN engagement, 247
Peacebuilding Commission, 150–152
    activities, 151–152
    and Annan, Kofi, 150, 195
    challenges and reform, 152
    country-specific configurations, 150, 151
    history and creation of, 26, 32, 44, 150, 247
    and multidimensional peacebuilding, 151
    Organizational Committee, 150–151
    responsibilities, 150
    structure, 150–151
Peaceful settlement, 249–250
    advances and challenges, 250
    and Charter of UN, 249
    and General Assembly, 249–250
    Manila Declaration on Peaceful Settlement of International Disputes, 249–250
    and Security Council, 249–250
    UN engagement, 249–250
Peacekeeping, 251–253
    advances and challenges, 252–253
    funding, 252
    and General Assembly, 252
    Report of the Panel on United Nations Peace Operations (Brahimi Report), 252
    and Security Council, 251
    top ten assessed contributors for UN peacekeeping operations, 252
    UN engagement, 251–252
    UN peacekeeping operations created by decade, 251
Pérez de Cuéllar, Javier, 190–192
    advances and challenges while in office, 191–192
    and Cold War politics, 191
    death of, 192
    early career, 190
    "The Role of the Secretary-General" (speech), 191
    and peaceful settlement, 191
    role as Secretary-General, 191
    as Special Representative to Cyprus, 204
    years as Secretary-General, 181
Permanent Court of Arbitration, 3, 37
Permanent Court of International Justice (PCIJ), 3, 13, 37, 306

Permanent Five (P-5), 22, 23, 27, 28, 38, 180, 205, 212, 243, 260, 261
Permanent Forum on Indigenous Issues, 152–155
  activities, 154
  challenges and reform, 154
  and Economic and Social Council, 44, 139, 153, 154
  funding, 153
  history and creation of, 152–153, 241
  responsibilities, 153
  and self-determination, 263
  structure, 153–154
Precursors to United Nations, 2–4
  Central Commission for the Navigation of the Rhine, 3
  Concert of Europe, 2–3, 4, 22
  Hague Conventions, 3, 4, 170, 220
  International Bureau of Weights and Measures, 3
  public international unions, 3
  and technology, 3
  Treaty of Westphalia, 2
  See also International Telecommunication Union (ITU); League of Nations; Universal Postal Union (UPU)
Preparatory Commission for the Comprehensive Nuclear-Test-Ban Treaty Organization (CTBTO), 173–175
  activities, 174
  budget and funding, 174
  challenges and reform, 174
  and Comprehensive Nuclear-Test-Ban Treaty, 173, 175
  history of, 173
  responsibilities, 173
  structure, 174
President of General Assembly, 205–207
  advances and challenges, 206
  and Charter of the UN, 205
  financial support for, 206
  funding, 206
  neutrality of, 206
  responsibilities, 205–206
President of Security Council, 207–209
  and Charter of UN, 207
  dual role of president and informal powers, 208
  responsibilities, 207–208

Quebec Conference, 5

Reagan, Ronald, 129, 191, 215
Refugees and migration, 253–255
  advances and challenges, 255
  and climate change, 255
  Convention Relating to the Status of Refugees, 120, 237, 254, 255
  and General Assembly, 254
  international agreements, 254
  International Organization for Migration, 254
  UN engagement, 254
  UN Relief and Works Agency for Palestinian Refugees in the Near East, 254
Regional Commissions, 155–157
  activities, 156
  budget and funding, 156
  challenges and reform, 156–157
  Economic and Social Commission for Asia and the Pacific, 155, 156
  Economic Commission for Africa, 155, 156, 194
  Economic Commission for Europe, 155, 156
  Economic Commission for Latin America, 155, 156
  Economic Commission for Western Asia, 155, 156
  and globalization, 156
  responsibilities, 155
  structure, 155–156
  and Sustainable Development Goals, 156
Regionalism, 255–257
  advances and challenges, 256–257
  and Cold War politics, 256
  and General Assembly, 256
  and Security Council, 256
  UN engagement, 256
  See also Regional Commissions
Research and training institutes
  budget and funding, 158, 159
  history and creation of, 157–158
  and Sustainable Development Goals, 159
  UN Institute for Disarmament Research, 157, 158
  UN Institute for Training and Research, 157, 158
  UN Interregional Crime and Justice Research Institute, 157, 158

Index

UN Research Institute for Social Development, 157, 158
UN System Staff College, 157, 158, 159
United Nations University, 157, 158–159
Research and Training Institutes, 157–159
  activities, 158–159
  challenges and reform, 159
  responsibilities, 158
  structure, 158
Responsibility to protect (R2P), 257–260
  advances and challenges, 259–260
  and Ban Ki-moon, 259
  and Convention on the Prevention and Punishment of the Crime of Genocide, 39, 237, 257, 258
  and General Assembly, 259
  Implementing the Responsibility to Protect, 259
  and Security Council, 257, 259–260
  and state sovereignty, 259
  UN engagement, 257–259
Rio+20 (UN Conference on Sustainable Development), 116, 141–142, 143, 229, 230, 265, 267
Rockefeller, John D., Jr., 8, 276
Role of great powers, 260–262
  advances and challenges, 261–262
  and climate change, 261
  and Cold War politics, 260
  and General Assembly, 260
  great power contribution to UN regular budget 2020, 261
  and Security Council, 260–262
  and Sustainable Development Goals, 262
  UN engagement, 260–261
Roosevelt, Franklin D.
  and Advisory Committee on Postwar Foreign Policy, 6
  and Atlantic Charter, 175
  and China's inclusion in UN, 5
  and creation of UN, 5–7
  death of, 7
  "four policemen" approach of, 6, 260, 262
  and Yalta Conference, 6
Roosevelt, Theodore, 4

San Francisco Conference on International Organization, 7, 8, 9
Secretariat, 33–36
  and Annan, Kofi, 36
  and civil servants, 33, 35
  debates and issues, 35
  reform, 36
  role and responsibilities, 34–35
  staffing, 33
  structure, 34
Secretary-General. *See* Office of Secretary-General
Security Council, 21–28
  activities, 24–26
  "Arria-formula" meetings, 26
  challenge and reform, 26–28
  and Cold War politics, 23
  decision-making process, 23–24
  and Democratic Republic of Congo, 26, 28
  and International Court of Justice, 23, 24–25
  and International Criminal Court, 24
  and Iran nuclear deal negotiations, 24
  and Iraq War, 25, 26
  and Korean War, 26
  meetings of, 22–23
  "on call," 22
  Peacebuilding Commission, 26
  and peacekeeping, 26
  Permanent Five members, 22, 23, 27, 28, 38, 180, 205, 212, 243, 260, 261
  and Persian Gulf War, 25
  President of, 22, 207–208
  proposed reforms, 27
  representation on, 27
  structure, 22–23
  and Syrian conflict, 24, 28
  and Trusteeship Council, 41, 304
  and "Uniting for Peace" Resolution, 18, 23, 222, 249, 260
  vetoes in, 24
Self-determination, 262–264
  advances and challenges, 263–264
  and Charter of UN, 262–263
  definition of, 262
  and General Assembly, 263
  UN engagement, 263
Smuts, Jan, 6
Special Representatives of the United Nations Secretary-General (SRSGs), 203–205
  advances and challenges, 204–205
  backgrounds, 204
  UN engagement, 203–204
  and world conflicts, 204

Specialized agencies, 47–48
  definition of, 47
  list of and dates when joined UN system, 48
  See also individual agencies
Stalin, Joseph
  and creation of UN, 6
  and death of Roosevelt, 7
  and League of Nations, 6
  and Tehran Conference, 6
  and Yalta Conference, 6
Sustainable development, 264–266
  advances and challenges, 265–266
  and climate change, 265
  funding, 265
  and General Assembly, 265
  history of, 264–265
  and Millennium Development Goals, 265
  UN engagement, 264–265
Sustainable Development Goals (SDGs), 266–269
  advances and challenges, 267–268
  and Ban Ki-moon, 197
  and climate change, 267, 268
  creation of, 141, 265, 266–267
  and Economic and Social Council, 30
  and environmental protection, 231
  and Food and Agriculture Organization, 50
  and General Assembly, 267
  and Guterres, António, 199
  and health, 234
  and human rights, 236
  and human security, 240
  and International Fund for Agricultural Development, 57
  and International Labour Organization, 61
  and Joint United Nations Programme on HIV/AIDS, 149
  list of seventeen, 268
  and Millennium Development Goals, 226, 265, 266–267
  and peacebuilding, 248
  and Regional Commissions, 156
  and research and training institutes, 159
  and role of great powers, 262
  and UN Conference on Sustainable Development, 141
  and UN Conference on Trade and Development, 106
  and UN Development Programme, 112
  and UN Educational, Scientific and Cultural Organization, 74
  UN engagement, 266–267
  UN General Assembly A/RES/73/241 on, 316
  and UN Human Settlements Programme, 124
  and UN Population Fund, 127
  and UN reform, 278
  and United Nations Children's Fund, 104
  and United Nations Industrial Development Organization, 79
  and World Health Organization, 89
  and World Tourism Organization, 99
  and World Trade Organization, 177
Syrian conflict
  and Annan, Kofi, 195, 204
  and human rights, 237
  and Human Rights Council, 146
  and Organization for the Prohibition of Chemical Weapons, 172
  and responsibility to protect, 260
  and role of great powers, 261
  and UN Relief and Works Agency for Palestine Refugees, 130
  and UN Security Council, 24, 28

Terrorism, 269–271
  advances and challenges, 271
  and General Assembly, 269–271
  international counter-terrorism Conventions, 270
  9/11, 269–270
  and Security Council, 269–271
  UN engagement, 269–271
Thant, U, 187–188
  advances and challenges while in office, 188
  and apartheid, 188
  and Cold War politics, 187, 188
  and Congolese crisis, 187
  death of, 188
  early career, 187
  and India-Pakistan war, 187
  role as Secretary-General, 187–188
  and Trust Fund for Population Activities, 127
  years as Secretary-General, 181
"Transforming our World: the 2030 Agenda for Sustainable Development," 231, 267, 316
Treaty of Versailles
  and collective security, 222

and International Labour Organization, 58–59
and League of Nations, 58–59, 222
Treaty of Westphalia, 2
Truman, Harry S.
  and creation of UN, 7
  on UN, 2
  on UN Development Programme, 109
Trump, Donald, 129, 131, 177, 200, 215
Trusteeship Council, 40–45
  Charter of the UN on, 41, 43, 44, 304, 305–306
  and International Trusteeship System, 263
  membership, 41
  past concerns and future possibilities, 43–45
  President and Vice-President, 41
  and Security Council, 41, 304
  and self-determination, 262, 263, 264
  suspension of operations, 40
  trust territories under Trusteeship Council, 43
  trust territory supervision and outcome, 42
  and UN Environment Programme, 119
  and UN reform, 279
  voting, 41–42
  voting procedures, 14

United Nations
  creation of, 5–8
  historical background, 2–8
  and League of Nations, 4–5
  precursors to, 2–4
  principles, 11–12
  purposes, 11
  resolutions, 14
  and San Francisco Conference on International Organization, 7, 8, 9
United Nations budget and funding, 272–273
  advantages and challenges, 273
  and General Assembly, 272, 273
  and Security Council, 272
  UN engagement, 272
United Nations Children's Fund (UNICEF), 101–105
  activities, 103–104
  budget and funding, 102, 103, 104
  challenges and reform, 104
  history and creation of, 101–102
  and Millennium Development Goals, 103
  Prince of Asturias Award, 104
  responsibilities, 102
  structure, 102–103
  and Sustainable Development Goals, 104
  and UN International Year of the Child (1979), 103
United Nations Conference on Sustainable Development, 141
United Nations Conference on Sustainable Development (Rio+20), 116, 141–142, 143, 229, 230, 265, 267
United Nations Conference on Trade and Development (UNCTAD), 105–109
  activities, 106–108
  budget and funding, 106
  challenges and reform, 108
  history and creation of, 105
  and Millennium Development Goals, 106
  Principles of the New International Economic Order, 107
  responsibilities, 105
  structure, 106
  and Sustainable Development Goals, 106
  Trade and Development Board, 106
United Nations conferences and summits, 274–275
  advances and challenges, 275
  Beijing Women's Conference, 274
  Conference on the Human Environment, 274
  International Conference on Trade and Employment, 274
  Millennium Summit, 274
  Ottawa Conference, 274
  UN engagement, 274
United Nations Declaration on the Rights of Indigenous Peoples, 153, 241–242
United Nations Development Programme (UNDP), 109–112
  activities, 111
  challenges and reform, 111–112
  funding, 109, 110, 111
  history and creation of, 109
  Human Development Report, 111, 239
  Jackson Report, 111
  and Millennium Development Goals, 112
  responsibilities, 109–110
  structure, 110
  and Sustainable Development Goals, 112

United Nations Educational, Scientific and Cultural Organization (UNESCO), 72–77
  activities, 74–76
  budget, 74
  budget and funding, 73, 74
  challenges and reform, 76
  Convention for the Protection and Promotion of the Diversity of Cultural Expressions, 74
  date joined UN, 48
  Director-General, 73, 210
  and education, 75
  and environmental protection, 228
  history and creations of, 72–73
  membership, 74
  and Millennium Development Goals, 74
  National Commissions, 73–74
  responsibilities, 73
  and Sustainable Development Goals, 74
  World Heritage Sites, 75, 101
United Nations Entity for Gender Equality and the Empowerment of Women (UN Women), 112–116
  activities, 114–115
  and Ban Ki-Moon, 197
  challenges and reform, 115
  funding, 114, 115
  and Hathaway, Anne, 216
  history and creation of, 112–113, 281–282
  and International Research and Training Institute for the Advancement of Women, 159
  responsibilities, 113
  structure, 113–114
  UN Trust Fund to End Violence against Women, 114
United Nations Environment Programme (UNEP), 116–119
  activities, 117–118
  challenges and reform, 118–119
  and climate change, 117
  funding, 117, 118
  Global Environmental Outlook, 117, 118
  history and creation of, 116
  and Intergovernmental Panel on Climate Change, 117
  and Multilateral Environmental Agreements, 117–118
  responsibilities, 116
  structure, 116–117

United Nations General Assembly A/RES/73/241
  on climate change, 317
  on International Labour Organization, 318
  on Millennium Development Goals, 317
  on Sustainable Development Goals, 316
  on "Transforming our world: the 2030 Agenda for Sustainable Development," 316
United Nations General Assembly A/RES/73/241 (document), 316–319
United Nations headquarters, 275–276
  advantages and challenges, 276
  and creation of UN, 7–8
  history of, 275–276
  UN engagement, 275–276
United Nations High Commissioner for Refugees (UNHCR), 119–123
  activities, 121–122
  challenges and reform, 122
  and climate change, 120, 122
  Convention Relating to the Status of Refugees, 120, 122
  funding, 121
  Grandi, Filippo, 121
  Guterres, António, 121
  history and creation of, 119–120
  responsibilities, 120
  Statistical Yearbook, 122
  structure, 121
United Nations Human Settlements Programme (UN-Habitat), 123–126
  activities, 125
  and climate change, 124, 126
  funding, 124, 125
  history and creation of, 123
  responsibilities, 123–124
  structure, 124–125
  and Sustainable Development Goals, 124
  UN Conference on Housing and Sustainable Urban Development, 124
  World Cities Report, 125
United Nations Industrial Development Organization (UNIDO), 77–80
  activities, 79
  budget and funding, 78–80
  challenges and reform, 79–80
  and climate change, 80
  date joined UN, 48
  Director-General, 78, 210
  history and creation of, 77
  and industrialization, 79

membership, 78, 79–80
and Montreal Protocol on Substances that Deplete the Ozone Layer, 78
responsibilities, 77–78
structure, 78–79
and Sustainable Development Goals, 79
United Nations Population Fund (UNFPA), 126–129
   activities, 128–129
   challenge and reform, 129
   funding, 128, 129
   Goodwill Ambassadors, 128
   history and creation of, 126–127
   and Millennium Development Goals, 127
   responsibilities, 127
   structure, 127–128
   and Sustainable Development Goals, 127
   and women's reproductive rights, 129
   and World Population Conferences, 127, 128
United Nations principal organs, 13–14
   Charter of the UN on, 9, 13, 289
   list of, 14
   purpose and role, 14
   resolutions, 14
   voting procedures, 14–15
   See also individual organs
United Nations reform, 277–279
   advances and challenges, 278–279
   and Security Council, 278
   and Sustainable Development Goals, 278
   UN engagement, 278
United Nations Relief and Works Agency for Palestine Refugees in the Near East (UNRWA), 130–133
   activities, 131–132
   challenges and reform, 132–133
   funding, 131, 132
   and Giacomelli, Georgio, 131
   history and creation of, 130
   responsibilities, 130
   structure, 130–131
United Nations Security Council S/RES/1325 (2000) (document), 320–323
   on appointments of women, 321
   on gender mainstreaming, 323
   on gender perspective in peace agreements, 322
   on gender-based violence, 322
   on genocide, 322
   on impact of conflict on girls and women, 323
   on participation of women in decision-making, 321
   on refugee camps and settlements, 322
   on representation of women, 321
   on rights of women and girls in armed conflict, 322
   on support for women, 321
United States ambassadors to the United Nations, 213–216
   Albright, Madeleine, 214, 215
   Bolton, John, 214, 215
   Bush, George H. W., 214, 215
   Craft, Kelly, 214, 215
   Haley, Nikki, 214, 215
   Kirkpatrick, Jeane, 214, 215
   list of, 214
   Moynihan, Daniel Patrick, 214, 215
   notable U.S. ambassadors to the UN, 215
   Power, Samantha, 214, 215
   Rice, Susan, 214, 215
   UN engagement, 213–215
Universal Declaration of Human Rights (document), 311–315
   on asylum, 313
   on criminal justice, 312
   on culture life of community, 315
   on education, 315
   on freedoms, 311–313
   on government participation, 314
   on marriage, 313
   on motherhood and childhood, 314
   on peaceful assembly, 314
   Preamble, 311
   on rest and leisure, 314
   on social security, 314
   on standard of living, 314
   on work, 314
Universal Postal Union (UPU), 80–84
   activities, 82–83
   challenges and reform, 83
   and creation of UN, 81
   date joined UN, 48
   Director-General, 81, 210
   funding, 82, 83
   history and creation of, 80–81
   membership, 81–82
   responsibilities, 81
   structure, 81–82
   and technology, 82–83
   and Treaty of Berne, 80, 81

Voting and negotiating blocs, 279–281
  advances and challenges, 280–281
  and Security Council, 280
  UN engagement, 279–280
Voting procedures of UN, 14–15
  consensus, 15
  majority, 14
  negative vote, 14
  unanimity, 15
  weighted voting, 15

Waldheim, Kurt, 188–190
  advances and challenges while in office, 189–190
  death of, 190
  early career, 188
  and Iranian hostage crisis, 189
  peacekeeping operations under, 189
  role as Secretary-General, 189
  "Waldheim Affair," 190
  and World War II, 190
  years as Secretary-General, 181
Wilson, Woodrow
  Fourteen Points speech, 4
  and League of Nations, 4
  on self-determination, 262
Women and gender, 281–283
  advances and challenges, 282–283
  Commission on the Status of Women, 281
  Convention on the Elimination of All Forms of Discrimination against Women, 236, 237, 282, 318, 322
  and Security Council, 282
  UN engagement, 281–282
World Bank Group, 84–87
  activities, 85–86
  challenges and reform, 86
  date joined UN, 48
  funding, 85
  and globalization, 86
  history and creation of, 65–66, 84, 86
  and International Bank for Reconstruction and Development, 84, 85
  and International Centre for Settlement and Investment Disputes, 84, 85
  and International Development Association, 84, 85
  and International Finance Corporation, 84, 85
  and International Monetary Fund, 65, 66, 67, 84, 85
  membership, 85
  and Multilateral Investment Guarantee Agency, 84, 85
  President, 85, 210
  responsibilities, 84
  structure, 85
World Food Programme (WFP), 133–136
  activities, 134–135
  challenges and reform, 135–136
  and corruption, 135–136
  and emergency food relief, 133–134
  and Food and Agriculture Organization, 49, 51, 133, 134, 135
  history and creation of, 133
  responsibilities, 133–134
  structure, 134
World Health Organization (WHO), 87–90
  activities, 88–89
  budget and funding, 88, 89–90
  challenges and reform, 89–90
  and communicable diseases, 88–89
  date joined UN, 48
  Director-General, 88, 210
  "Health for All" approach, 88
  history and creation of, 87
  Regional Directors, 88
  responsibilities, 87–88
  structure, 88
  and Sustainable Development Goals, 89
World Heritage Sites, 75, 101
World Intellectual Property Organization (WIPO), 90–94
  activities, 92–93
  Agreement on Trade-Related Intellectual Property Rights, 92–93
  Arbitration and Mediation Center, 92
  budget and funding, 91–92, 93
  challenges and reform, 93
  date joined UN, 48
  Director-General, 92, 210
  history and creation of, 90–91
  membership, 92
  Patent Cooperation Treaty, 92
  responsibilities, 91
  structure, 91–92
  and United International Bureaux for the Protection of Intellectual Property, 90–91

World Meteorological Organization
  (WMO), 94–97
 activities, 96
 budget and funding, 96
 challenges and reform 96–97
 and climate change, 96, 97
 date joined UN, 48
 history and creation of, 94
 and Intergovernmental Panel on Climate
  Change, 96
 membership, 95–96
 responsibilities, 94–95
 Secretary-General, 95, 210
 structure, 95–96
 World Climate Programme, 96
World Summit Outcome Document, 18,
  32, 150, 259
World Tourism Organization (UNWTO),
  97–101
 activities, 99–100
 budget and funding, 98–99, 100
 challenges and reform, 100–101
 and climate change, 101
 date joined UN, 48
 Global Code of Ethics for Tourism, 100
 history and creation of, 97–98
 membership, 99, 100
 responsibilities, 98
 Secretary-General, 98, 210
 structure, 98–99
 and Sustainable Development Goals, 99
World Trade Organization (WTO),
  175–178
 activities, 177
 budget and funding, 177
 challenges and reform, 177–178
 and General Agreement on Tariffs and
  Trade, 176
 history and creation of, 175–176
 membership, 176–177
 responsibilities, 176
 and Sustainable Development Goals,
  177
 structure, 176–177

Yalta Conference, 6

About the Authors

Kent J. Kille is professor of political science and global and international studies at The College of Wooster. Dr. Kille is an expert on UN Secretary-General leadership. He authored *From Manager to Visionary: The Secretary-General of the United Nations* and served as editor of and contributor to *The UN Secretary-General and Moral Authority: Ethics and Religion in International Leadership.* He is editor (with Bob Reinalda) of *IO BIO: Biographical Dictionary of Secretaries-General of International Organizations.* He has also explored the connections between the United Nations and regional organizations in several journal articles. He serves on the editorial board of *Global Governance: A Review of Multilateralism and International Organizations.* His work on active teaching and learning is widely published, and in 2010 (along with colleagues Matthew Krain and Jeffrey Lantis) he was awarded the International Studies Association's Deborah Gerner Innovative Teaching in International Studies Award. He is the academic adviser for The College of Wooster's Model UN team.

Alynna J. Lyon is professor of political science at the University of New Hampshire (UNH). She is the author of *U.S. Politics and the United Nations*, is coauthor of *The United Nations in the 21st Century*, 5th ed. (with Karen Mingst and Margaret Karns), and coeditor of two books, *Pope Francis as a Global Actor: Where Politics and Theology Meet* and *Religion and Politics in a Global Society.* Her scholarship also appears in many journals, including *Foreign Policy Analysis, Global Society, Ethnic and Racial Studies,* and *Journal of International Organization Studies.* She is past chair of the International Organization Section of the International Studies Association (2016–18) and is a faculty fellow for the Office of Senior Vice Provost, Engagement, and Academic Outreach at UNH. She is coeditor in chief for *Global Governance: A Review of Multilateralism and International Organizations* and serves as faculty adviser for UNH's Model UN.

Printed in the USA
CPSIA information can be obtained
at www.ICGtesting.com
LVHW081026171024
794074LV00007B/46